ASCENT®

CENTER FOR TECHNICAL KNOWLEDGE

# CATIA V5-6R2017:
# Introduction to Surface Design

*Learning Guide*
*1st Edition*

# ASCENT - Center for Technical Knowledge®
## CATIA V5-6R2017: Introduction to Surface Design
1st Edition

Prepared and produced by:

ASCENT Center for Technical Knowledge
630 Peter Jefferson Parkway, Suite 175
Charlottesville, VA 22911

866-527-2368
www.ASCENTed.com

Lead Contributor: Scott Hendren

ASCENT - Center for Technical Knowledge is a division of Rand Worldwide, Inc., providing custom developed knowledge products and services for leading engineering software applications. ASCENT is focused on specializing in the creation of education programs that incorporate the best of classroom learning and technology-based training offerings.

We welcome any comments you may have regarding this learning guide, or any of our products. To contact us please email: feedback@ASCENTed.com.

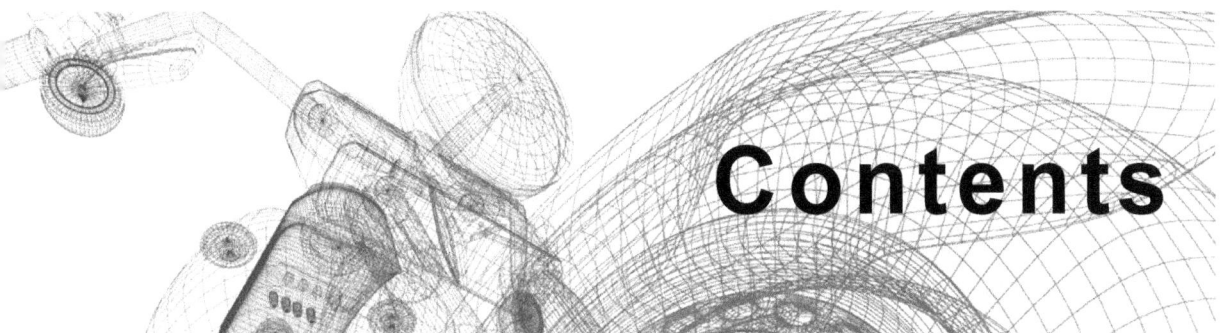

# Contents

# Preface

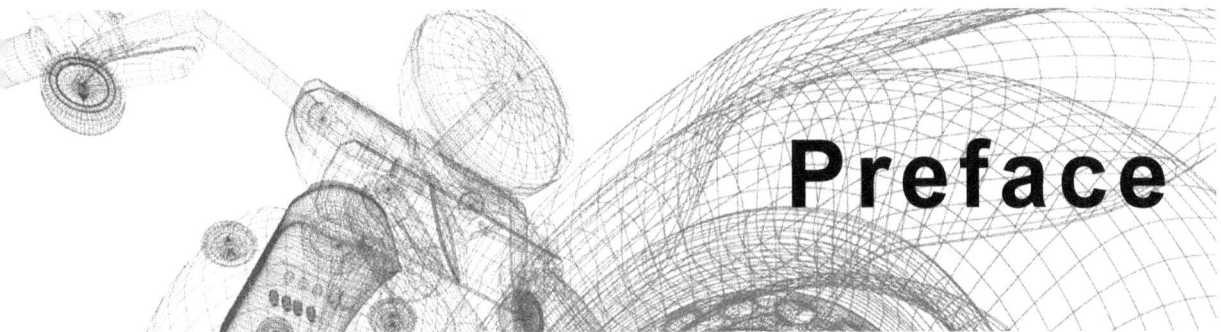

The *CATIA V5-6R2017: Introduction to Surface Design* learning guide introduces the fundamentals of creating wireframe and surface geometry. This guide takes an in-depth look at process-based modeling techniques used to develop robust and flexible surface geometry. With the design intent as the focus, students learn about shape and continuity settings for simple and complex geometry types.

## Topics Covered:

- Surfacing terminology

- Surface design process

- Creating wireframe geometry

- Creating simple surfaces

- Creating complex surfaces

- Performing operations on wireframe and surface geometry

- Working with surface geometry in the Part Design Workbench

- Geometrical Element Management

- Surface Fillets

- Boundary Representations

- Best practices for surface modeling

## Note on Software Setup

This learning guide assumes a standard installation of the software using the default preferences during installation. Lectures and practices use the standard software templates and default options for the Content Libraries.

This guide was developed against CATIA V5-6R2017, Service Pack 1.

## Lead Contributor: Scott Hendren

Scott Hendren has been a trainer and curriculum developer in the PLM industry for almost 20 years, with experience on multiple CAD systems, including Pro/ENGINEER, Creo Parametric, and CATIA. Trained in Instructional Design, Scott uses his skills to develop instructor-led and web-based training products.

Scott has held training and development positions with several high profile PLM companies, and has been with the Ascent team since 2013.

Scott holds a Bachelor of Mechanical Engineering Degree as well as a Bachelor of Science in Mathematics from Dalhousie University, Nova Scotia, Canada.

Scott Hendren has been the Lead Contributor for *CATIA: Introduction to Surface Design* since 2013.

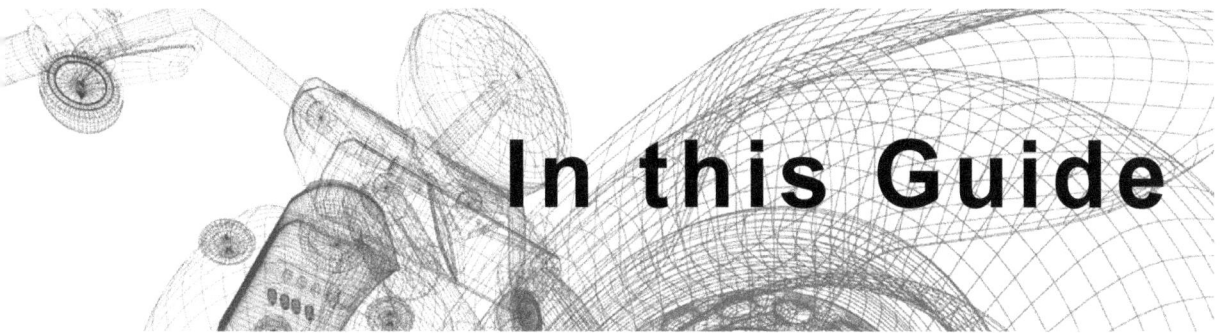

# In this Guide

The following images highlight some of the features that can be found in this Learning Guide.

## Practice Files

To download the practice files for this student guide, use the following steps

1. Type the URL shown below into the address bar of your Internet browser. The URL must be typed **exactly as shown**. If you are using an ASCENT ebook, you can click on the link to download the file.

*Address bar*

http://www.ASCENTed.com/getfile?id=xxxxxxxx

File    Edit    View    Favorites    Tools    Help

2. Press <Enter> to download the .ZIP file that contains the Practice Files

3. Once the download is complete, unzip the file to a local folder. The unzipped file contains an .EXE file

4. Double-click on the .EXE file and follow the instructions to automatically install the Practice Files on the C:\ drive of your computer.

**Do not** change the location in which the Practice Files folder is installed. Doing so can cause errors when completing the practices in this student guide

http://www.ASCENTed.com/getfile?id=xxxxxxxx

**Stay Informed!**
Interested in receiving information about upcoming promotional offers, educational events, invitations to complementary webcasts, and discounts? If so, please visit: www.ASCENTed.com/updates/

**Help us improve our product by completing the following survey:**
www.ASCENTed.com/feedback
You can also contact us at: feedback@ASCENTed.com

**FTP link for practice files**

### Practice Files

The Practice Files page tells you how to download and install the practice files that are provided with this learning guide.

## Chapter 1

### Getting Started

In this chapter you learn how to start the AutoCAD® software, become familiar with the basic layout of the AutoCAD screen, how to access commands, use your pointing device, and understand the AutoCAD Cartesian workspace. You also learn how to open an existing drawing, view a drawing by zooming and panning, and save your work in the AutoCAD software.

**Learning Objectives in this Chapter**

· Launch the AutoCAD software and complete a basic initial setup of the drawing environment.
· Identify the basic layout and features of AutoCAD interface including the Ribbon, Drawing Window, and Application Menu.
· Locate commands and launch them using the Ribbon, shortcut menus, Application Menu, and Quick Access Toolbar.
· Locate points in the AutoCAD Cartesian workspace.
· Open and close existing drawings and navigate to file locations.
· Move around a drawing using the mouse, Zoom and Pan commands, and the Navigation Bar.
· Save drawings in various formats and set the automatic save options using the Save commands.

**Learning Objectives for the chapter**

### Chapters

Each chapter begins with a brief introduction and a list of the chapter's Learning Objectives.

---

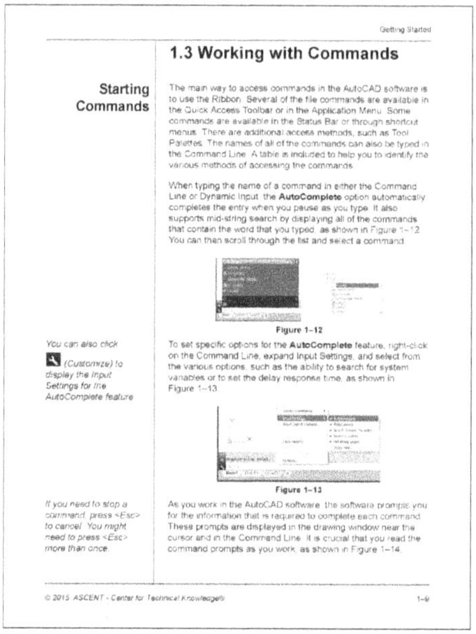
Getting Started

1.3 Working with Commands

Starting Commands

The main way to access commands in the AutoCAD software is to use the Ribbon. Several of the file commands are available in the Quick Access Toolbar or in the Application Menu. Some commands are available in the Status Bar or through shortcut menus. There are additional access methods, such as Tool Palettes. The names of all of the commands can also be typed in the Command Line. A table is included to help you to identify the various methods of accessing the commands.

When typing the name of a command in either the Command Line or Dynamic Input, the **AutoComplete** option automatically completes the entry when you pause as you type. It also supports mid-string search by displaying all of the commands that contain the word that you typed, as shown in Figure 1–12. You can then scroll through the list and select a command.

Figure 1–12

*You can also click (Customize) to display the Input Settings for the AutoComplete feature.*

To set specific options for the **AutoComplete** feature, right-click on the Command Line, expand Input Settings, and select from the various options, such as the ability to search for system variables or to set the delay response time, as shown in Figure 1–13.

Figure 1–13

*If you need to stop a command, press <Esc> to cancel. You might need to press <Esc> more than once.*

As you work in the AutoCAD software, the software prompts you for the information that is required to complete each command. These prompts are displayed in the drawing window near the cursor and in the Command Line. It is crucial that you read the command prompts as you work, as shown in Figure 1–14.

© 2015, ASCENT - Center for Technical Knowledge® 1–9

### *Instructional Content*

Each chapter is split into a series of sections of instructional content on specific topics. These lectures include the descriptions, step-by-step procedures, figures, hints, and information you need to achieve the chapter's Learning Objectives.

### *Side notes*

Side notes are hints or additional information for the current topic.

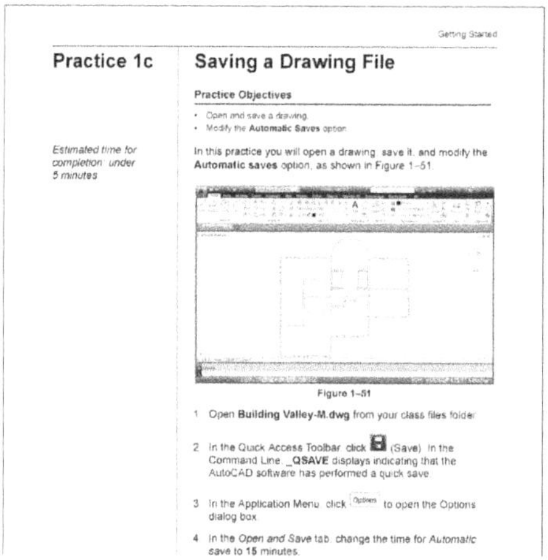
Getting Started

Practice 1c Saving a Drawing File

Practice Objectives

- Open and save a drawing.
- Modify the **Automatic Saves** option.

*Estimated time for completion: under 5 minutes*

In this practice you will open a drawing, save it, and modify the **Automatic saves** option, as shown in Figure 1–51.

Figure 1–51

1. Open **Building Valley-M.dwg** from your class files folder.
2. In the Quick Access Toolbar, click (Save). In the Command Line, **_QSAVE** displays indicating that the AutoCAD software has performed a quick save.
3. In the Application Menu, click Options to open the Options dialog box.
4. In the *Open and Save* tab, change the time for *Automatic save* to 15 minutes.

### *Practice Objectives*

### *Practices*

Practices enable you to use the software to perform a hands-on review of a topic.

Some practices require you to use prepared practice files, which can be downloaded from the link found on the Practice Files page.

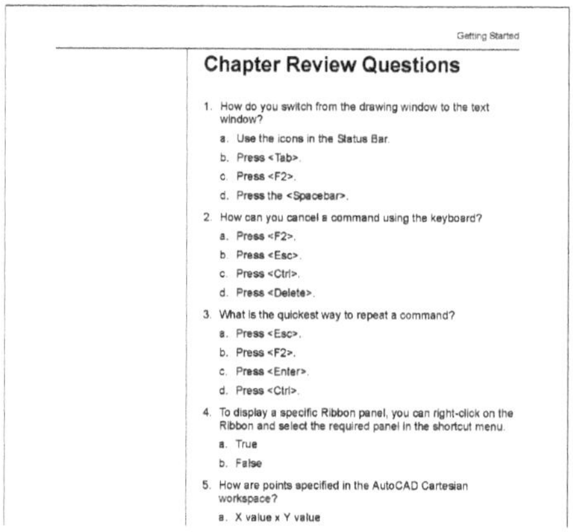
Getting Started

Chapter Review Questions

1. How do you switch from the drawing window to the text window?
   a. Use the icons in the Status Bar.
   b. Press <Tab>.
   c. Press <F2>.
   d. Press the <Spacebar>.
2. How can you cancel a command using the keyboard?
   a. Press <F2>.
   b. Press <Esc>.
   c. Press <Ctrl>.
   d. Press <Delete>.
3. What is the quickest way to repeat a command?
   a. Press <Esc>.
   b. Press <F2>.
   c. Press <Enter>.
   d. Press <Ctrl>.
4. To display a specific Ribbon panel, you can right-click on the Ribbon and select the required panel in the shortcut menu.
   a. True
   b. False
5. How are points specified in the AutoCAD Cartesian workspace?
   a. X value x Y value

### *Chapter Review Questions*

Chapter review questions, located at the end of each chapter, enable you to review the key concepts and learning objectives of the chapter.

# Practice Files

To download the practice files for this learning guide, use the following steps:

1. Type the URL shown below into the address bar of your Internet browser. The URL must be typed **exactly as shown**. If you are using an ASCENT ebook, you can click on the link to download the file.

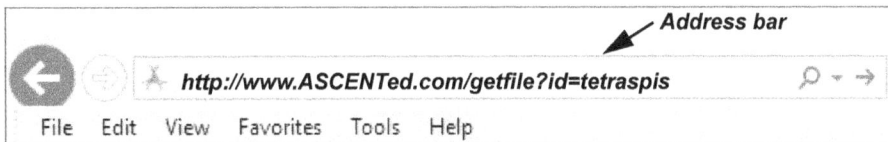

*Address bar*

> http://www.ASCENTed.com/getfile?id=tetraspis

File    Edit    View    Favorites    Tools    Help

2. Press <Enter> to download the .ZIP file that contains the Practice Files.

3. Once the download is complete, unzip the file to a local folder. The unzipped file contains an .EXE file.

4. Double-click on the .EXE file and follow the instructions to automatically install the Practice Files on the C:\ drive of your computer.

   **Do not** change the location in which the Practice Files folder is installed. Doing so can cause errors when completing the practices in this learning guide.

## http://www.ASCENTed.com/getfile?id=tetraspis

**Stay Informed!**

Interested in receiving information about upcoming promotional offers, educational events, invitations to complimentary webcasts, and discounts? If so, please visit:

*www.ASCENTed.com/updates/*

**Help us improve our product by completing the following survey:**

*www.ASCENTed.com/feedback*

You can also contact us at: *feedback@ASCENTed.com*

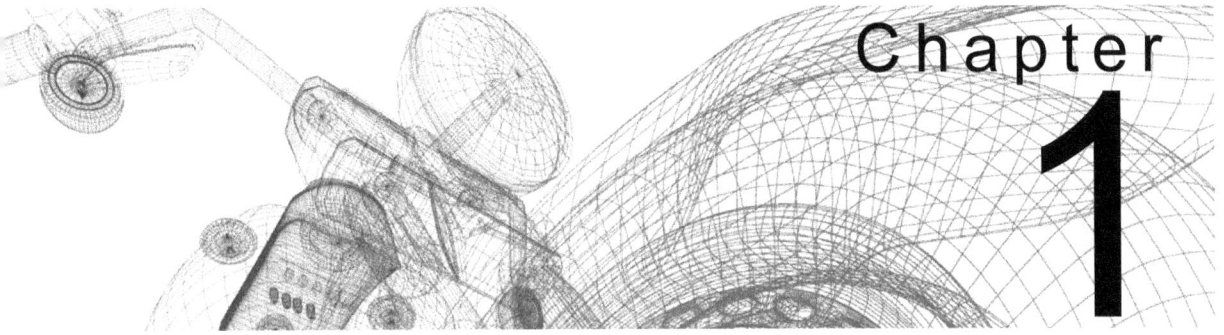

# Introduction to Surfacing

Several tools are required to construct basic wireframe and surface geometry. Many parts can be designed using only solid geometry. Using solid modeling tools might be limiting as parts become more complex in shape. In these cases, surface features can be used to define more complex shapes. Parts can be completely designed using surface features, or a surface model can be brought into the Part Design workbench to integrate into a solid part.

## Learning Objectives in this Chapter

- Understand the definition of a surface in the context of a CATIA model.
- Recognize the components of the surface interface.
- Review surfacing terminology.
- Create a surface model.

# 1.1 Surface Definition

A surface is a non-solid, zero-thickness feature that can define a contoured shape. Surfaces help capture the design intent of complex shapes that are not easily defined with solid features. Once defined, surfaces can be used as references to aid in the creation of other features (solid and non-solid). Figure 1–1 shows an example of a single surface feature.

**Figure 1–1**

CATIA uses the term *surface* in several different contexts depending on the functionality being discussed. A surface can refer to any of the following:

- A non-solid feature created using the Wireframe and Surface or Generative Shape Design workbenches, commonly referred to as surfaces.

- A bounded face defined by a solid feature, commonly referred to as a face.

- A reference plane (infinite flat surface), commonly referred to as a plane.

Examples of different types of surfaces are shown in Figure 1–2.

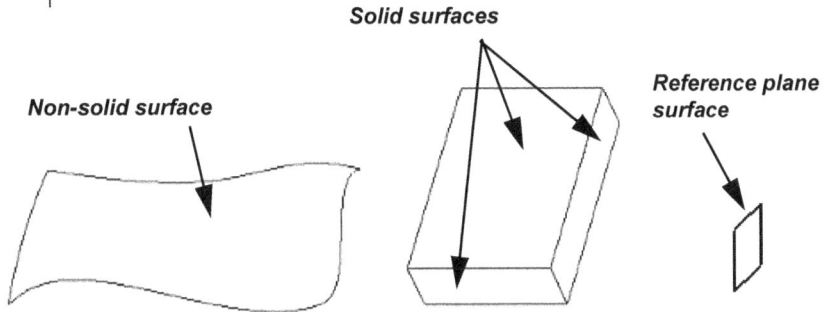

**Solid surfaces**

**Non-solid surface**

**Reference plane surface**

**Figure 1–2**

Surfaces in CATIA are primarily used to create complex shapes that are not easily created using solid geometry. Creating geometry with surfaces requires a basic understanding of surface modeling styles and an understanding the process used to create complex surfaces to ensure robust surface models.

# 1.2 Surface Interface

CATIA contains several workbenches that enable you to create surface features. This section introduces the basic tools of the Generative Shape Design (GSD) workbench.

## Access the GSD Workbench

To use this workbench, open a part model that was last saved in the GSD workbench or select **Start>Shape>Generative Shape Design**. The workbench symbol changes to [ ].

## GSD User Interface

The interface for the GSD workbench is very similar to that of the Part Design workbench. The primary difference is that the toolbar options change to GSD-specific tools, as shown in Figure 1–3.

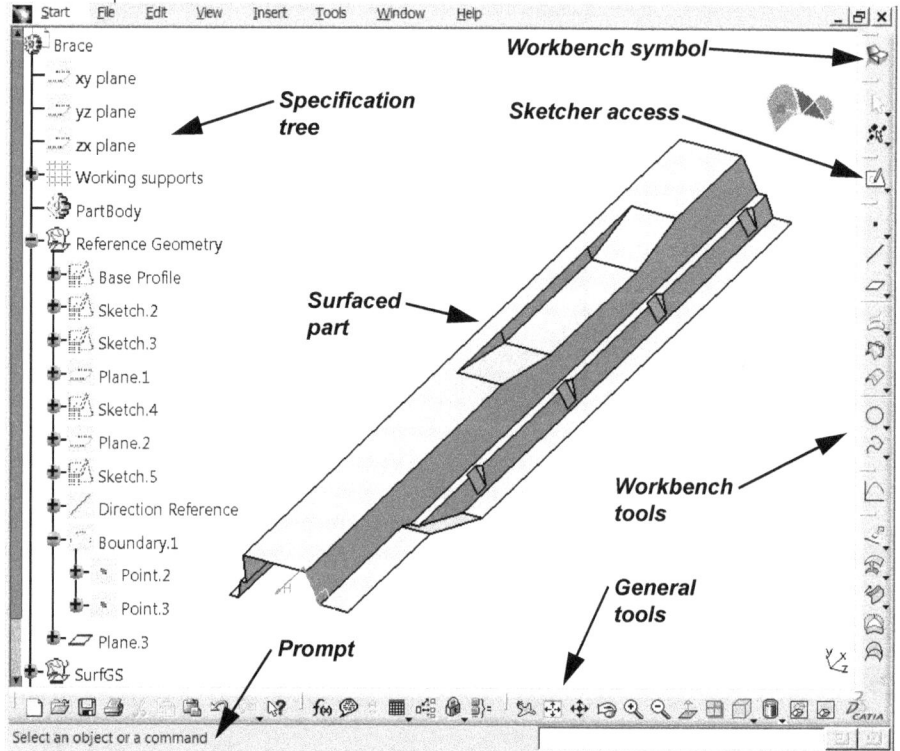

**Figure 1–3**

# 1.3 Surfacing Terminology

The following terms are commonly used in surfacing:

- Curvature

- Curvature Continuity

- Inflection point

- Geometrical set

## Curvature

The curvature of a surface or curve is equal to the inverse of the radius at any point on the surface. Therefore, a smaller radius results in a greater curvature. An example is shown in Figure 1–4.

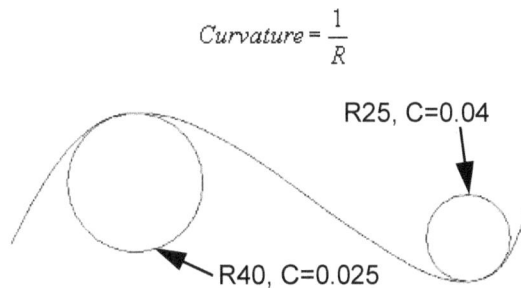

$$Curvature = \frac{1}{R}$$

R25, C=0.04

R40, C=0.025

**Figure 1–4**

*These tools are discussed in more depth later.*

To detect changes in curvature, you can use a combination of curve and surface analysis tools.

When designing surfaces with curvature, keep the following information in mind:

- The curvature for a straight line is zero.

- The curvature for a true arc is constant at all points along the curve.

- The curvature of a spline is constantly changing.

## Curvature Continuity

Curvature Continuity refers to how two curves or two surfaces meet. An edge is generated where two surfaces meet and a vertex is generated where two curves meet. Continuity between entities plays an important role in the appearance of a surface.

The connections between curves and surfaces are defined as follows:

| Classification | Description |
| --- | --- |
| **G0** | The curves or surfaces share a common end point or edge. They are not tangent to one another as shown below. |

*No tangency*

| Classification | Description |
| --- | --- |
| **G1** | The curves or surfaces are tangent to each other, share a common end point or edge, and have differing curvature magnitudes at their intersections, as shown below. |

*Magnitude of curvatures is different.*

*Entities are tangent*

| Classification | Description |
| --- | --- |
| **G2** | The curves or surfaces are tangent and have a constant curvature at their shared end point or edge as shown below. G2 continuity produces a smooth connection. G2 continuity is usually only required for surfaces in which light reflection is an issue. |

*Tangent and curvature continuous*

# Inflection Point

An inflection point of a curve or surface is a point at which the curvature changes from concave to convex, or conversely. An inflection point is shown in Figure 1–5.

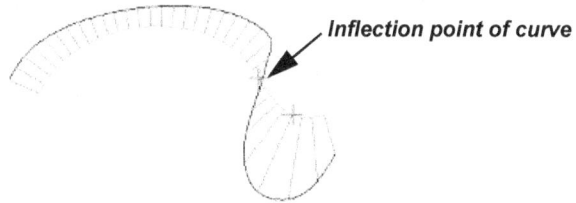

Inflection point of curve

**Figure 1–5**

# Geometrical Set

As you build your surface model, the display of wireframe, surface, and even solid geometry can make the model difficult to visualize. Geometrical sets are used to group geometry by function or type, and to organize the model.

You can have as many geometrical sets as required to suit your design intent. Geometrical sets do not affect the mass properties of the model. To add a new geometrical set, select **Insert>Geometrical Set**.

A new geometrical set added to the model becomes the current set, as shown in Figure 1–6.

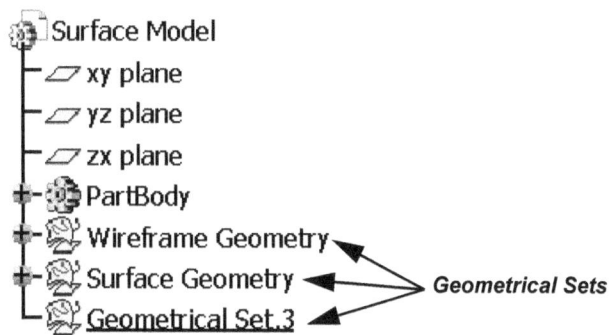

Surface Model
— xy plane
— yz plane
— zx plane
— PartBody
— Wireframe Geometry
— Surface Geometry
— Geometrical Set.3

Geometrical Sets

**Figure 1–6**

To set a geometrical set as the active set, right-click on the set in the specification tree and select **Define In Work Object**.

New features created in the GSD workbench are added to the active set. To switch a feature to a different set, use **Change geometrical set** as shown in Figure 1–7. A feature can only belong to one geometrical set at a time.

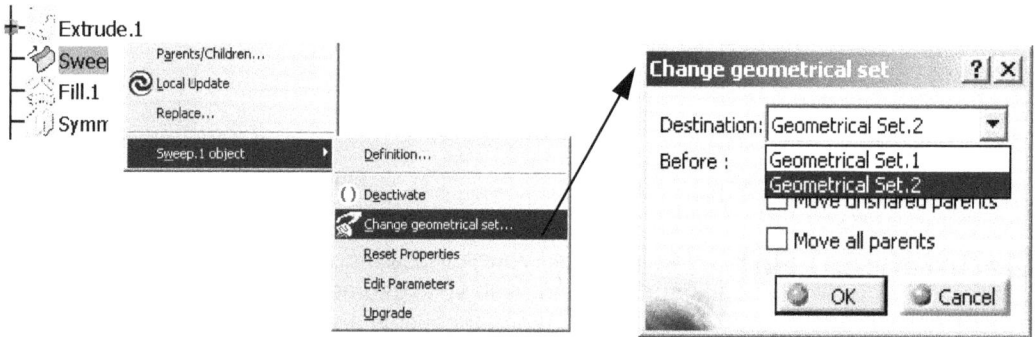

**Figure 1–7**

The display of the contents of a geometrical set can be controlled by right-clicking on it in the specification tree and selecting **Hide/Show**. The display of all of the geometrical sets can be controlled using **Tools>Hide>All geometrical sets** and **Tools>Show>All geometrical sets**.

# 1.4 Creating a Surface Model

The process of creating surface features differs slightly from that for creating solid features in CATIA. With solid modeling, you can often visualize the final shape of a feature and create the geometry with individual construction features (e.g., Pad, Pocket, fillet, hole, etc.). With surfaces, you must frequently create reference geometry (e.g., points and curves) before creating a single surface feature. Planning ahead is essential to achieving the required results when designing with surfaces.

When you create solid features, all of the faces of the feature are defined in one step. The intersections of solid features are immediately calculated and consumed in the model. With surfaces, the contours of the model can be created individually as separate features. These multiple surfaces can then be joined to generate a final solid feature. As a result, simple surfaces have the benefit of being able to yield complex results.

A model does not necessarily have to be constructed entirely of surface geometry. Solid features can be used in combination with surface geometry to generate the shape of the model. Operations are performed on the solid geometry to intersect the surface geometry and add or remove material.

## General Steps

Use the following general steps to create a model from surface features:

1. Create wireframe geometry.
2. Create surface geometry.
3. Perform surface operations.
4. (Optional) Create solid geometry.

## Step 1 - Create wireframe geometry.

Wireframe geometry is the backbone on which surface features are created. You can use wireframe features to define construction elements, intersections, and common boundaries of the surfaces that define the shape of the model. Wireframe geometry can consist of simple features, such as sketches, points, lines, and planes, as well as more complex geometry, such as splines or circles.

Figure 1–8 shows an example of a group of wireframe features that are used to develop a surface model.

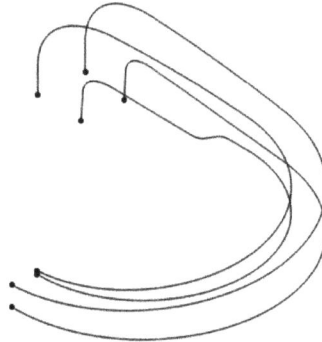

**Figure 1–8**

## Step 2 - Create surface geometry.

Once the wireframe geometry has been created, surface features are required to define the internal and external boundaries of the model. Surface features can be created independent of the rest of the model, or by using existing wireframe and surface geometry as references. You can create the following types of surface features:

- Extrude
- Revolve
- Sphere
- Cylinder
- Offset

- Sweep
- Fill
- Multi-sections
- Blend

The boundaries of the model shown in Figure 1–9 are completely defined. Although the surfaces look like they form a closed body surface, they still need to be joined before the solid model is created.

Figure 1–9

## Step 3 - Perform surface operations.

Many surfaces might be required to achieve the required geometry. For example, the geometry shown in Figure 1–9 was created using eight surface features. In addition, operations such as joining and trimming might be required.

Surface operations can be used to combine various surfaces into one feature, correct overlap and improve connections between surfaces, and move surfaces to different locations and orientations. Basic surface operations include:

- Join

- Split

- Trim

- Extract

- Transform

The model shown in Figure 1–10 uses the **Join** option to define the resulting join feature. Note that the construction surfaces (such as Blend.1) are hidden. Surface operations consume the surfaces used in the feature so that Join.8 represents the collection of surfaces for all future modeling operations.

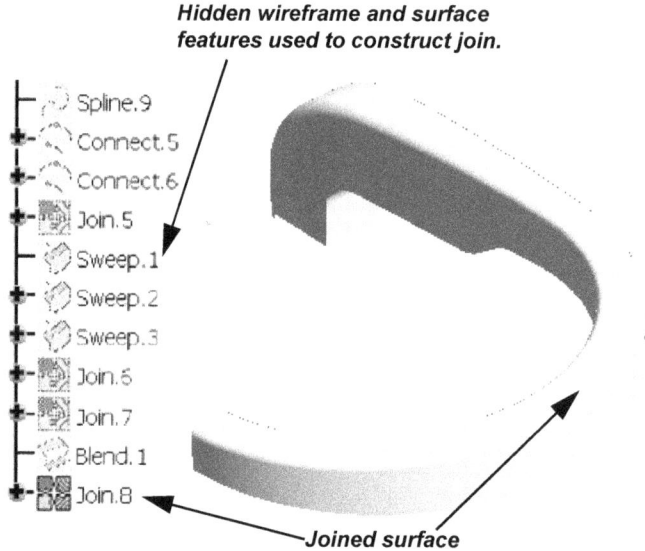

**Figure 1–10**

## Step 4 - (Optional) Create solid geometry.

When you finish creating surface features, you can create solid geometry, if required. At this point, your model contains a surface representation of the 3D model. This model is termed *water tight*, indicating that the surfaces form a closed skin. However, parts modeled with surfaces do not necessarily need to be converted into solid geometry. For some applications, leaving the model as surface geometry is acceptable.

If the mass properties of your model are required or you intend on performing additional solid modeling, you must create solid geometry from the surfaces. You must take the model back to the Part Design workbench and use the Surface-Based Features toolbar options to create solid geometry. These options include features, such as **Close Surface** (which fills a surface model with solid geometry) or **Thick Surface** (which adds solid material to either side of a surface). The solid geometry is added to the PartBody, as shown in Figure 1–11.

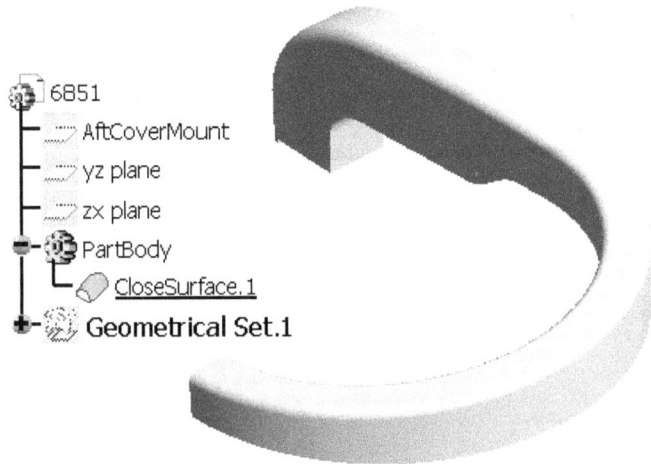

**Figure 1–11**

# Chapter Review Questions

1. Which of the following is a characteristic of surface features?

    a. A non-solid, zero-thickness feature that can define a contoured shape.

    b. Helps to capture the design intent of complex shapes.

    c. Can be used as references to aid in the creation of other features.

    d. All of the above.

2. In CATIA, the term Surface can refer to a Non-solid surface, a solid surface or face, or a reference plane surface.

    a. True

    b. False

3. The symbol for the Generative Design workbench is:

    a.

    b.

    c.

    d.

4. In surface models, you are limited to a single geometrical set.

    a. True

    b. False

# Basic Wireframe Features

Wireframe features can form the foundation for future surface elements. Here you learn how to create wireframe geometry, such as lines, circles, and curves. The wireframe geometry can then be used to create surface features.

## Learning Objectives in this Chapter

- Recognize wireframe elements.
- Create Points, Lines, and Planes to help develop wireframe models.
- Use Axis Systems as locators in 3D space for wireframe, surface, and solid entities to reference.
- Review Sketcher functionality.
- Use Work on Support planes.
- Create polylines, circles, and corners to create wireframe geometry.
- Use Connect Curve to quickly create a two-point spline between two existing curves.
- Create Splines.

# 2.1 Wireframe Elements

Wireframe elements are accessed in the Wireframe toolbar in the GSD workbench. Figure 2–1 shows the Wireframe toolbar icons. Refer to the following image any time you need to find a specific icon.

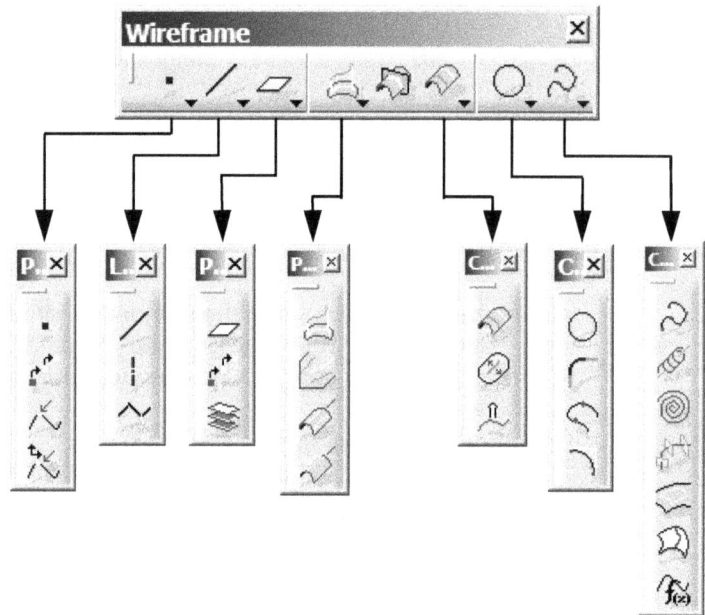

**Figure 2–1**

This section discusses the creation of the following elements:

• Points, Lines, and Planes

• Polyline

• Circle

• Corner

• Connect Curve

• Spline

# 2.2 Points, Lines, and Planes

Point, line, and plane features are normally used as references that facilitate the creation of other elements.

**Points**

Points are geometry markers located in 3D space. They can be the building blocks of solid geometry or surface geometry, but are often used to create other wireframe elements.

To create a single point, click  (Point) in the Wireframe toolbar. In the Point Definition dialog box that opens, select an option in the Point type drop-down list, as shown in Figure 2–2.

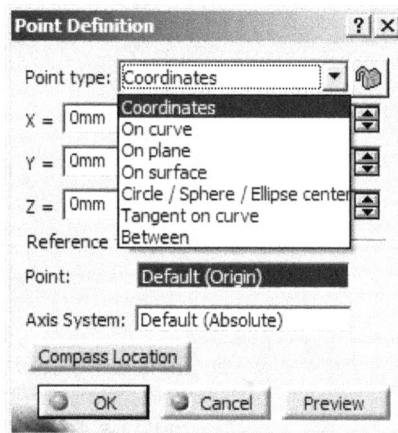

**Figure 2–2**

## How To: Create Multiple Points Along a Curve, Line, or Edge

1. Click [icon] (Points and Planes Repetition). The Points & Planes Repetition dialog box opens, as shown in Figure 2–3.

**Points & Planes Repetition** ? X

| | |
|---|---|
| First Point: | No selection |
| Curve: | Sketch.1 |
| Parameters: | Instances ▼ |
| Instance(s): | 10 |
| Spacing: | 1mm |
| Second point: | Default (Extremity) |

Mode for Repetition
● Absolute  ○ Relative

Reverse Direction
☐ With end points
☐ Create normal planes also
☐ Create in a new editable Body

OK     Cancel     Preview

**Figure 2–3**

2. Define the start point for the repetition. This is done by selecting an edge, line, curve, or point. If a point is selected, it must be created using the **On Curve** option.

3. To obtain evenly-spaced points, select **Instances** in the Parameters drop-down list. Figure 2–4 shows five points created using the **Instances** option.

**Figure 2–4**

To obtain points spaced at a specific distance relative to one another, select **Instances and Spacing**. The **Instances and Spacing** option is only available if you have selected a point to define the start of the repetition. Figure 2–5 shows four points spaced apart by 0.5in using the **Instances and Spacing** option.

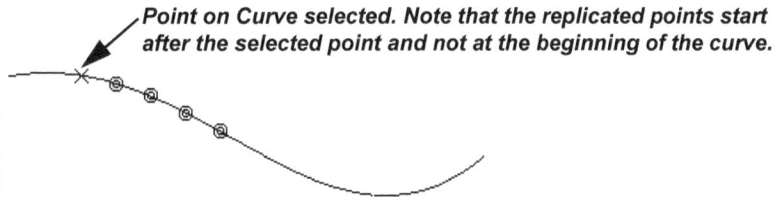

*Point on Curve selected. Note that the replicated points start after the selected point and not at the beginning of the curve.*

**Figure 2–5**

## Lines

Lines can be used as a reference to align two components in an assembly, or as a reference to define a rotational plane in a part model. To create a line feature, click (Line) in the Wireframe toolbar. In the Line Definition dialog box, select an option in the Line type drop-down list as shown in Figure 2–6.

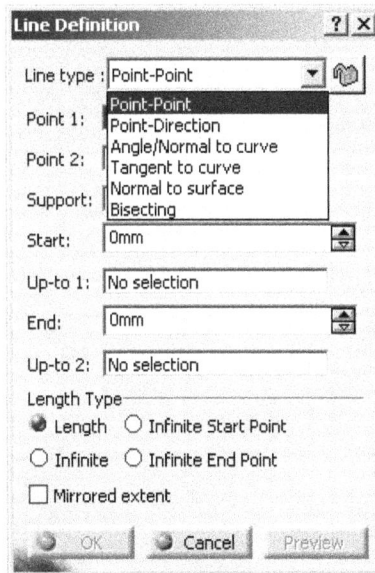

**Figure 2–6**

## Planes

Plane features can be used as a placement and dimensional reference for all types of features. To create a plane, click

⬜ (Plane) and select an option in the Plane type drop-down list as shown in Figure 2–7.

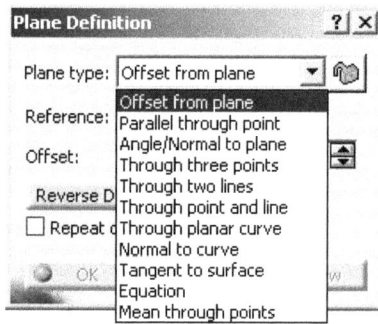

**Figure 2–7**

# 2.3 Axis Systems

**Definition**

An axis system is a locator in 3D space that wireframe, surface, and solid entities reference. Every axis system consists of a point that defines the origin, and three orthogonal vectors that make up the X-, Y-, and Z-axes of the system.

Axis systems are created in a part to provide the model with a stable reference entity. Multiple axis systems can be created in a part. You can specify which axis system is active.

Each part model automatically has default datum planes and a global axis system. A local axis system is not automatically created in the model.

A *global axis system* is system-defined. This axis system defines the origin of the part. The default datum planes are oriented about the global axis system and cannot be edited. The global axis system is displayed in the lower right corner of the screen.

A *local axis system* is user-defined. You select a point to define the origin. The X-, Y-, and Z-axes can be manually defined or automatically computed.

The two types of axis systems are shown in Figure 2–8.

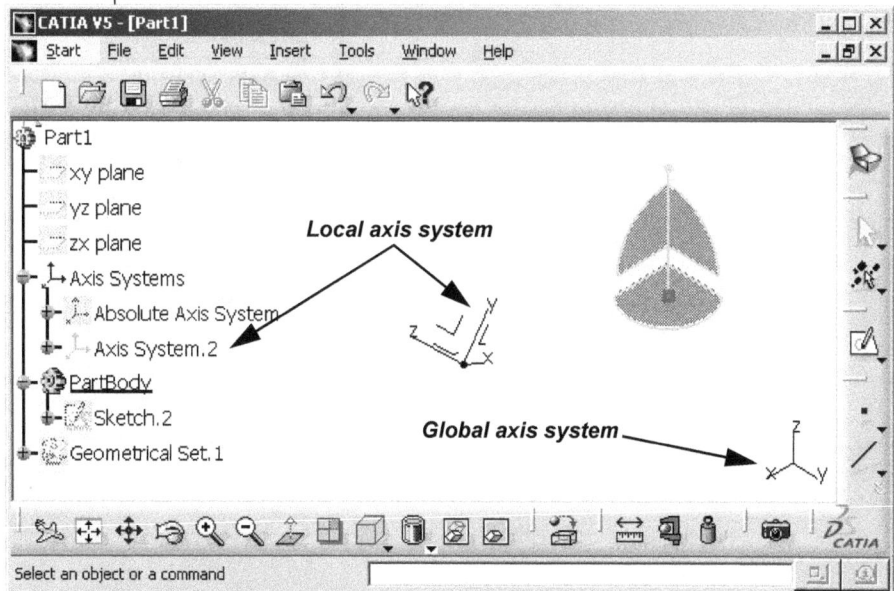

**Figure 2–8**

## Default Options

If you want to have a local axis system created when you create a new part, you can make this a default:

1. Select **Tools>Options>Infrastructure>Part Infrastructure**, and select the *Part Document* tab.
2. Select **Create an axis system**.
3. Click **OK** to set the option, as shown in Figure 2–9.

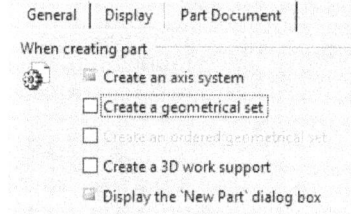

**Figure 2–9**

When a new part is created, the specification tree and part display as shown in Figure 2–10. Note that the default planes are automatically hidden, but are still in the tree. An axis system name, Absolute Axis System, is created in the tree. It is located at the origin of the global axis system and uses the XY, YZ and XZ datum planes to define the orthogonal axes.

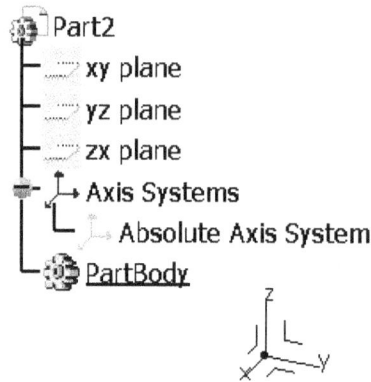

**Figure 2–10**

## Creating a Local Axis System

*If the **Create a geometrical set** option shown in Figure 2–9 is checked, the **Under the Axis System node** option will not display in the Axis System Definition dialog box.*

To create an axis system, click ⬚ (Axis System) in the Tools toolbar. The Axis System Definition dialog box opens as shown in Figure 2–11.

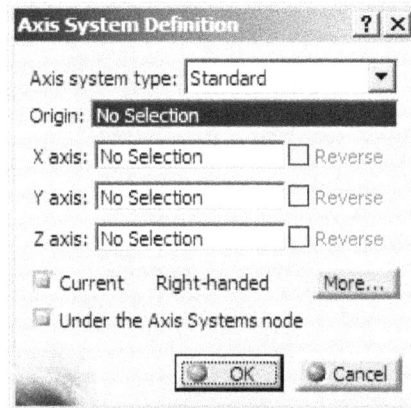

**Figure 2–11**

The origin for each type of axis system is defined by selecting a point or vertex on the model. The origin can also be defined by right-clicking in the *Origin* field, as shown in Figure 2–12.

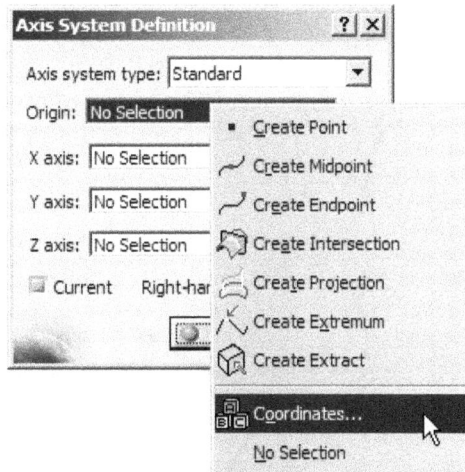

**Figure 2–12**

To introduce flexibility into the axis system, the origin is typically defined using the **Coordinates** option, which enables you to define the X-, Y-, and Z-coordinates relative to the part origin. The system can then be translated by modifying these coordinates.

All axis systems start in a default orientation about the origin and can be further defined by specifying the type and orientation references described as follows:

| Type | Orientation References |
|---|---|
| **Standard** | Select a reference to define the orientation of up to two axes (X, Y, Z). The orientation can be defined by selecting a point (the axis is oriented along a line between the point and the origin), a line, or a plane (defining a normal vector). |
| **Axis rotation** | Select a reference for the X-, Y-, or Z-axis. The axis system is then rotated about this axis by the specified angle measured from the specified reference, as shown in Figure 2–13. |
| **Euler Angle** | Define the origin and then enter an angle to define the orientation of the X-, Y-, and Z-axes, as shown in Figure 2–14. |

*Axis rotation*

**45 Degrees from global XY**

*Y-axis created parallel to global Y-axis*

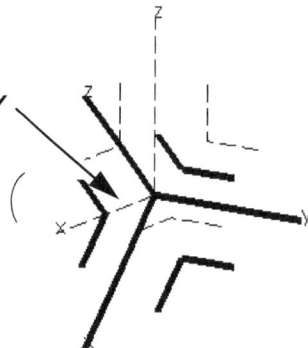
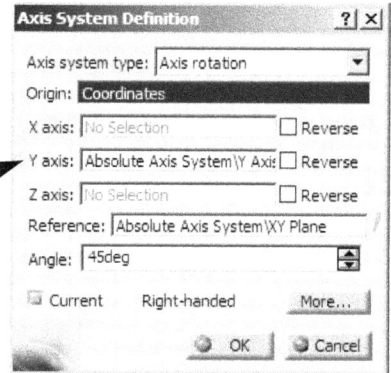

**Figure 2–13**

*Rotation around global Z axis*

*Rotation around local axis "a"*

*Rotation around local axis "c"*

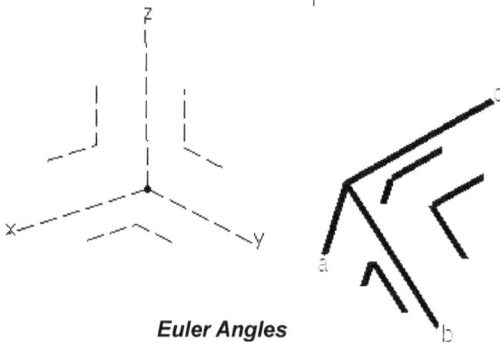

***Euler Angles***

**Figure 2–14**

## Active Axis System

More than one local axis system can be created in a part, but only one axis system can be active (or current).

When a local axis system is current:

- The quick view's orientation adapts to the local axis system.

- Points created by coordinate dimensions use the origin of the current system by default.

The active local axis system is orange in the specification tree. In the model, the active axis system has solid lines. The non-active or non-current axis system displays with dashed lines, as shown in Figure 2–15.

*Not current*                    *Current*

**Figure 2–15**

To change the active axis system, you can right-click on the axis system in the specification tree and select **Set As Current** or **Set As Not Current**, as shown in Figure 2–16.

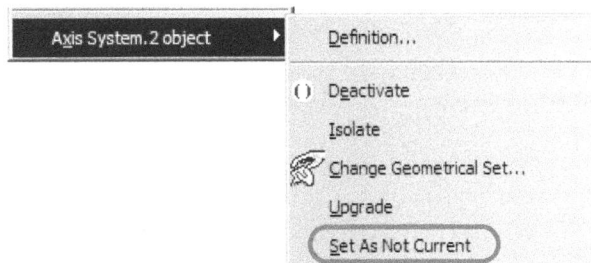

**Figure 2–16**

## Isolated

Local axis systems are associative to the geometry that defines its placement.

To lock or fix the local axis system in space so that it is no longer associative, it can be isolated. To isolate the local axis system, right-click on local axis system and select *<axis system name>.object>Isolate.*

An isolated axis system displays with a different icon in the specification tree, as shown in Figure 2–17.

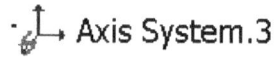 Axis System.3

**Figure 2–17**

One or more axis systems are created for the following reasons:

- To use as references for sketching, and feature creation.

- To define or locate the part's center of gravity

- To aid in top-down design or modeling the in body position.

- To alter the orientation/view of a part in accordance with Automotive, Aerospace, or company specific standards.

- Feature definition:

  - Symmetric part (right and left parts)
  - Spherical surfaces
  - Transformation functions

# 2.4 Sketcher Review

The Sketcher workbench is typically used for surface modeling. The commonly used tools in the Sketcher workbench are discussed below.

## Auto Search

The **Auto Search** tool enables quick selection of multiple elements in a closed loop of geometry. This tool does not display by default in the Sketcher toolbars. You might use this function quite often and you can customize the toolbars to add it as a shortcut. By adding the icon, the command icon can be selected rather than using the shortcut menu. You must be in the Sketcher workbench to do this.

### How To: Add the Auto Search Icon

1. Select **Tools>Customize**.
2. Select the *Toolbars* tab.
3. In the Customize dialog box, select **Sketch tools** in the list on the left.
4. Click **Edit commands**, as shown in Figure 2–18.
5. Select **Auto Search** in the list on the right and click **OK**.

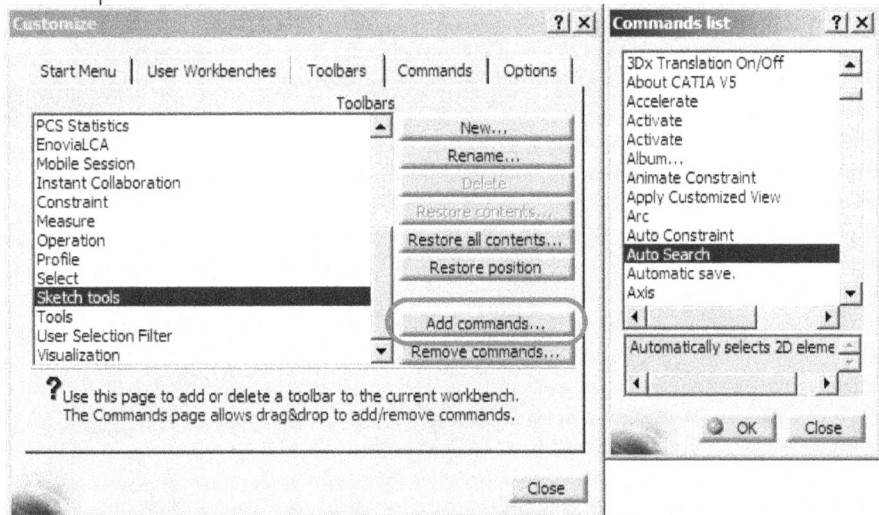

**Figure 2–18**

The **Auto search** icon is added to the Sketch tools toolbar, as shown in Figure 2–19.

**Figure 2–19**

## Sketch Analysis

The **Sketch Analysis** tool (shown in Figure 2–20) is important because it analyzes the sketch for issues that could potentially cause problems.

**Figure 2–20**

The status of the profile is displayed in the *Geometry* tab, indicating whether the shape is open, closed, or isolated. The *Use-edges* tab lists any entities that are associative to geometry outside the sketch.

The **Sketch Analysis** tool enables you to check your sketch for any items that could result in the sketch failing. For example, you can find out if you have trimmed lines or added lines to the sketch. It is almost impossible to see a line if it is on top of another line. The **Sketch Analysis** tool quickly displays where those lines are and provides the tools to remove them.

Select **Tools>Sketch Analysis** or click . The Sketch Analysis dialog box opens as shown in Figure 2–21.

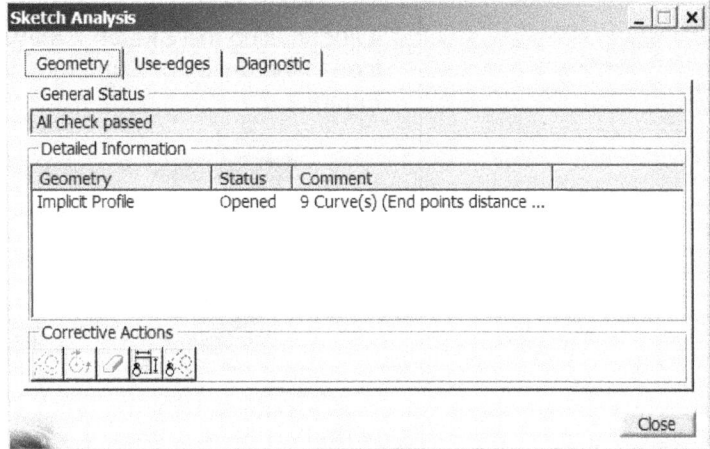

**Figure 2–21**

You can use the **Sketch Analysis** tool to analyze any of the following:

- Verify that sections meet the design intent.

- Display any duplicate lines.

- Check that the section is fully constrained.

- Check the status of the projections and intersections.

- Perform corrective actions, if required.

A common reason for sketch failure is duplicate lines. Duplicate lines display as Isolated lines in the Sketch Analysis dialog box. For example, the simple sketch shown in Figure 2–22 displays correctly but the Sketch Analysis dialog box indicates a problem with the sketch.

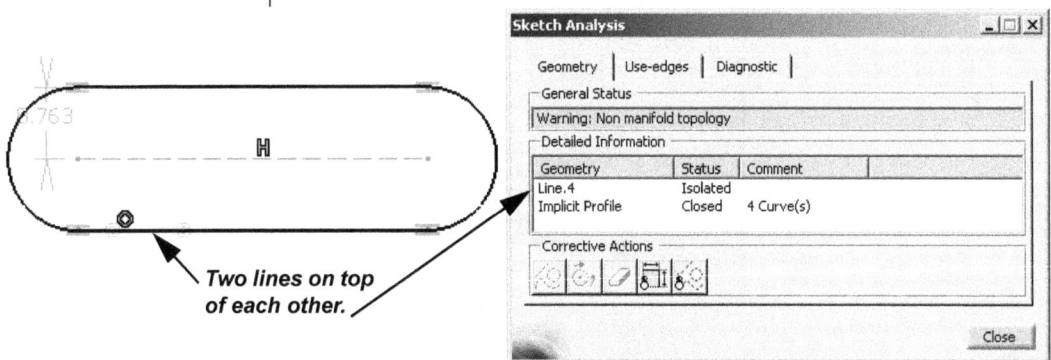

Two lines on top of each other.

**Figure 2–22**

The sketch contains duplicate lines that might have been missed without using the **Sketch Analysis** tool. You can use the **Delete** icon in the dialog box to remove duplicate lines, as shown in Figure 2–23.

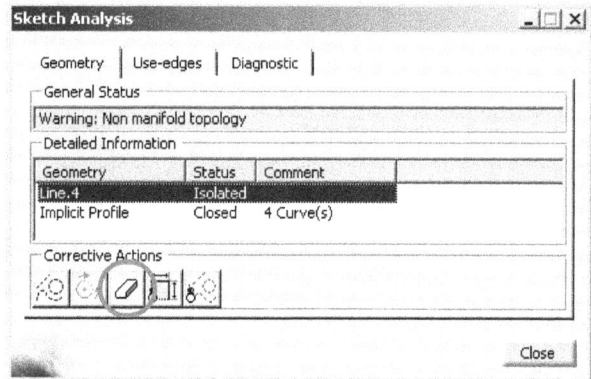

**Figure 2–23**

Once the duplicate line has been removed, the sketch can be used for feature creation.

# 2.5 Work on Support

A Work on Support is a plane or surface that is automatically used during feature creation for the Support reference. When work on support is activated, you can select a surface or plane as the active support. The support can be planar or curved. Multiple Work on Supports can be defined in a model, but only one can be active at a time. It is also possible for none of the Work on Supports to be activated.

If a Work on Support is active, any wireframe geometry that has an optional support parameter uses the active support. For example, consider a curve (such as a spline or circle) that is created while a support is active. The curve geometry lies on the surface or plane that has been designated as the support for the active Work on Support.

The **Work on Support** icon can be found in the Tools toolbar, as shown in Figure 2–24.

Figure 2–24

## How To: Define a Work on Support

1. Click ▦ (Work on Support).
2. Select a surface or a reference plane as a support. The point is optional as shown in Figure 2–25.

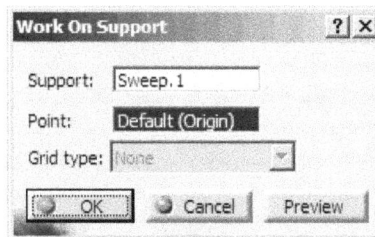

Figure 2–25

3. Click **OK** to complete the Work on Support definition.

4. If a plane was selected as the support element another dialog box opens, as shown in Figure 2–26. Use this dialog box to specify specifics about the resulting grid. If you do not want to create a grid, select **None** in the Grid type drop-down list.

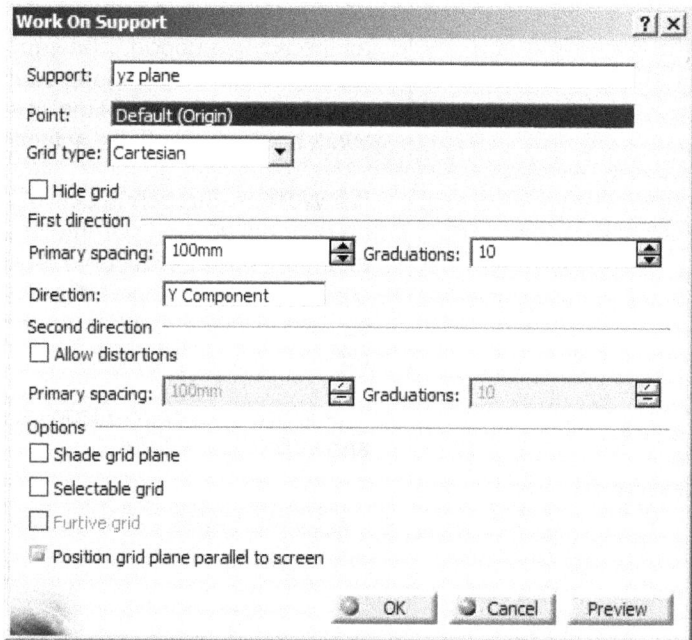

**Figure 2–26**

5. The Work on Support is added to the specification tree as shown in Figure 2–27.

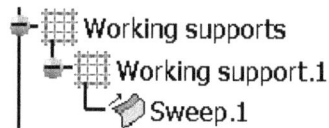

**Figure 2–27**

# 2.6 Polyline

A polyline is similar to a spline. The polyline feature is defined by selecting points through which the curve passes. A radius value can be defined at each point to control the shape of the curve.

Click ⌃ (Polyline) to create a polyline feature. The Polyline Definition dialog box opens, as shown in Figure 2–28.

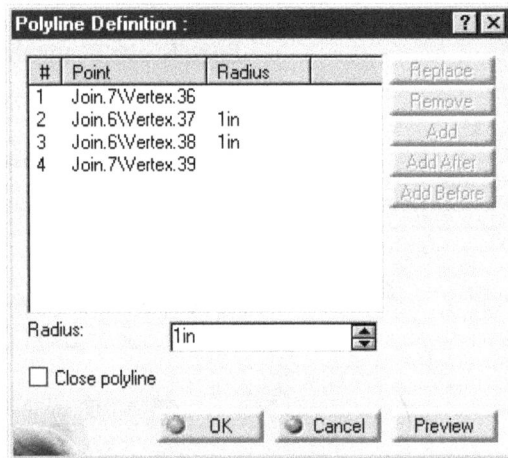

**Polyline Definition :**

| # | Point | Radius | |
|---|-------|--------|---|
| 1 | Join.7\Vertex.36 | | |
| 2 | Join.6\Vertex.37 | 1in | |
| 3 | Join.6\Vertex.38 | 1in | |
| 4 | Join.7\Vertex.39 | | |

Replace / Remove / Add / Add After / Add Before

Radius: 1in

☐ Close polyline

OK   Cancel   Preview

**Figure 2–28**

The polyline shown on the left in Figure 2–29 is created using the default straight edges. When a radius is applied at Point 2 and 3 of the polyline, it displays as shown on the right in Figure 2–29.

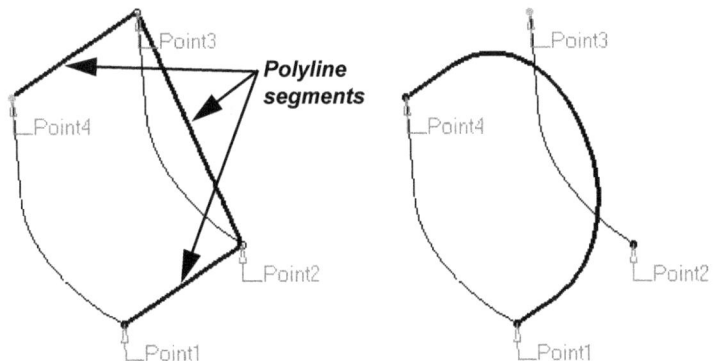

**Figure 2–29**

# 2.7 Circles

The circle feature can be used to define a closed circular curve or an open arc curve.

**General Steps**

Use the following general steps to create a circle feature:

1. Start the creation of a circle feature.
2. Select a circle type.
3. Specify circle parameters.
4. Specify circle limitations.

---

### Step 1 - Start the creation of a circle feature.

---

In the Wireframe toolbar, click ⭕ (Circle). The Circle Definition dialog box opens as shown in Figure 2–30.

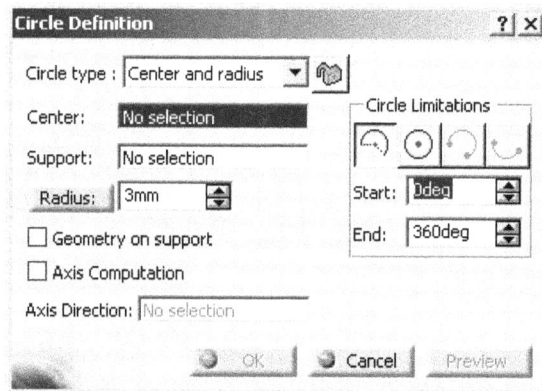

**Figure 2–30**

# Step 2 - Select a circle type.

In the Circle type drop-down list, select an option. Commonly used options are described as follows:

| Method | Orientation References |
|---|---|
| **Center and radius** | A curve is defined by selecting a reference point or vertex to locate the center and entering a radius value as shown below. 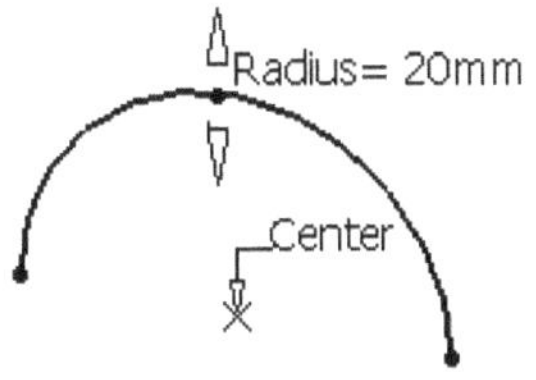 |
| | |
| **Center and point** | A curve is defined by selecting a reference point or vertex to locate the center and a point to define the radius and start point as shown below. 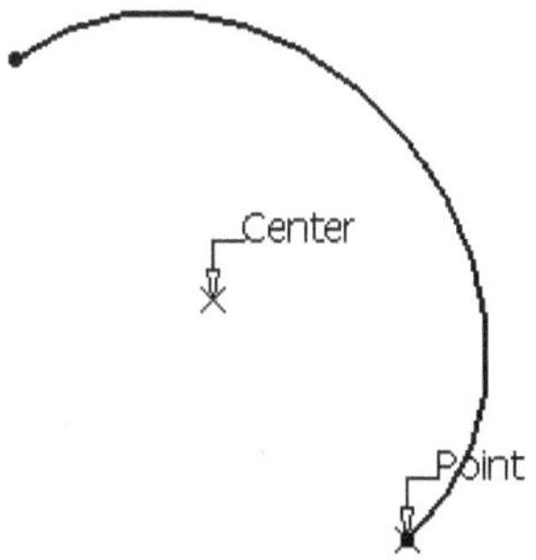 |
| | |
| **Two points and radius** | A curve is defined by selecting two reference points or vertices to define the start and end. The radius value entered determines the size of the arc as shown below. 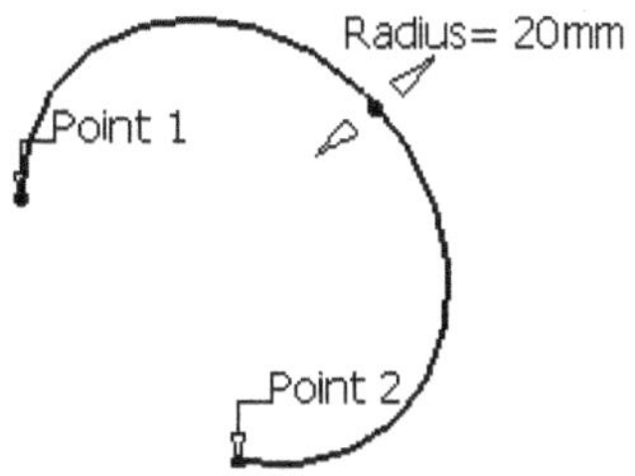 |
| | |

| Three points | A curve is defined by three reference points or vertices: the start (Point 1), radius (Point 2), and end (Point 3) as shown below. If a support is defined, the circle is projected onto the selected geometry. 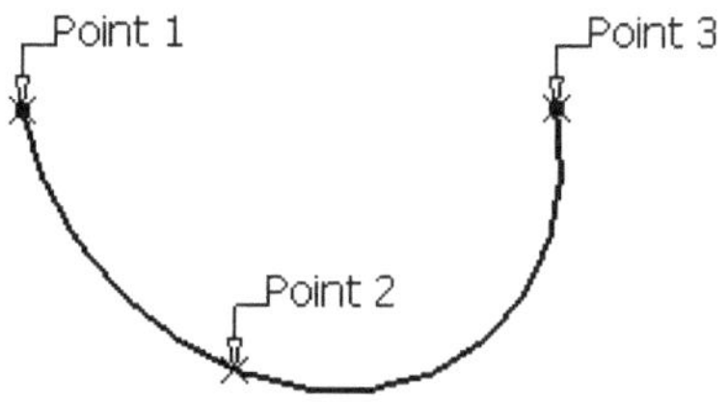 |
|---|---|
| | |
| **Center and axis** | A curve is defined by selecting a reference point or vertex to locate the center and a reference line to which the circle is perpendicular as shown below. Only full circles are available with this circle type. 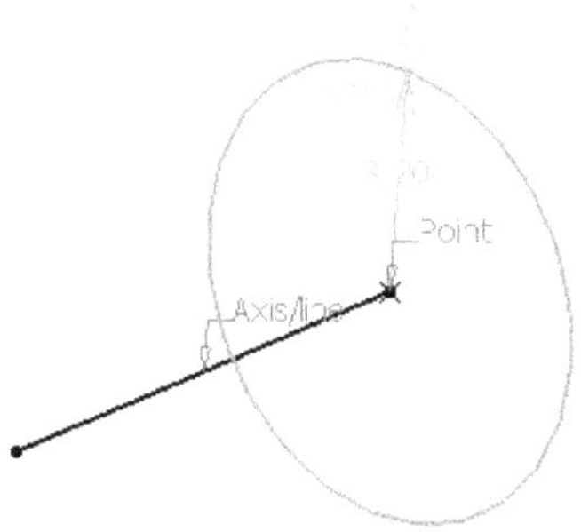 |
| | |
| **Bitangent and radius** | A curve is created tangent to two selected elements and with a specified radius as shown below. Click **Next Solution** to toggle to the required solution. 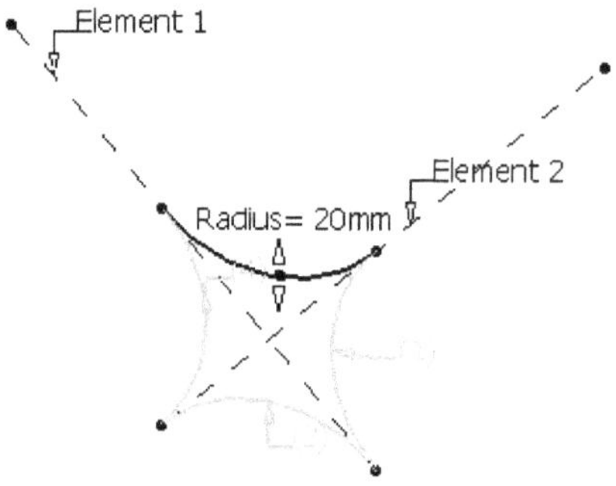 |
| | |
| **Bitangent and point** | This option is similar to **Bitangent and radius**, except that the radius of the bitangent curve is defined by selecting a reference point or vertex. |

| | |
|---|---|
| **Tritangent** | A curve is created tangent to three selected elements as shown below. Click **Next Solution** to toggle to the required solution. |

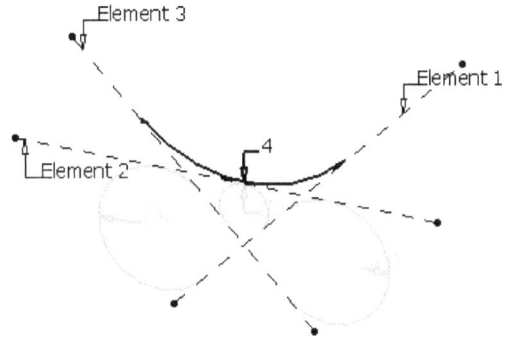

**Figure 2–31**

| | |
|---|---|
| **Center and Tangent** | A circle is defined by selecting a reference point or vertex to define the center, and a curve to which the circle is tangent as shown below. |

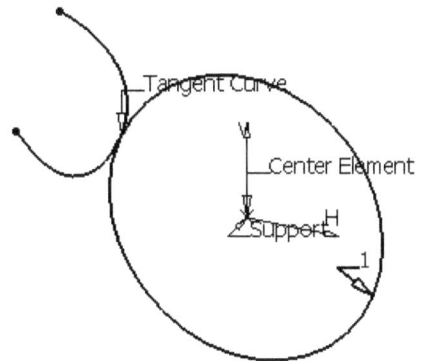

## Step 3 - Specify circle parameters.

If required, specify a center, support, and radius to define the curve as shown in Figure 2–32. A support is a planar reference on which the circle is constrained.

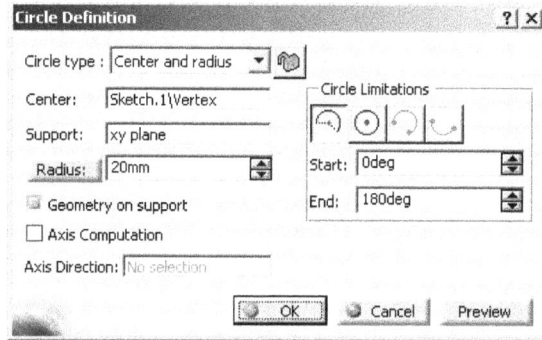

**Figure 2–32**

## Step 4 - Specify circle limitations.

The *Circle Limitations* area determines the start and end of the circle or arc being created. The limitation options are described in the table below. Depending on the Circle type selected, only the applicable circle limitations are available.

| Option | Orientation References |
|---|---|
| (Part Arc) | The start and end points of the arc are defined by the Start and End angular values entered. |
| (Whole Circle) | A closed circle is created. |
| (Trimmed Circle) | An arc is generated based on the reference geometry specified. A Start or End value is not required. |
| (Complementary Circle) | This option is the same as **Trimmed Circle**, but generates the opposite side of the arc. |

# 2.8 Create Corners

A corner element is a wireframe feature that creates a radius between two other wireframe elements.

**General Steps**

Use the following general steps to create a corner feature:

1. Start the creation of a corner.
2. Select the corner type and reference geometry.
3. Specify a radius and complete the feature.

## Step 1 - Start the creation of a corner.

Click ⌐ (Corner). The Corner Definition dialog box opens as shown in Figure 2–33.

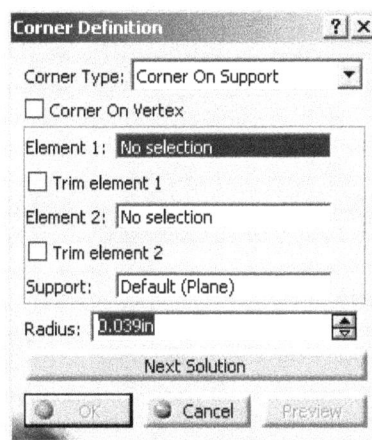

**Corner Definition**                                     ? | ✕

Corner Type: | Corner On Support | ▼

☐ Corner On Vertex

Element 1: | No selection

☐ Trim element 1

Element 2: | No selection

☐ Trim element 2

Support: | Default (Plane)

Radius: | 0.039in | ⬍

Next Solution

OK    Cancel    Preview

Figure 2–33

## Step 2 - Select the corner type and reference geometry.

You can create two types of corners by selecting an option in the Corner type drop-down list: **Corner On Support** or **3D Corner**.

## Corner On Support

*Select **Trim element 1** or **Trim element 2** if you want to remove the portion of the elements that extends beyond the corner. When this option is enabled, the original wireframe element is automatically hidden.*

A Corner On Support curve is created between two wireframe features lying on a surface or plane. The corner element follows the contour of the surface on which the reference curves lie. An example of a Corner On Support curve is shown in Figure 2–34.

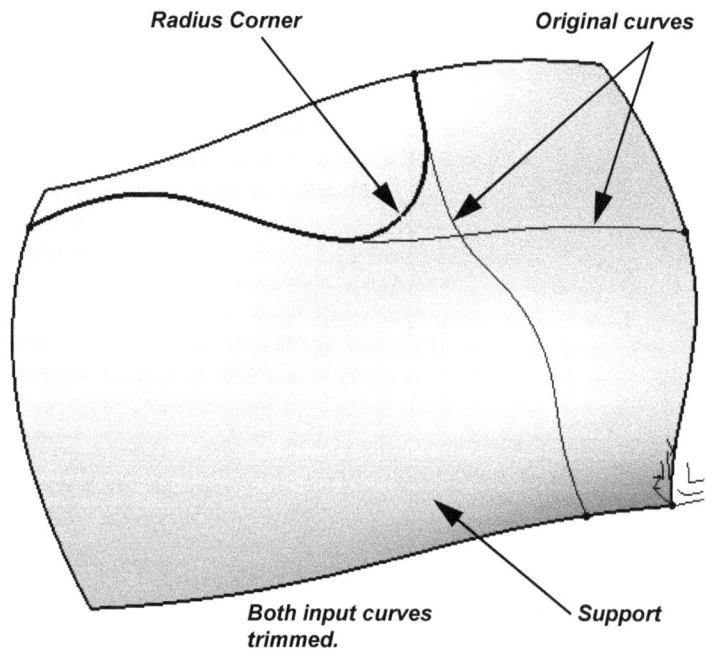

Radius Corner    Original curves

Both input curves trimmed.    Support

**Figure 2–34**

## 3D Corner

A 3D Corner is created by selecting two wireframe elements and a line or plane that defines the direction of the curve. The corner is developed in two steps.

First, the two wireframe elements are projected onto the Direction reference (either a selected plane or a plane normal to a selected line) and the corner is built in 2D. The 2D corner and the projected wireframe elements are not displayed and are only used to construct the final geometry.

The first step is shown in Figure 2–35. The 2D construction geometry is shown for demonstration purposes only.

To create the 3D corner, the 2D corner is projected onto the selected wireframe elements. An example of a completed 3D Corner is shown in the bottom center of Figure 2–35.

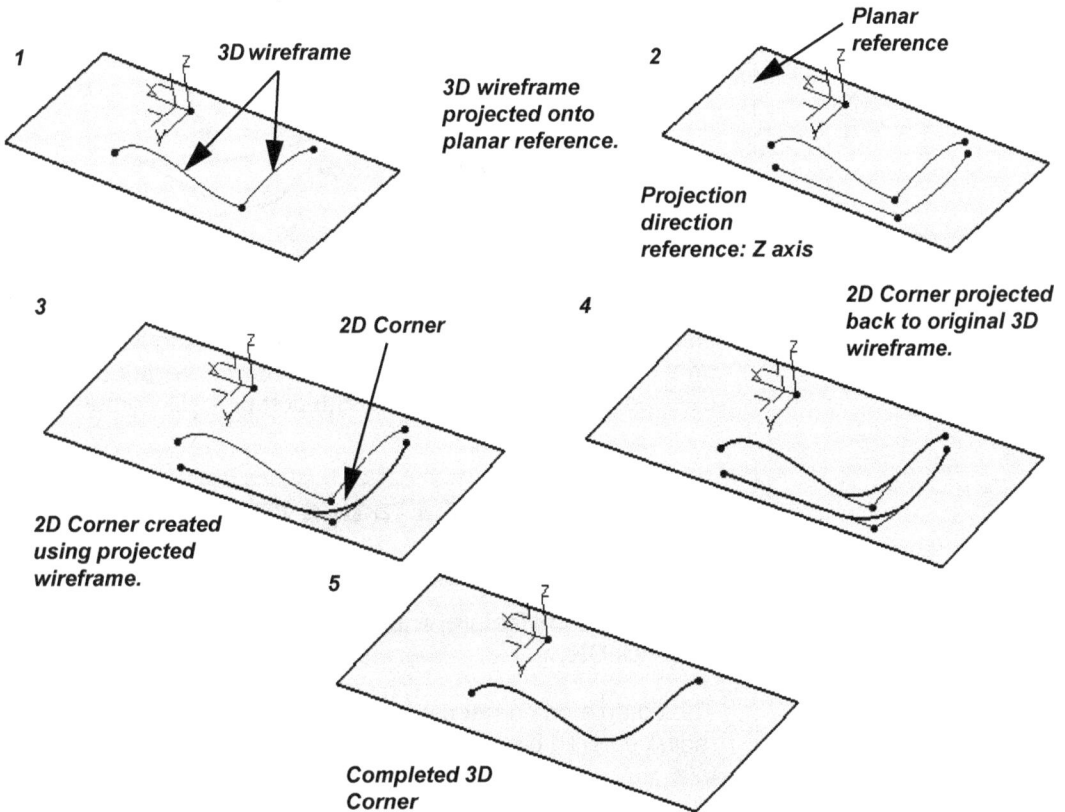

1  **3D wireframe**

**3D wireframe projected onto planar reference.**

2  **Planar reference**

**Projection direction reference: Z axis**

3  **2D Corner**

**2D Corner created using projected wireframe.**

4  **2D Corner projected back to original 3D wireframe.**

5

**Completed 3D Corner**

**Figure 2–35**

Two 3D Corners are shown in Figure 2–36. One uses the Z axis as its direction reference, while the other uses a line.

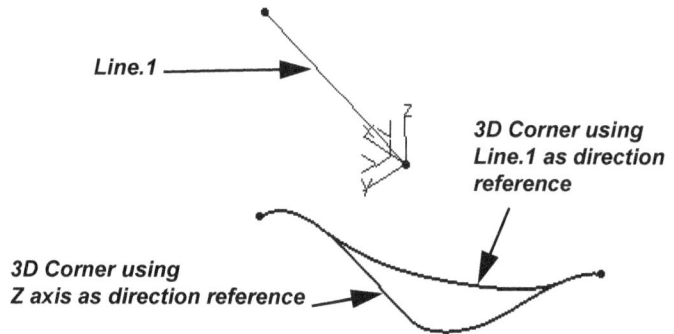

**Figure 2–36**

The **Corner On Vertex** option is used to define a corner by selecting the point of intersection between two wireframe elements. This is especially useful when creating the final corner on a closed group of curves. The **Corner on vertex** option can be used for either a Corner On Support or a 3D Corner.

## Step 3 - Specify a radius and complete the feature.

To complete the feature, enter a radius value for the corner curve and click **OK**.

The completed corner curve is G1 tangent continuous. If the radius entered does not enable tangent continuity, the curve fails.

# 2.9 Connect Curve

Connect curves is a quick way of creating a two-point spline between two existing curves. Once the two points have been selected, CATIA automatically searches for and applies tangency conditions. Click ⟳ (Connect Curve) to create a connect curve. The Connect Curve Definition dialog box opens as shown in Figure 2–37 and the options are described in the following table.

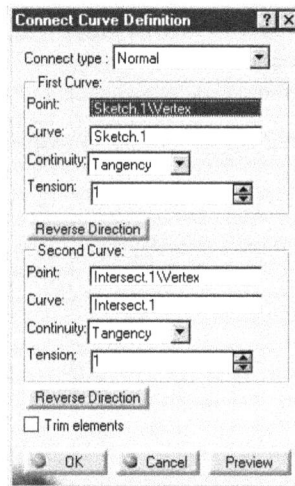

**Figure 2–37**

| Option | Orientation References |
|---|---|
| **Connect type** | Defines the type of connect curve. It can be set to **Normal** (default) or **Base Curve**. |
| **Point** | Used to select the points that the curve is to connect. |
| **Curve** | Used to select the curves to be connected. These curves must support the selected points. |
| **Continuity** | Used to select the type of continuity between the connect curve and the existing curve at each point. |
| **Tension** | Increases or decreases the amount by which the shape of the connect curve can change to maintain the continuity settings. |
| **Reverse Direction** | Reverses the direction of the connect curve at each point. |
| **Trim elements** | Removes the portion of the existing curve that extends past the connect curve. |

*The geometry can also be created using the Spline function, but the Connect Curve function is faster.*

The curves shown in Figure 2–38 need to be connected at one end. A connect curve is created to satisfy the requirement.

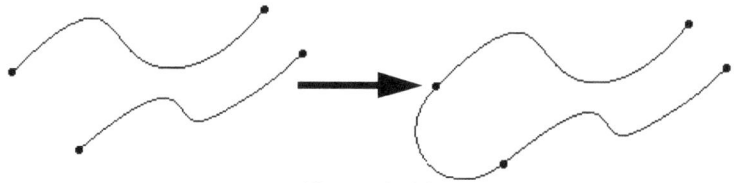

**Figure 2–38**

Figure 2–39 shows a default spline created through the same points. The tangency tensions can be modified on either feature to achieve the required geometry.

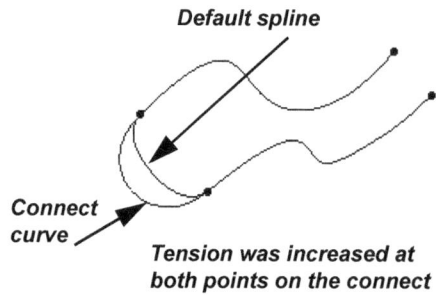

*Default spline*

*Connect curve*

*Tension was increased at both points on the connect*

**Figure 2–39**

# 2.10 Creating Splines

Splines are curves that pass smoothly through two or more points. The selected points can be point elements or vertices of previous features, including sketched points. These points must be present before initiating the creation of the spline. Once the points have been selected, additional points can be inserted or replaced. A spline can be created as either 2D or 3D and is a great tool for creating complex wireframe shapes.

**General Steps**

Use the following general steps to create a spline feature:

1. Start the creation of a spline.
2. Select reference points.
3. Define spline parameters.
4. Complete the feature.

## Step 1 - Start the creation of a spline.

Click ![spline icon] (Spline) to create a spline. The Spline Definition dialog box opens as shown in Figure 2–40.

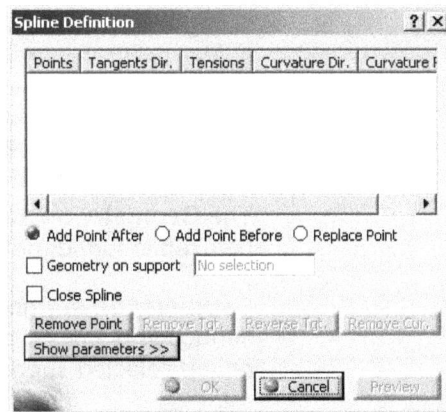

**Figure 2–40**

## Step 2 - Select reference points.

Once you start the creation of the spline, you can select reference points, end points, and vertices. Add points to the spline by selecting them in the specification tree or main window. The options in the Spline Definition dialog box enable you to perform operations on the current point that is highlighted. For example, you can rearrange the order of the points, close the spline, or remove a point.

The **Add Point After**, **Add Point Before**, and **Replace Point** options enable you to control the position of the next selected point. Points can be added before, after, or to replace the current point.

The **Close Spline** option automatically selects the last point of the spline using the first point selected to close the spline.

**Remove Point** enables you to remove the current point from the spline.

Figure 2–41 shows a spline passing through five points.

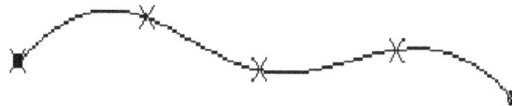

**Figure 2–41**

## Step 3 - Define spline parameters.

The **Geometry on support** option and Tangency conditions can be used to further define the shape of the spline.

**Geometry on support** forces the spline to lie on the selected surface or plane. All points selected for the spline must also lie on the selected support.

Tangency can be defined for any point specified in the spline. To specify tangency or curvature conditions, click **Show Parameters** in the Spline Definition dialog box and select a line, plane, or curve to which the spline is to be tangent at the selected point.

At the top in Figure 2–42 a spline has been created between two surfaces with no tangency constraints added. At the bottom a spline has been created between the same surfaces with tangency constraints added at both ends of the spline. The direction of tangency can be set as required.

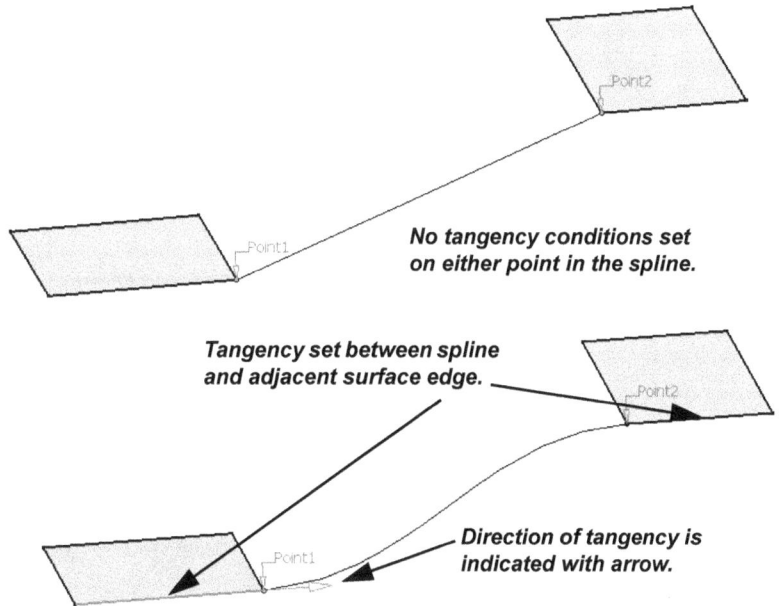

*Tangency specification is not limited to end points.*

Point2

Point1

**No tangency conditions set on either point in the spline.**

**Tangency set between spline and adjacent surface edge.**

Point2

Point1

**Direction of tangency is indicated with arrow.**

**Figure 2–42**

## Step 4 - Complete the feature.

To complete the feature, click **OK**.

# Practice 2a

# Basic Wireframe

## Practice Objectives

- Create various types of points and lines.
- Create splines and connect curves.
- Create circles and planes.

In this practice, you will create wireframe features, such as points, lines, curves, and planes. Different subtypes of each of these elements will be shown. The completed model displays as shown in Figure 2–43.

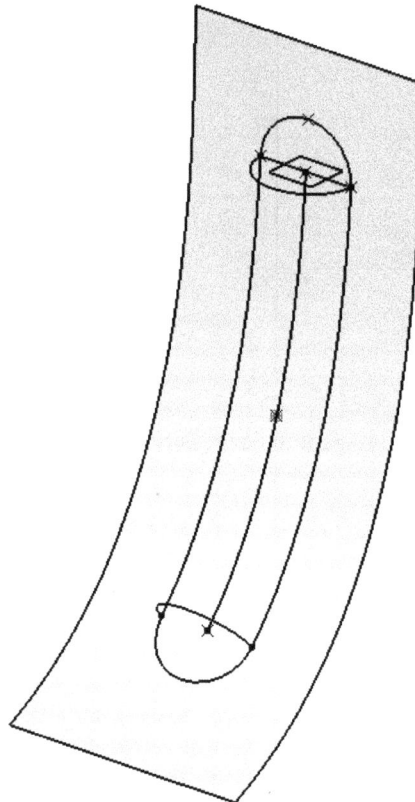

**Figure 2–43**

## Task 1 - Open a part.

1. Open **Wireframel_Start.CATPart**. The model displays as shown in Figure 2–44.

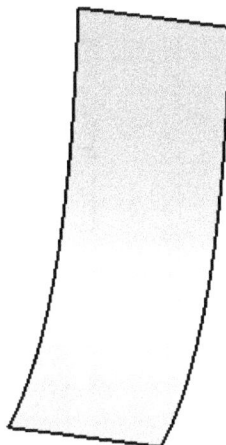

**Figure 2–44**

2. Verify that the model units are set to **mm**.

## Task 2 - Create a Work on Support.

1. In the Tools toolbar, click  (Work on support).

2. In the specification tree, select the surface or feature named Base. The Work On Support dialog box opens as shown in Figure 2–45.

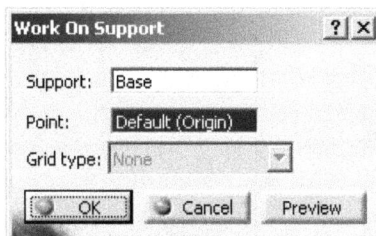

**Figure 2–45**

3. Click **OK** to complete the Work on support. Note that a new branch, **Working supports**, has been added to the specification tree. Expand the branch and note the newly created **Working support.1**, as shown in Figure 2–46. This support is active. When a wireframe element is created that contains a *Support* input field, this working support will be automatically used.

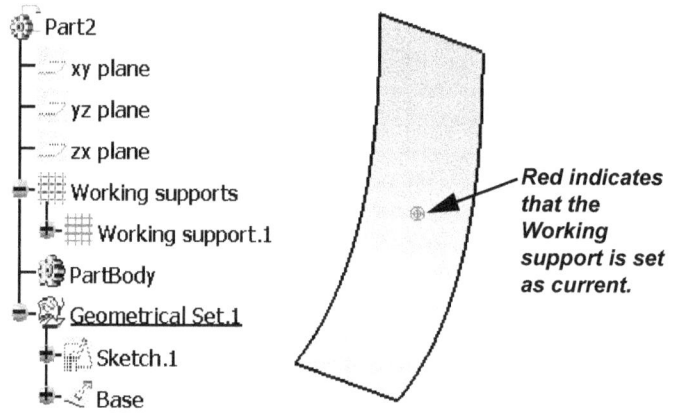

*Red indicates that the Working support is set as current.*

**Figure 2–46**

## Task 3 - Create On Surface type points.

1. Click ▣ (Point). The Point Definition dialog box opens as shown in Figure 2–47. Note that **Base** is automatically selected as the Surface reference. This is because **Base** was defined as the active Working support.

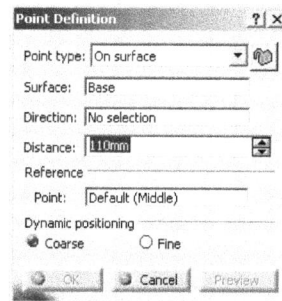

**Figure 2–47**

2. Select the **XY plane** as the Direction reference.

3. Enter **0mm** for the *Distance*.

4. Click **OK** to complete the point.

5. Rename *Point.1* as **Center**.

6. Click on the screen to ensure that no geometry is selected.

7. Click [■] (Point).

8. Verify that the **On surface** *Point type* is selected.

9. Right-click in the *Direction* field and select **Z Component**, as shown in Figure 2–48. Selecting the Z Axis provides the same result as selecting the XY plane.

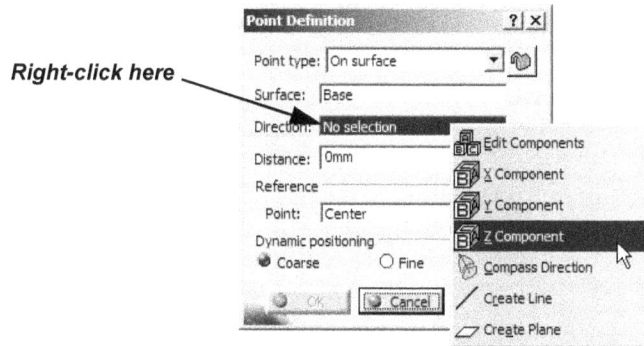

**Figure 2–48**

10. Enter a *Distance* value of **90mm**. The dialog box displays as shown in Figure 2–49.

**Figure 2–49**

11. Click **OK** to complete the point. The model displays as shown in Figure 2–50.

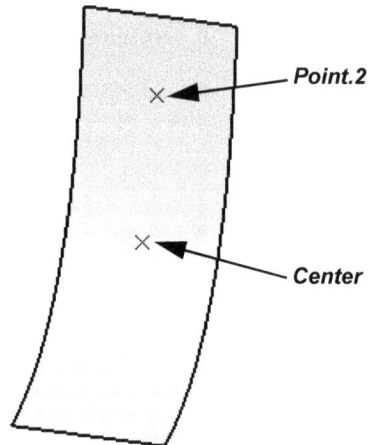

**Figure 2–50**

## Task 4 - Create a Point-Point line.

1. Click  (Line). The Line Definition dialog box opens as shown in Figure 2–51.

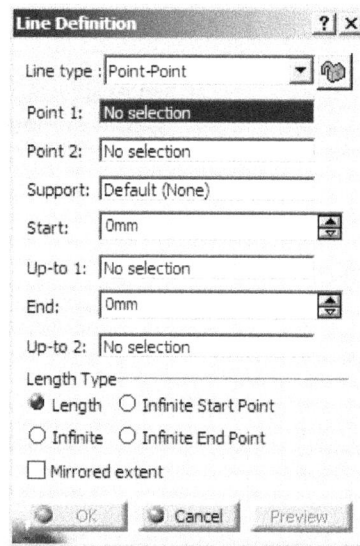

**Figure 2–51**

2. In the Line type drop-down list, select **Point-Point**, if not already selected.

3. In the specification tree, select **Point.2**.

4. In the specification tree, select the point named **Center**.

5. Enter an *End* value of **80mm**.

6. Click **OK** to complete the line. The model displays as shown in Figure 2–52.

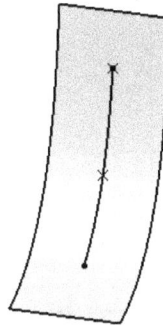

Figure 2–52

7. Rename *Line.1* as **Point to Point**.

---

**Task 5 - Create an On curve type point.**

---

1. Click  (Point).

2. In the Point type drop-down list, select **On curve**.

3. Select **Point to Point** as the curve reference.

4. Select **Ratio of curve length**.

5. Enter a *Ratio* of **1**. It might be required to click **Reverse Direction** so that your point displays as shown in Figure 2–53.

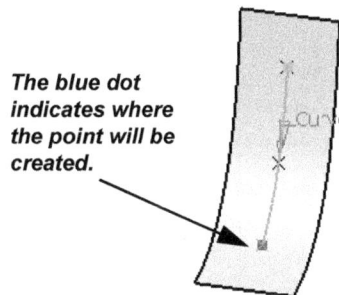

*The blue dot indicates where the point will be created.*

Figure 2–53

6. Click **OK** to complete the point. The model displays as shown in Figure 2–54.

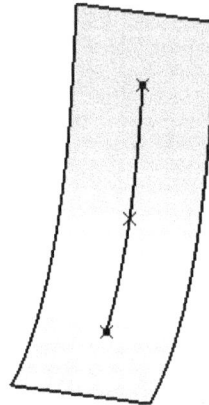

**Figure 2–54**

7. Rename the point as **On Curve1**.

---

**Task 6 - Create a circle.**

---

1. In the Wireframe toolbar, click [icon] (Circle).

2. Verify that **Center and radius** is the selected Circle type.

3. Select **On curve1**. The Circle Definition dialog box opens as shown in Figure 2–55. Note that the surface named **Base** is automatically selected as the support because it is the active Working Support.

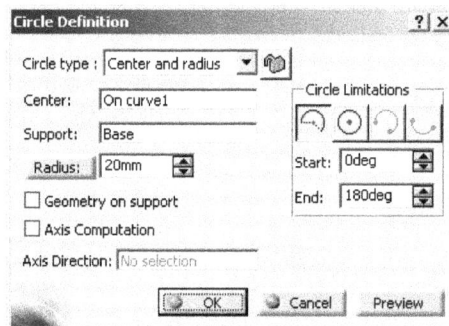

**Figure 2–55**

4. Enter a *Radius* value of **20mm**.

5. Enter a *Start* value of **-90deg**.

6. Enter a *End* value of **90deg**. The start and end values might be different on your model. Adjust your values accordingly so that you create a 180 degree arc.

7. Click **OK** to complete the circle. The model displays as shown in Figure 2–56.

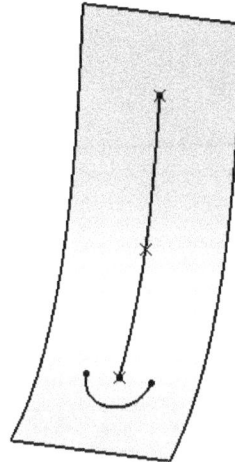

**Figure 2–56**

## Task 7 - Create a Point-Direction line.

1. Click [ / ] (Line).

2. In the Line type drop-down list, select **Point-Direction**.

3. In the specification tree, select **Point.2**.

4. Select the **ZX plane**. It will act as the Direction reference. Remember that **Base** is the active working support, so the Support reference is automatically assigned.

5. Select **Mirror extent**.

6. Enter an *End* value of **20mm**, as shown in Figure 2–57.

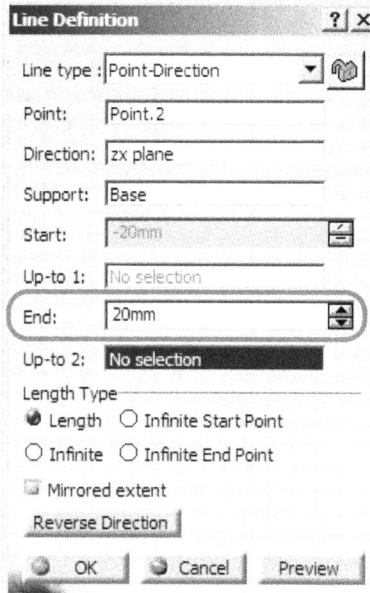

**Figure 2–57**

7. Click **OK** to complete the line. The model displays as shown in Figure 2–58.

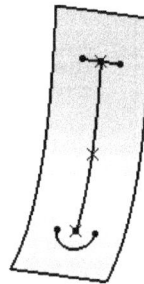

**Figure 2–58**

8. Rename the line as **Point Direction Line**.

## Task 8 - Create more On curve points.

1. Click  (Point).

2. In the Point type drop-down list, select **On curve**.

3. Select **Point Direction Line** as the curve reference.

4. Select **Ratio of curve length**.

5. Enter a *Ratio* of **1**. The dialog box updates as shown in Figure 2–59.

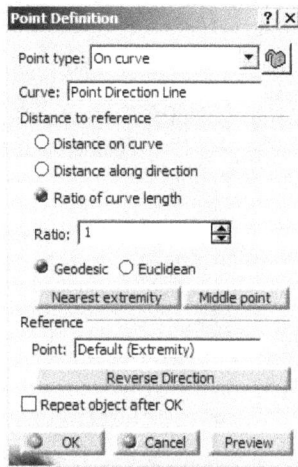

**Point Definition** ? X

Point type: On curve ▼ 📖

Curve: Point Direction Line

Distance to reference
○ Distance on curve
○ Distance along direction
● Ratio of curve length

Ratio: 1

● Geodesic ○ Euclidean

Nearest extremity | Middle point

Reference

Point: Default (Extremity)

Reverse Direction

☐ Repeat object after OK

OK | Cancel | Preview

**Figure 2–59**

6. If required, click **Reverse Direction** to flip the direction from which the ratio is measured. The model displays as shown in Figure 2–60.

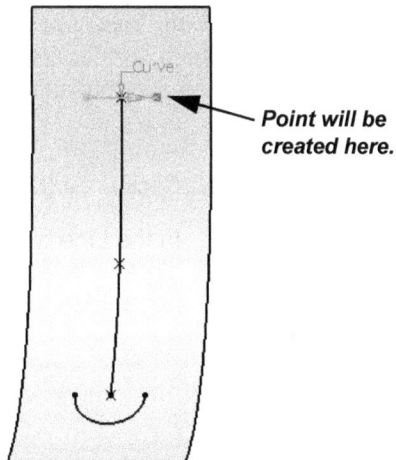

Curve

*Point will be created here.*

**Figure 2–60**

7. Click **OK** to complete the point. Rename the point as **On Curve2**.

8. Create another **On curve** point using the following references:

   - *Curve:* **Point Direction Line**
   - *Distance to reference:* **Ratio of curve length**
   - *Ratio:* **1**

9. The completed point displays as shown in Figure 2–61. Rename the point as **On Curve3**.

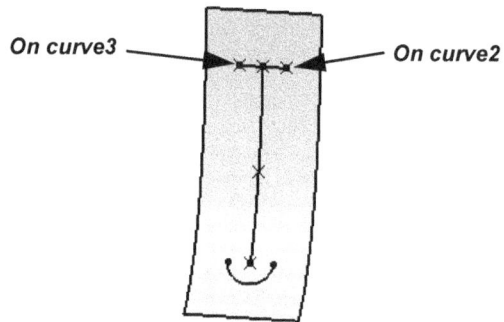

**Figure 2–61**

---

### Task 9 - Create a line using the active support.

---

In this task, you will create a line. It will follow the curvature of the **Base** surface. Because **Base** is the active working support, the line automatically uses **Base** as the support reference.

1. Click [ / ] (Line).

2. In the Line type drop-down list, select **Point-Point** if it is not already selected. In the specification tree, select the point named **On Curve 2**.

3. Right-click in the *Point 2* reference field and select **Create Endpoint**, as shown in Figure 2–62. This technique is helpful when a reference that is required to complete the feature is not already created. The shortcut menu provides a way to create the required reference on the fly.

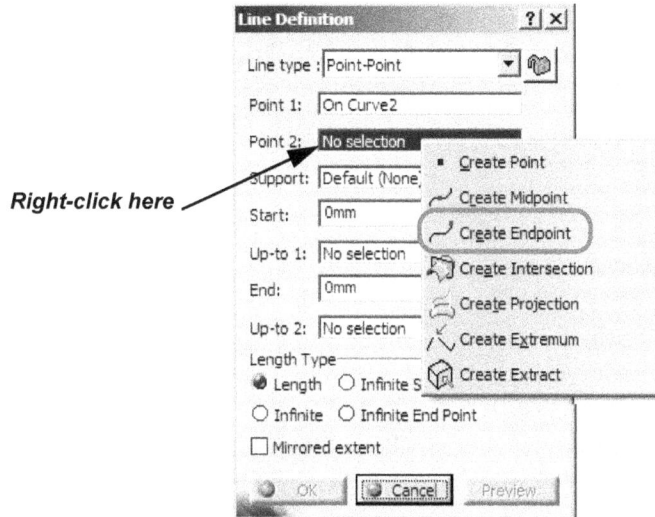

**Figure 2–62**

4. Select the point shown in Figure 2–63.

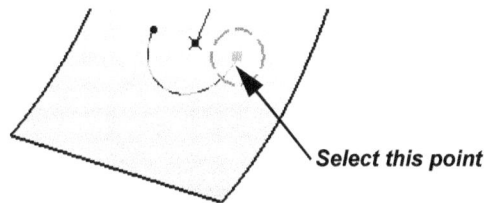

**Figure 2–63**

5. Verify that the *Start* and *End* values of the line are both **0mm**. Note that the support reference uses the **Base** surface. **Base** is the active working support, so the line will be created on this surface. The dialog box updates as shown in Figure 2–64.

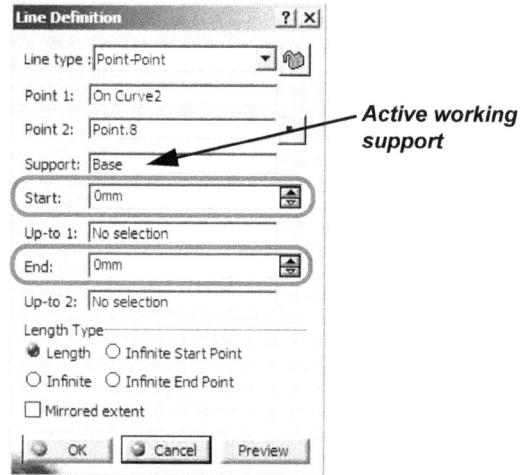

Figure 2–64

6. Click **OK** to complete the line. The model displays as shown in Figure 2–65.

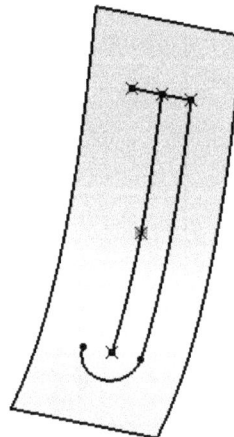

Figure 2–65

7. Rename the line as **Point to Point 2**.

## Task 10 - Create a spline.

1. Click ⟳ (Spline). The Spline Definition dialog box opens as shown in Figure 2–66.

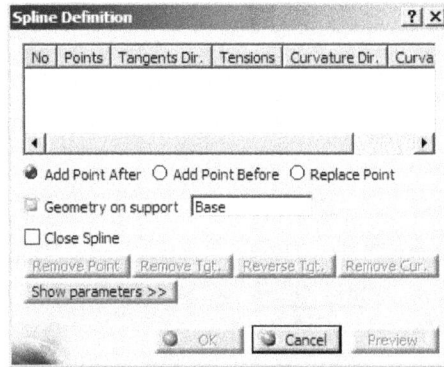

**Figure 2–66**

2. In the specification tree, select **On Curve3**.

3. Right-click where indicated in Figure 2–67 and select **Create Endpoint**.

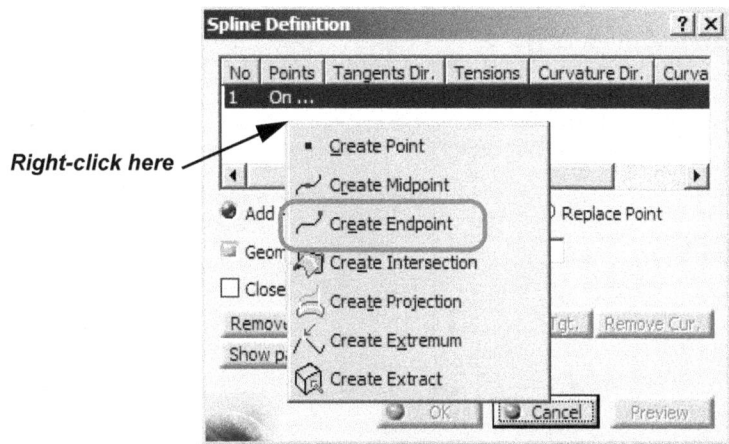

**Figure 2–67**

4. Select the point shown in Figure 2–68. The dialog box updates.

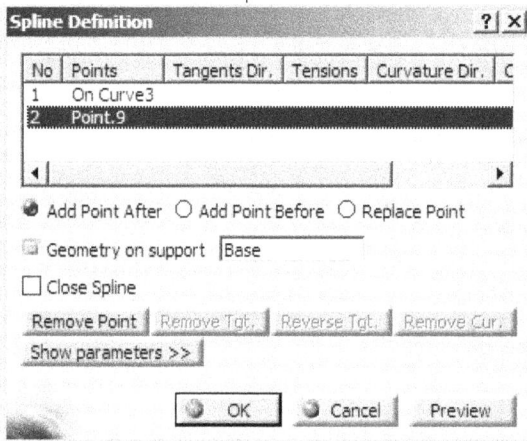

Figure 2–68

5. Click **OK** to complete the spline. The model displays as shown in Figure 2–69.

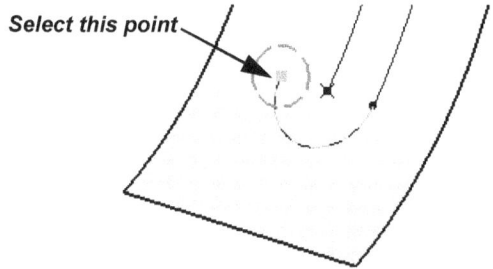

Figure 2–69

---

**Task 11 - Create an On surface point.**

---

1. Click 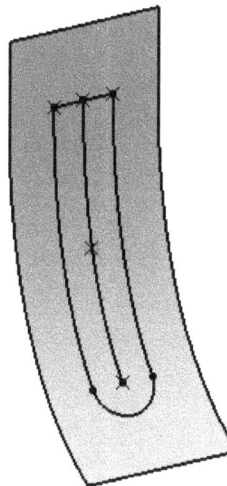 (Point).

2. Verify that the **On surface** *Point type* is selected.

3. Select the XY plane as the direction reference.

4. Enter a *Distance* of **110mm**.

5. Click **OK** to complete the point. The model displays as shown in Figure 2–70.

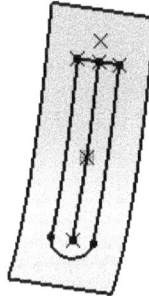

**Figure 2–70**

6. Rename the point as **On Surface1**.

---

**Task 12 - Create another circle.**

---

1. In the Wireframe toolbar, click [ ] (Circle). The Circle Definition dialog box opens as shown in Figure 2–71.

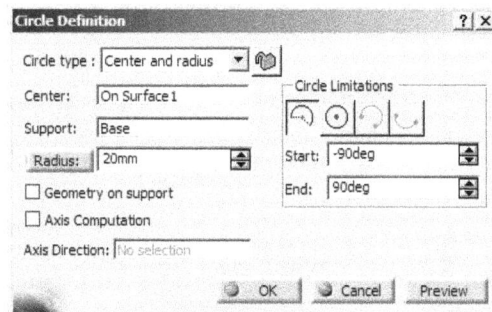

**Figure 2–71**

2. In the Circle type drop-down list, select **Three points**.

3. Select the point named **On Curve2**.

4. Select the point named **On Surface1**.

5. Select the point named **On Curve3**.

6. Click **OK** to complete the Circle. The model displays as shown in Figure 2–72.

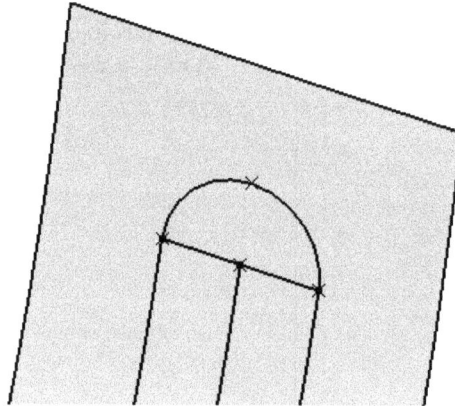

**Figure 2–72**

---

**Task 13 - Create three lines.**

---

1. Click ![Line icon] (Line).

2. In the Line type drop-down list, select **Normal to surface**.

3. Right-click in the *Point* reference field and select **Create Endpoint**.

4. Select the point shown in Figure 2–73.

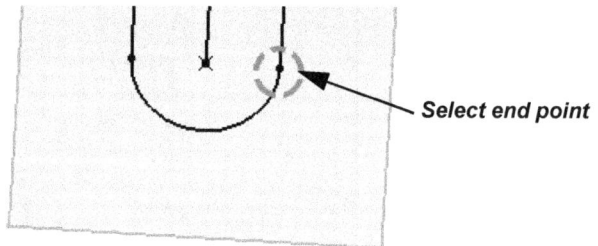

*Select end point*

**Figure 2–73**

5. Enter an *Start* value of **0mm**.

6. Enter an *End* value of **20mm**.

7. Verify that the direction of the line is as shown in Figure 2–74. If required, click **Reverse Direction**.

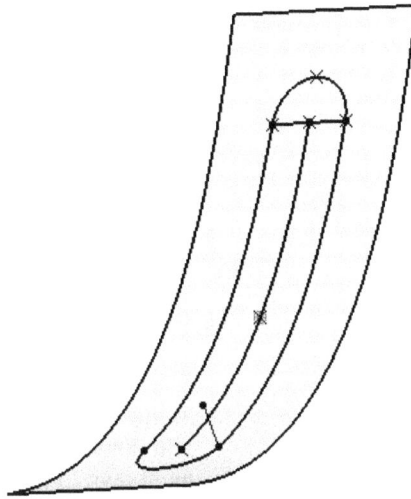

**Figure 2–74**

8. Click **OK** to complete the line.

9. Rename the line as **Line Normal to Surface 1**.

10. Repeat Steps 1 through 8 to create another line. The only difference is that the line will use the point indicated in Figure 2–75.

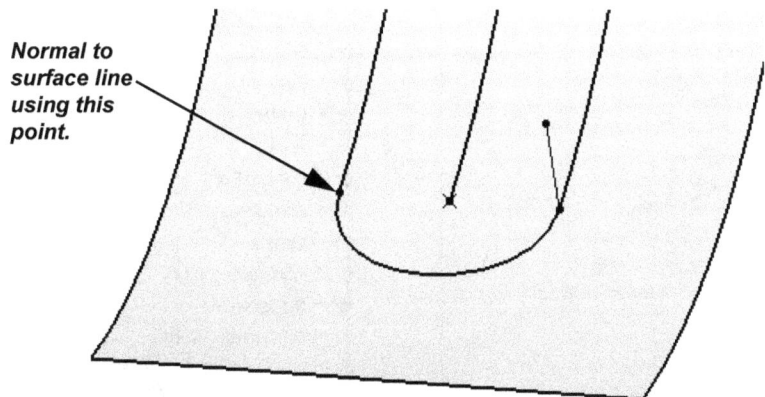

*Normal to surface line using this point.*

**Figure 2–75**

11. Rename the line as **Line Normal to Surface 2**. The model displays as shown in Figure 2–76.

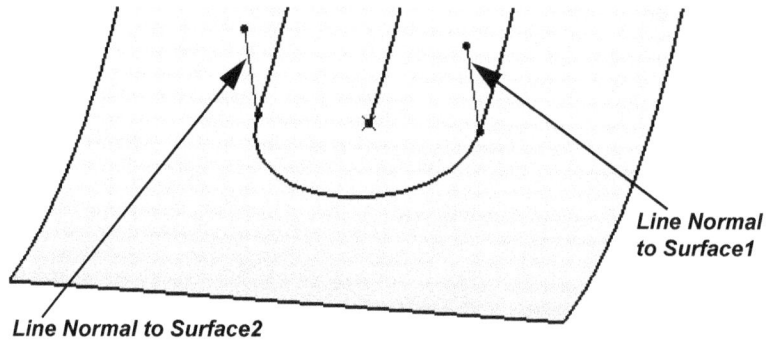

**Figure 2–76**

12. In the specification tree, right-click on **Working support.1** and select **Working support.1 object> Set as Not Current**, as shown in Figure 2–77. Note that the color of the Working support changes to blue.

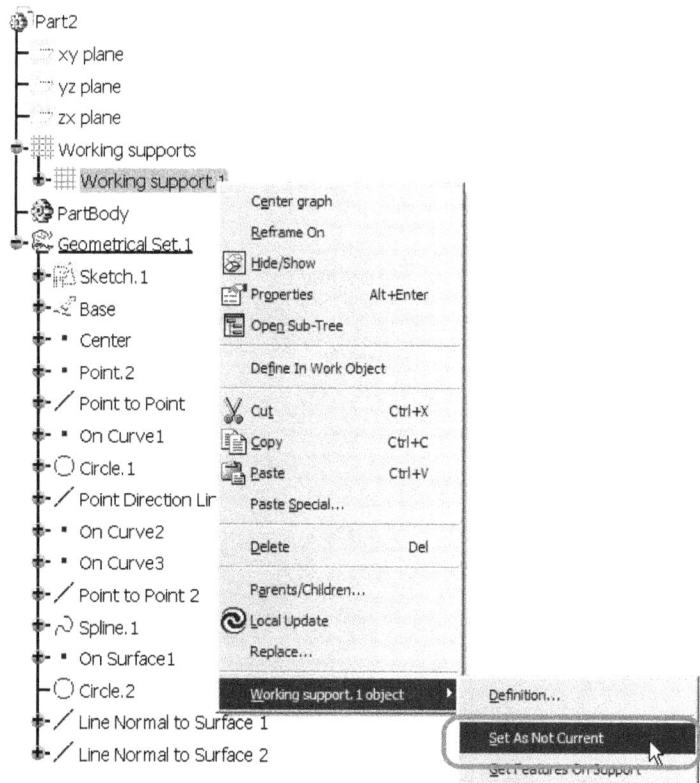

**Figure 2–77**

**Task 14 - Create points and a line for the tritangent circle.**

1. Create two **On Curve** points using a ratio of **0**. Rename them as shown in Figure 2–78.

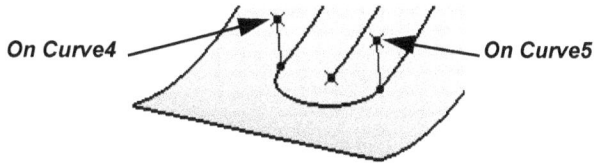

**Figure 2–78**

2. Create a **Point-Point** line using On Curve 4 and On Curve 5. The model displays as shown in Figure 2–79.

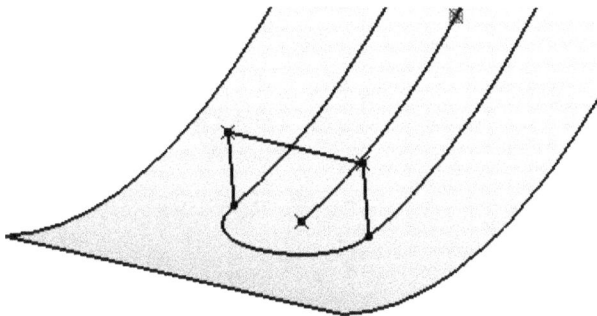

**Figure 2–79**

3. Rename the line as **Point to Point 3**.

4. Click ⬜ (Circle).

5. In the Circle type drop-down list, select **Tritangent**.

6. In the specification tree, select **Line Normal to Surface 1**.

7. In the specification tree, select **Point to Point 3**.

8. In the specification tree, select **Line Normal to Surface 2**. The dialog box updates as shown in Figure 2–80.

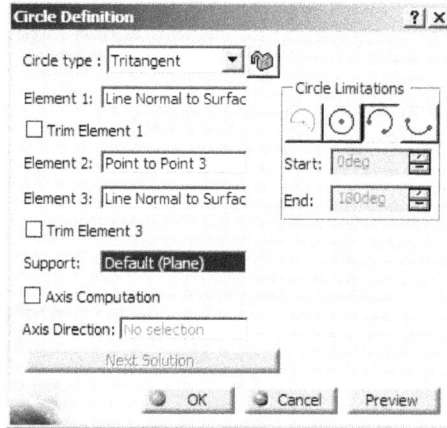

**Figure 2–80**

9. Click **OK** to complete the circle. The model displays as shown in Figure 2–81.

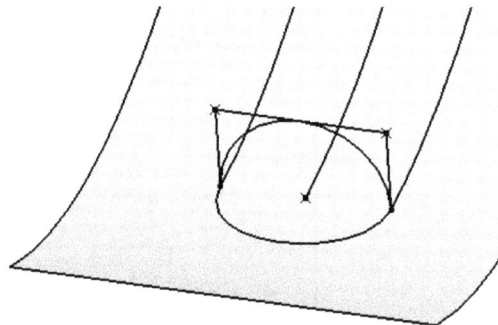

**Figure 2–81**

10. Hide the following elements:

   • Line Normal to Surface 1
   • Line Normal to Surface 2
   • Point to Point 3
   • On Curve 4
   • On Curve 5

## Task 15 - Create another circle.

1. Click [⬦] (Plane). The dialog box opens as shown in Figure 2–82.

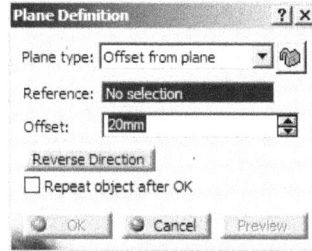

**Figure 2–82**

2. In the Plane type drop-down list, select **Normal to curve**. Select **Point to Point** as the Curve reference. Select **Point.2** as the Point reference.

3. Click **OK** to complete the plane. The model displays as shown in Figure 2–83.

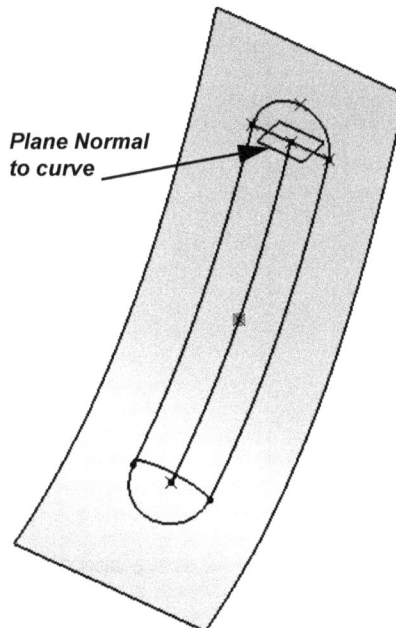

*Plane Normal to curve*

**Figure 2–83**

4. Click [○] (Circle).

5. In the Circle type drop-down list, select **Two points and radius**.

6. Select **On Curve2** as the *Point 1* reference.

7. Select **On Curve3** as the *Point 2* reference.

8. Select **Plane.1** as the Support reference.

9. Enter a *Radius* value of **20mm**.

10. Verify that the **Geometry on support** option is selected.

11. Click **OK** to complete the circle. The completed model displays as shown in Figure 2–84.

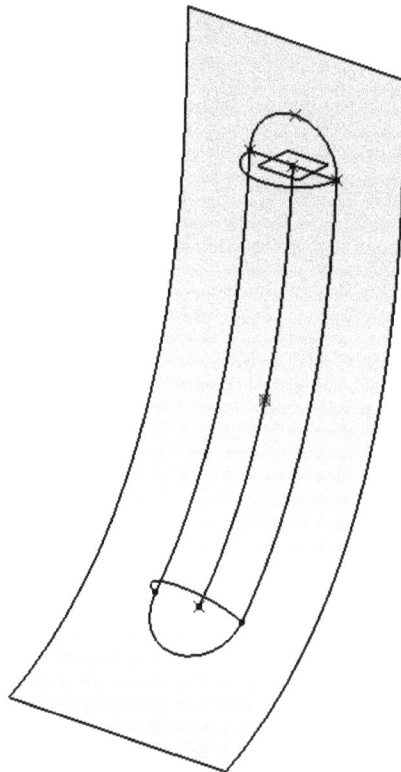

**Figure 2–84**

12. Save and close the model.

# Practice 2b | Sketch Review

## Practice Objective

- Sketch a profile without any instruction.

In this practice, you will review creating sketches. The shapes in this practice will challenge your memory and knowledge of the sketcher. These sketches do not represent profiles that are recommended for creating surfaces or solids. They are used in this practice as a tool to review the Sketcher workbench.

1. Create a new part called **Sketch Review**. Sketch the profile shown in Figure 2–85 on the XY plane.

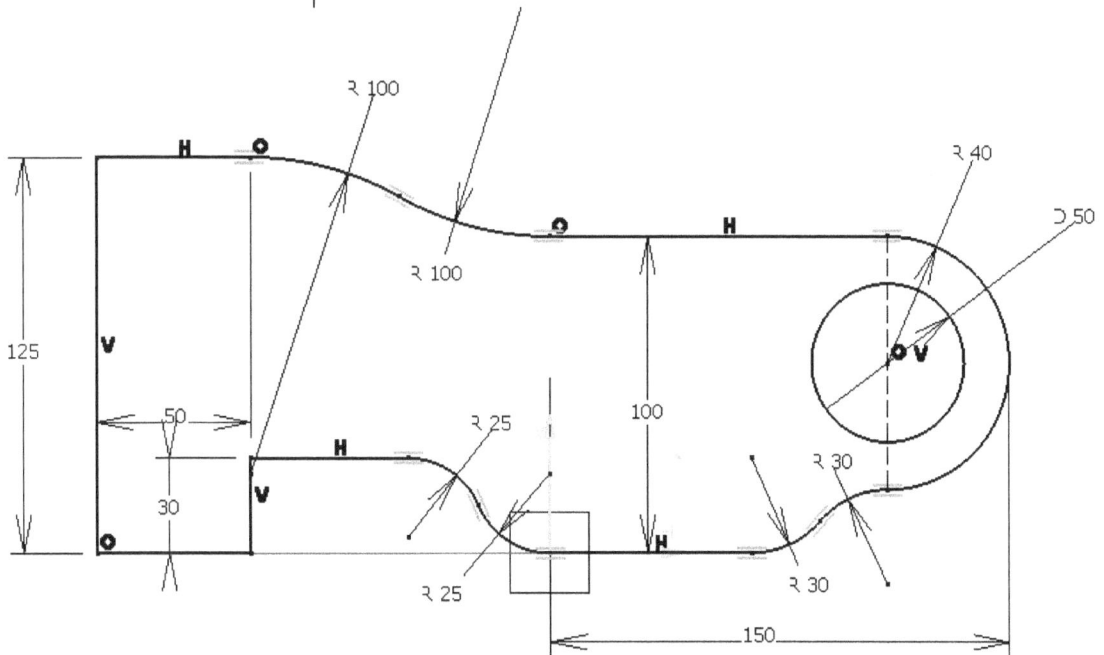

Figure 2–85

2. Sketch the profile shown in Figure 2–86 on the YZ Plane.

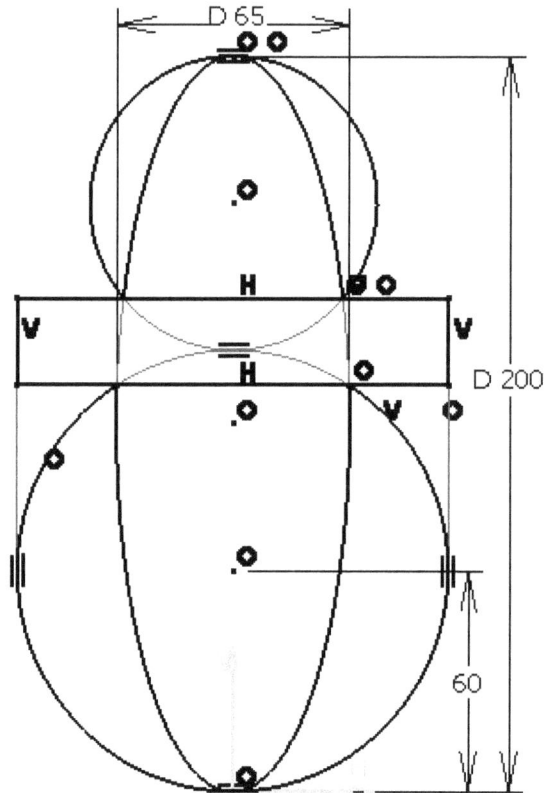

**Figure 2–86**

When the sketch is Iso-constrained, perform a Sketch Analysis. The Sketch Analysis dialog box opens as shown in Figure 2–87.

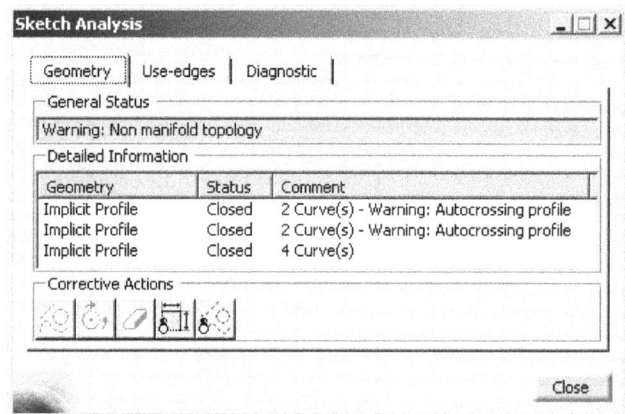

**Figure 2–87**

The Autocrossing profile indicates two profiles that are touching. This would cause a problem if a surface or solid feature was built from this profile.

If you see something different in the Sketch Analysis, check whether the geometry was correctly constrained and dimensioned.

## Hints for creating the profile:

- Start by creating the ellipse. Sketch the two circles second. Dimension and constrain them as shown in Figure 2–88.

- The top circle is tangent to the ellipse. It is also tangent to the larger bottom circle.

- The bottom circle is tangent to the ellipse.

- No radii values are required for the two circles.

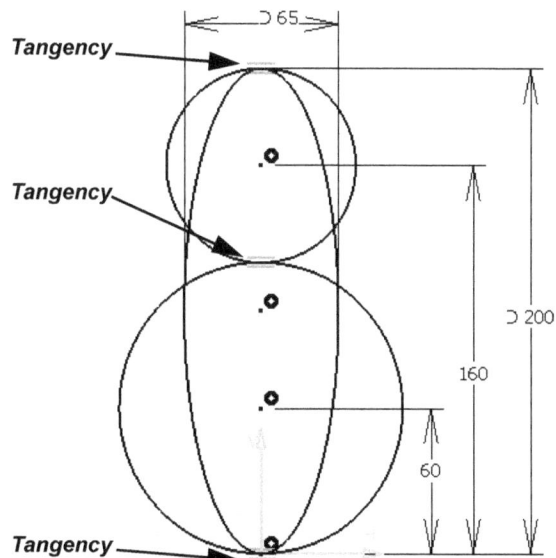

**Figure 2–88**

- Use the **Trim** or **Quick Trim** tool to remove unwanted portions of the Ellipse and the two circles, as shown in Figure 2–89.

*The dimensions and constraints are hidden in Figure 2–89.*

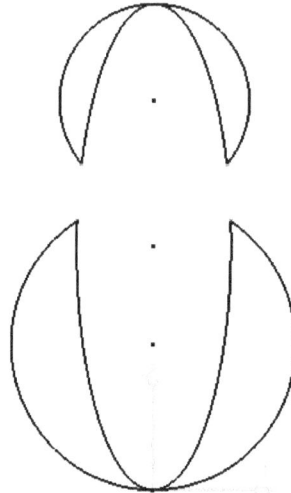

**Figure 2–89**

- Create a rectangle.

- Ensure that the rectangle is coincident to the end points shown in Figure 2–90, and tangent to the bottom circle.

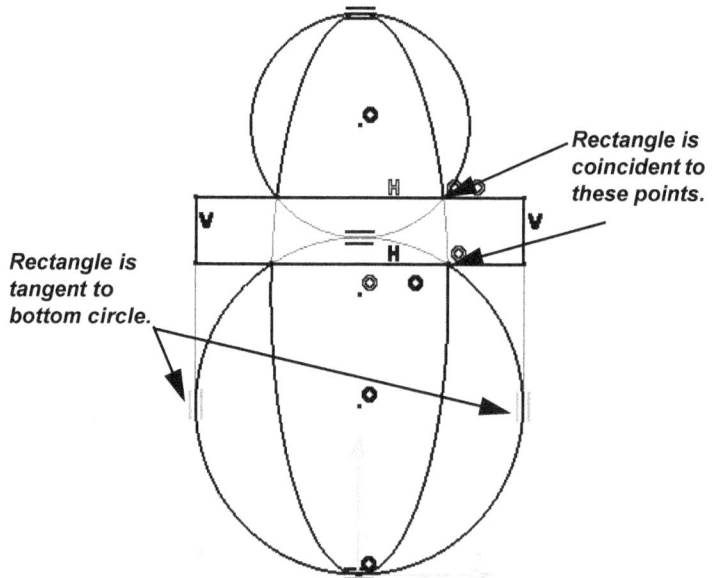

Rectangle is coincident to these points.

Rectangle is tangent to bottom circle.

**Figure 2–90**

| Practice 2c | # Positioned Sketch Review |
| --- | --- |

### Practice Objectives

- Create positioned sketches.
- Change sketch supports.

In this practice, you will create a profile that is projected from a face of the model using a positioned sketch. You will then change the support of the sketch and modify the profile using a different face of the model according to the design changes.

### Task 1 - Open a part.

1. Open **Positioned_Sketch_Start.CATPart**. The model displays as shown in Figure 2–91.

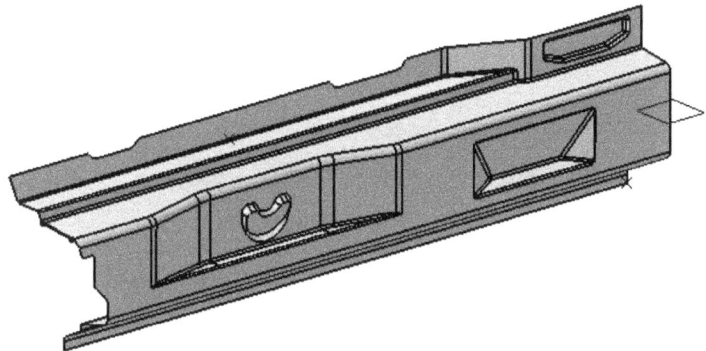

**Figure 2–91**

Note that the reference elements and an imported surface are present in the model, as shown in Figure 2–92.

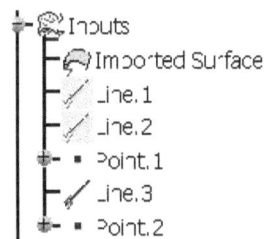

**Figure 2–92**

2. Verify that the model units are set to **mm**.

**Task 2 - Create the first positioned sketch.**

In this task, you will create the first positioned sketch. The absolute axis of the sketch is based on the Barycenter of a selected surface from the model.

1. Click ⛏️ (Position Sketch). The Sketch Positioning dialog box opens. Verify that the Type in *Sketch Positioning* area is set to **Positioned** as shown in Figure 2–93.

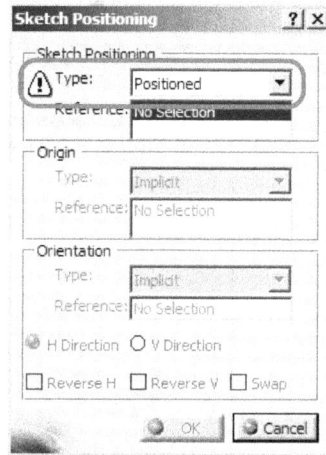

**Figure 2–93**

2. Select the surface shown in Figure 2–94. This is defined as the Sketch Positioning reference (the sketching plane).

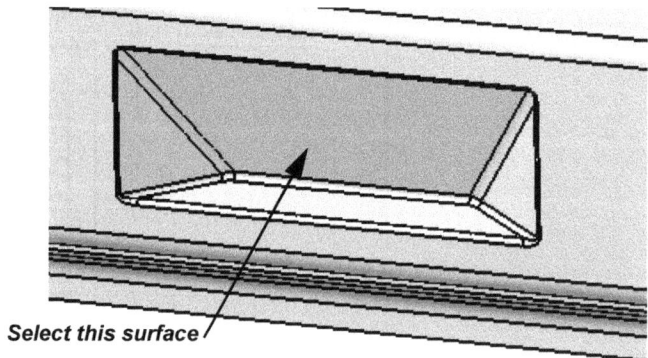

*Select this surface*

**Figure 2–94**

3. In the Origin type drop-down list, select **Barycenter**.

4. Select the surface shown in Figure 2–95 as the Barycenter reference. This places the origin of the sketch at the center of the selected surface.

5. Verify that the Vertical Axis and Horizontal Axis are pointing in the directions shown in Figure 2–95.

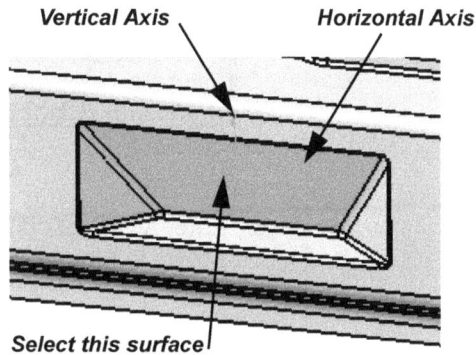

**Figure 2–95**

6. In the Sketch Positioning dialog box, click **OK**. You will automatically enter the Sketcher in the orientation shown in Figure 2–96.

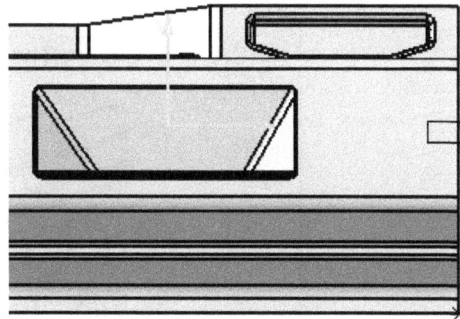

**Figure 2–96**

7. Click  (Offset).

8. Select the surface shown in Figure 2–97.

*Select surface*

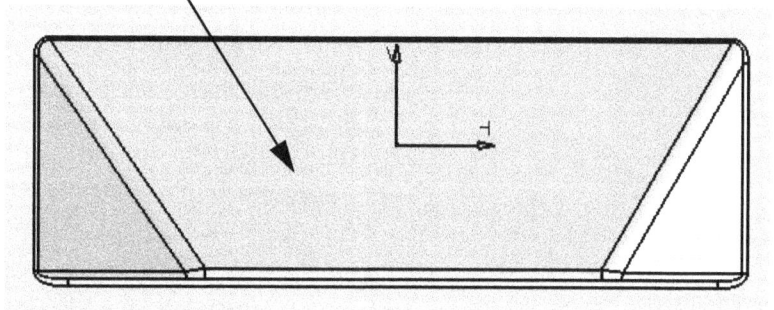

**Figure 2–97**

9. Enter an offset distance of **5mm**. The model displays as shown in Figure 2–98.

**Figure 2–98**

10. Exit Sketcher. The model displays as shown in Figure 2–99.

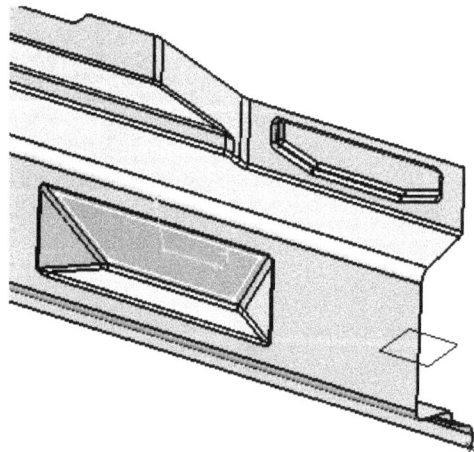

**Figure 2–99**

11. Rename the sketch as **Sketch - Barycenter**.

## Task 3 - Edit the Sketch support and references.

In this task, a design change calls for the sketch plane to be changed. The geometry must also be offset from a new reference. You will change the sketch plane and origin of the sketch. To edit the sketch geometry, you will replace the 3D reference that is used by the offset.

1. Right-click on **Sketch - Barycenter** and select **Sketch - Barycenter object>Change Sketch Support**.

2. In the Warning box, click **OK** as shown in Figure 2–100. The warning displays because the offset in the sketch is considered a projection. This is because you referenced geometry that was outside the sketch.

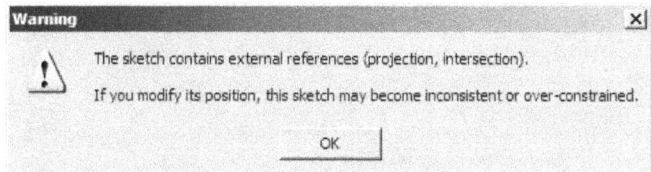

**Figure 2–100**

3. In the Sketch Positioning dialog box, select the surface shown in Figure 2–101 for the **Sketch Positioning Reference** and the **Origin Reference**. This changes the sketch plane to the selected surface. You will also redefine the Barycenter surface. This will adjust the origin of the sketch.

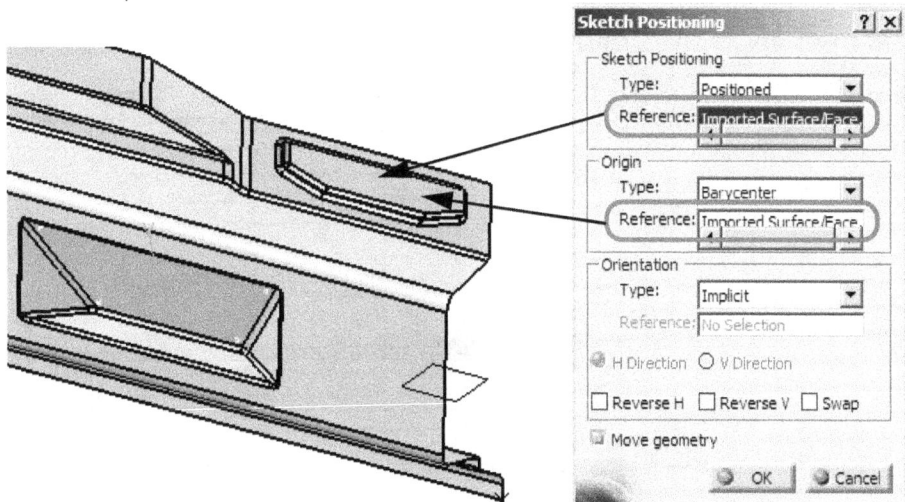

**Figure 2–101**

4.  It might be required to adjust the Horizontal Axis of the sketch, as shown in Figure 2–102. If your Vertical and Horizontal Axis already look like the *After* image, you do not need to adjust the axis.

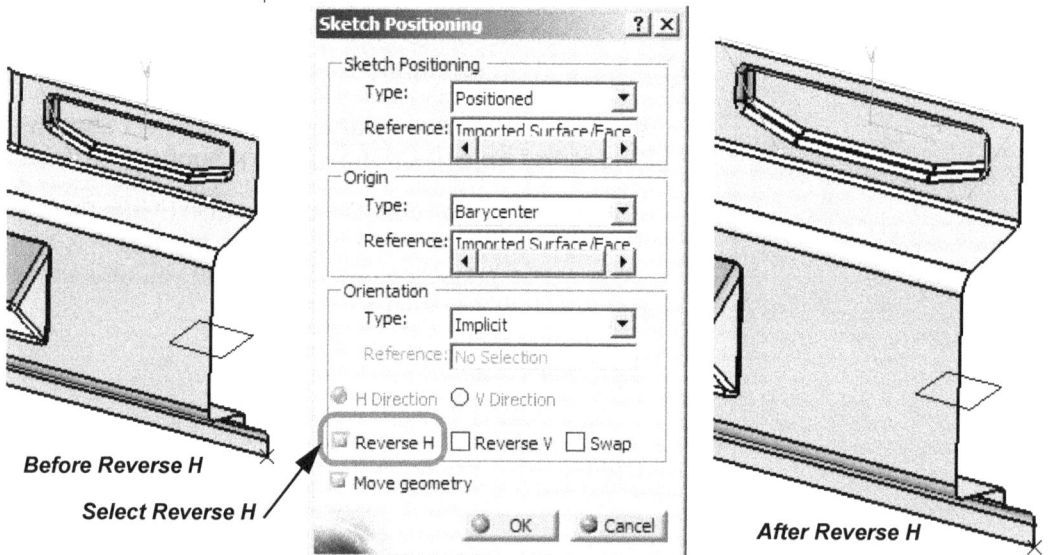

**Figure 2–102**

5.  In the Sketch Positioning dialog box, click **OK**.

6.  Edit **Sketch - Barycenter** by double-clicking on it. The model displays as shown in Figure 2–103.

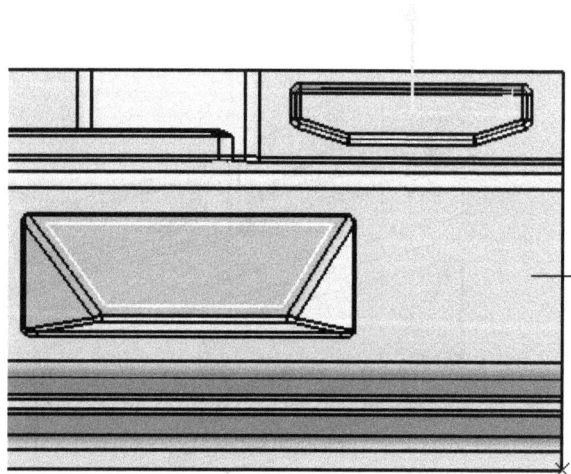

**Figure 2–103**

7. Select **Tools>Sketch Analysis**.

8. In the Sketch Analysis dialog box, select the *Use-edges* tab.

9. Select **Offset.1** in the list, as shown in Figure 2–104.

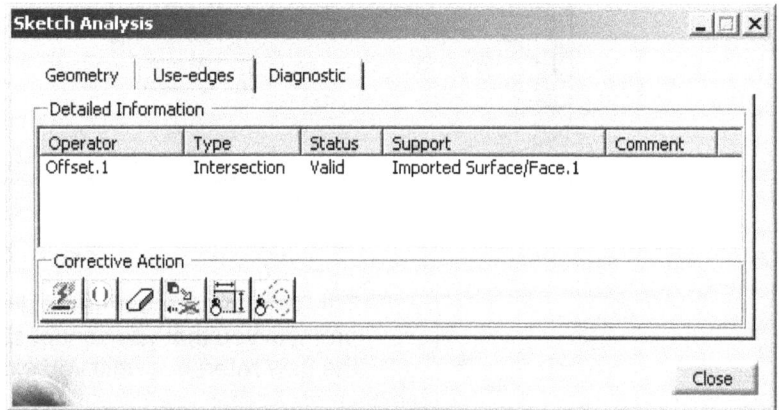

**Figure 2–104**

The referenced face highlights on the model, indicating where the projected geometry originated, as shown in Figure 2–105. You no longer want the offset geometry to reference the highlighted face.

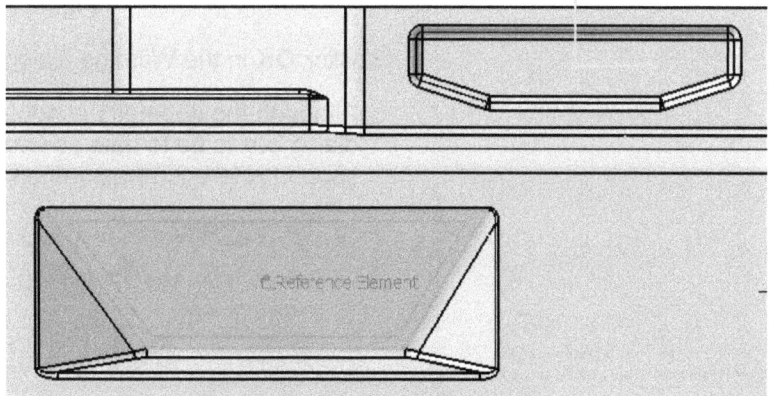

**Figure 2–105**

10. In the Sketch Analysis dialog box, click ⬛ (Replace 3D Geometry). This enables you to select a new surface to reference for the offset geometry.

11. Select the surface shown in Figure 2–106.

**Select surface**

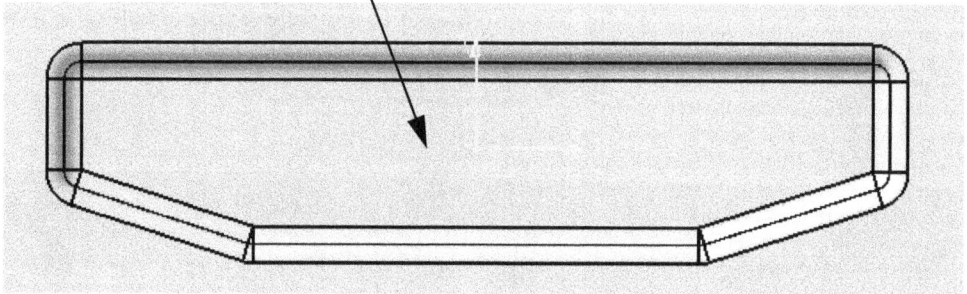

**Figure 2–106**

12. The Warning box opens as shown in Figure 2–107. It prompts you that you cannot see the changes when selecting the new reference until you exit Sketcher.

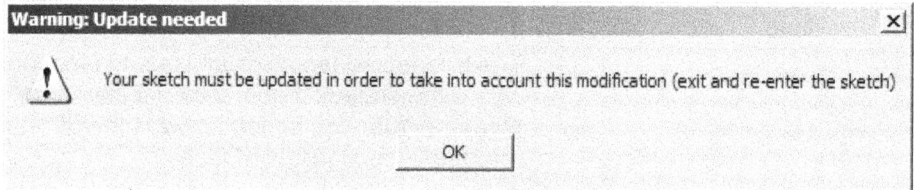

**Figure 2–107**

13. Click **OK** in the Warning dialog box.

Although the geometry is not up to date, the Sketch Analysis dialog box is up to date as shown in Figure 2–108. The old support reference was named **Imported Surface\Face.1**.

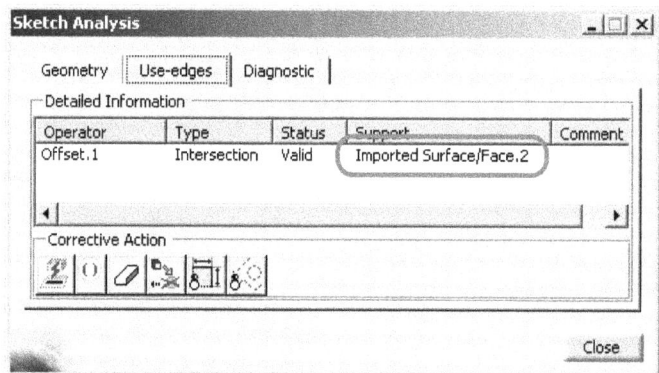

**Figure 2–108**

14. Close the Sketch Analysis dialog box and exit Sketcher. The geometry updates automatically. The model displays as shown in Figure 2–109.

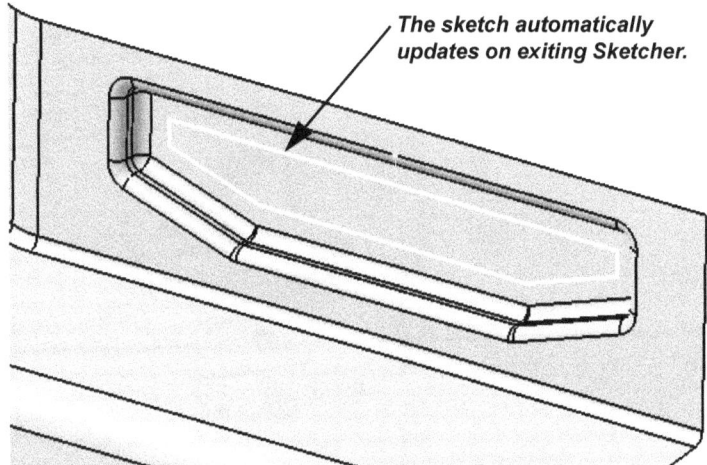

*The sketch automatically updates on exiting Sketcher.*

**Figure 2–109**

**Task 4 - Create a Positioned Sketch located by a point.**

1. Click  (Positioned Sketch). The dialog box displays as shown in Figure 2–110. Verify that the **Positioned** option is selected in the Type drop-down list.

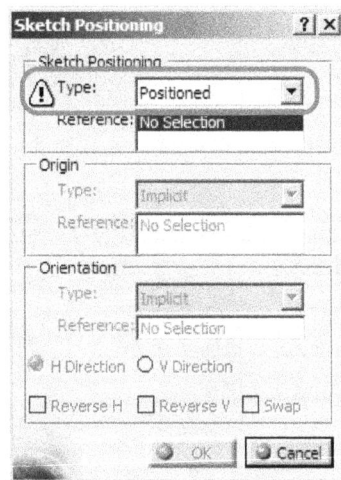

**Figure 2–110**

2. Select the surface shown in Figure 2–111.

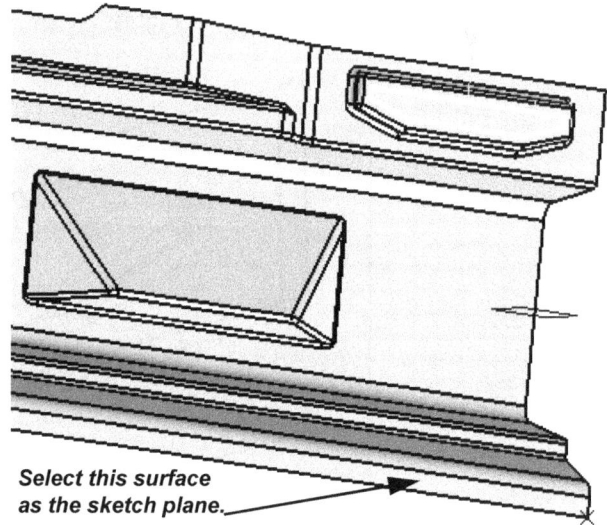

Select this surface
as the sketch plane.

**Figure 2–111**

Note the location of the Absolute Axis of the sketch, as shown in Figure 2–112.

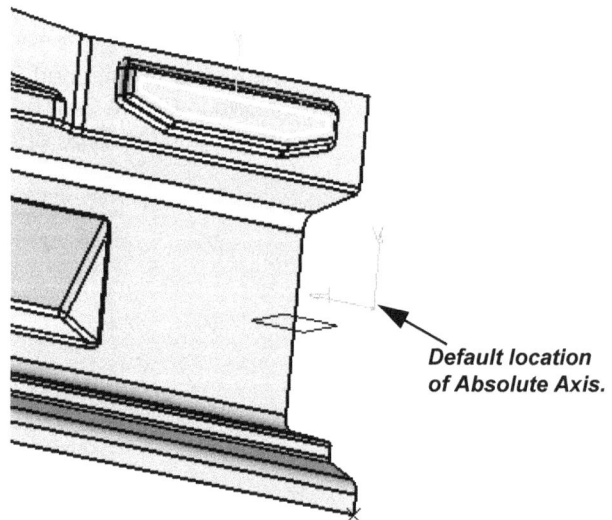

Default location
of Absolute Axis.

**Figure 2–112**

3. In the Origin Type drop-down list, select **Projection Point**.

4. Select **Point.2** as the *Projection Point* reference. **Point.2** is located under the geometrical set named **Inputs**. Note the location of the Absolute Axis, as shown in Figure 2–113.

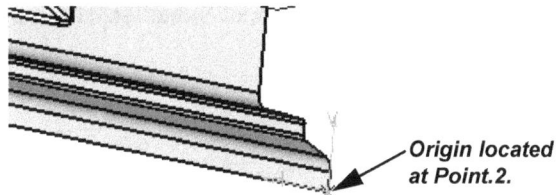

Origin located
at Point.2.

**Figure 2–113**

5. In the Sketch Positioning dialog box, select **Reverse H**, as shown in Figure 2–114.

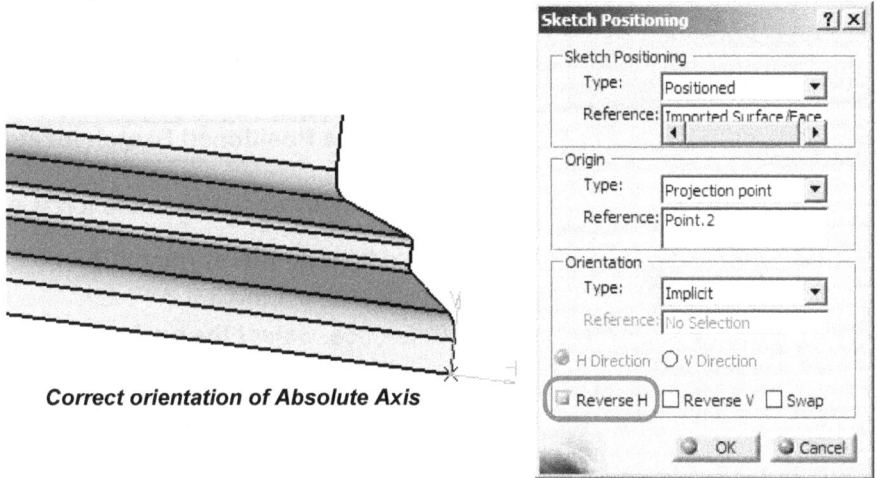

Correct orientation of Absolute Axis

**Figure 2–114**

6. Click **OK**.

7. Sketch and constrain the geometry, as shown in Figure 2–115.

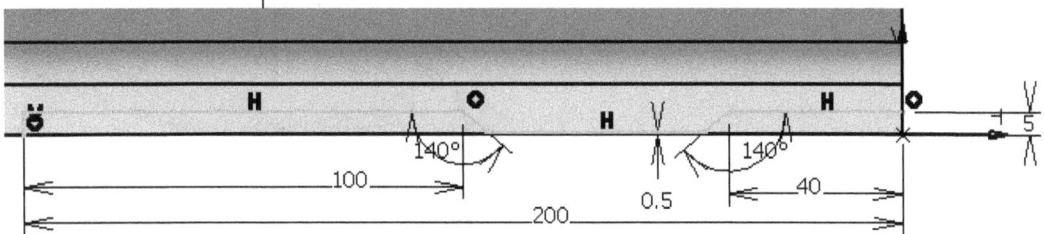

**Figure 2–115**

8. Exit Sketcher. The model displays as shown in Figure 2–116.

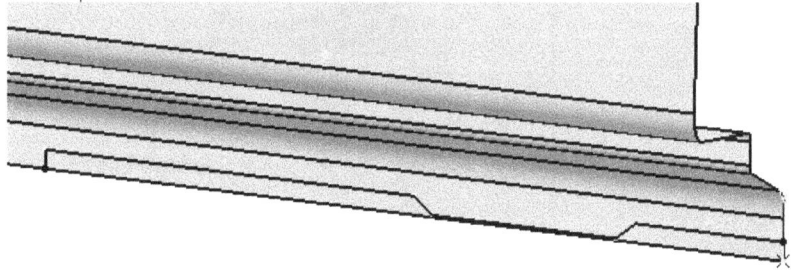

**Figure 2–116**

9. Rename the sketch as **Sketch - Projection Point**.

**Task 5 - Create a Positioned Sketch located by a midpoint.**

1. Create a reference plane with the following selections:

   • *Plane type:* **Angle/Normal to plane**
   • *Rotation axis:* **Line.3**
   • *Reference:* **Select the surface shown in Figure 2–117**
   • *Angle:* **35deg**

   The model displays as shown in Figure 2–117.

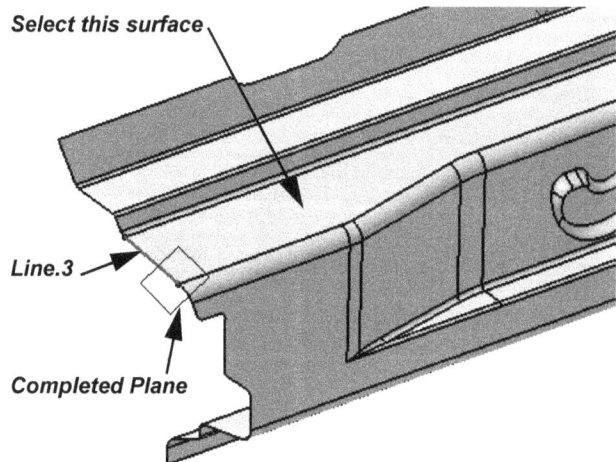

**Figure 2–117**

2. Create a Positioned Sketch using the newly created Plane.

3. In the *Origin* area, set *Type* to **Middle point**, and select **Line.3** as the *Middle point* reference.

4. In the *Orientation* area, set *Type* to **Parallel to line**. Verify that the **H Direction** option is selected, as shown in Figure 2–118.

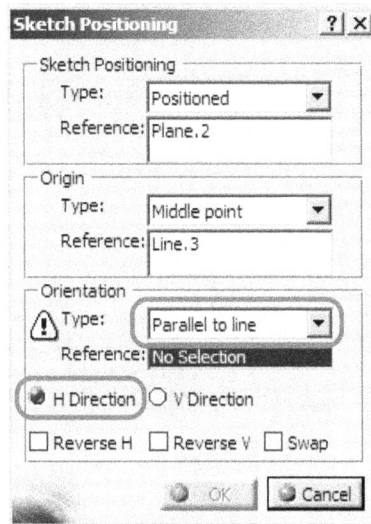

**Figure 2–118**

5. Select **Line.3** as the Orientation Reference.

6. You might need to select **Reverse H** and **Reverse V** to verify that the Absolute Axis displays as shown in Figure 2–119.

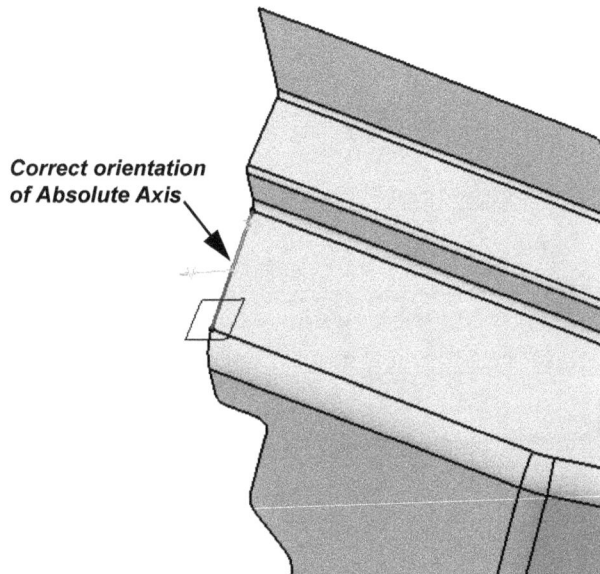

*Correct orientation of Absolute Axis*

**Figure 2–119**

7. In the Sketch Positioning dialog box, click **OK**.

8. Sketch and constrain the geometry, as shown in Figure 2–120. The geometry is symmetrical to the Vertical sketch axis.

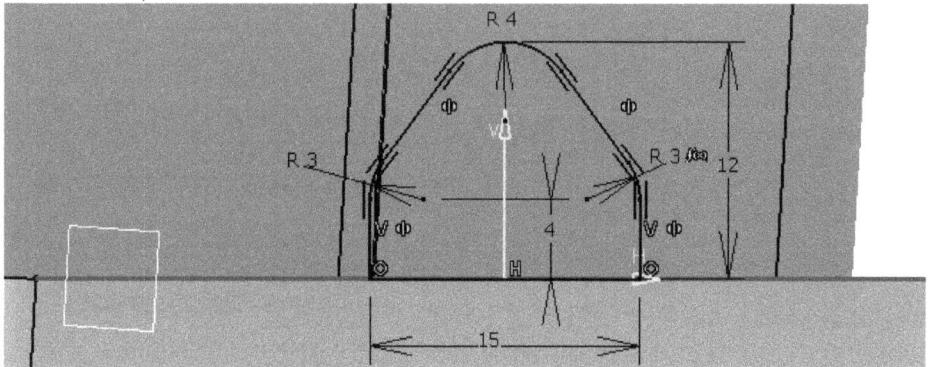

**Figure 2–120**

9. Exit Sketcher. The model displays as shown in Figure 2–121.

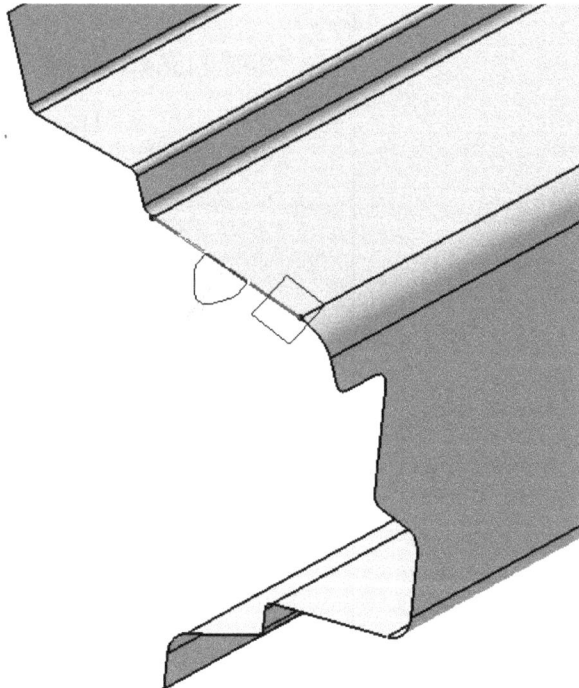

**Figure 2–121**

10. Save and close the model.

# Chapter Review Questions

1. Three options that enable you to create points are:

   a. Coordinates, On Curve, Center.

   b. Tangent on curve, On point, Midpoint

   c. On curve, On plane, Tangent on curve

   d. Between, Mid Point, On line

2. When creating a series of points using the Points and Planes Repetition option, use _____ to space the points at a specified distance relative to one another.

   a. **Instances and Distance**

   b. **Instances and Spacing**

   c. **Distance and Spacing**

   d. None of the above

3. Axis systems consist of a point and any two of the X-, Y-, or Z- axes.

   a. True

   b. False

4. The global axis system is system-defined and defines the origin of the part.

   a. True

   b. False

5. More than one local axis system can be created in a part, but only one can be active.

   a. True

   b. False

6. Axis systems are created to:

   a. Use as references for sketching and feature creation.

   b. Define or locate a part's center of gravity

   c. Aid in top-down design or modeling the in body position

   d. All of the above.

7. A polyline is defined by selecting points through which the curve passes. A unique radius value can be applied at each point to smooth the curve.

   a. True

   b. False

8. The two types of wireframe corners are:

   a. **Radius Corner** and **Sharp Corner**

   b. **Corner on Support** and **3D Corner**

   c. **Trim Corner** and **Support Corner**

   d. None of the above.

9. Connect Curves are a quick way of creating a spline between any number of points.

   a. True

   b. False

10. A spline requires a minimum of _____ points.

   a. One

   b. Two

   c. Three

   d. No Minimum

# Simple Surfaces

Simple surfaces help capture the design intent of complex shapes that are not easily defined with solid features. For example, surfaces enable you to design a part with smoother curve definition that might not be available or might be too difficult to create as a solid feature. Once surfaces have been defined, they can be joined together using surface operations and made into solid geometry. Here you learn about the different methods used to create simple surface shapes in CATIA.

## Learning Objectives in this Chapter

- Understand the surface creation process.
- Create various surface types such as Extruded, Revolved, Spherical and Cylindrical Surfaces.
- Create Offset Surfaces and Planes.
- Create Fill Surfaces.

# 3.1 Creating a Surface

To successfully create a surfaced part, you must be able to visualize a part divided into a group of construction elements. Each construction element represents a surface. You seldom need to create an entire part using a single complex surface. The final surfaced part often consists of many simple surface features.

When using surfaces to model a part, each surface might initially be created larger than required. This technique is useful because it ensures that the surfaces contain enough working material to define the part. For example, the surfaces shown in Figure 3–1 have been defined to be oversized to ensure complete intersection between all simple surfaces.

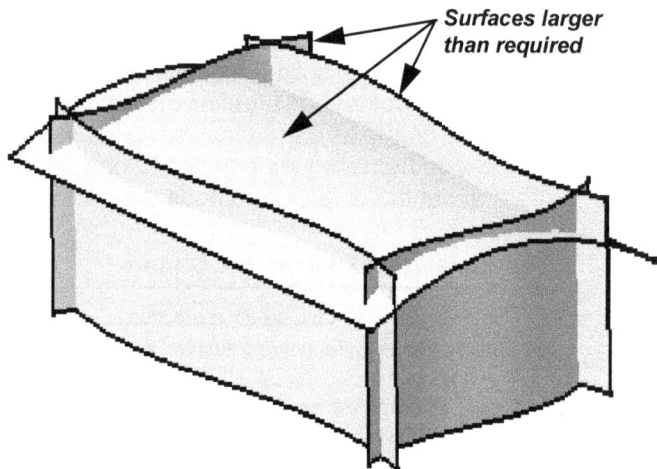

**Surfaces larger than required**

**Figure 3–1**

# 3.2 Surface Types

You can create a variety of different types of surfaces using the Surfaces toolbar, as shown in Figure 3–2. This toolbar is accessed in the Generative Shape Design workbench.

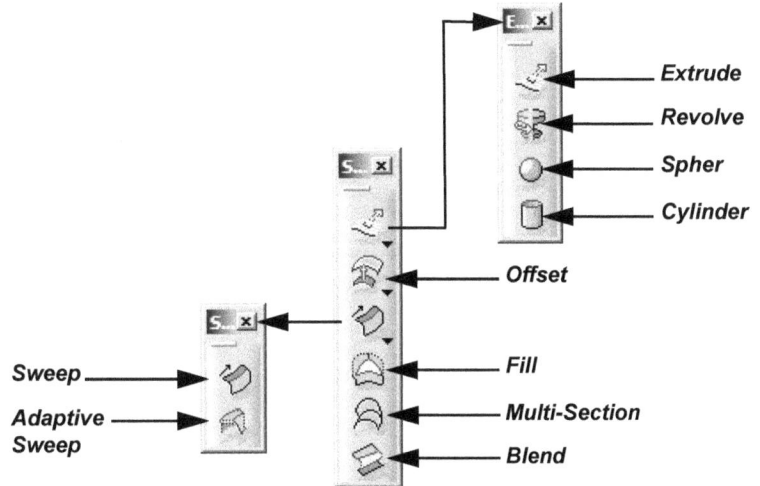

**Figure 3–2**

The following sections discuss how to create the following six simple surfaces:

- Extruded Surfaces
- Revolved Surfaces
- Sphere Surfaces
- Cylinder Surface
- Offset Surfaces
- Fill Surfaces

*The Sweeps, Multi-sections, and Blend surfaces in the Surfaces toolbar are discussed later.*

# 3.3 Extruded Surfaces

An extruded surface is created similar to Pad and Pocket features. An extruded surface is a sketched profile that is extruded to a specific length in one or two directions. In the example shown in Figure 3–3, the main body of a cover for a cellular phone is created using an extruded surface.

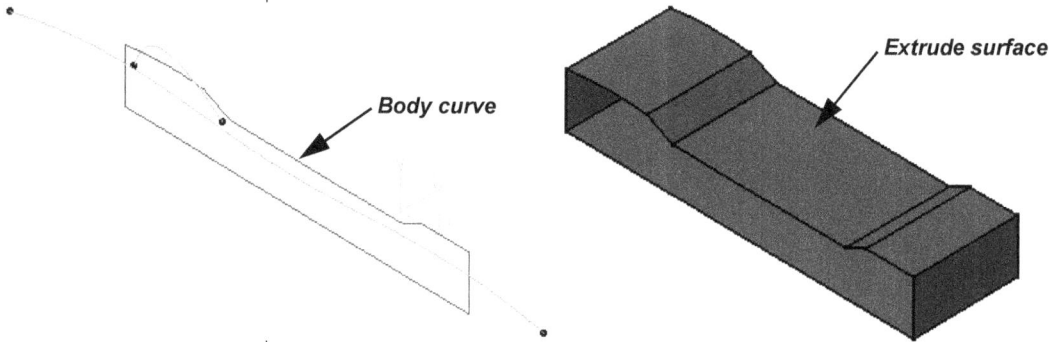

*Body curve*

*Extrude surface*

**Figure 3–3**

## How To: Create an Extruded Surface

1. In the Surfaces toolbar, click  (Extrude). The Extruded Surface Definition dialog box opens, as shown in Figure 3–4.

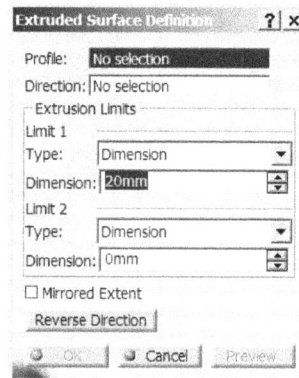

**Figure 3–4**

2. Select or create a profile to extrude.

3. By default, the profile is extruded normal to the sketch plane. You can change the direction of the extrusion by selecting the *Direction* field and selecting another plane or line. Alternatively, the direction can be changed by right-clicking in the *Direction* field and selecting one of the options shown in Figure 3–5.

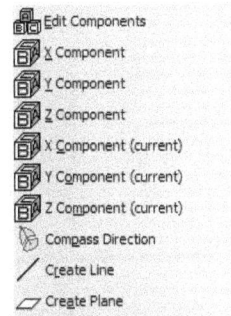

**Figure 3–5**

*You can also click and drag the limit handles to modify the length.*

4. Enter the length of the extrusion in the *Limit 1* and *Limit 2* fields. *Limit 1* defines the length extruded from the profile in one direction and *Limit 2* defines the length extruded from the profile in the opposite direction. To extrude the surface symmetrically about the profile, select **Mirrored Extent**. The total length of the extruded surface is twice the *Limit 1 Dimension* value entered in the Extruded Surface Definition dialog box. An extruded surface is shown in Figure 3–6.

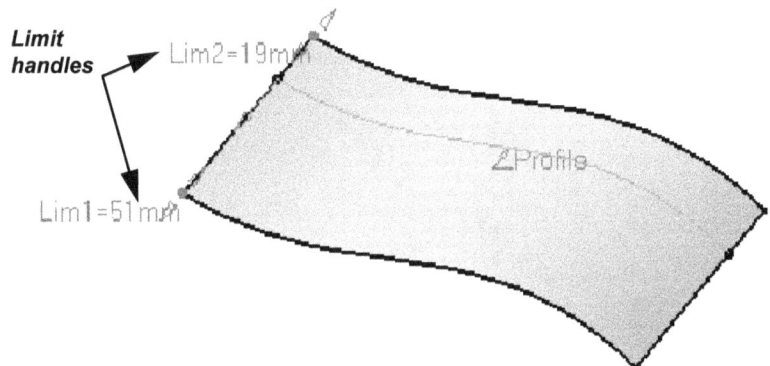

**Figure 3–6**

5. If required, the direction of extrusion can be flipped by using **Reverse Direction**.
6. Click **OK** to complete the feature.

# 3.4 Revolved Surfaces

A Revolved surface is created similar to Shaft and Groove
features. A revolved surface is a sketched profile that is revolved
about an axis. An example of a revolved surface is shown in
Figure 3–7.

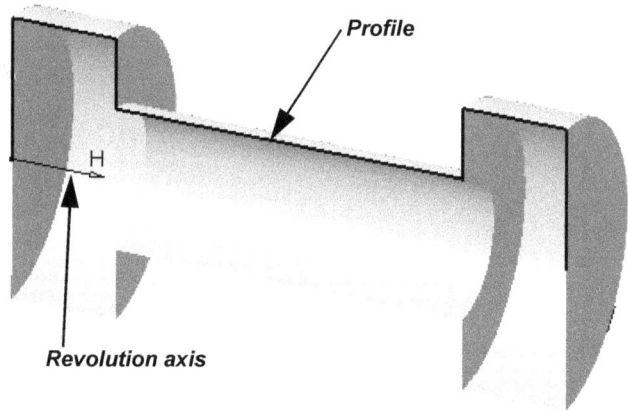

Figure 3–7

## How To: Create a Revolved Surface

1.  Click ⟨icon⟩ (Revolve). The Revolution Surface Definition dialog
    box opens as shown in Figure 3–8.

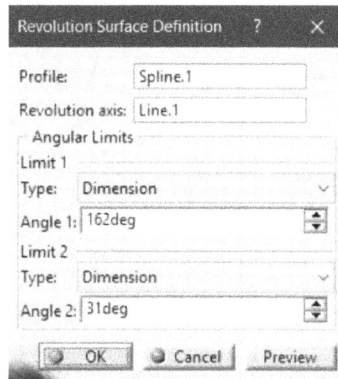

Figure 3–8

2.  Select or create a profile.
3.  Select an axis about which to revolve. The axis of revolution
    can be a line feature or sketched axis or it can be selected
    from the horizontal or vertical axes of the profile sketch.

4. In the Revolution Surface Definition dialog box, select the limit type (**Dimension** or **Up-to element**) and enter the angles of the revolved surface. Alternatively, you can click and drag the limit handles as shown in Figure 3–9.

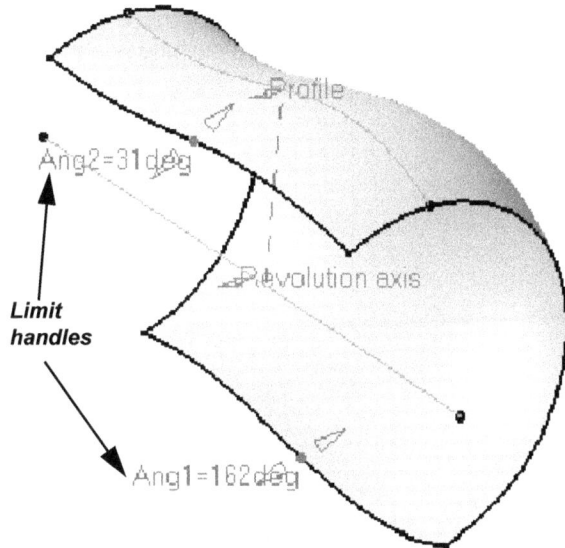

**Figure 3–9**

5. Click **OK** to complete the feature.

# 3.5 Sphere Surfaces

A Sphere surface creates a sphere-shaped surface that is centered on a selected reference point. The surface can be a complete sphere or a portion of a sphere. An example of a sphere surface is shown in Figure 3–10.

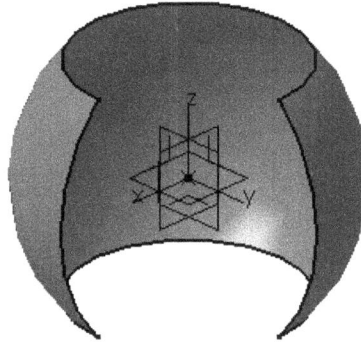

**Figure 3–10**

## How To: Create a Sphere Surface

1. In the Surfaces toolbar, click ⬤ (Sphere). The Sphere Surface Definition dialog box opens, as shown in Figure 3–11.

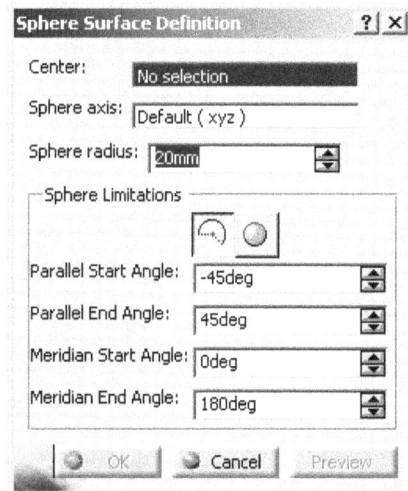

**Figure 3–11**

2. Select a point to locate the center of the surface.
3. Select an axis system (if one or more exists).
4. Enter a sphere radius.

5. Specify sphere limitations. To create a limited sphere, click [icon] . To create a complete sphere, click [icon].

6. When creating a limited sphere, values for the parallel and meridian start and end angles must be defined. The parallel angles are measured relative to the plane derived from the X- and Y-axes of the sphere axis system. The meridian angles are perpendicular to the parallel angles. The orientation of these angles is determined by the axis system used to define the sphere axis. If an axis system is not selected, a system default axis is used based on the three default reference planes.

7. Click **OK** to complete the sphere surface. An example of a sphere surface is shown in Figure 3–12.

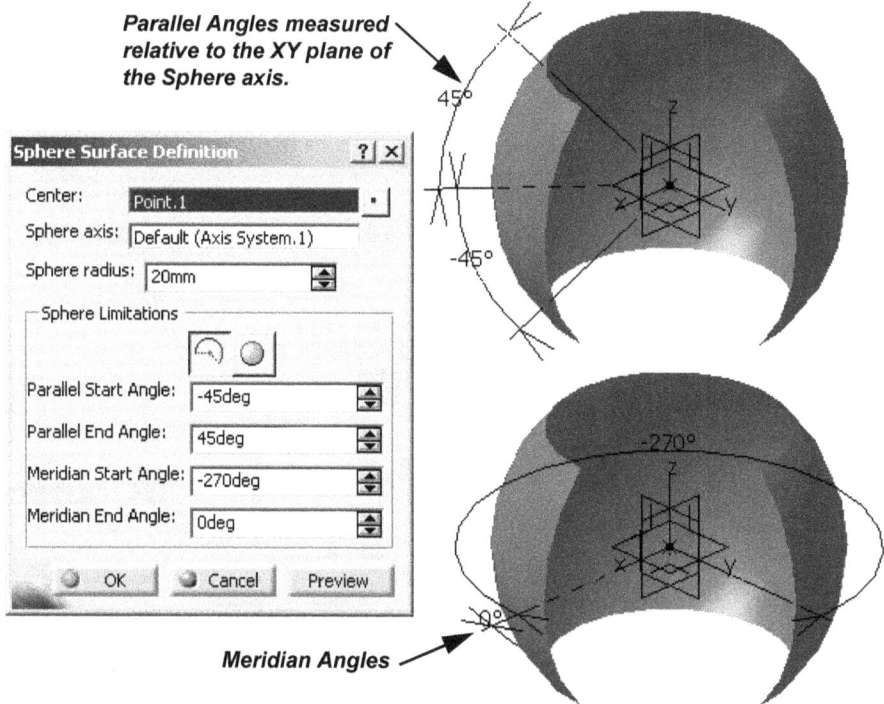

Figure 3–12

# 3.6 Cylindrical Surfaces

A Cylinder surface creates a circle that is centered on a selected reference point and extrudes it in the direction of a line, plane, or axis. The resulting surface is a cylinder with open ends. An example of a cylinder surface is shown in Figure 3–13.

**Figure 3–13**

## How To: Create a Cylinder Surface

1. In the Surfaces toolbar, click [icon] (Cylinder). The Cylinder Surface Definition dialog box opens, as shown in Figure 3–14.

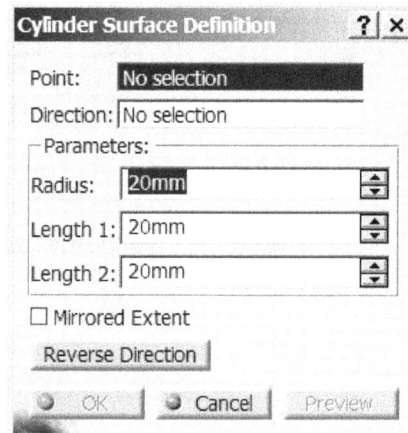

**Figure 3–14**

2. Select a point to locate the center of the cylinder.
3. Select a direction to define the extrusion direction of the cylinder.
4. Enter a radius.

5. Enter values for *Length 1* and/or *Length 2* to define the length of the cylinder. To create a cylinder that is symmetrical about the profile, select **Mirrored Extent**. The total length of the cylinder surface is twice the Length 1 Dimension value entered in the Cylinder Surface Definition dialog box.

6. Click **Reverse Direction** to toggle the positive and negative directions of Length 1 and Length 2. An example of the Cylinder surface is shown in Figure 3–15.

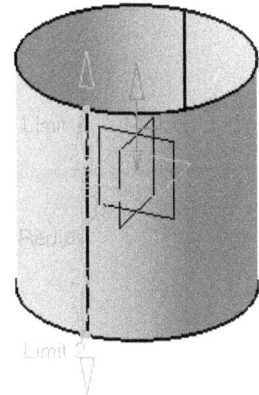

**Figure 3–15**

7. Click **OK** to complete the feature.

# 3.7 Offset Surfaces and Planes

An Offset surface creates a copy of the selected part surface, surface feature, or reference plane by a specified offset distance.

To create an Offset surface, click [icon] (Offset). The Offset Surface Definition dialog box opens as shown in Figure 3–16.

**Figure 3–16**

When the offset feature is displayed, enter an offset value in the Offset Surface Definition dialog box or click and drag the limit handles. The **Repeat object after OK** option enables you to create multiple parallel elements at the same time. The **Both sides** option creates two offset features on either side of the element being offset. An example of an offset surface is shown in Figure 3–17.

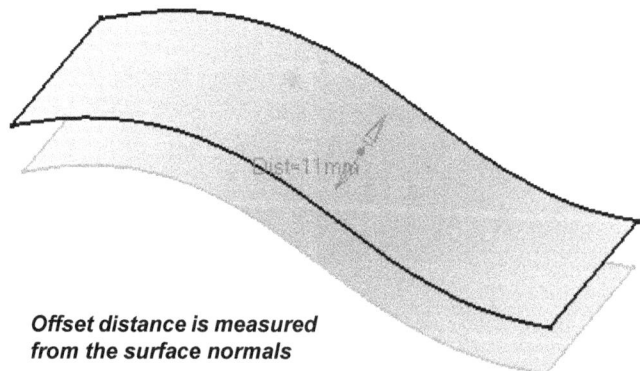

*Offset distance is measured from the surface normals*

**Figure 3–17**

# 3.8 Fill Surfaces

A Fill surface creates a surface inside a closed boundary. The closed boundary can consist of curves or surface edges. An example of a Fill surface feature is shown in Figure 3–18.

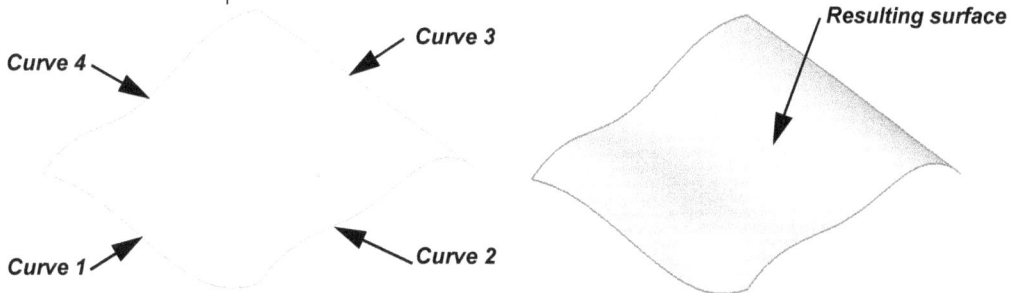

**Figure 3–18**

To create a fill surface, click ⬚ (Fill). The Fill Surface Definition dialog box opens, as shown in Figure 3–19.

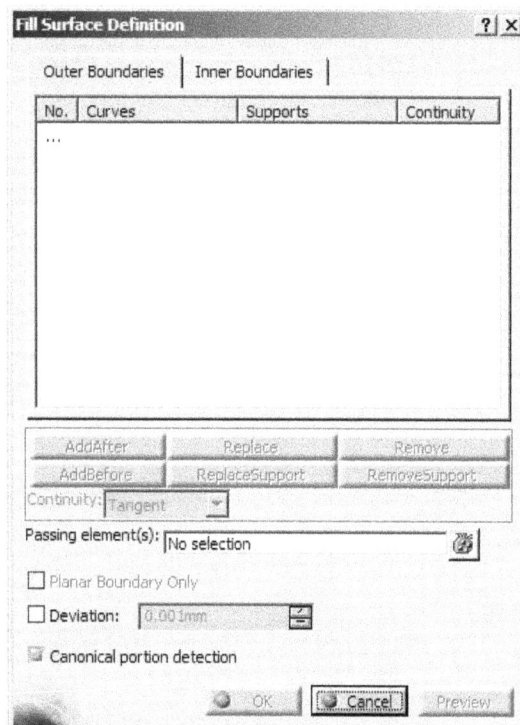

**Figure 3–19**

In some cases, you might want to constrain the curvature properties at specific boundaries of the fill surface to a surface adjacent to it, as shown in Figure 3–20.

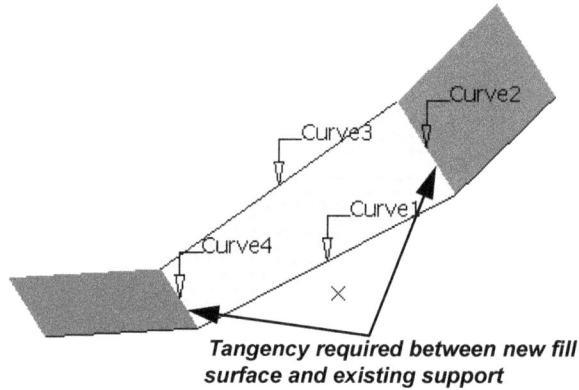

**Tangency required between new fill surface and existing support**

**Figure 3–20**

Selecting a surface after selecting a boundary curve adds the surface as a support surface for that boundary. This is shown for Curve 2, Curve 4, and the Support Surface in Figure 3–21.

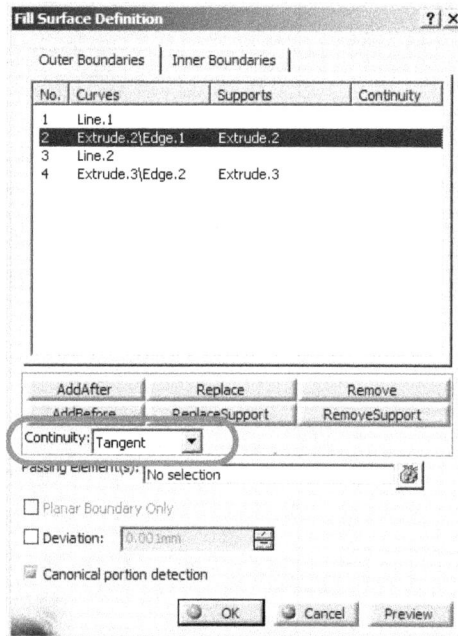

**Figure 3–21**

Continuity is defined for the selected element (Extrude.2\Edge.1 is highlighted) and can be set to **Point**, **Tangent** or **Curvature**.

In the Continuity drop-down list, if you select **Tangent** for the selected boundary curve-support surface combination, the fill surface is created tangent to the support surfaces (**Extrude.1** and **Extrude.2**), at the second and fourth boundary curve. The resulting surface is shown in Figure 3–22 with a tangent intersection between the three surfaces.

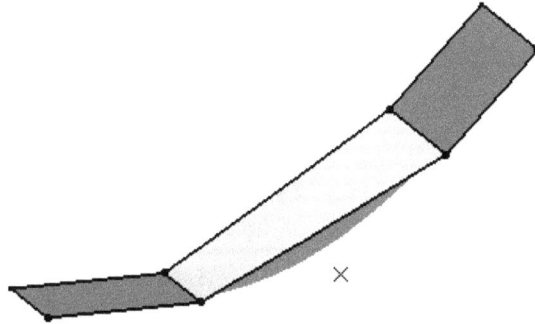

**Figure 3–22**

A passing element can be selected to define a location through which the fill surface must pass. The passing element is used to add a constraint to the fill surface creation. An example is shown in Figure 3–23.

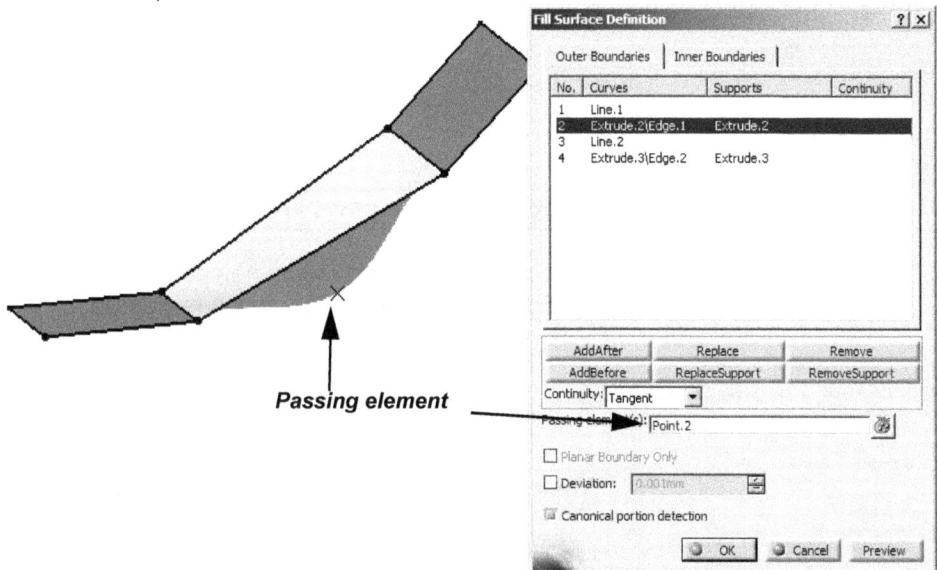

**Figure 3–23**

| Practice 3a | # Simple Surfaces |
|---|---|

### Practice Objectives

- Create wireframe elements.
- Create simple surface elements.

In this practice, you will create some basic wireframe and surface elements. You will start by extruding several surfaces from spline and projected curves, and then connect these with additional splines with tangency conditions. Finally, you will fill the gap between them with a Fill surface and set tangency constraints on the surface. The completed surfaces display as shown in Figure 3–24.

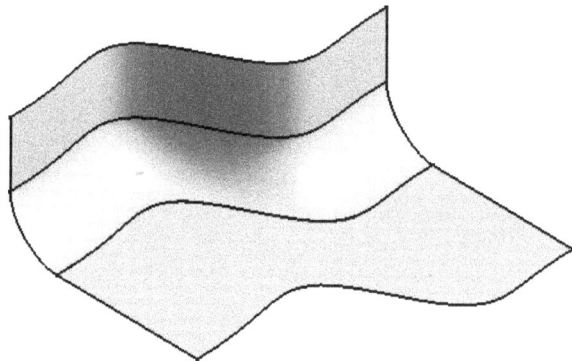

**Figure 3–24**

### Task 1 - Create a new part.

1. Create a new part model named **Wireframe**. Verify that the **Enable hybrid design** option is cleared.

2. Activate the GSD workbench.

3. Set the units to **mm**.

### Task 2 - Create a spline through points.

1. Using [icon] (Point), create four points at coordinate locations **(125,-50,0)**, **(25,-50,0)**, **(-25,25,0)** and **(-100,25,0)**.

2. Click [icon] (Spline) to open the Spline Definition dialog box.

3. Select the four point features in the order in which they were created. A spline is dynamically created through the selected points, as shown in Figure 3–25.

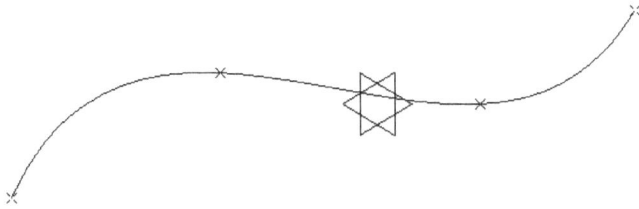

**Figure 3–25**

4. To make the spline perpendicular to the YZ plane at its end points, in the Spline Definition dialog box, select **Point.1**, and select the **YZ plane**. A red arrow displays on Point1 on the screen. Select the point to switch the direction if required so that it points toward Point4, as shown in Figure 3–26.

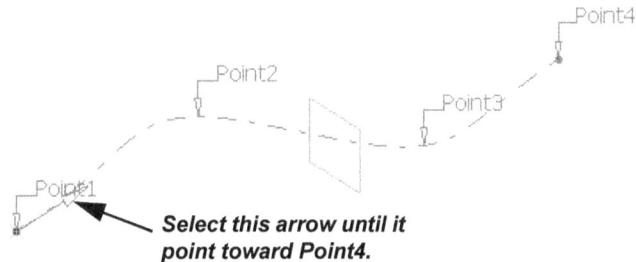

*Select this arrow until it point toward Point4.*

**Figure 3–26**

5. Repeat Step 4 for **Point4**. Toggle the red arrow that displays until the arrow points away from Point4 on the screen, in the same direction as the arrow for Point1.

6. Click **OK**. The completed Spline feature displays as shown in Figure 3–27.

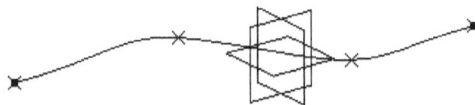

**Figure 3–27**

---

**Task 3 - Create an extruded surface from the spline curve.**

---

1. In the Surfaces toolbar, click  (Extrude).

2. Select the spline curve to create an extruded surface. The spline curve is used as the profile.

3. Select the **XY plane** to define the extrude direction.

4. Enter **125** for *Limit 1* and click **OK**. The resulting surface displays as shown in Figure 3–28.

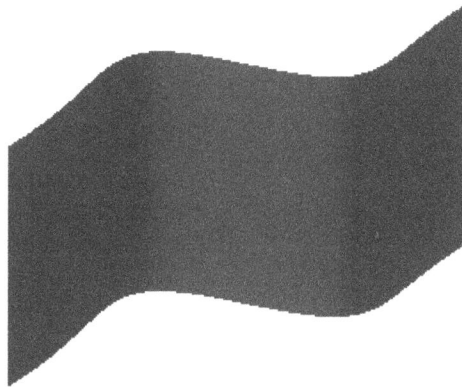

Figure 3–28

---

**Task 4 - Create a new plane using the offset surface and project the spline onto it.**

---

1. Select the **XY plane** and click (Offset). Offset the plane upward by a distance of **38**.

2. Select **Spline.1** and click (Projection). Project the spline onto the offset plane created in Step 1.

   The model displays as shown in Figure 3–29.

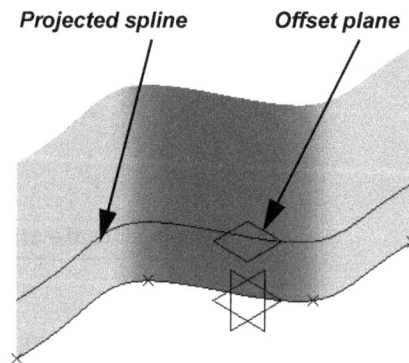

*Projected spline*      *Offset plane*

Figure 3–29

In the following tasks, you will create a fillet-shaped surface that connects the two extruded surface features. You will create a gap between the surfaces and use the edges of the surface to join them. Consequently, you will need to modify the first extruded surface to create a similar gap.

## Task 5 - Create an extruded surface from the projected curve.

1.  In the Surfaces toolbar, click  (Extrude).

2.  Select the projected spline curve as the profile.

3.  Select the **ZX plane** to define the extrude direction.

4.  Enter **150** for *Limit1* and **-38** for *Limit2* and click **OK**. The resulting surface displays as shown in Figure 3–30.

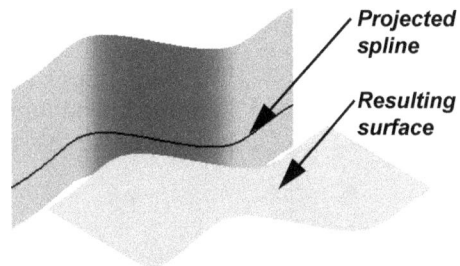

*Projected spline*

*Resulting surface*

Figure 3–30

## Task 6 - Modify the first extruded surface.

1.  In the specification tree, double-click on **Extrude.1**.

2.  Enter **-75** for *Limit2* and click **OK**. The model displays as shown in Figure 3–31.

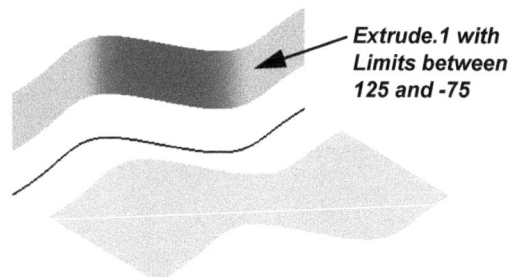

*Extrude.1 with Limits between 125 and -75*

Figure 3–31

## Task 7 - Create splines connecting the extruded surface edges to define the fillet surface.

1. Create a spline using the two vertices indicated in Figure 3–32.

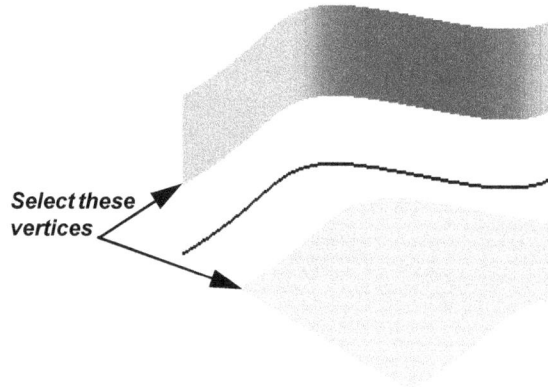

**Select these vertices**

**Figure 3–32**

2. Use the edges of the surface to enforce tangency conditions for the spline. Verify that the arrows point in the correct direction so that the spline displays as shown in Figure 3–33.

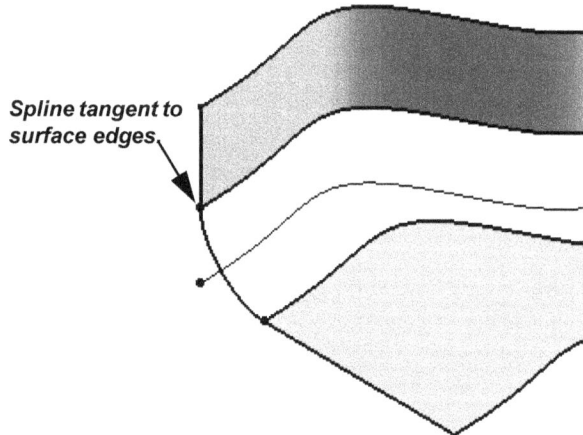

**Spline tangent to surface edges**

**Figure 3–33**

3. Repeat Steps 1 and 2 to create a spline on the other side of the surfaces. The model displays as shown in Figure 3–34.

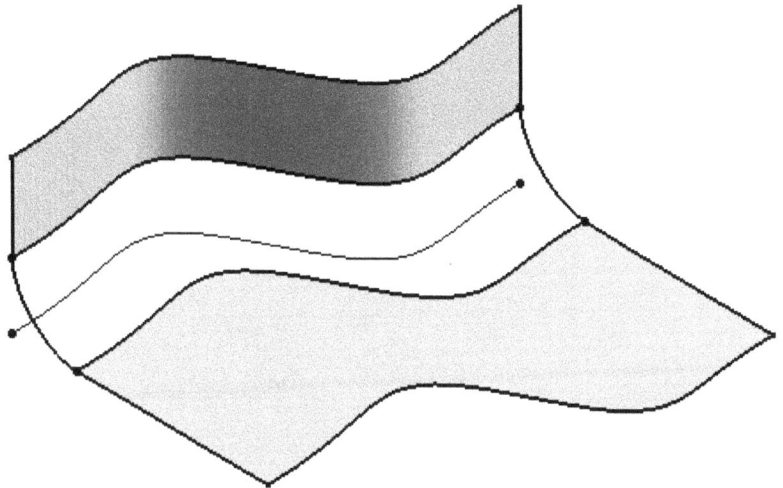

Figure 3–34

## Task 8 - Create a fill surface using the splines and edges of the extruded surfaces.

1. Click ⬚ (Fill) to create a fill surface.

2. Select the four curves shown in Figure 3–35.

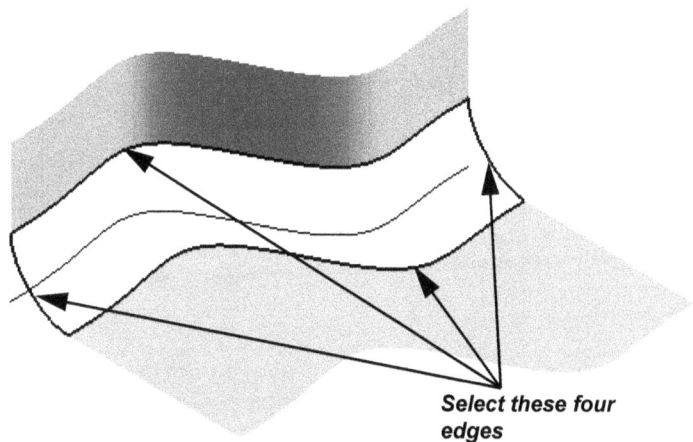

*Select these four edges*

Figure 3–35

3. Click **OK** to complete the feature.

4. Hide all of the wireframe geometry. The model displays as shown in Figure 3–36.

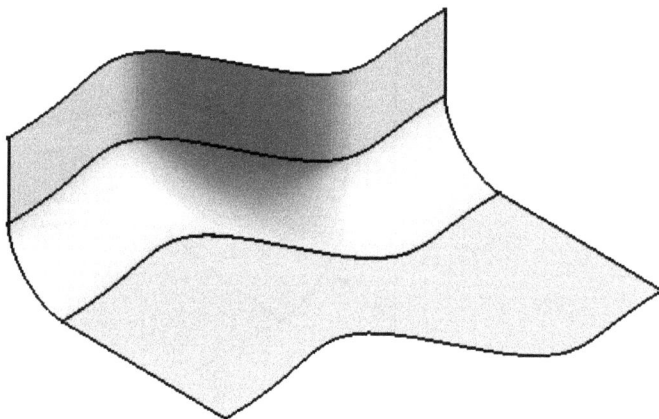

**Figure 3–36**

5. Save the model and close the file.

# Practice 3b

# Phone

### Practice Objective

• Create basic surfaces from wireframe geometry.

In this practice, you will create surfaces based on wireframe geometry for the cover of a cell phone. You use the Extrude and Fill features to create the body surfaces and the Sphere feature to generate the ear piece. The completed model is shown in Figure 3–37.

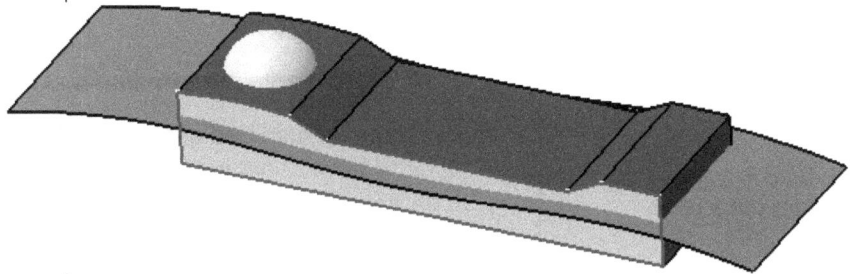

**Figure 3–37**

### Task 1 - Open a part.

1. Open **Cover_Start.CATPart**. The model displays as shown in Figure 3–38.

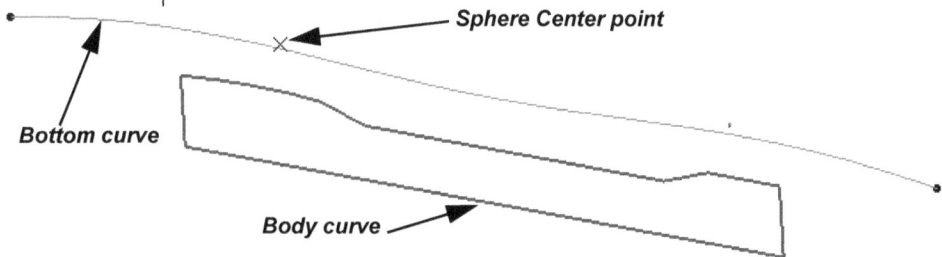

**Figure 3–38**

This wireframe geometry will be used to create the following surfaces:

• **BodySurf:** An extruded surface that uses Body curve to define the body of the phone.

• **Sphere Center:** A sphere to define the ear piece of the phone.

• **Bottom:** An extruded surface that uses Bottom curve to define the bottom surface of the phone.

2. Set the units to **mm**.

3. Expand **Geometrical Set.1** and investigate the wireframe geometry that will be used to create the surfaces of this model.

---

**Task 2 - Create the main body surface by extruding the body curve.**

---

1. Click [Extrude icon] (Extrude) and select the **Body Curve** shown in Figure 3–38 to use it as a profile for an extruded surface.

2. Set *Limit 1* to **76 mm**.

3. Click **OK** to create the extruded surface.

4. Rename the extruded surface as **BodySurf** and change the color of the surface to blue. The model updates as shown in Figure 3–39.

*You might need to reverse the direction of the extrude so that the surface is created going toward the X-axis.*

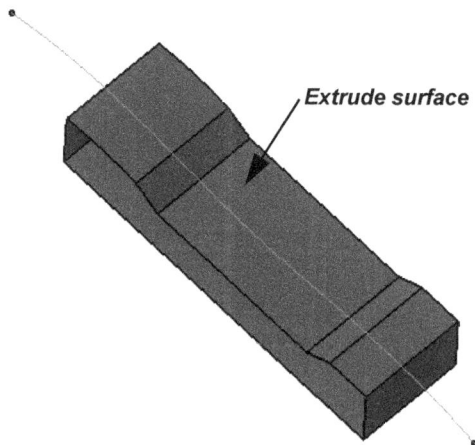

Extrude surface

**Figure 3–39**

---

**Task 3 - Create the bump geometry using a revolved surface.**

---

1. Hide **BodySurf** to simplify the display.

2. In the specification tree, expand the **Axis Systems** branch.

3. Show **Sphere Axis 1**.

4. Click ⬜ (Sphere) to open the Sphere Surface Definition dialog box.

5. Select the point named **Sphere Center** and the axis system named **Sphere Axis 1**.

6. Enter the following values in the dialog box, as shown in Figure 3–40.

   - *Sphere radius:* **25mm**
   - *Parallel Start Angle:* **-90deg**
   - *Parallel End Angle:* **90deg**

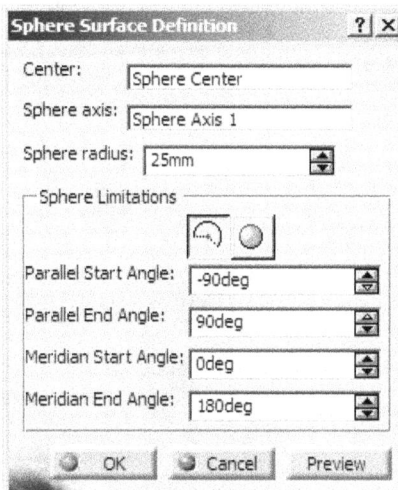

**Figure 3–40**

7. Click **OK** to complete the Sphere. The model displays as shown in Figure 3–41. Note that the Parallel Start and End Angles are measured about the X-axis of the Sphere axis. The Meridian Start and End Angles measure from Z-axis of the Sphere axis.

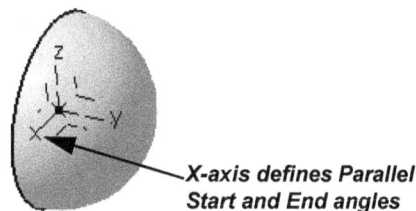

*X-axis defines Parallel Start and End angles*

**Figure 3–41**

8. Hide **Sphere Axis 1** and show **Sphere Axis 2**. Note that **Sphere Axis 2** has a different Y- and Z-axis orientation when compared to **Sphere Axis 1**.

9. Double-click on the newly created Sphere surface.

10. Select the *Sphere axis* field. In the specification tree, select **Sphere Axis 2** as shown in Figure 3–42.

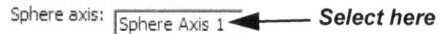

Sphere axis: [Sphere Axis 1 ◄──── *Select here*

Figure 3–42

11. Click **OK** to complete the sphere. The model displays as shown in Figure 3–43.

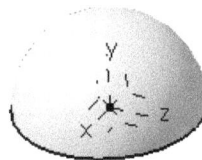

Figure 3–43

---

## Task 4 - Create the bottom using an extruded surface.

---

1. Hide **Sphere.1**, **Sphere Center**, and **Sphere Axis.2** to simplify the display.

2. Create an extruded surface using the following parameters:

   - *Profile:* **Bottom Curve**
   - *Direction:* **YZ plane**
   - *Limit 1 Dimension:* **50mm**
   - Select **Mirrored Extent**.

3. Rename the surface as **Bottom** and change its color to red. The model updates as shown in Figure 3–44.

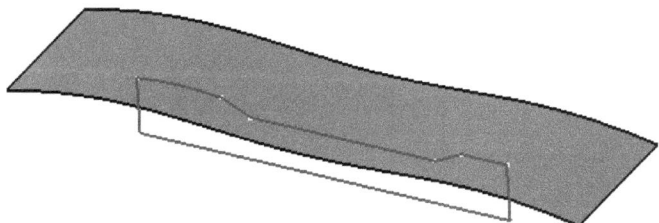

Figure 3–44

**Task 5 - Create the side of the cover using a fill surface.**

1. Hide **Bottom** and **Bottom Curve**.

2. Click [icon] (Fill) to create a fill surface.

3. Select **Body Curve** as shown in Figure 3–45.

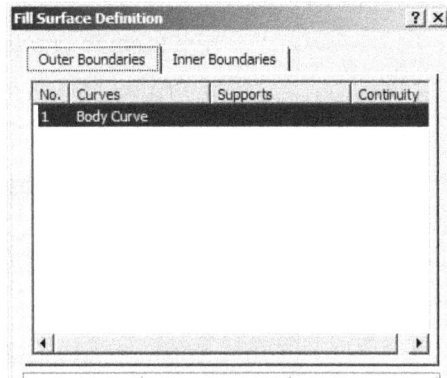

Figure 3–45

4. Click **OK** to complete the Fill surface. The model displays as shown in Figure 3–46.

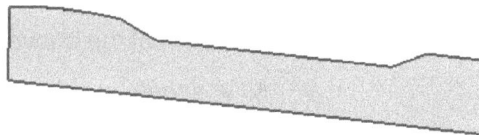

Figure 3–46

5. Hide **Body Curve**.

6. Show **Sphere.1**, **Bottom**, and **Body Surf** features. The model displays as shown in Figure 3–47.

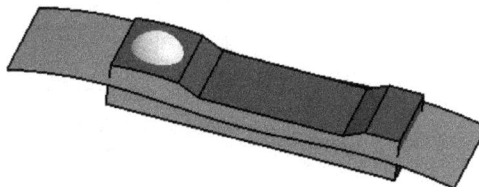

Figure 3–47

7. Save the model and close the window.

# Chapter Review Questions

1. Typically, a surface model consists of multiple simple surfaces combined together to create a final complex model.

   a. True

   b. False

2. A common surface technique is to overbuild surfaces and trim them to create the final model.

   a. True

   b. False

3. Extruded surfaces are always extruded normal to the sketch support plane.

   a. True

   b. False

4. Which of the following can be used as an axis of revolution for a revolved surface?

   a. Line

   b. Sketched Axis

   c. Axis of the profile sketch

   d. All of the above.

5. A sphere surface must result in a closed volume.

   a. True

   b. False

6. An Offset surface creates a copy of the selected part surface, surface feature, or reference plane by a specified offset distance.

   a. True

   b. False

7. When creating a fill surface, you can define continuity for a selected element as:

   a. Point

   b. Tangent

   c. Curvature

   d. All of the above.

# Operations

Operations are tasks that create a new feature by referencing the geometry of existing wireframe or surface features. When you perform an operation on any feature, the original feature does not change. Instead, a new feature is created and the original features are automatically hidden.

## Learning Objectives in this Chapter

- Understand tools for manipulating surfaces such as Split, Trim and Sew.
- Use Remove Face to remove a surface from a model.
- Use Join to combine surfaces.
- Use transformation operations such as Translate, Rotate and Scale, among others.
- Create Extract Surfaces.
- Add Chamfers to surface geometry.

# 4.1 Split

The **Split**, **Trim**, **Sew Surface**, and **Remove Face** options are found in the **Trim-Split** fly-out menu, shown in Figure 4–1.

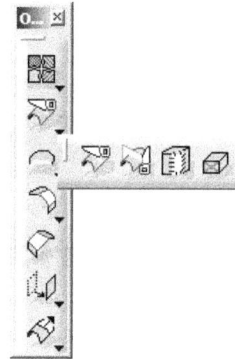

**Figure 4–1**

The **Split** operation divides a surface at its intersection with another surface or curve element.

## How To: Perform a Split Operation

1. Click  (Split) and the Split dialog box opens, as shown in Figure 4–2.

**Figure 4–2**

2. Select a surface to split.
3. Select the cutting elements to intersect the surface. Use **Remove** and **Replace** to edit the elements added to the *Cutting elements* area.
4. Click **Other side** to toggle to the side to remove or select **Keep both sides** to keep both sides.
5. If required, select **Intersections computation** to add an intersection curve to the feature.
6. Click **OK** to complete the **Split** operation.
7. Figure 4–3 shows two extruded surfaces. A Split operation is performed at their intersection.

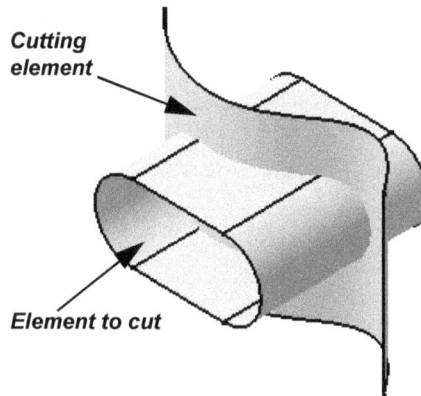

**Figure 4–3**

Figure 4–4 shows the resulting split feature.

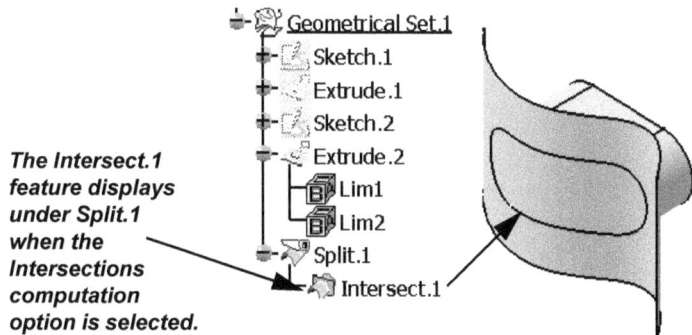

**Figure 4–4**

# 4.2 Trim

The **Trim** operation with the Standard mode trims overlapping geometry between intersecting surface features.

## How To: Perform a Trim Operation

1. Click  (Trim).
2. In the Trim Definition dialog box, in the Mode drop-down list, select **Standard**, as shown in Figure 4–5.

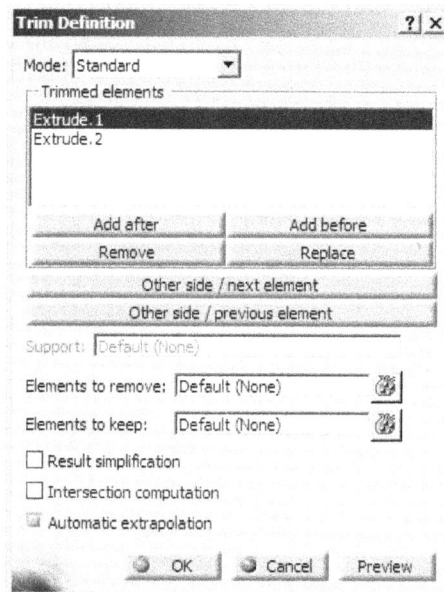

Figure 4–5

3. Select the two features with overlapping geometry for the *Element.1* and *Element.2* fields. Four different results can be achieved by clicking **Other side / next element** and/or **Other side / previous element**.

Examples of overlapping geometry are shown in Figure 4–6.

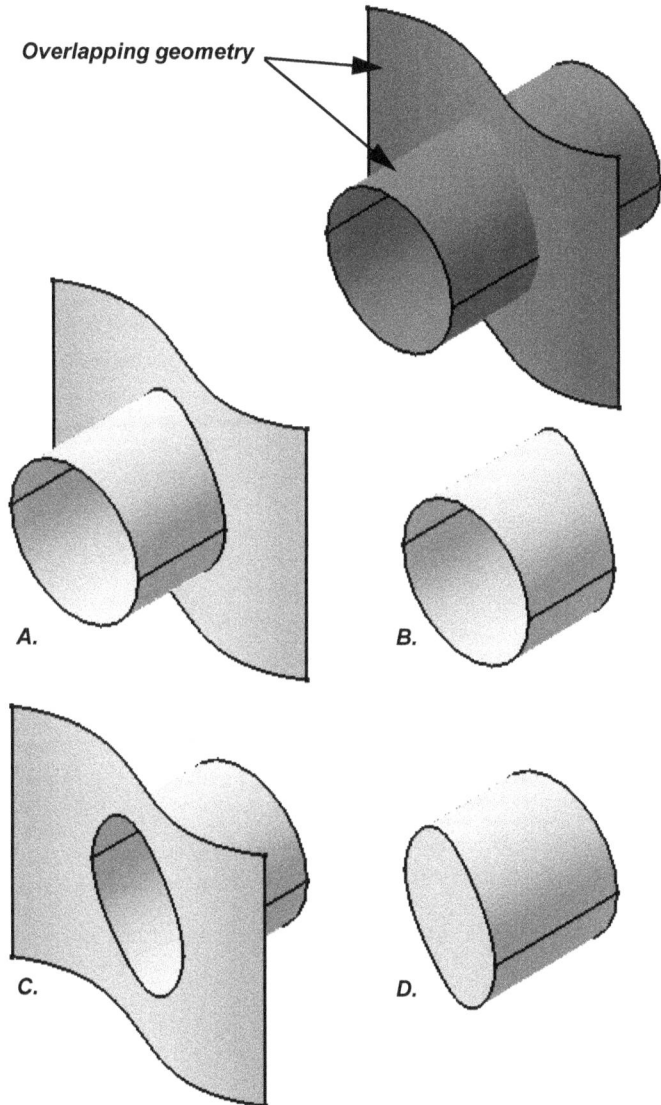

Overlapping geometry

A.

B.

C.

D.

**Figure 4–6**

4. Use the **Add After**, **Add Before**, **Remove**, and **Replace**
   buttons to modify the elements included in the **Trim**
   operation.

# 4.3 Sew Surface

The **Sew Surface** operation adds or removes a surface by combining a selected surface with an existing support.

## How To: Perform a Sew Surface Operation

1. Click ▦ (Sew Surface). The Sew Surface Definition dialog box opens, as shown in Figure 4–7.

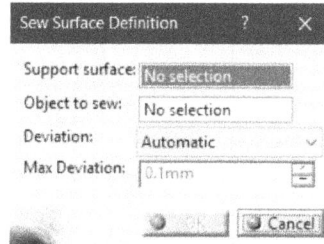

**Figure 4–7**

2. Select a support surface.
3. Select the surface you want to sew onto the support surface.
4. Select the direction for the **Sew** operation.
5. Click **OK** to complete the **Sew** operation.

Figure 4–8 shows two surfaces. A Sew Surface operation is performed between the support surface and the revolved surface.

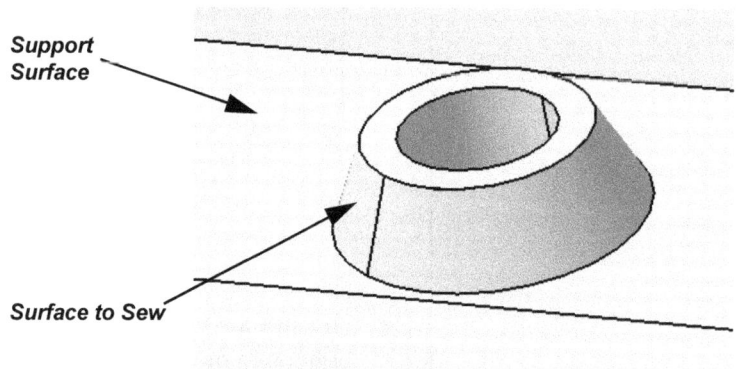

*Support Surface*

*Surface to Sew*

**Figure 4–8**

Figure 4–9 shows the direction arrows and the resulting Sew Surface feature. The arrows indicate the surface that will be either added or removed.

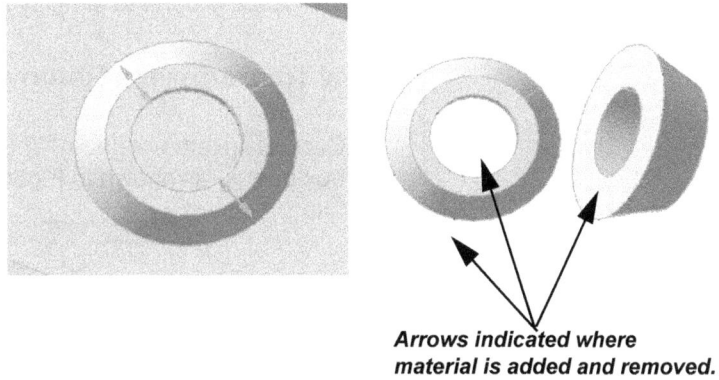

*Arrows indicated where material is added and removed.*

**Figure 4–9**

You can click the arrows to change the direction, and therefore change what material is kept and what is removed, as shown in Figure 4–10.

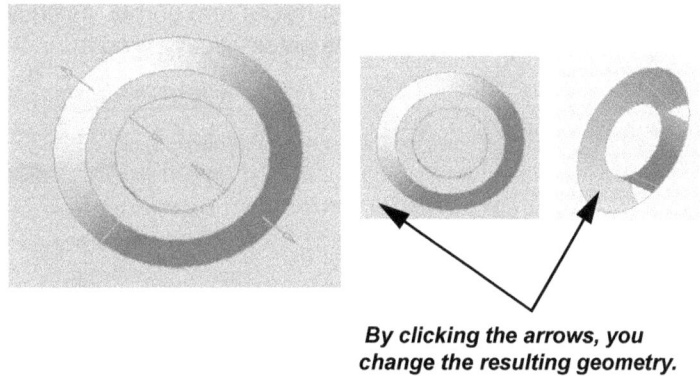

*By clicking the arrows, you change the resulting geometry.*

**Figure 4–10**

The **Deviation** option, used to define the tolerance value, can be set to **Automatic** (recommended), **None** and **Manual** deviation modes.

With the **Manual** option, you can set the Max Deviation value in the *Max Deviation* field.

# 4.4 Remove Face

The **Remove Face** operation removes surfaces from the model. This is typically done to simplify the model for FEA purposes.

## How To: Perform a Remove Face Operation

1. Click 📦 (Remove Face). The Remove Face Definition dialog box opens, as shown in Figure 4–11.

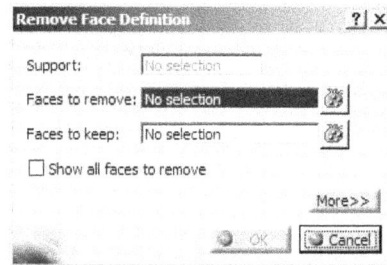

**Figure 4–11**

2. Select the surfaces you want to remove. The selected surfaces turn purple, as shown in Figure 4–12. The Support is automatically filled in.

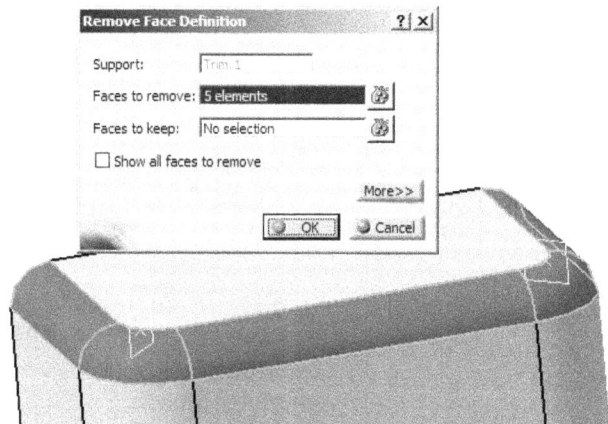

**Figure 4–12**

3. Click **OK** and the faces are removed, as shown in Figure 4–13.

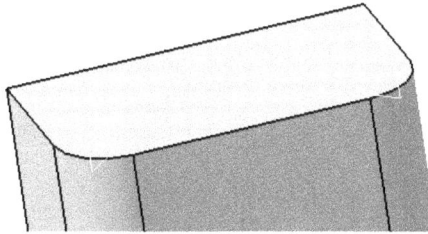

**Figure 4–13**

There are several methods for selecting surfaces. You can select individual surfaces, or you can right-click in the *Faces to remove* field and select **Tangency Propagation**, which will select all tangent surfaces.

Alternatively, when you select a surface, you can select surfaces using the *Faces to keep* field. The system will automatically select all surfaces except those selected as faces to keep, as shown in Figure 4–14. If you enable the **Show all faces to remove** option, the system highlights the faces to remove in purple, and the faces to keep in cyan.

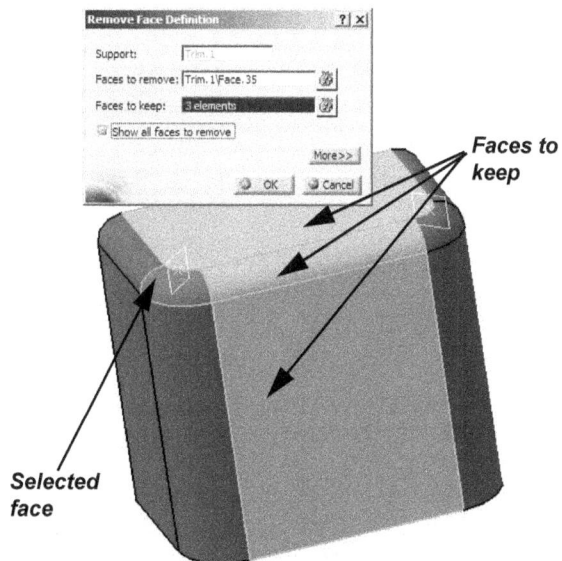

**Figure 4–14**

You can also define a limit on how much of a surface can be removed by clicking **More** to expand the Remove Face Definition dialog box, as shown in Figure 4–15.

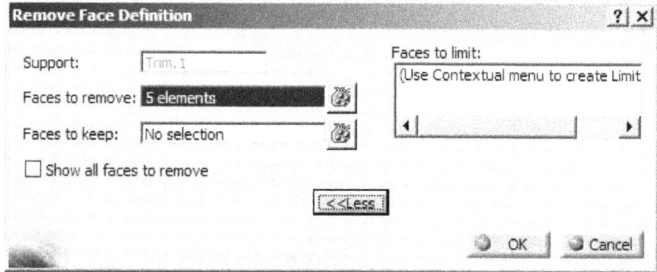

**Figure 4–15**

You can create limiting surfaces by selecting or creating entities to establish boundaries. Right-click in the *Faces to limit* field and select **Create**. In the Face to Limit dialog box, select a face you want to set a limit on, then select or create a reference, as shown in Figure 4–16. The arrow indicates the portion of the face to remove. Click the arrow to change the portion to remove.

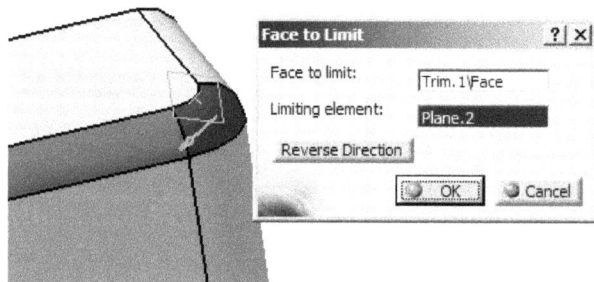

**Figure 4–16**

You can create multiple limits, as shown in Figure 4–17.

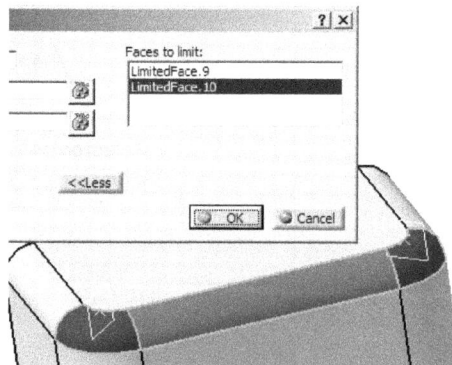

**Figure 4–17**

The resulting geometry is displayed in Figure 4–18.

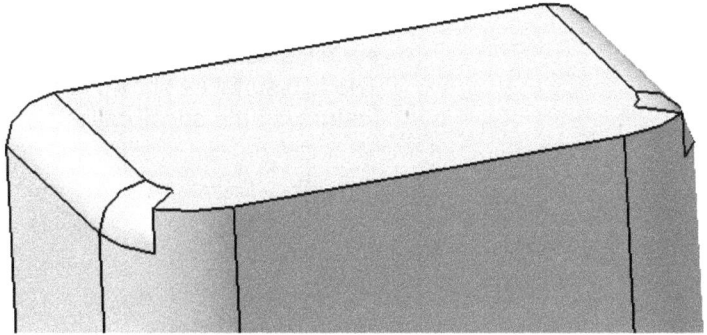

**Figure 4–18**

# 4.5 Join

The **Join surface** operation joins two or more adjacent curves or surfaces so that they can be selected as one curve or surface. The two surfaces shown in Figure 4–19 represent two separate features in the specification tree.

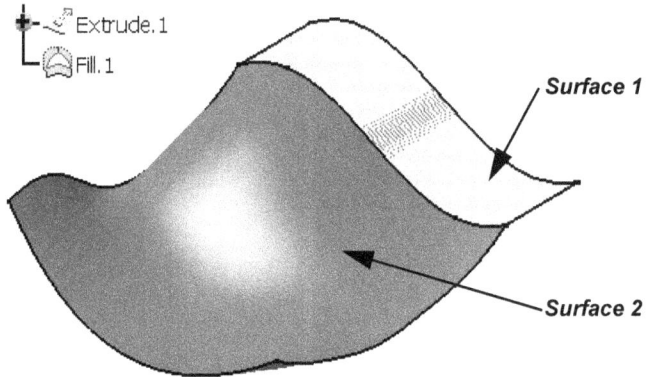

Figure 4–19

To join two surfaces, select both surfaces using <Ctrl> and click

 (Join) from the Operations toolbar. You can specify additional parameters using optional elements in the Join Definition dialog box, as shown in Figure 4–20.

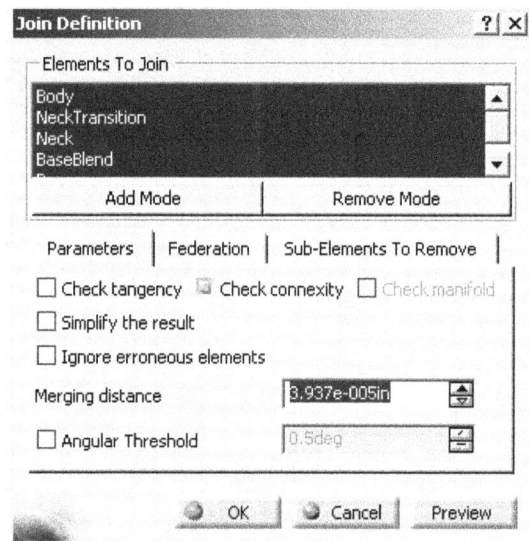

Figure 4–20

Some of these options are described as follows:

| Option/Tabs | Description |
|---|---|
| **Check connexity** | If selected, this option enables you to enter a value in the *Merging Distance* field. If this option is not selected, any two surfaces or curves can be joined into a single element, regardless of the Merging distance value. |
| **Simplify the result** | Reduces the number of elements in the Join feature, if possible. |
| **Ignore erroneous elements** | Ignores any elements that do not enable the Join feature to be created. |
| **Merging Distance** | Determines the maximum separation permitted between elements if the **Check connexity** option is selected. Merging distance has a maximum value of 0.1mm. |
| **Federation tab** | Defines groups of elements in the Join feature. By default, **No Federation** is selected. In this situation, each surface in the Join can be selected individually. If **All** is selected, all elements in the Join are selected together. |
| **Sub-Elements to Remove tab** | Enables you to exclude sub-elements of elements that have been included in the Join feature. For example, an individual face of a surface to be joined can be removed from the Join feature. |

Accept the default results in a new Join surface feature, as shown in Figure 4–21. Note that the initial two surfaces now display grayed out in the specification tree. The new Join surface represents these two surfaces.

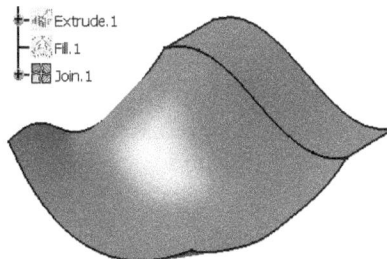

**Figure 4–21**

Curves selected for a **Join** operation must share a common end point. Surfaces must share an edge but the edges do not need to have the same length. Features that do not meet these requirements can still be joined by clearing the **Check connexity** option.

# 4.6 Transformation Operations

Transformations change the orientation and position of wireframe and surface elements. The toolbar is shown in Figure 4–22.

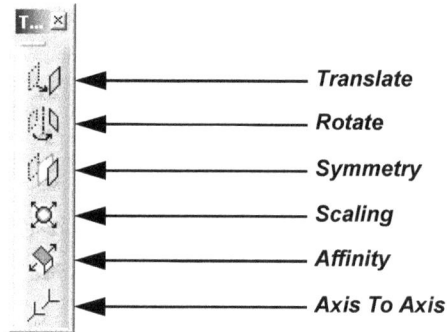

*Translate*

*Rotate*

*Symmetry*

*Scaling*

*Affinity*

*Axis To Axis*

**Figure 4–22**

The **Translate**, **Rotate**, **Symmetry**, and **Scaling** operations are identical to those in the Part Design workbench. This section reviews these operations and introduces the **Affinity** and **Axis to Axis** operations.

## Translate

A **Translate** operation moves or translates a wireframe or surface feature. To perform a **Translate** operation, click

(Translate). The Translate Definition dialog box opens as shown in Figure 4–23.

*The original feature can be hidden using Hide/Show initial element.*

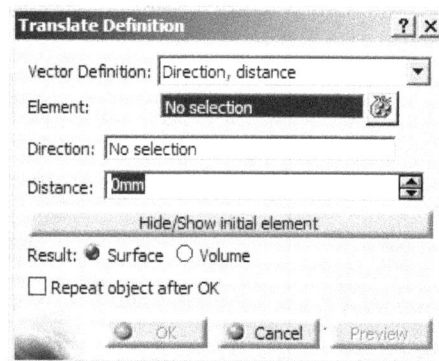

**Figure 4–23**

In the *Direction* field, you can right-click to display the X, Y, Z options. The **Repeat object after OK** option enables you to duplicate the object multiple times. Each duplication is created in a separate feature.

## Rotate

The **Rotate** operation enables you to rotate a feature around an axis. To perform a **Rotate** operation, click ![Rotate icon] (Rotate). The Rotate Definition dialog box opens as shown in Figure 4–24, enabling you to define a rotational axis or line and enter an angular value.

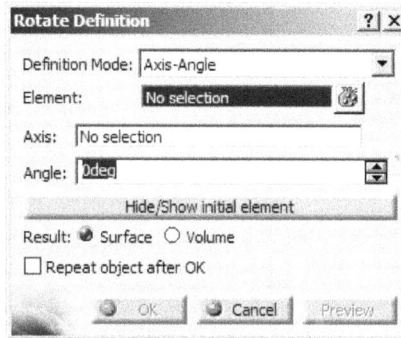

**Figure 4–24**

## Symmetry

The **Symmetry** operation creates a mirrored copy of a feature about a point, line, or plane. To perform a **Symmetry** operation, click ![Symmetry icon] (Symmetry). The Symmetry Definition dialog box opens, as shown in Figure 4–25.

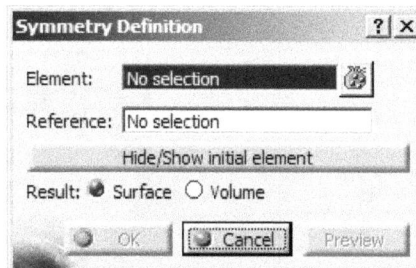

**Figure 4–25**

## Scaling

The **Scaling** operation scales a feature about a point or plane.

To perform a **Scaling** operation, click [⊠] (Scaling). The Scaling Definition dialog box opens as shown in Figure 4–26. The scaling factor is applied equally in all directions.

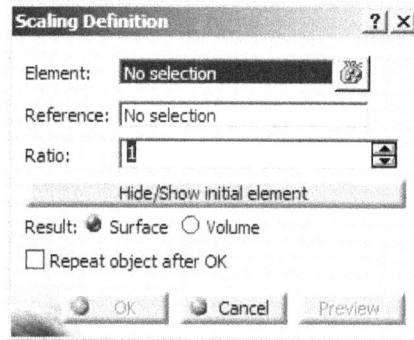

**Figure 4–26**

## Affinity

The **Affinity** operation scales a selected feature in the X-, Y- or Z-direction relative to a selected Axis System. Click

[⚛] (Affinity) to open the Affinity Definition dialog box, as shown in Figure 4–27.

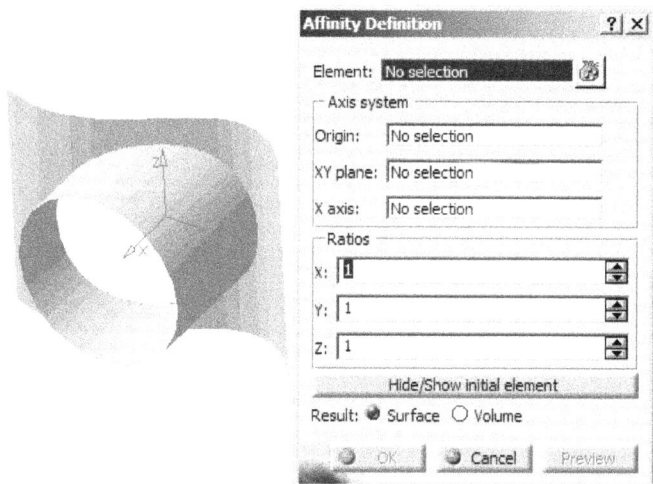

**Figure 4–27**

Figure 4–28 shows a Trim feature with a ratio of **2** in the X-direction.

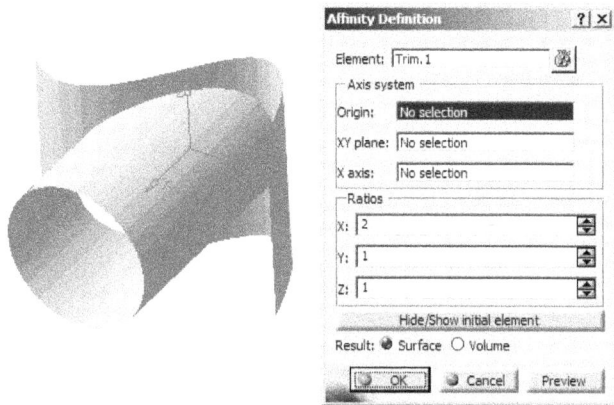

**Figure 4–28**

Figure 4–29 shows a Trim feature with a ratio of **2** in the Y-direction.

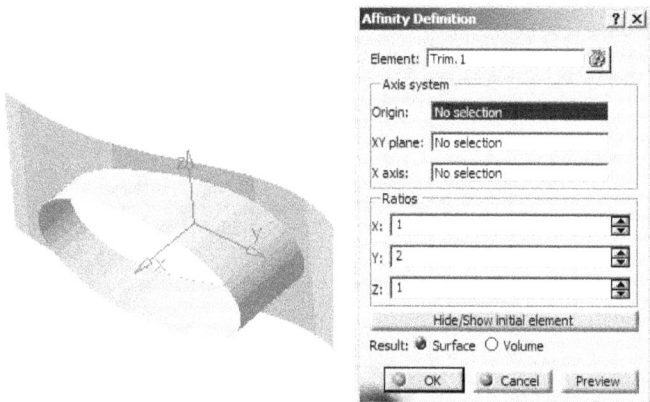

**Figure 4–29**

Figure 4–30 shows a Trim feature with a ratio of **2** in the Z-direction.

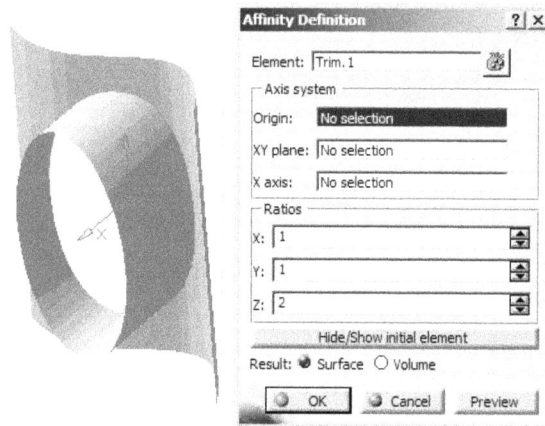

Figure 4–30

## Axis to Axis

The **Axis To Axis** operation transforms a surface feature between two axis systems. Click [icon] (Axis to Axis) to open the Axis To Axis Definition dialog box, as shown in Figure 4–31.

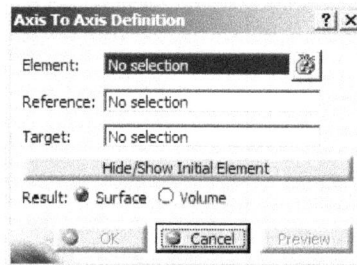

Figure 4–31

The feature shown in Figure 4–32 is copied to the target axis system.

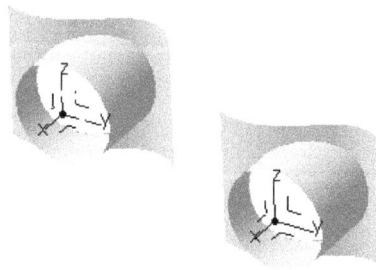

Figure 4–32

# 4.7 Creating Extract Surfaces

The **Extract** operation creates new surface elements by copying surface or solid faces. The resulting surface is a duplicate of the original element that was selected. Examples of the **Extract** tool are shown in Figure 4–33, Figure 4–34, and Figure 4–35.

Figure 4–33 shows the solid model of a wing.

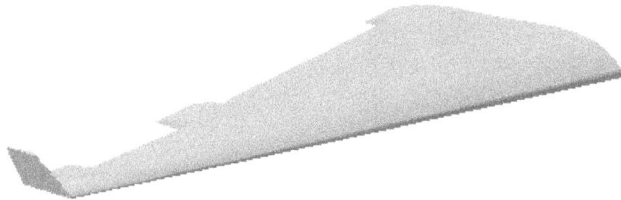

**Figure 4–33**

Figure 4–34 shows a preview of the selected surface to be extracted.

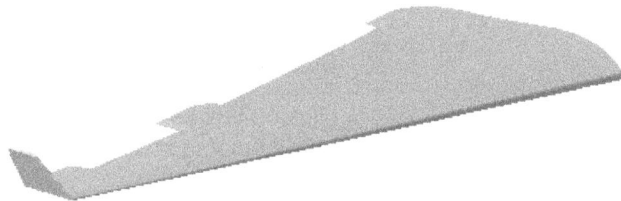

**Figure 4–34**

Figure 4–35 shows the resulting extracted surface. The solid geometry is hidden.

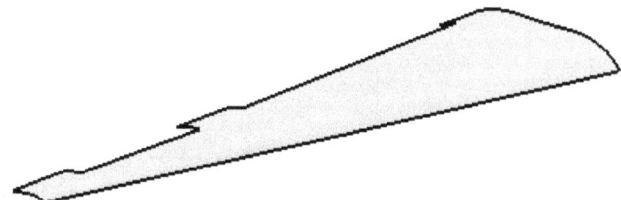

**Figure 4–35**

**General Steps**

Use the following steps to perform an **Extract** operation:

1. Start the **Extract** operation.
2. Select the entities to extract.
3. Specify the propagation type.
4. (Optional) Define additional settings.

## Step 1 - Start the Extract operation.

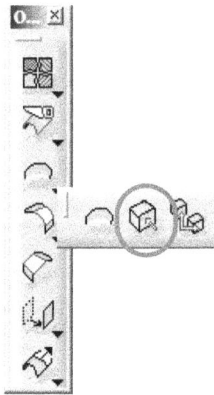

Click  (Extract). The Extract definition dialog box opens as shown in Figure 4–36.

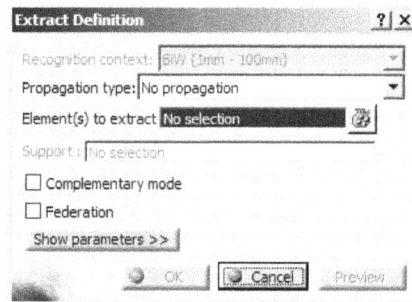

Figure 4–36

## Step 2 - Select the entities to extract.

Select a face in the model. Multiple faces can be selected by clicking  as shown in Figure 4–37. Once the Element(s) to extract dialog box opens you can select multiple entities.

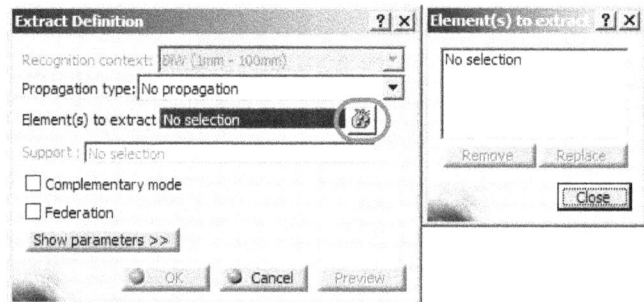

Figure 4–37

## Step 3 - Specify the propagation type.

In the Propagation type drop-down list, select one of the following:

- No propagation
- Point continuity

- Tangent continuity

- Curvature continuity

- Depression propagation

- Protrusion propagation

Figure 4–38 shows the different propagation settings used in the **Extract** operation. Only one face was selected for each of the propagation settings.

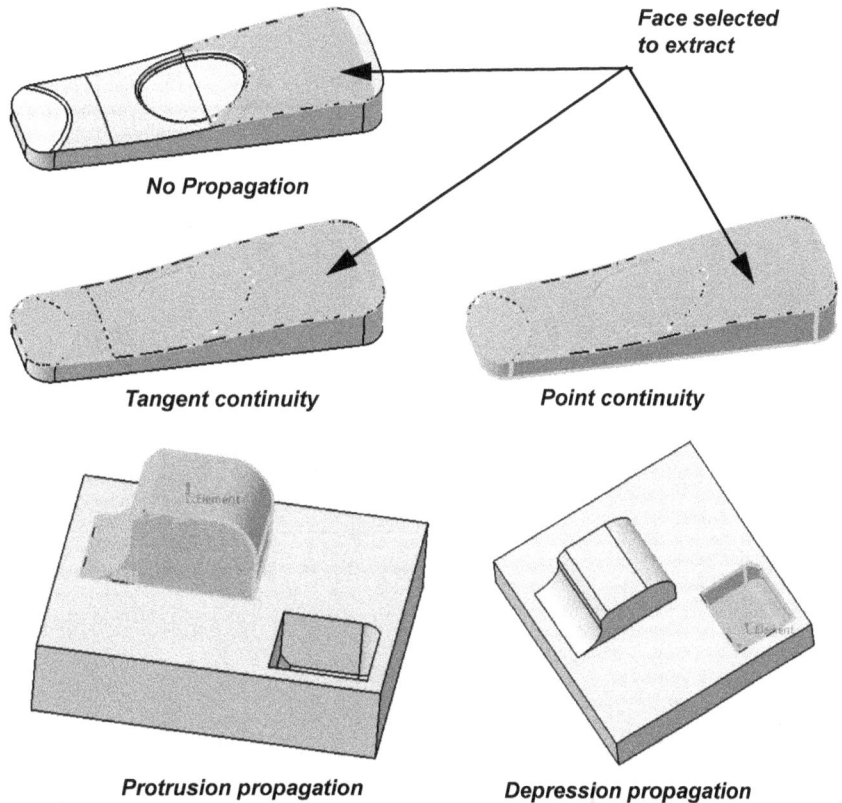

*No Propagation*

*Face selected to extract*

*Tangent continuity*

*Point continuity*

*Protrusion propagation*

*Depression propagation*

**Figure 4–38**

The Recognition context option is only available with **Protrusion propagation** or **Depression propagation**.

- With propagation type **Protrusion propagation**, after selecting a face or cell, all surrounding faces or cells are included in the extract if the shared boundaries are convex.

- With propagation type **Depression propagation**, after selecting a face or cell, all surrounding faces or cells are included in the extract if the shared boundaries are concave.

The **Recognition context** option (default value **BiW (1mm – 100mm)**) can be used to add surrounding Fillets or Chamfers to the Protrusion or Depression propagation based on size. The values are as shown as follows:

| Industry | Fillets size range | Chamfers size range |
|---|---|---|
| Power Train | 0mm - 15mm | 0mm - 15mm |
| BiW (Body in White) | 0mm - 15mm | 1mm - 100mm |
| Consumer Goods | 0mm - 50mm | 0mm - 50mm |
| Ship Building | 0mm - infinity | 0mm - infinity |
| High Tech | 0mm - 1.5mm | 0mm - 1.5mm |
| Building | 1mm - 100mm | 1mm - 100mm |
| Machine Design (see User Assistance) | 0mm - 15mm | 0.03mm - 1.5mm<br>angles range: 30deg - 60deg |

## Step 4 - (Optional) Define additional settings.

Optional settings can be applied when using the **Extract** tool.

They are located in the Extract Definition dialog box as shown in Figure 4–39.

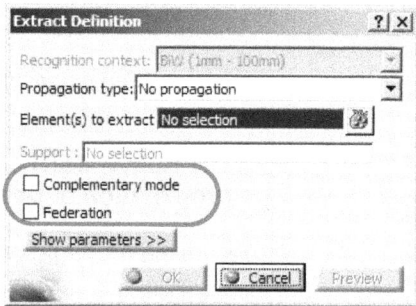

**Figure 4–39**

Select **Complementary mode** to extract the opposite surfaces selected by the **Propagation** tool. An example is shown in Figure 4–40.

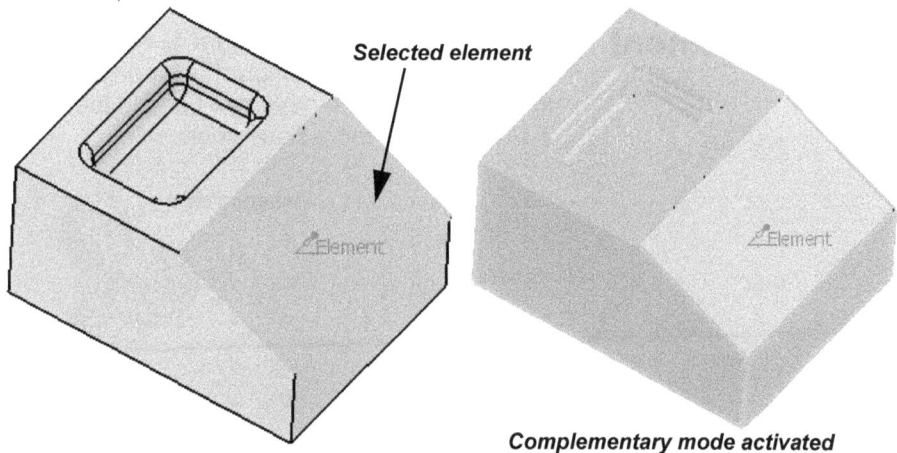

*Complementary mode activated*

**Figure 4–40**

Select **Federation** if the resultant surface is considered a representation of all surfaces added to the extract. Do not select the **Federation** option if the resultant surface is used as a collection of patches representing each surface added to the extract.

The **Federation** option determines whether the resultant surface can mathematically represent all surfaces added to the extract. For example, if a Pad is extruded up to an extract surface, the **Federation** option should be selected. This enables the stop surface of the Pad to be calculated at any location on the Extract. If the **Federation** option is not selected and the Pad moves to a new location on the Extract, the Pad feature could fail.

Click **OK** to complete the Extract.

## Extracting in a Top-Down Design Environment

In a top-down design environment, extracted surfaces can be selected to create geometry that uses external references at the assembly level. Solid or surface geometry can then be built from the extracted face.

In the example shown in Figure 4–41, Part A is being modeled in the context of the assembly. Part A does not have any geometry in Figure 4–41. The other two parts in the assembly are a Y-shaped pipe and a Base connector.

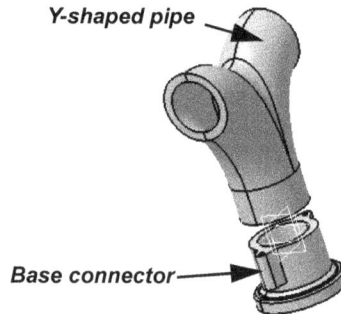

*Y-shaped pipe*

*Base connector*

Figure 4–41

Instead of sketching shapes that already exist in the assembly, the **Extract** tool is used. With Part A active, a Pad feature is being created. Right-click in the *Selection* field and select **Create Extract**. The top face of the Base connector is selected to extract. The extracted face then defines the shape of the Pad feature as shown in Figure 4–42.

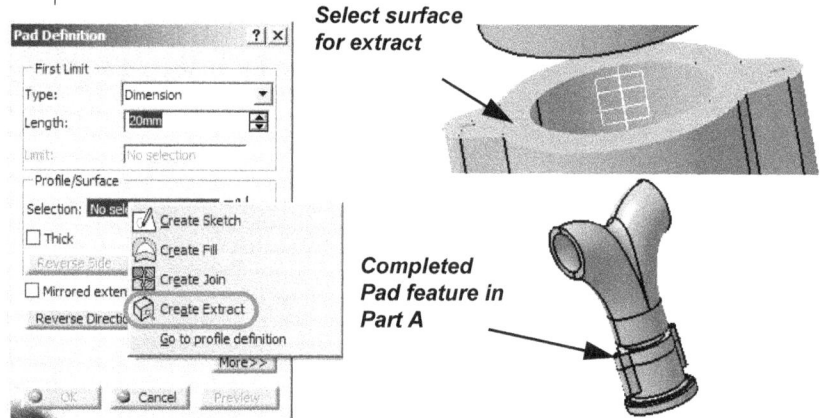

*Select surface for extract*

*Completed Pad feature in Part A*

Figure 4–42

By extracting a surface at the assembly level, you create an external reference. Select **Edit>Links** to investigate the multi-model links that are created when extracting from another part.

# 4.8 Chamfer

A Chamfer feature creates a flat, beveled surface between two faces that are adjacent to an edge. Chamfers are created by clicking  (Chamfer) in the Operations toolbar.

**Figure 4–43**

Chamfers have the following characteristics:

- Chamfers can be added to concave or convex edges, as shown in Figure 4–44.

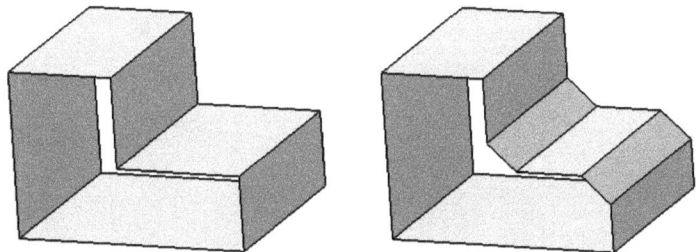

**Figure 4–44**

- You can select edges or surfaces to be chamfered. When you select a surface, all of the edges on the surface's boundary that are adjacent to other surfaces are chamfered.

## General Steps

Use the following general steps to create a Chamfer feature:

1. Select the edges to chamfer.
2. Define the Dimension mode.
3. Complete the feature.

### Step 1 - Select the edges to chamfer.

Edges can be selected individually or propagated using propagation methods.

### Step 2 - Define the Dimension mode.

The Dimension mode for a chamfer can be defined in the Mode drop-down list in the Chamfer Definition dialog box. It determines how the chamfer is dimensioned.

The **Length1/Angle** option in the Mode drop-down list creates a chamfer in which the length equals the distance from the edge to be chamfered to the edge of the bevel. The angle is measured with respect to Length1. An example is shown in Figure 4–45.

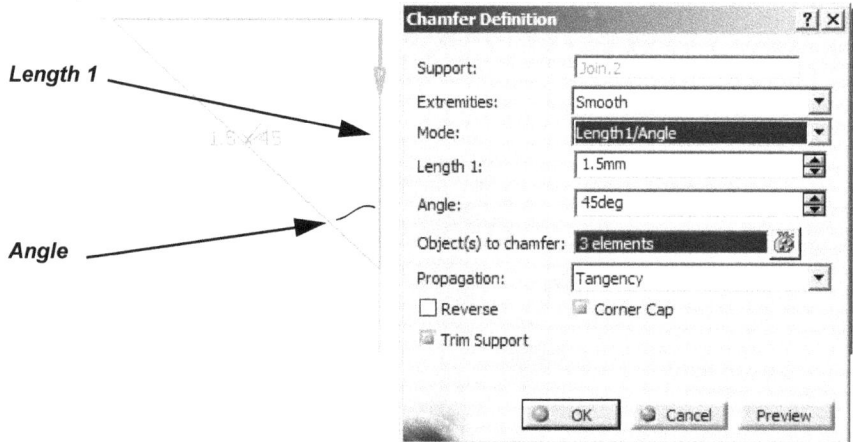

Figure 4–45

Another method of defining the size of the chamfer is to select **Length1/Length2** in the Mode drop-down list. You enter the distance from the edge to be chamfered to the edge of the bevel on each side. An example is shown in Figure 4–46.

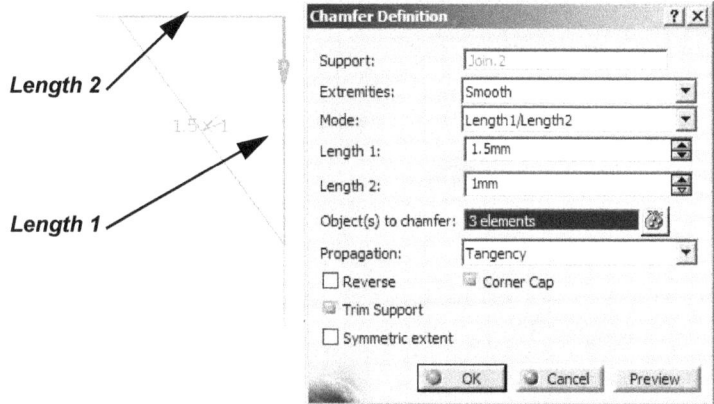

**Figure 4–46**

The two other Modes are **Chordal Length/Angle** and **Height/Angle**. For **Chordal Length/Angle**, you enter a chordal length and angle. The Chordal length is the chamfer width. For **Height/Angle**, you enter a height value and an angle. The height is the distance between the intersection of the two adjacent faces and the chamfer face.

You can define the Propagation as either **Tangency** or **Minimal**. Tangency will include all edges tangent to the selected edge, while minimal will include only as much geometry as required to blend the chamfer in, as shown in Figure 4–47.

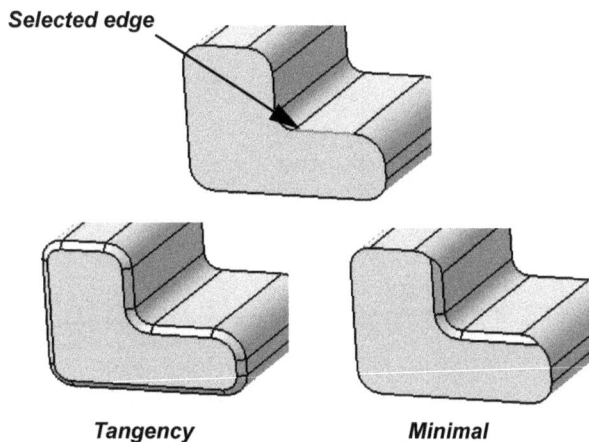

**Figure 4–47**

You can select **Reverse** in the Chamfer Definition dialog box to flip the direction of the chamfer.

The **Corner Cap** option will create a clean corner when more than two edges converge, as shown in Figure 4–48.

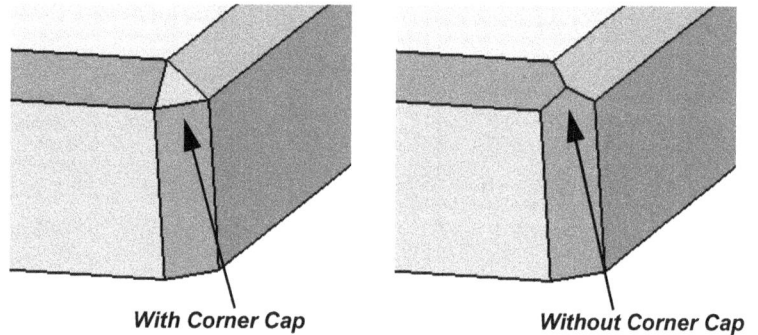

*With Corner Cap*          *Without Corner Cap*

**Figure 4–48**

The **Trim Support** option will remove material from the support and join the support and chamfer.

If you enable the **Symmetric extent** option (only available for Length1/Length2 chamfers), Length 2 will be set to match Length 1, then Length 2 will be grayed out in the Chamfer Definition dialog box.

## Step 3 - Complete the feature.

Click **OK** to complete the feature.

# Practice 4a

# Surface Operations I

### Practice Objectives

- Mirror and translate surface features.
- Use the Split and Trim operations.
- Add a chamfer.

In this practice, you will create some generic geometry to practice using surface operations. The geometry will be created in a new part model and will consist of two independent volumes that are symmetrical about the ZX reference plane. Operations are performed on the left and right sides to compare the similarities and differences between features in the Operations toolbar. The completed model displays as shown in Figure 4–49.

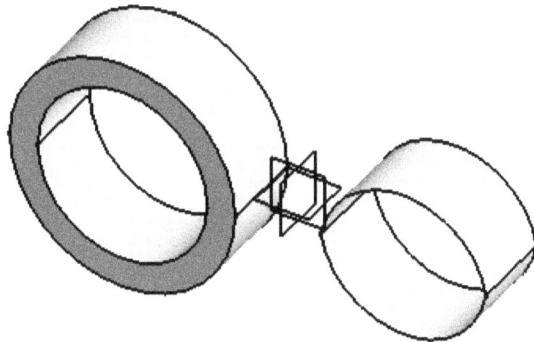

Figure 4–49

### Task 1 - Create a new part.

1. Create a new part model and access the GSD workbench.

2. Change the *Part Number* to **Operations** and save the model with the default name.

3. Set the units to mm.

### Task 2 - Create a cylinder surface.

1. Create a reference point using the Coordinates type. Enter the coordinates **0, -50, 0** using the origin as the reference.

2. Click ⬚ (Cylinder) to create a cylinder surface.

3. Select **Point.1** as the point and the YZ plane as the direction.

4. Enter a *Radius* of **40** and extrude the surface **20** in both directions. The model displays as shown in Figure 4–50.

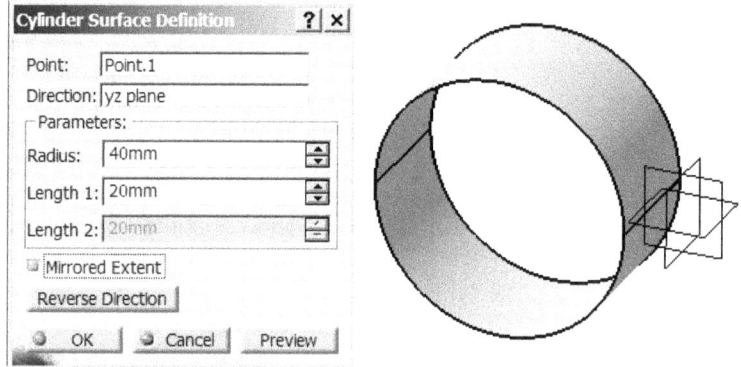

**Figure 4–50**

5. Hide the **Point** feature.

---

**Task 3 - Mirror the extruded surface.**

---

1. In the Transformations toolbar, click ⬚ (Symmetry). The Symmetry Definition dialog box opens as shown in Figure 4–51.

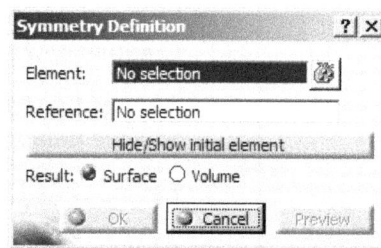

**Figure 4–51**

2. Select the cylinder surface as the element.

3. Select the ZX plane as the reference.

4. Click **OK** to complete the operation. The model displays as shown in Figure 4–52.

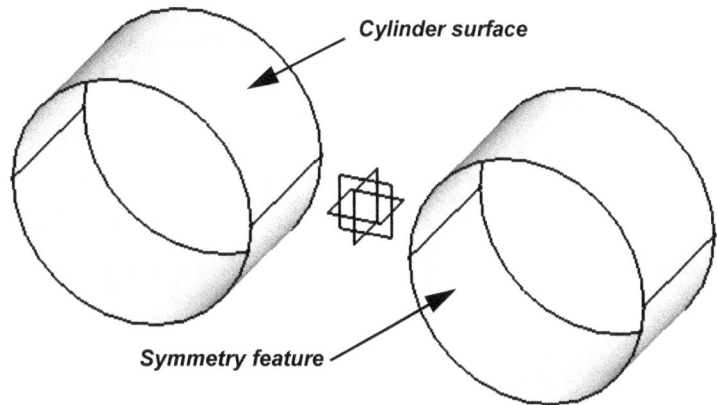

Figure 4–52

5. Using the specification tree, modify the *Radius* of **Cylinder.1** to **30mm**. Note that both cylinder features are updated.

## Task 4 - Create an offset surface.

1. Create an offset surface using the cylinder surface. Offset outwards by a value of **10mm**. The resulting surface displays as shown in Figure 4–53.

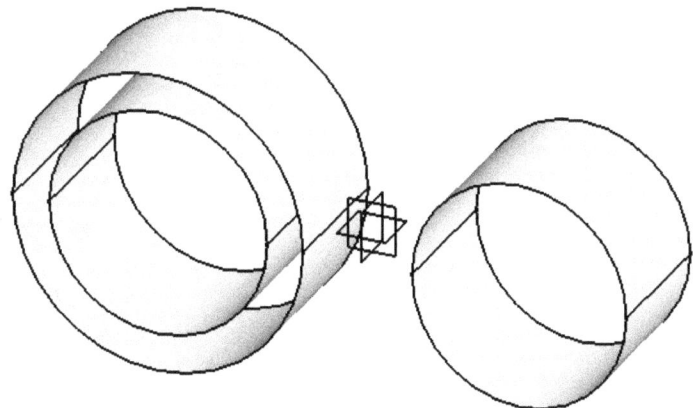

Figure 4–53

## Task 5 - Create a translated surface.

1. Click  (Translate). The Translate Definition dialog box opens as shown in Figure 4–54.

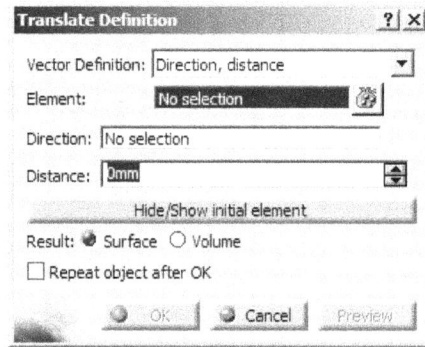

**Figure 4–54**

2. Select the symmetry surface as the surface to translate.

3. Select the XY plane as the Direction reference.

4. Enter a *Distance* of **10mm** upwards and complete the feature. The translated surface displays as shown in Figure 4–55.

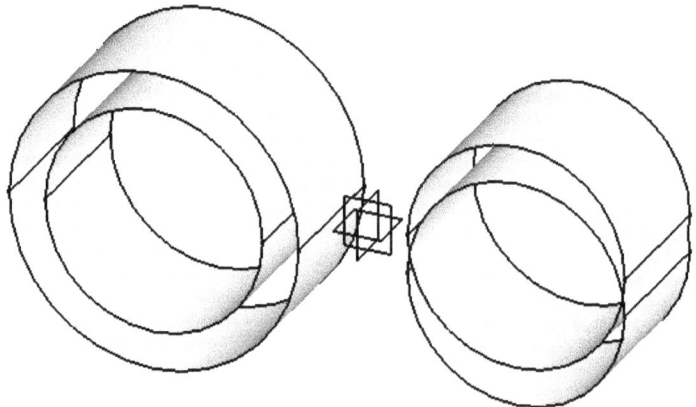

**Figure 4–55**

## Task 6 - Trim the right surfaces.

1. Click ![Trim icon] (Trim). The Trim Definition dialog box opens, as shown in Figure 4–56.

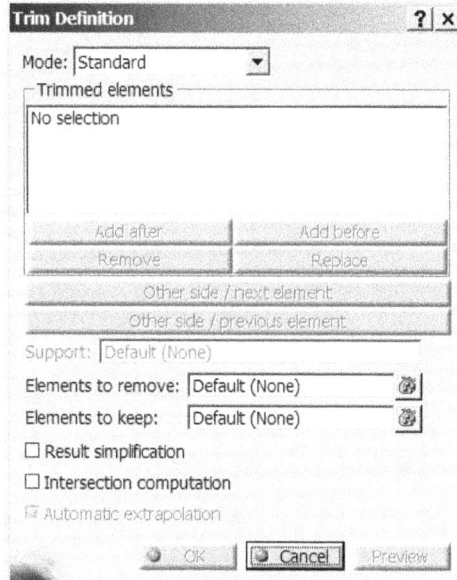

**Figure 4–56**

2. Select the two surfaces shown in Figure 4–57 as **Element 1** and **Element 2**.

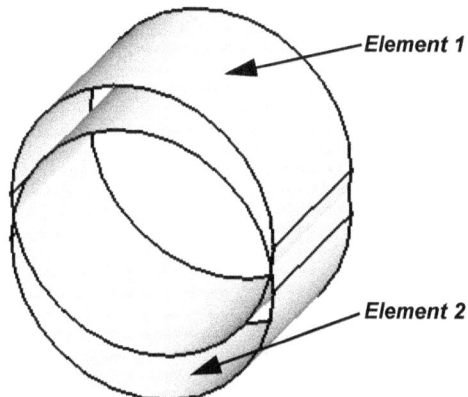

**Figure 4–57**

3. Use **Other side / next element** and/or **Other side / previous element** to toggle the side to keep of each trimmed surface. There are four possible solutions as shown in Figure 4–58. Verify that your result is the same as the one in the bottom right corner.

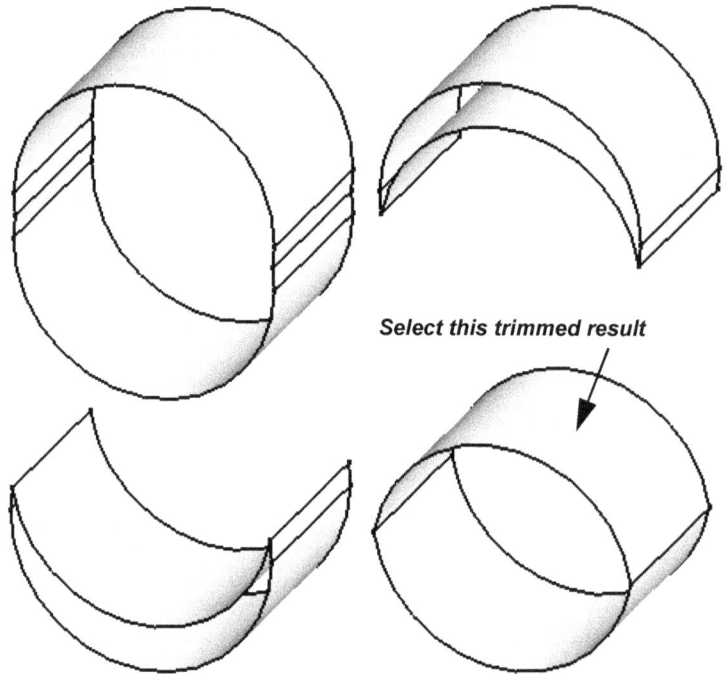

**Select this trimmed result**

Figure 4–58

## Task 7 - Split and fill the outer circular surface.

1. Orient the model, as shown in Figure 4–59.

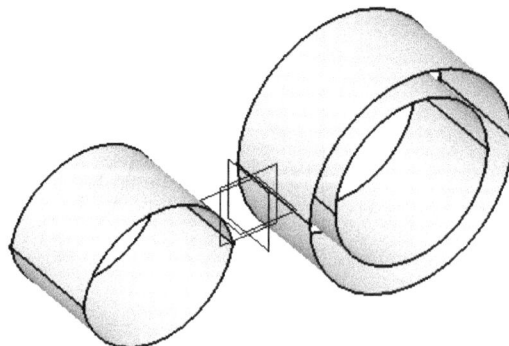

Figure 4–59

2.  Create a reference plane offset from the YZ plane by -**10mm**.

3.  Click  (Split) to split a feature.

4.  In the *Element to cut* field, select the **Offset.1** surface and in the *Cutting elements* area, select **Plane.1**, as shown in Figure 4–60.

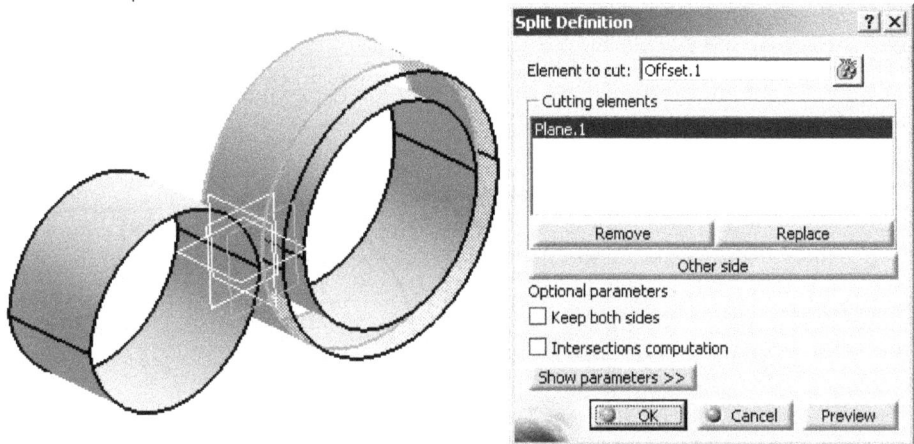

**Figure 4–60**

5.  Create a fill surface inside the edge of the outer circular surface on the side that it was split, as shown in Figure 4–61.

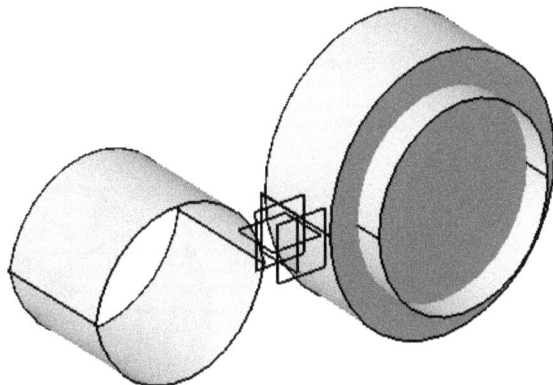

**Figure 4–61**

## Task 8 - Trim the fill surface.

1. Click ⬚ (Trim) and select the fill surface and the inner circular surface.

2. Select the appropriate sides so that the trimmed model displays as shown in Figure 4–62.

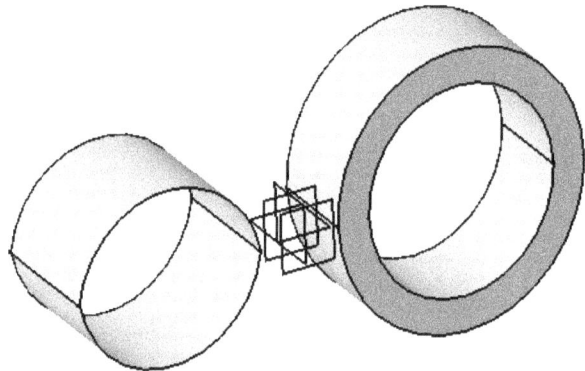

Figure 4–62

## Task 9 - Create another fill surface and join the surfaces.

1. Click ⬚ (Isometric View) to reorient the model to the default Isometric view.

2. Create a fill surface using the edge of **Split.1** as the Outer Boundaries and the edge of **Trim.1** as the Inner Boundaries, as shown in Figure 4–63.

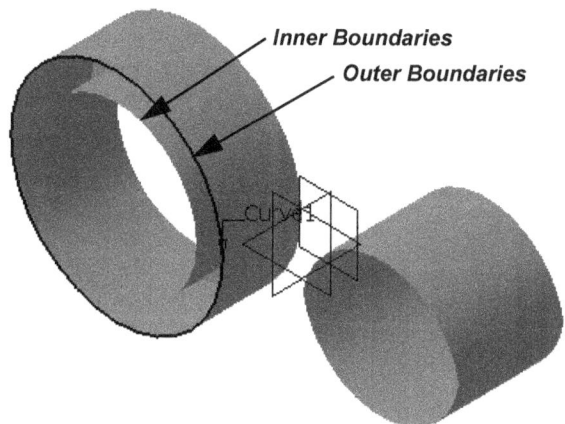

Figure 4–63

3. The resulting geometry displays as shown in Figure 4–64.

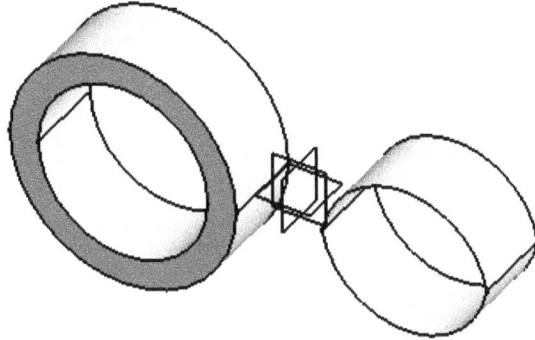

**Figure 4–64**

4. Click ▓ (Join). The Join Definition dialog box opens.

5. In the specification tree, select **Split.1**, **Trim.2**, and **Fill.2** as the elements to be joined and complete the feature.

**Task 10 - Add a chamfer to the outer edge of the joined surfaces.**

1. Click ⬦ (Chamfer).

2. Select the outer edge of the joined surfaces.

3. Enter **3** for *Length1* and **60** for the *Angle*.

4. Click **Preview**. The model displays as shown in Figure 4–65.

**Figure 4–65**

5. Select **Length1/Length2** in the Mode drop-down list.

6. Enter **6** for *Length 2* and click **OK**. The model display as shown in Figure 4–66.

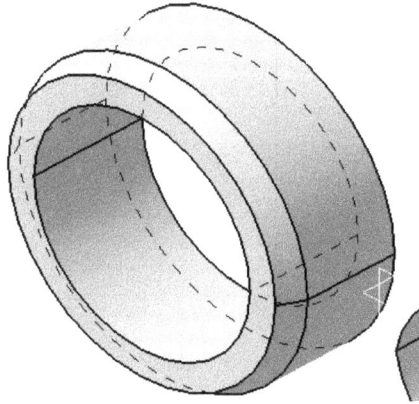

**Figure 4–66**

7. Double-click on the surface of the chamfer.

8. Select **Trim Support** to disable it and click **OK**. Note that the material from the support surface has not been removed, as shown in Figure 4–67.

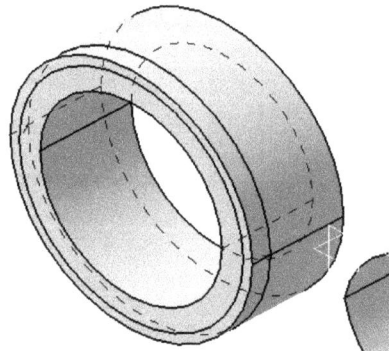

**Figure 4–67**

9. Double-click on **Chamfer.1** in the Specification Tree.

10. Select **Trim Support** to enable it and click **OK**.

11. Save the model and close the window.

# Practice 4b

# Panel

### Practice Objectives

- Create Extract surfaces.
- Create Offset surfaces.

In this practice, you will complete the part by creating surfaces using the Extract and Offset features. The completed model displays as shown in Figure 4–68.

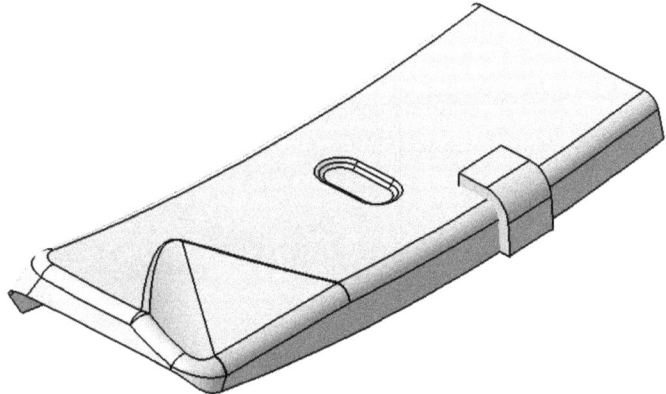

**Figure 4–68**

### Task 1 - Open a part.

1. Open **Trim_ Panel.CATPart**. The model displays as shown in Figure 4–69.

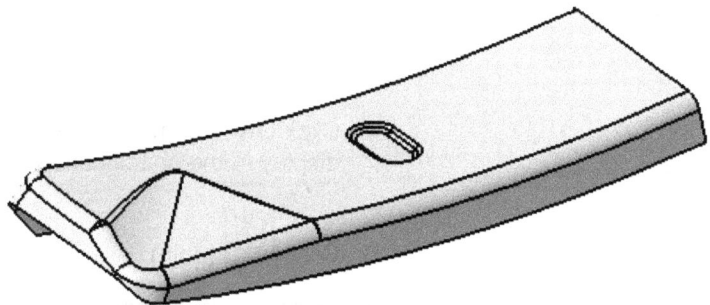

**Figure 4–69**

2. Verify that the model units are set to **mm**.

## Task 2 - Extract surfaces from the model.

1. In the Operations toolbar, click 🔲 (Extract). The Extract Definition dialog box opens, as shown in Figure 4–70.

2. In the dialog box, click 🔲, as shown in Figure 4–70. This enables multiple entities to be extracted.

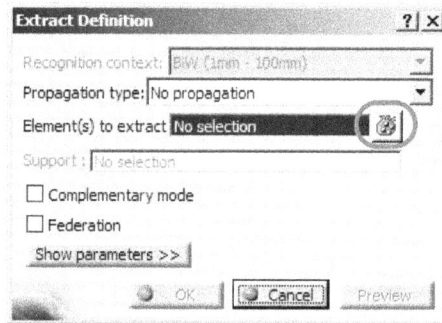

**Figure 4–70**

3. Select the surfaces shown in Figure 4–71.

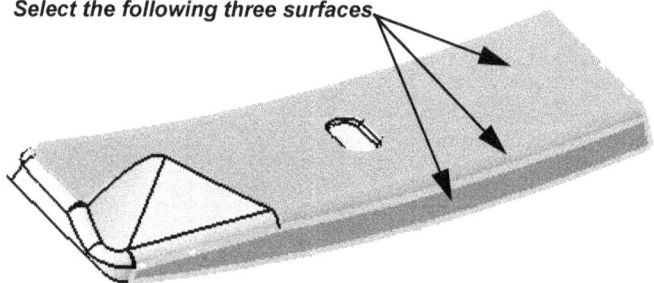

*Select the following three surfaces.*

**Figure 4–71**

4. Click **OK** to complete the extract. Three new extract features display in the specification tree.

5. Click 🔲 (Join).

6. Select the three newly created Extract features.

7. Click **OK** to complete the Join.

## Task 3 - Offset surfaces.

1. In the Surfaces toolbar, click [icon] (Offset). The Offset Surface Definition dialog box opens as shown in Figure 4–72.

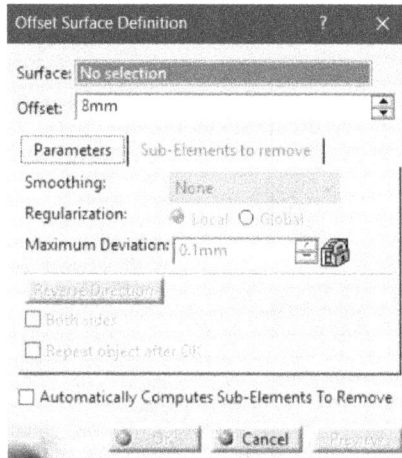

**Figure 4–72**

2. In the specification tree, select the newly created Join feature.

3. Enter an *Offset* value of **8mm**.

4. Click **OK** to complete the Offset.

5. Change the color of the Offset to green. The model displays as shown in Figure 4–73.

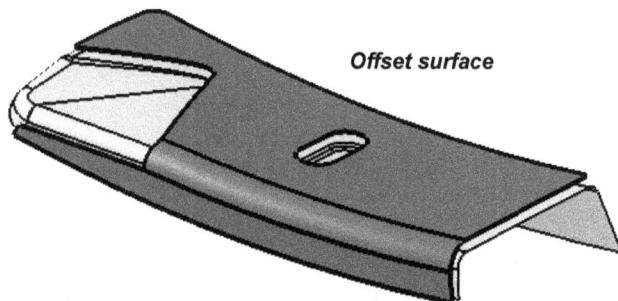

*Offset surface*

**Figure 4–73**

## Task 4 - Create an extruded surface.

1. Show **Sketch.5**. This sketch will become the profile for the extruded surface in the next steps.

2. Click [Extrude icon] (Extrude).

3. Select **Sketch.5** as the Profile. The XY plane is automatically used as the direction reference because that was the sketching plane for Sketch.5.

4. Enter **34mm** for *Limit 1*, and **50mm** for *Limit 2*.

5. Click **OK** to complete the Extruded surface. The model displays as shown in Figure 4–74.

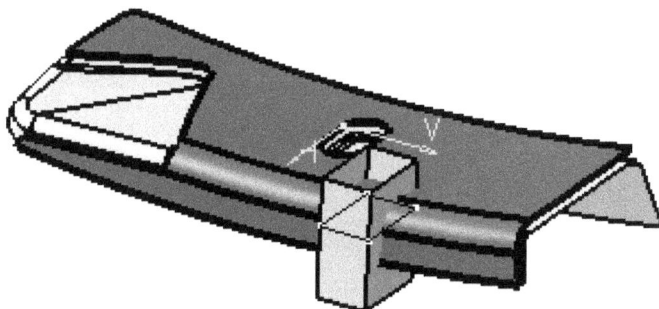

**Figure 4–74**

## Task 5 - Trim and split surfaces.

1. Hide **Sketch.5**.

2. Click [Trim icon] (Trim).

3. Select **Offset.1** and the newly created extruded surface, as shown in Figure 4–75.

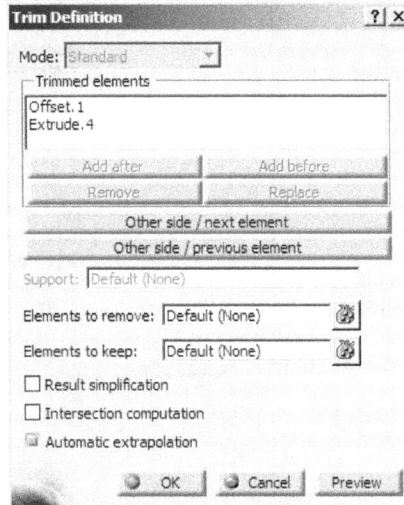

**Figure 4–75**

4. It might be required to click **Other side / next element** and/or **Other side / previous element** in the Trim Definition dialog box. These buttons toggle which side of the surfaces to keep in the **Trim** operation. Figure 4–76 shows the portions of the surfaces to keep.

5. Click **OK** to complete the Trim feature.

6. When the **Trim** operation is completed, the model displays as shown in Figure 4–76.

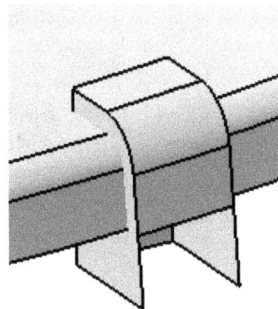

**Figure 4–76**

7. Rename *Trim.3* as **Trimmed Surf**.

8. In the specification tree, select **Split Surf**. It will be used in the **Split** operation.

9. Click  (Split). The Split Definition dialog box opens, as shown in Figure 4–77.

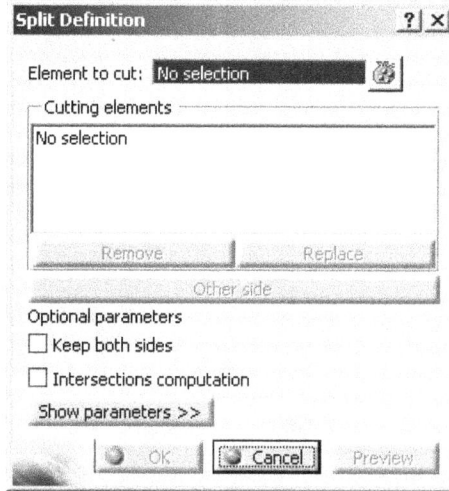

**Figure 4–77**

10. Select **Trimmed Surf** as the Element to cut, and select **Split Surf** as the Cutting Element, as shown in Figure 4–78.

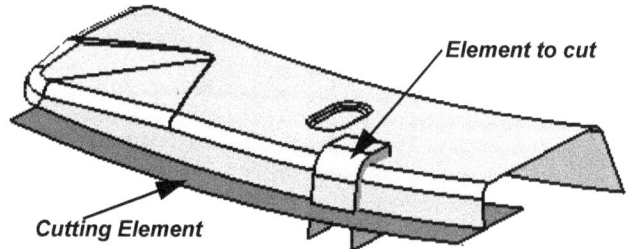

**Figure 4–78**

11. In the Split Definition dialog box, you might need to click **Other side**. This button toggles which side of the geometry to keep. The completed Split feature displays as shown in Figure 4–79.

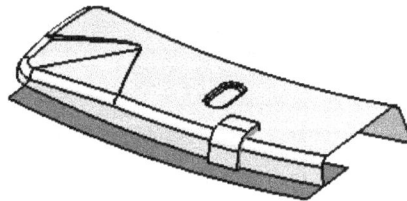

**Figure 4–79**

12. Hide **Split Surf**. The finished model displays as shown in Figure 4–80.

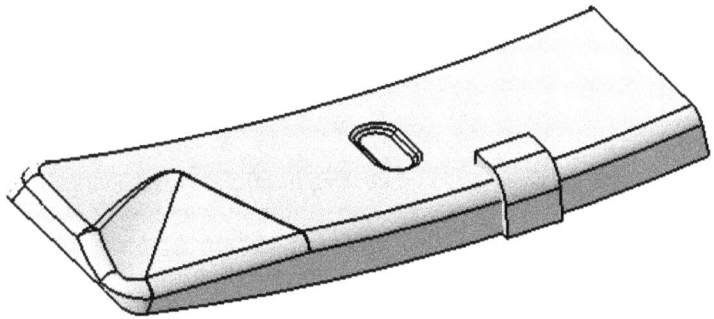

**Figure 4–80**

13. Save the model and close the file.

# Practice 4c

# Surface Operations II

### Practice Objectives

- Use the Join feature.
- Use the Split and Trim features.
- Extract and offset surfaces.

In this practice, you will create basic surface features. Wireframe and surfaces are used in surface operations, such as trimming, splitting, joining, and extracting. The completed model displays as shown in Figure 4–81.

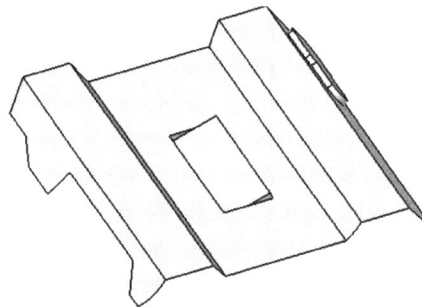

**Figure 4–81**

### Task 1 - Open a part.

1. Open **Surf_Operations_Start.CATPart**. The model displays as shown in Figure 4–82.

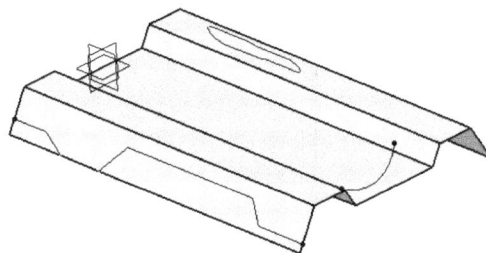

**Figure 4–82**

2. Verify that the model units are set to **mm**.

## Task 2 - Split a surface with a curve.

1. In the Operations toolbar, click ⬚ (Split). The Split
   Definition dialog box opens as shown in Figure 4–83.

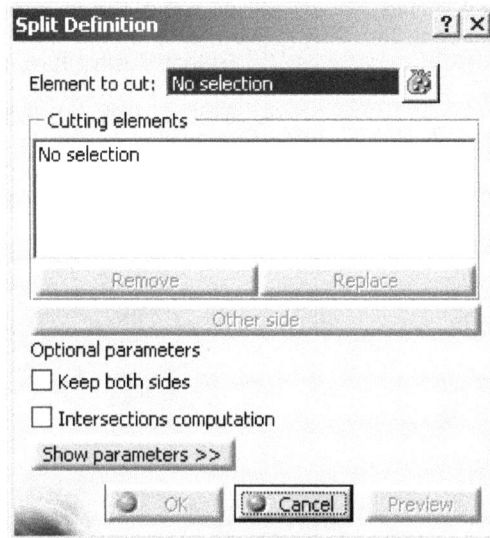

**Figure 4–83**

2. Select **Base Extrude** as the Element to cut, and select **Split
   Profile** as the Cutting element.

3. Click **Preview**. The model displays as shown in Figure 4–84.

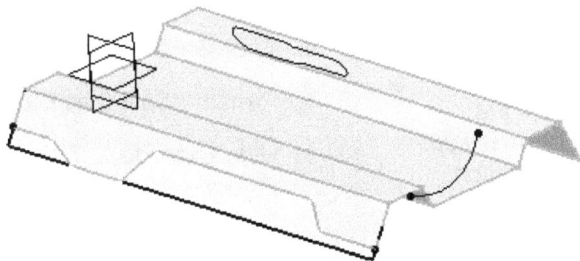

**Figure 4–84**

4. If the geometry does not display as shown in Figure 4–84,
   click **Other side** to toggle the side of the Element to cut to
   keep in the **Split** operation.

5. Click **OK**. **Split.1** now displays in the specification tree.

6. Hide **Split Profile**.

## Task 3 - Split a surface with another surface.

1. Click [icon] (Extrude).

2. In the specification tree, select **Arc Profile**. It will define the shape of the Extrude.

3. Enter **150mm** for *Limit 1*.

4. Select **Mirrored Extent**.

5. Click **OK** to complete the Extrude. The model displays as shown in Figure 4–85.

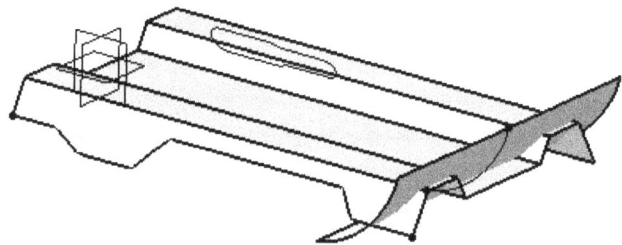

**Figure 4–85**

6. Hide **Arc Profile**.

7. Click [icon] (Split).

8. Select **Split.1** as the Element to cut, and select **Extrude.2** as the Cutting element.

9. Click **OK** to complete the Split.

*You might need to click* ***Other side*** *to toggle which side of the Element to cut is kept in the* ***Split*** *operation.*

10. Rename *Split.2* as **Base Surface**.

11. Hide **Extrude.2**. The model displays as shown in Figure 4–86.

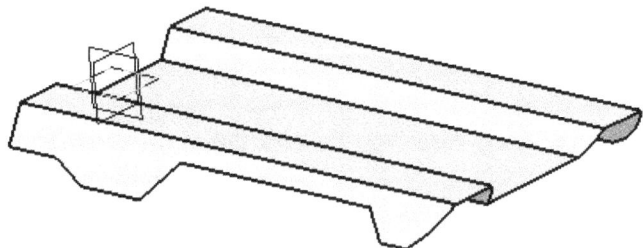

**Figure 4–86**

## Task 4 - Create stamp geometry.

1. Click ⬚ (Extrude).

2. In the specification tree, select **Side Profile**. This will define the shape of the Extrude.

3. Enter **5mm** for *Limit 1.*

4. Click **OK** to complete the Extrude. The model displays as shown in Figure 4–87.

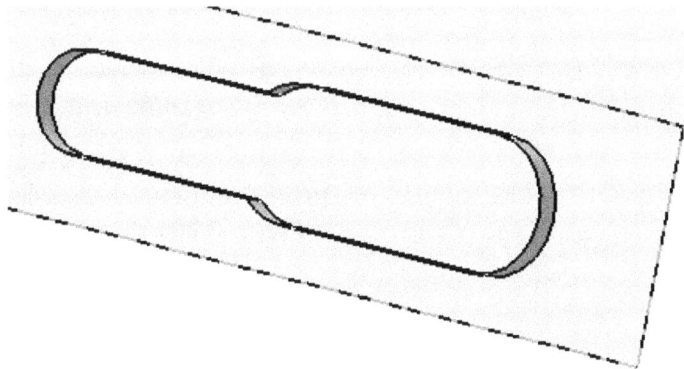

**Figure 4–87**

5. In the Operations toolbar, click ⬚ (Extract).

6. In the Extract Definition dialog box, in the Propagation type drop-down list, select **No propagation**, as shown in Figure 4–88.

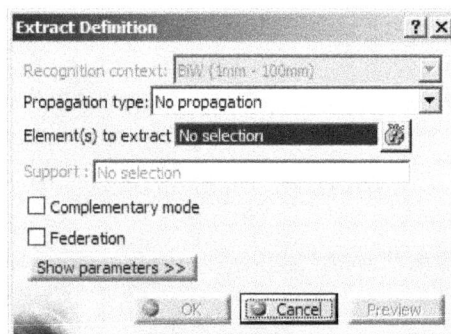

**Figure 4–88**

7. Select the surface shown in Figure 4–89.

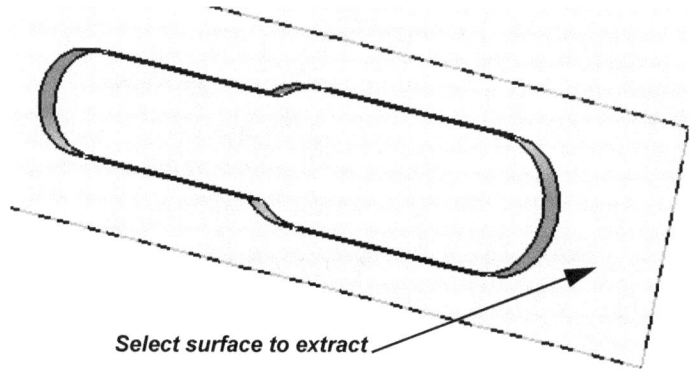

**Select surface to extract**

**Figure 4–89**

8. Click **OK** to complete the Extract.

9. In the Surfaces toolbar, click  (Offset). The Offset Surface Definition dialog box opens as shown in Figure 4–90.

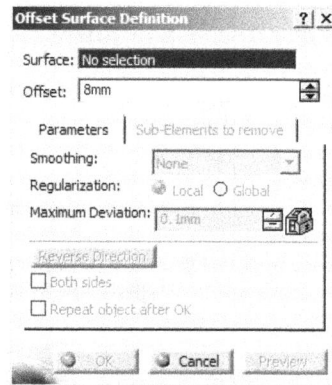

**Figure 4–90**

10. In the specification tree, select **Extract.1** as the *Surface* to offset.

11. Enter an *Offset* value of **10mm**.

12. Click **OK** to complete the Offset. The model displays as shown in Figure 4–91.

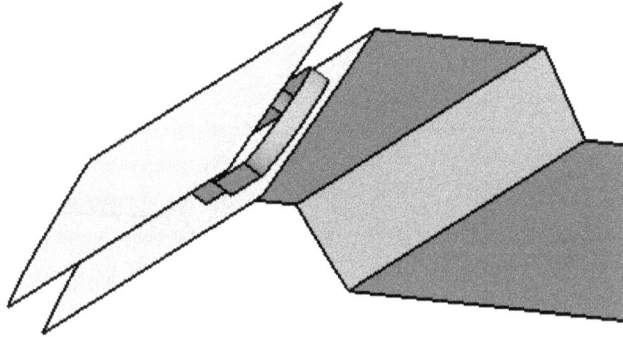

**Figure 4–91**

**Design Considerations**

The **Extrude.3** depth and **Offset.1** values are not equal. You will create a formula to set these two dimensions to be equal to one another.

13. In the specification tree, double-click on the feature and edit **Offset.1**.

14. In the dialog box, right-click on the **10mm** value and select **Edit Formula**.

15. In the specification tree, select **Extrude.3**.

16. In the Formula Editor, double-click on **Geometrical Set.1\Extrude.3\Lim1**, as shown in Figure 4–92.

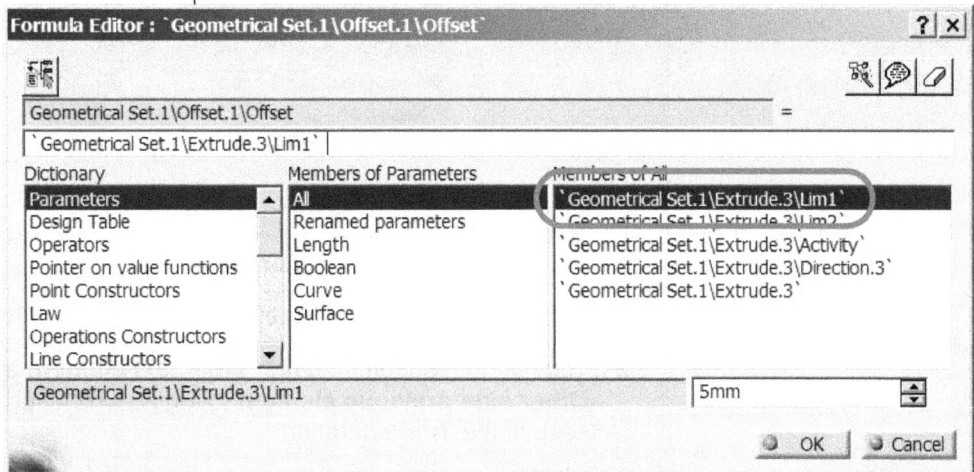

**Figure 4–92**

17. In the Formula Editor, click **OK**.

18. In the Offset Surface Definition dialog box, click **OK**. The model updates as shown in Figure 4–93.

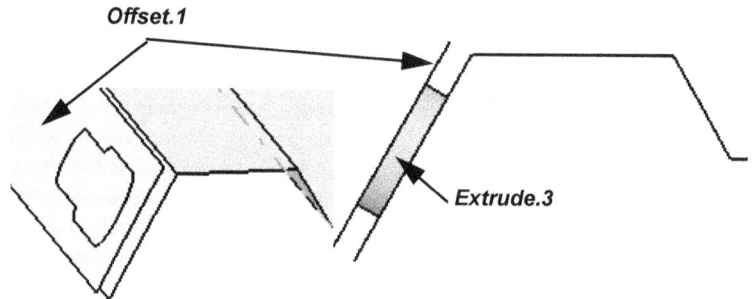

**Figure 4–93**

19. In the Operations toolbar, click [icon] (Trim). The Trim Definition dialog box opens as shown in Figure 4–94.

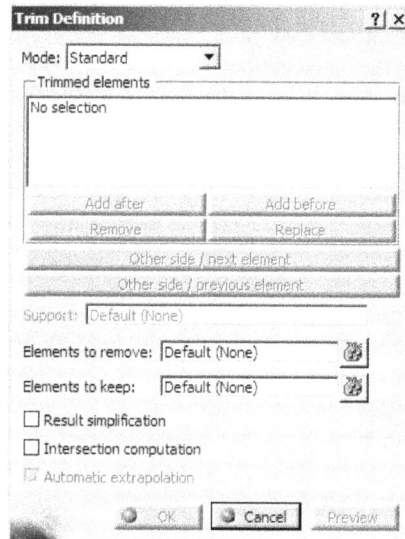

**Figure 4–94**

20. Select **Extrude.3** and **Offset.1**.

21. You might need to use **Other side/next element** and/or **Other side/previous element** to toggle which surfaces to keep in the **Trim** operation.

22. Click **OK** to complete the Trim. The model displays as shown in Figure 4–95.

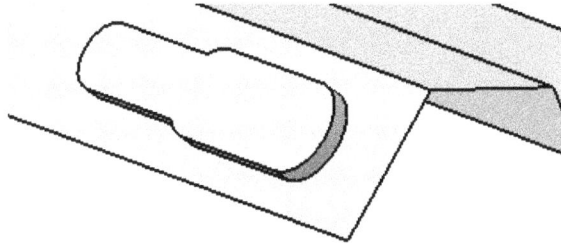

**Figure 4–95**

## Task 5 - Create extrude surface and reference geometry.

1. Click ⬜ (Plane).

2. In the Plane type drop-down list, select **Angle/Normal to plane**.

3. Right-click in the *Rotation axis* field and select **Y Axis**, as shown in Figure 4–96.

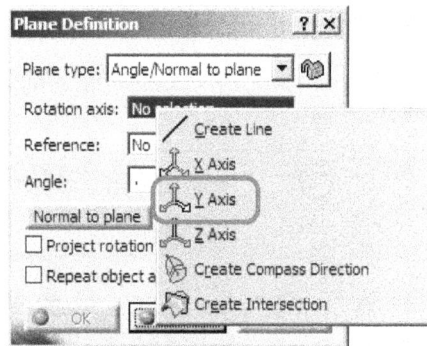

**Figure 4–96**

4. Select the XY plane.

5. In the *Angle* field, enter **15deg**.

6. Click **OK** to complete the Plane.

7. Create a point with the following coordinates:

   • X= 0mm
   • Y= 200mm
   • Z= 0mm

8. Click ▣ (Position Sketch).

9. Select **Plane.1**. This is the angled plane that was created in the previous steps.

10. In the Origin Type drop-down list, select **Projection point**.

11. Select **Point.1**.

12. Note the Absolute Axis of the sketch as shown in Figure 4–97. It shows the orientation that the sketch will take inside the sketching environment. If required, select **Reverse H**, **Reverse V**, or **Swap** to change the orientation of the Vertical or Horizontal Axis.

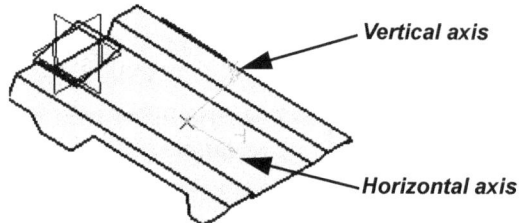

**Figure 4–97**

13. In the Sketch Positioning dialog box, click **OK**.

14. Create the sketch shown in Figure 4–98.

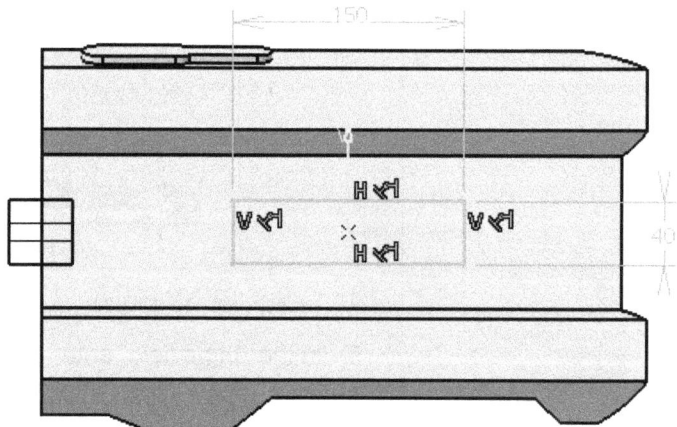

**Figure 4–98**

15. Exit the Sketcher workbench.

16. Rename the sketch as **Top Profile**.

17. Extrude Top Profile by **10mm** in each direction. The model displays as shown in Figure 4–99.

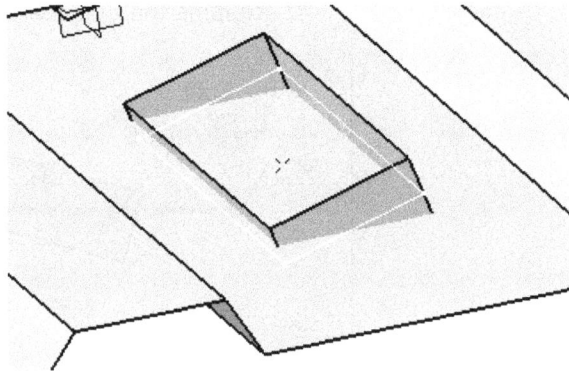

**Figure 4–99**

18. Click ⬚ (Split).

19. Select **Base Surface** as the Element to cut, and select **Extrude.4** as the Cutting element.

*You might need to click* **Other side** *to toggle which side of the Element to cut is kept in the* **Split** *operation.*

20. Click **OK** to complete the Split. The model displays as shown in Figure 4–100.

**Figure 4–100**

21. Rename the Split feature as **Split A**.

22. Hide **Top Profile**.

23. Click ⬚ (Split).

24. Select **Extrude.4** as the Element to cut and select **Split A** as the Cutting element.

25. Select **Keep both sides**.

26. Click **OK** to complete the Split. The model displays as shown in Figure 4–101.

27. Rename the Split features, as shown in Figure 4–101.

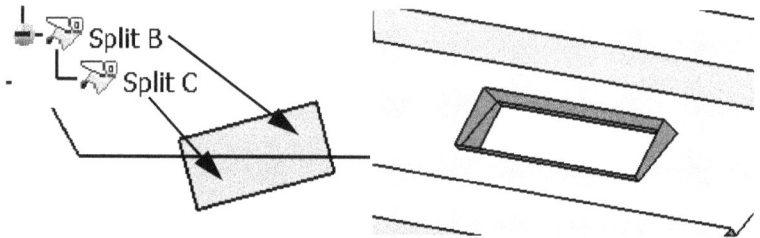

**Figure 4–101**

28. In the Surfaces toolbar, click  (Fill).

29. In the specification tree, select **Top Profile**.

30. Click **OK** to complete the Fill. The model displays as shown in Figure 4–102.

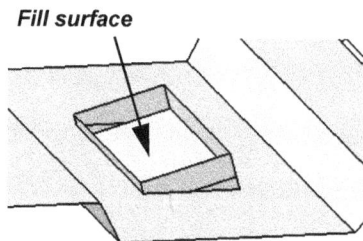

**Figure 4–102**

31. Click  (Split).

32. Select **Split B** as the Element to cut and select **Fill.1** as the Cutting element.

33. Click **OK** to complete the Split. The model displays as shown in Figure 4–103.

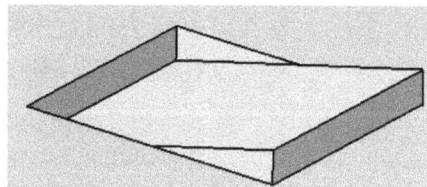

*You might need to click **Other side** to toggle which side of the Element to cut is kept in the **Split** operation.*

**Figure 4–103**

34. Rename the Split feature as **Split D**.

35. Click ⬚ (Split).

36. Select **Split C** as the Element to cut and select **Fill.1** as the Cutting element.

37. Click **OK** to complete the Split. The model displays as shown in Figure 4–104.

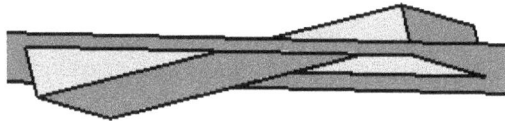

**Figure 4–104**

38. Rename the Split feature as **Split E**.

## Task 6 - Complete the model

1. Hide **Extract.1**.

2. Click ⬚ (Trim).

3. Select **Trim.1** and **Split A**.

4. You might need to use **Other side / next element** and/or **Other side / previous element** to toggle which surfaces to keep in the **Trim** operation.

5. Click **OK** to complete the Trim. The model displays as shown in Figure 4–105.

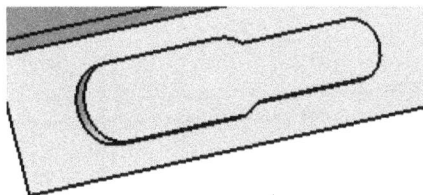

**Figure 4–105**

6. Click ⬚ (Join).

7. Select **Trim.2**, **Fill.1**, **Split D**, and **Split E**.

8. Click **OK** to complete the Join. The model displays as shown in Figure 4–106.

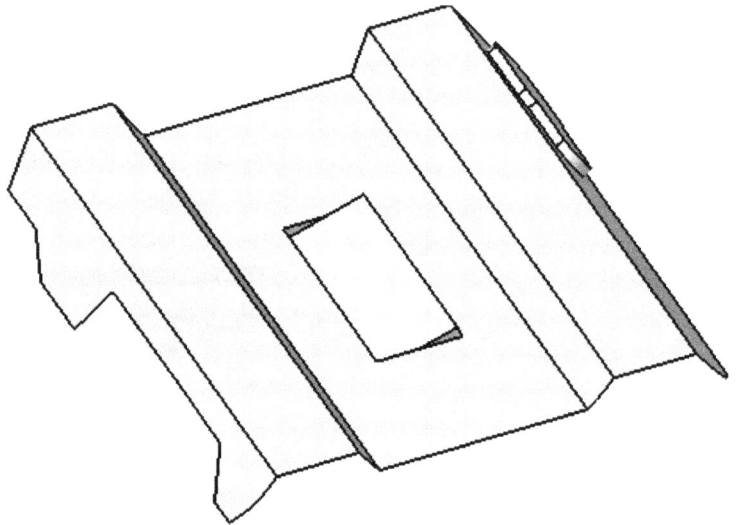

**Figure 4–106**

9. Save and close the model.

# Chapter Review Questions

1. To divide a surface at its intersection with another surface, use the _____ option.

   a. **Join**

   b. **Split**

   c. **Trim**

   d. **Merge**

2. With the **Trim** operation, the cutting element stays whole, but both elements are affected with the **Split** operation.

   a. True

   b. False

3. When using the **Sew Surface** operation, the object to sew always removes material from the support surface.

   a. True

   b. False

4. When using the **Remove Face** operation, you can right-click in the *Faces to remove* field and select **Tangency Propagation** to select all tangent surfaces.

   a. True

   b. False

5. In the Remove Face Definition dialog box, what does the **Faces to limit** option do?

   a. Select all tangent surfaces.

   b. Display the faces to be removed.

   c. Define the portion of a surface to remove.

   d. None of the above.

6. To reduce the number elements in a Join feature, use the _____option.

   a. **Ignore erroneous elements**

   b. **Simplify the result**

   c. **Check connexity**

   d. None of the above.

7. The Scaling operation scales a feature in the X-, Y-, or Z-direction, relative to a selected Axis System.

    a. True

    b. False

8. The **Extract** operation creates new surface elements by copying surface or solid faces.

    a. True

    b. False

9. Chamfer features can only be added to concave edges.

    a. True

    a. False

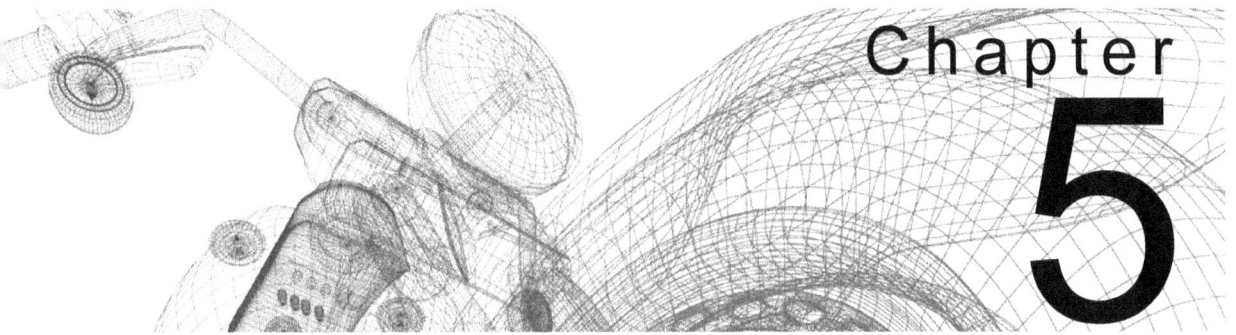

# Geometrical Element Management

This chapter focuses on suggested techniques for grouping elements in geometrical sets and in groups, as well as using visualization and investigation tools.

## Learning Objectives in this Chapter

- Understand the difference between Geometrical Sets and Bodies.
- Understand how objects are organized in the Specification Tree.
- Understand Feature Naming and graphic properties.
- Use the Visualization tools to control object display.
- Use various tools to investigate a model.
- Use the various Operation Tools.
- Replace elements in features.

# 5.1 Geometrical Sets vs. Bodies

When working with a solid part body, features are updated in a linear order. New features can only reference existing geometry. Because the system updates the solid part body from top to bottom, a feature cannot reference geometry that is located after it in the specification tree. If a feature must reference geometry that is placed later in the specification tree, the feature needs to be reordered.

However, a geometrical set does not list features in its update order. An existing feature can be modified to reference geometry that was added later. For example, a line can be modified to reference a point that did not exist when the line was originally created. Because of the non-linear update order, features do not have to be reordered or rearranged in the specification tree.

A spline is created using five points in the example shown in Figure 5–1.

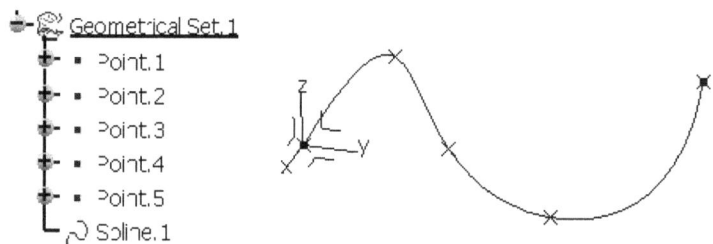

**Figure 5–1**

After the creation of the spline, another point is created as shown in Figure 5–2.

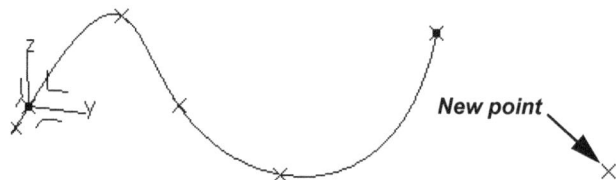

**Figure 5–2**

The new point is added to modify the spline, as shown in Figure 5–3.

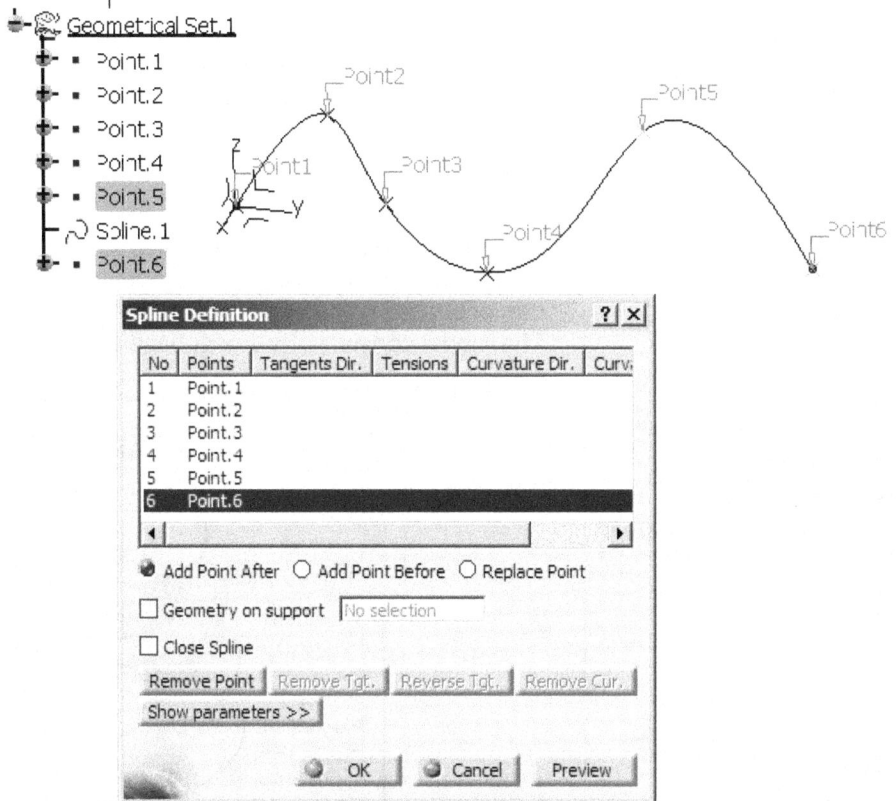

Figure 5–3

## Properties of a Consumed Feature

- Consumed features are inputs to operation-based features. Common examples include:

  - Trim
  - Split
  - Join
  - Shape Fillets

- Consumed features are automatically placed in No Show mode. They can be Shown or edited at any time.

- Consumed features are still located in the specification tree.

# 5.2 Tree Organization

## Geometrical Sets

In the specification tree, solid geometry is stored in a Part Body. Each unique group of solid geometry can be divided into its own Body. Similarly, geometrical sets are used to group wireframe and surface geometry by function or type; they also organize the surface model. You can have as many geometrical sets as required.

Adding geometrical sets and bodies simplifies the location, modification, and update of the geometry. This structure is demonstrated in the specification tree as shown in Figure 5–4. The model consists of a swept base and a helical fin.

*The wireframe and surface geometry used to create the geometry is stored under each Part Body by selecting the Part Body when inserting the Geometrical set.*

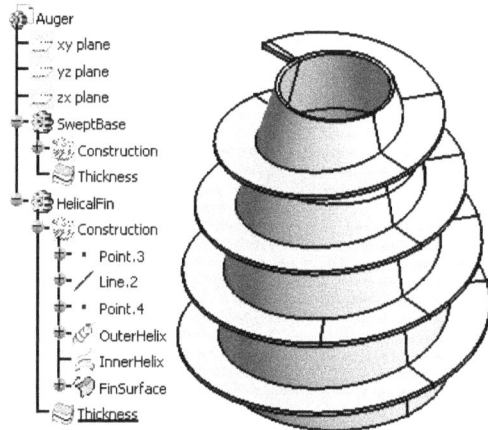

Figure 5–4

To create a new geometrical set, select **Insert>Geometrical Set**. The Insert geometrical set dialog box opens as shown Figure 5–5.

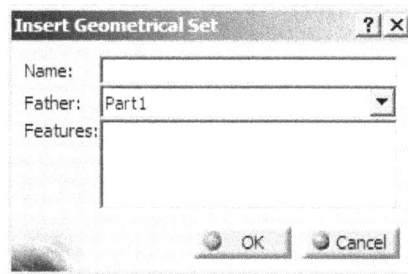

Figure 5–5

In this dialog box, you can specify a Name, select a Father, and select existing features for location in the new geometrical set.

In the example shown in Figure 5–6, different Fathers are selected for the new geometrical set named DEMO. The placement of the new geometrical set in the specification tree is dependent on the selected Father.

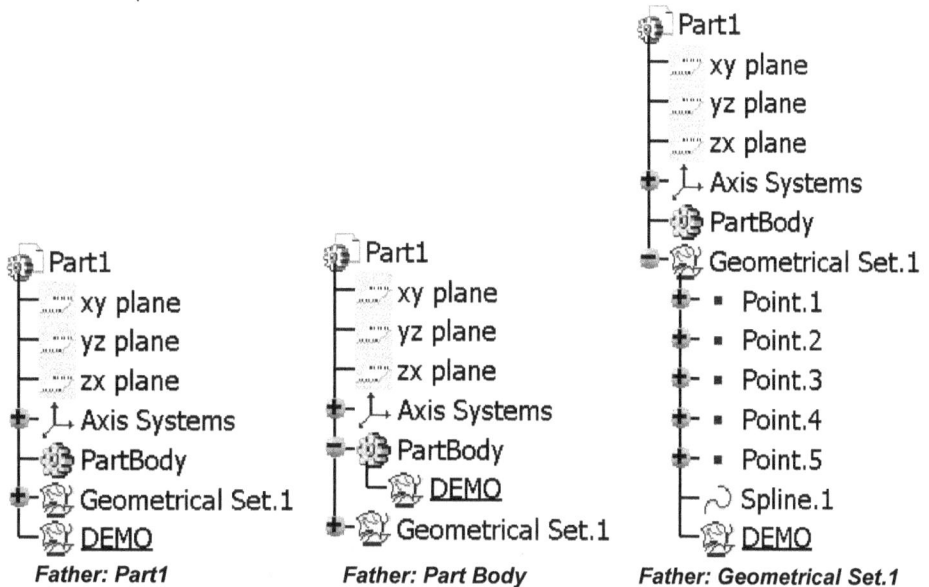

**Father: Part1**

**Father: Part Body**

**Father: Geometrical Set.1**

**Figure 5–6**

## Best Practices

Organize wireframe and surface features into different geometrical sets. This structure makes searching for specific features easier. It also enables the display of the groups elements to act together if required. For instance, a geometrical set can be set to **Hide** when the geometry is not required at a specific time.

Organizing a part using geometrical sets makes reviewing and editing the part easier. Please check your company standards and best practices regarding specification tree organization before putting these methods into practice.

A typical organizational structure for geometrical sets is shown in Figure 5–7. The following geometrical sets are created:

- **Inputs** contain imported geometry.

- **Working** contains wireframe geometry and surfaces.

- **Trim** contains surface operations, such as Split and Trim features.

- **Final** contains the final geometry to create the solid.

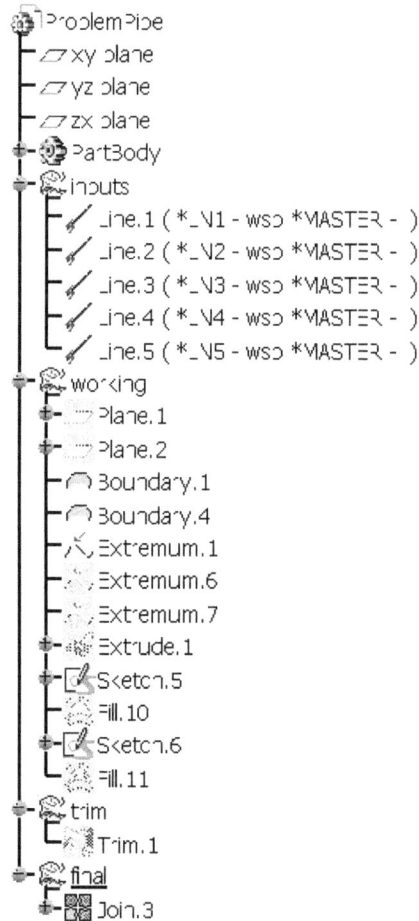

```
ProblemPipe
├── xy plane
├── yz plane
├── zx plane
├── PartBody
├── inputs
│   ├── Line.1 ( *_N1 - wso *MASTER - )
│   ├── Line.2 ( *_N2 - wso *MASTER - )
│   ├── Line.3 ( *_N3 - wso *MASTER - )
│   ├── Line.4 ( *_N4 - wso *MASTER - )
│   └── Line.5 ( *_N5 - wso *MASTER - )
├── working
│   ├── Plane.1
│   ├── Plane.2
│   ├── Boundary.1
│   ├── Boundary.4
│   ├── Extremum.1
│   ├── Extremum.6
│   ├── Extremum.7
│   ├── Extrude.1
│   ├── Sketch.5
│   ├── Fill.10
│   ├── Sketch.6
│   └── Fill.11
├── trim
│   └── Trim.1
└── final
    └── Join.3
```

**Figure 5–7**

# 5.3 Feature Naming

CATIA uses a default naming convention for the features created in the GSD workbench. However, renaming these features based on their intended use is recommended. For example, another user can tell that the features shown in Figure 5–8 are used as construction geometry for a helical curve because they have been appropriately named.

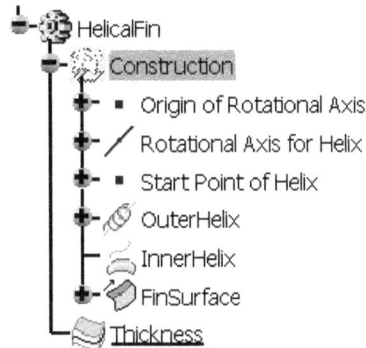

**Figure 5–8**

To name a feature in the model or specification tree, right-click on the feature and select **Properties**. The feature can be renamed in the *Feature Properties* tab, as shown in Figure 5–9.

*The Properties dialog box can also be accessed by pressing <Alt> and <Enter> simultaneously.*

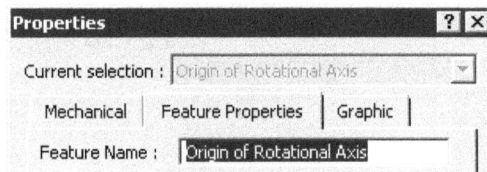

**Figure 5–9**

## 5.4 Graphic Properties

**Graphical Properties of a Geometrical Set**

By changing the graphical properties of a geometrical set, you can change the properties of all features under that geometrical set at the same time. As a result, you can control the properties of multiple features more easily.

To change the graphical properties of a geometrical set, right-click on a geometrical set in the specification tree and select **Properties**. The graphical properties can be changed in the *Graphic* tab, as shown in Figure 5–10.

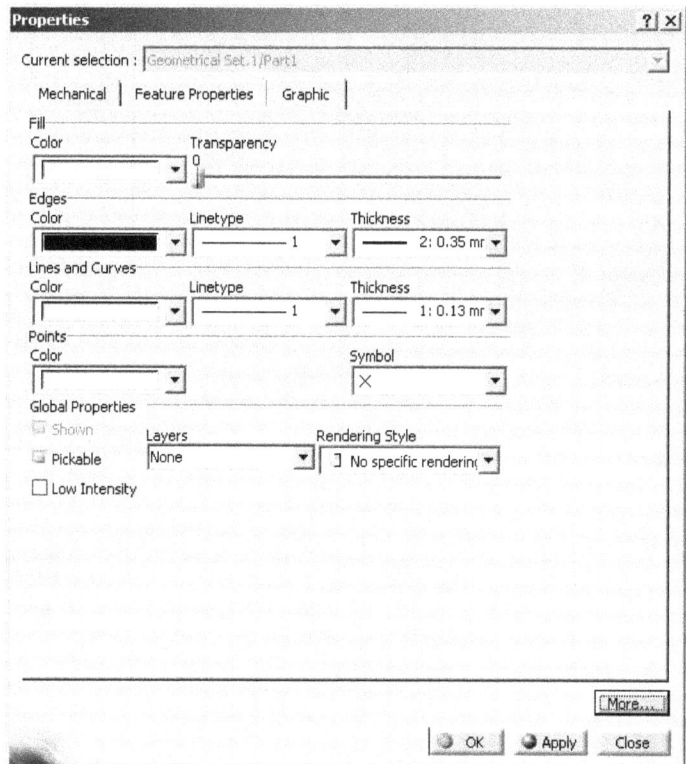

**Figure 5–10**

Another way to change the graphical properties of a geometrical set is to use the Graphic Properties toolbar. It is easily accessible and provides commonly used options as shown in Figure 5–11. The full set of options can be found in the Properties dialog box.

**Figure 5–11**

## Graphical Properties of Individual Features

The graphical properties of an individual feature can be modified using the Properties dialog box. Right-click on a feature in the specification tree and select **Properties**. Make changes in the *Graphic* tab.

The graphical properties of a feature can also be reset to its default values. To reset the defaults, right-click on a feature in the specification tree and select **Reset Properties** to open the Reset Properties dialog box, as shown in Figure 5–12.

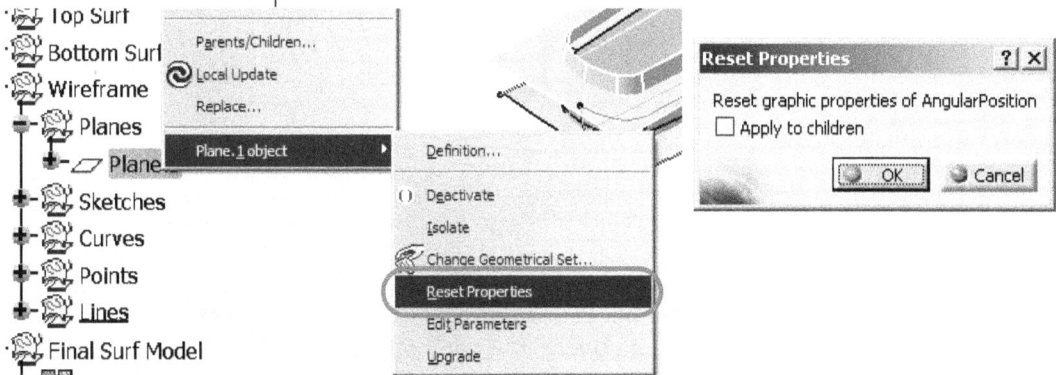

**Figure 5–12**

# 5.5 Visualization

## Hide/Show

The display of a complicated model can be simplified by using the Hide/Show feature. To hide/show a geometrical set, right-click on a geometrical set in the specification tree and select **Hide/Show**, as shown in Figure 5–13.

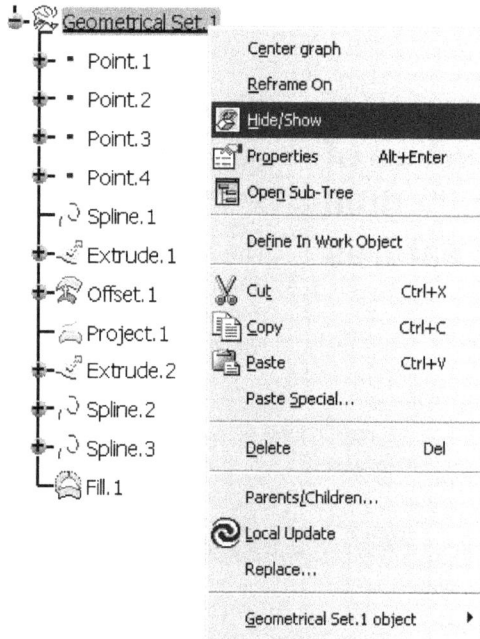

**Figure 5–13**

Note that when a geometrical set is hidden, all of the individual features under that geometrical set are also hidden.

When a feature is hidden, the feature icon turns dull and gray, indicating that the feature is hidden. To show these features again, right-click on the geometrical set in the specification tree or on the feature that you want to show and select **Hide/Show**.

## Only Current Body

You can also show only the body or geometrical set that you are working on while the rest of the model is hidden.

This option only controls the display of solid geometry. The system only displays the contents of the active solid body. When using a structured modeling approach, you can display (and therefore select) geometry from a specific area of the design part you are working on. It does not control the display of geometrical sets. Any geometrical set that is shown is displayed regardless of its position in the tree.

To show only the current body or geometrical set, click

(Only Current Body) in the Tools toolbar. To make the entire model display again, click the icon again.

You can also display only the current body by changing the display option. Select **Tools>Options>Infrastructure>Part Infrastructure**, and select the *Display* tab to access the display options, as shown in Figure 5–14.

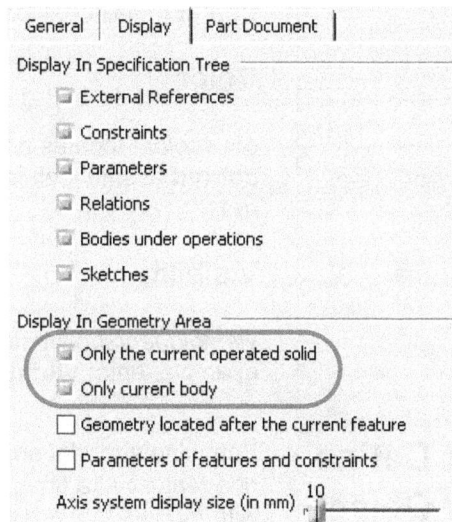

**Figure 5–14**

# 5.6 Model Investigation

**Search**

The **Search** tool can be used to locate features by name, type, or color. The tool is accessed by selecting **Edit>Search** and specifying the search parameters for the element's name, feature type, or color. As an alternative to the Search dialog box, the *Power Input* field in the bottom right corner of the CATIA window can be used.

Use the following syntax to search and select features:

### Name

*n:<feature name>* locates a feature by name. For example, enter **n:sketch\*** to select features whose name starts with *sketch*.

### Type

*t:<feature type>* locates a feature by type. For example, enter **t:point** to select all points in the model.

### Color

*col:<color>* locates a feature by color. For example, enter **col:red** to select all features that have been assigned the color red.

### Visibility

*vis:<hidden/shown>* locates a feature by its display status. For example, enter **vis:hidden** to select all hidden features.

**Scan or Define In Work Object**

Scanning a model enables you to review its construction history, one feature at a time. This is particularly helpful when working with models that are created by other users. The **Scan** tool can reveal the modeler's design intent and modeling techniques by replaying and reviewing the design.

To use the **Scan** tool, select **Edit>Scan or Define In Work Object** in the menu bar. The Scan dialog box is shown in Figure 5–15. The two different scan modes are **Structure** and **Update**.

Figure 5–15

## Structure

Structure scan mode scans features of a model in the order in which they are displayed in the specification tree. Click

(Display Graph) to show all features belonging to the Scan, as shown in Figure 5–16.

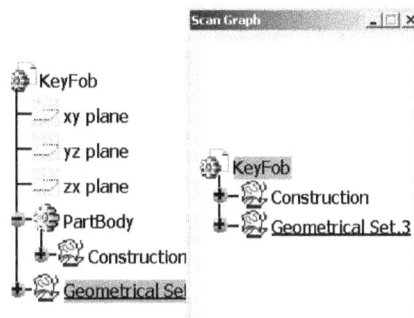

Figure 5–16

Note that the specification tree and the tree in the Scan Graph dialog box are almost identical, except that some elements are missing from the Scan Graph dialog box. This is because in Structure scan mode, internal elements of sketches, part bodies, ordered geometrical sets, and elements that belong to a certain geometrical set are ignored.

## Update

Update mode scans features of a model in the order of the update. Therefore, the scanning order might be different from the order of the specification tree.

Note that in Update mode, datum elements always display at the top of the Scan Graph, while geometrical sets (including ordered geometrical sets) and deactivated features are not displayed, as shown in Figure 5–17.

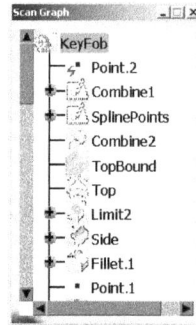

Figure 5–17

## Quick Select

Quick Select enables you to quickly access sub-elements in the model without having to scroll through the specification tree. Click on the final element and Quick Select follows the update cycle of a model by selecting the Parents or Children from the windows in the Quick Select dialog box. To use Quick Select, click ![icon] (Quick Select) in the Select toolbar, and select the element. The Quick Select dialog box opens as shown in Figure 5–18.

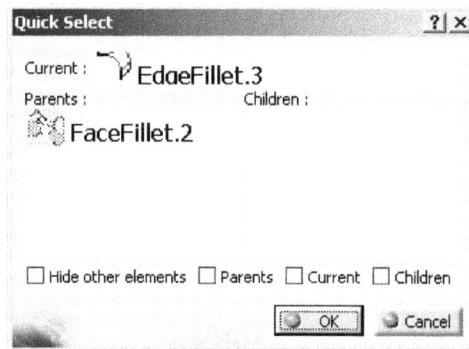

Figure 5–18

The Quick Select dialog box indicates the currently selected element, along with the parent and child elements. In Figure 5–18, no elements are listed in the *Children* area because the EdgeFillet.3 element does not have any children. You can further explore using the Parents/Children graph to retrieve the required feature.

Note the four options at the bottom of the dialog box:

- Hide other elements

- Parents

- Current

- Children

Select the required option to show or hide a number of elements in the geometry.

Quick Select is a very useful tool when searching for specific elements. You can easily access sub-elements in the specification tree without having to go through all of the parent and child traces. This function is also useful when looking for sub-elements that are not visible.

# 5.7 Operation Tools

## Datum Elements

In some cases, the design intent might require that you break the associativity between elements of your model. Datum elements are wireframe elements that are not modifiable or associative to the reference geometry used to create them.

Since datum elements are not associative, you cannot modify the parameters used to create the datum element. If any referenced geometry is modified, the datum element does not update.

*Existing geometry cannot be converted to a datum element.*

To create a datum element, click  (Create Datum) in the Tools toolbar, and create the required geometry. In the specification tree, the datum element displays with an icon as shown in Figure 5–19.

**Figure 5–19**

A spline created through five reference points is shown in Figure 5–20.

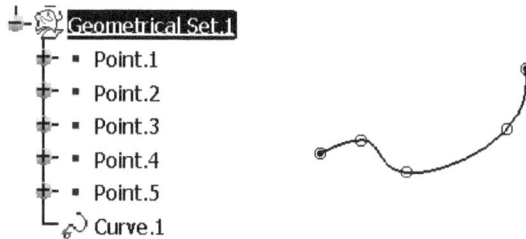

**Figure 5–20**

The datum curve does not update when the position of the points is modified, as shown in Figure 5–21.

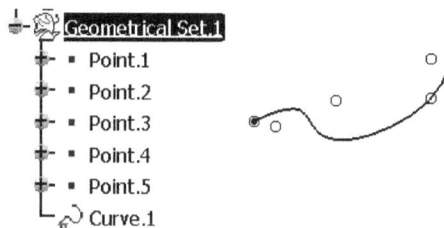

*Points, lines, planes, and local axis systems can be made parametric again after being isolated.*

**Figure 5–21**

# Paste Special

The **Paste Special** option offers various duplication options that are helpful when working with wireframe and surfaces.

The **As Result** option isolates the duplicated element. This is useful in a situation where an element is associative to other geometry, but needs to be made non-associative or isolated. In this case, you can copy the entity and then use **Paste Special** with the **As Result** option. The pasted element is then isolated, as shown in Figure 5–22.

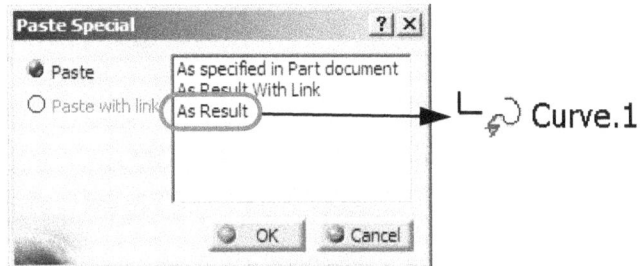

Figure 5–22

## How To: Take an Existing Element and Make it Non-associative using Paste Special

1. Copy the element.
2. Select **Edit>Paste Special**.
3. Select **As Result**.
4. Click **OK** to paste the entity.

Note that an entity duplicated through **Paste Special>As Result** and an entity created with the **Datum Feature** option are both isolated.

# Multi-Result Management

When more than one possible solution is available to create a feature, CATIA prompts you to select the sub-element(s) to keep. The Multi-Result Management dialog box contains new options for selecting which sub-element(s) to keep.

For example, two possible lines can be created when a plane intersects a cylinder surface. In the Intersection dialog box, once you click **OK**, the Multi-Result Management dialog box opens as shown in Figure 5–23.

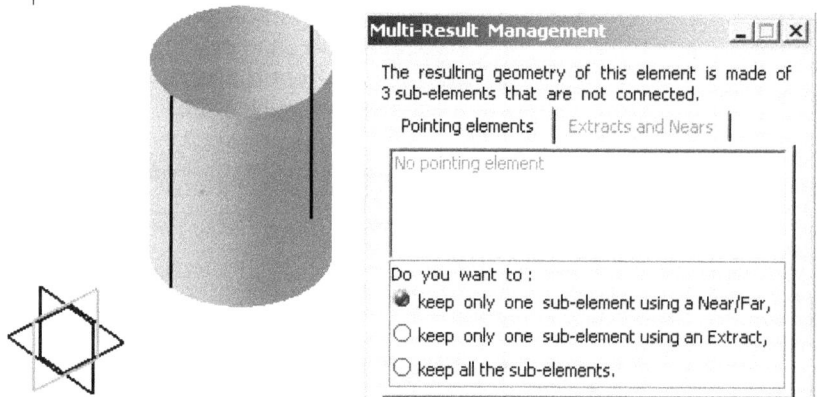

**Figure 5–23**

The following options are available in the Multi-Result Management dialog box:

*   Keep only one sub-element using a Near/Far

*   Keep only one sub-element using an Extract

*   Keep all the sub-elements

## Keep only one sub-element using a Near/Far

This option opens the Near/Far Definition dialog box, where you select one element that is closest to (or farthest from) the required output. For example, the ZX plane is selected to keep the sub-element shown in Figure 5–24.

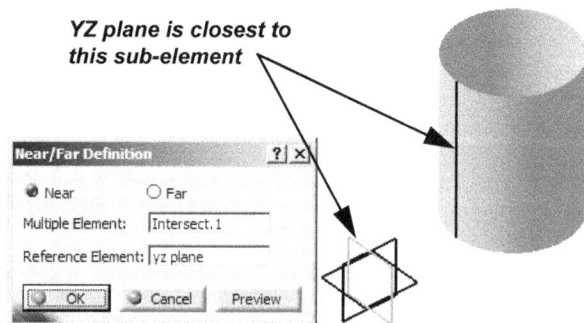

**Figure 5–24**

The original feature is no longer displayed and the geometry is now stored under the Near feature, as shown in Figure 5–25.

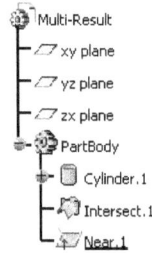

**Figure 5–25**

## Keep only one sub-element using an Extract

You can directly select the element to keep using an **Extract** operation. This option opens the Extract Definition dialog box in which you can select one of multiple results. For example, the opposite line is selected in Figure 5–26.

*Select this element to keep using an Extract*

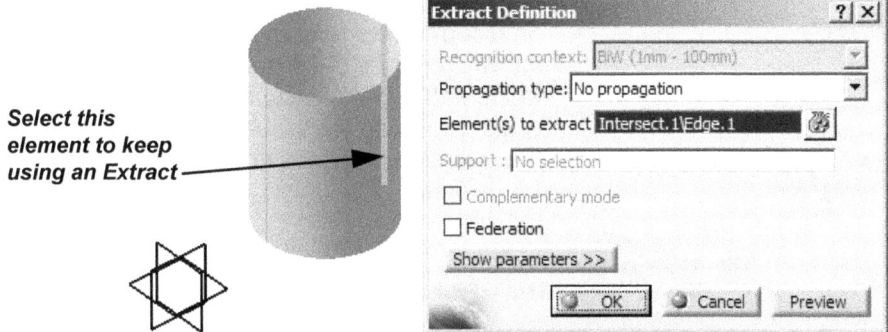

**Figure 5–26**

The original feature is no longer displayed and the geometry is now stored under the Extract feature, as shown in Figure 5–27.

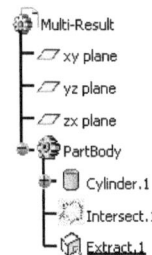

**Figure 5–27**

## Keep all the sub-elements

This option keeps all of the sub-elements. For example, for an intersection between a cylinder and a plane, the Intersection feature consists of two disconnected lines.

**Keeping the Initial Element**

The Keep Mode functionality enables you to maintain or replace an element on which you are performing operations. Two modes can be enabled before the operation is performed:

- Keep Mode

- No Keep Mode

### Keep Mode

To enable Keep Mode, in the KeepNoKeep flyout in the Tools toolbar, click (Keep Mode).

Once Keep Mode has been enabled, operations are performed on a copy of the referenced element. For example, the surface shown in Figure 5–28 is split by a reference plane with Keep Mode enabled. As a result, the system keeps the original surface while displaying the resulting split surface. This is the same as the referenced surface not being placed in No Show mode.

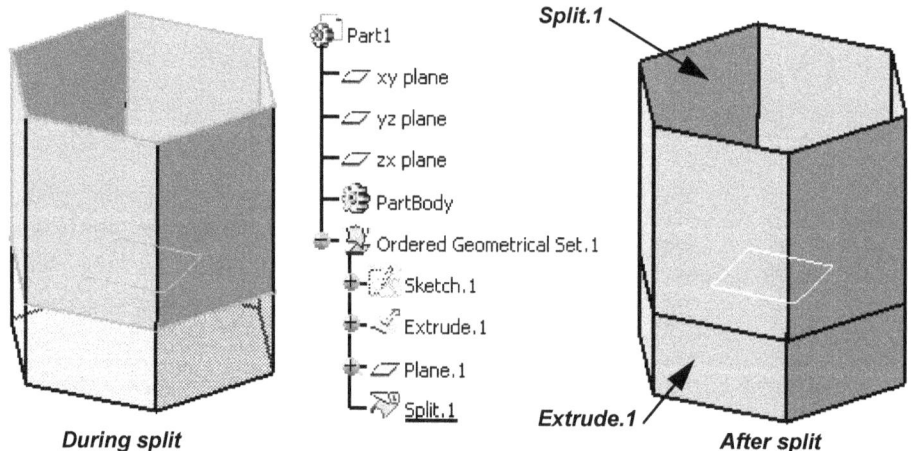

*During split*

Part1
— xy plane
— yz plane
— zx plane
— PartBody
— Ordered Geometrical Set.1
— Sketch.1
— Extrude.1
— Plane.1
— Split.1

*Split.1*

*Extrude.1*

*After split*

**Figure 5–28**

The ability to keep a referenced element is important when working with ordered geometrical sets. In an ordered geometrical set, Surface.1 would be consumed by the **Split** operation. You can preserve the original surface by creating the split with Keep Mode enabled.

## No Keep Mode

To enable No Keep Mode, in the KeepNoKeep flyout in the Tools toolbar, click [icon] (No Keep Mode). Once selected, the operation replaces the referenced element with a datum element. For example, consider an extruded surface that has been made solid using the **ThickSurface** command. If the surface is split with No Keep Mode and Create Datum enabled, the **Split** operation is not kept. Instead, the original surface is replaced with the split datum surface, as shown in Figure 5–29.

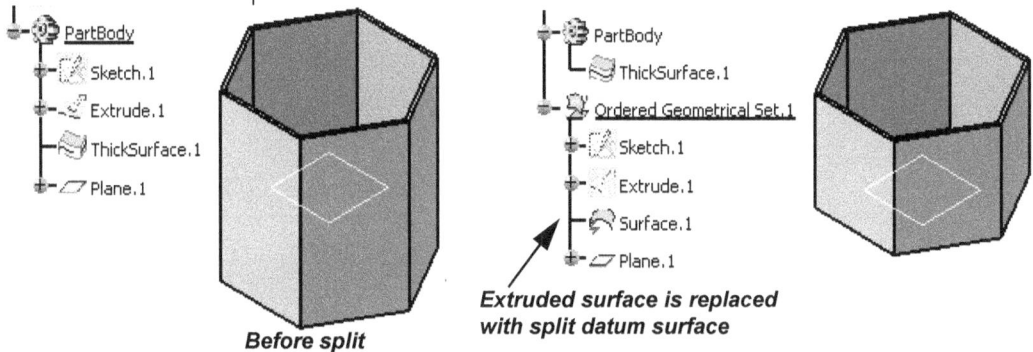

*Before split*

*Extruded surface is replaced with split datum surface*

**Figure 5–29**

# 5.8 Element Replacement

When a complex model consisting of curve or surface features requires a late specification change, the element(s) that define the specification might be replaced, avoiding the need to recreate the model.

Right-click on the feature that you want to swap out and select **Replace**, as shown in Figure 5–30.

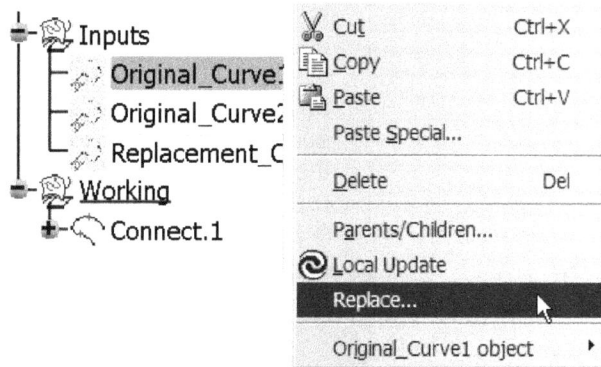

**Figure 5–30**

The Replace dialog box opens as shown in Figure 5–31.

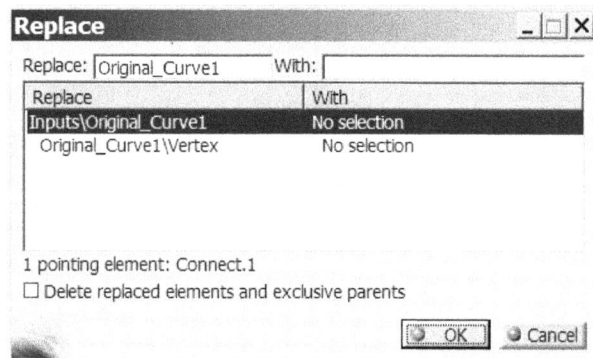

**Figure 5–31**

Select the new feature and verify that the orientation of the original and new features match. Invert the orientation by selecting the green arrow from the screen if required, as shown in Figure 5–32.

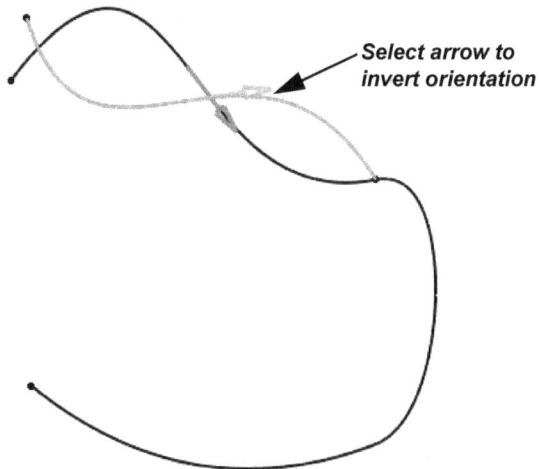

Select arrow to
invert orientation

Figure 5–32

You can automatically delete the original element and its
exclusive parents by selecting **Delete replaced elements and
exclusive parents** in the Replace dialog box, as shown in
Figure 5–33.

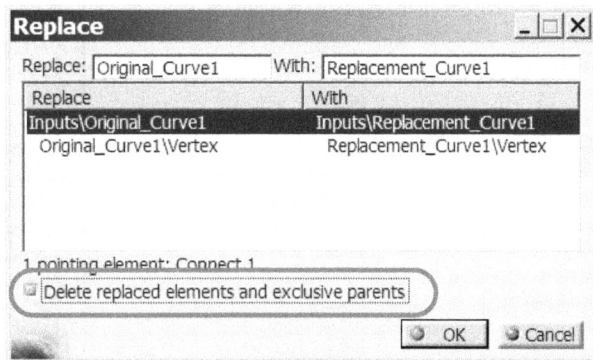

Figure 5–33

## Multi-Model Links vs. Replace

Using datum (as result) elements and doing a **Replace** operation
when changes occur can be used as an alternative to copying
features using the **As Result With Link** option. This is useful in
a multi-model design environment, where multi-model links
might not be required. This might be due to the nature of sharing
proprietary files between suppliers and OEM's and the unreliable
nature of maintaining links using some PDM systems.

# Practice 5a

# Organization and Quick Select

## Practice Objectives

- Scan the model to display the update cycle.
- Use AutoSort.
- Create geometrical sets.
- Organize features into geometrical sets.
- Use Quick Select to modify a feature.

In this practice, you will investigate the update cycle of a surface model and sort the features in the specification tree to reflect the update cycle. You will also organize the features into geometrical sets to only display the required features in the specification tree. You will use Quick Select to select a feature that you need to modify. The specification tree of the completed model is shown in Figure 5–34.

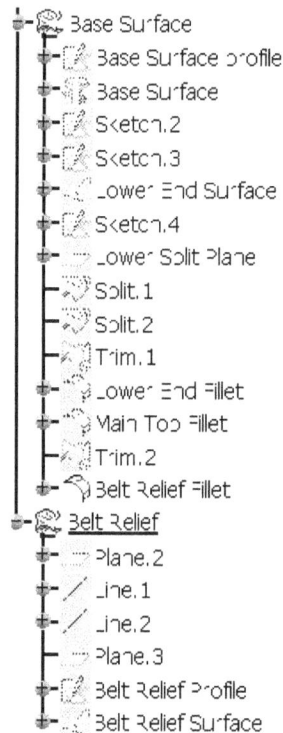

**Figure 5–34**

## Task 1 - Open a part.

1. Open **Feature_Management.CATPart**. The model displays as shown in Figure 5–35.

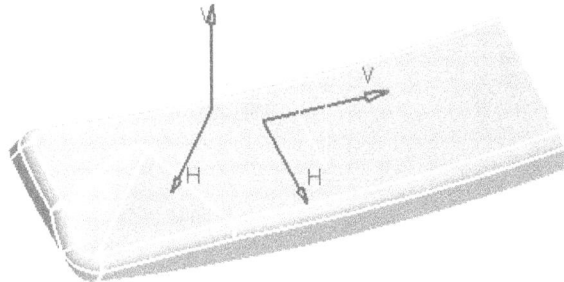

**Figure 5–35**

## Task 2 - Investigate the specification tree structure.

1. In the menu bar, select **View>Tree Expansion>Expand First Level**. The specification tree displays as shown in Figure 5–36.

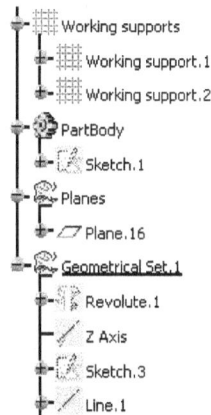

**Figure 5–36**

**Design Considerations**

Review the specification tree and note the following:

- There are two working supports.

- There is a single sketch listed under the PartBody.

- No elements have been renamed.

- The only geometrical set is the default one named **Geometrical Set.1**.

## Task 3 - Organize features in the specification tree.

In this task, you will organize the specification tree so that it reflects the model structure and enables all users to quickly find elements in the model.

1. The working supports are no longer required and can be deleted. Delete the working supports, as shown in Figure 5–37.

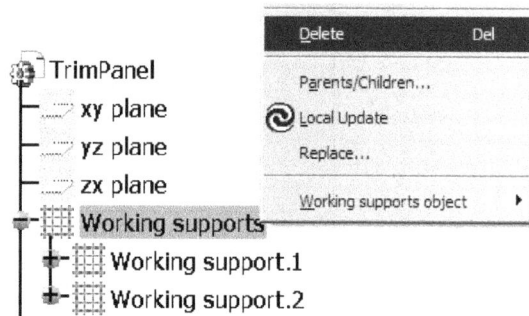

**Figure 5–37**

Since the model does not contain any solid geometry, the single sketch should not be listed under the Partbody. It should be under the geometrical set that holds the feature that references it.

2. Right-click on Sketch.1 and select **Sketch.1 object>Change Geometrical Set**, as shown in Figure 5–38.

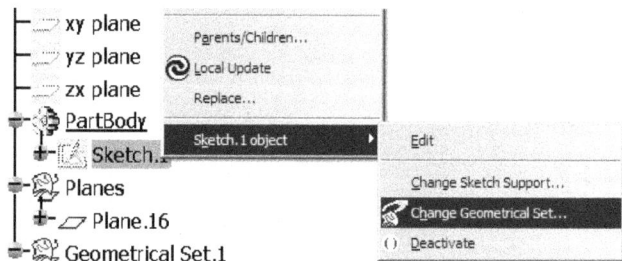

**Figure 5–38**

3. In the specification tree, select **Geometrical Set.1**.

In the Change geometrical set dialog box, **Geometrical Set.1** might already display in the *Destination* field. However, the *Before* field will not populate with **Last position** until **Geometrical Set.1** has been selected in the specification tree or **Last position** is selected in the Destination drop-down list in the Change geometrical set dialog box.

4. Accept the **Last position** by clicking **OK**, as shown in Figure 5–39.

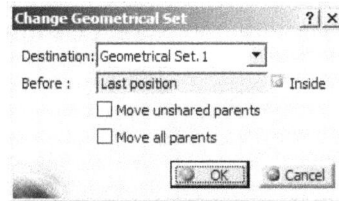

**Figure 5–39**

---

**Task 4 - Investigate the update cycle.**

---

1. Select **Edit>Scan or Define in Work Object**.

2. Change the scan type to **Update**, as shown in Figure 5–40.

**Figure 5–40**

3. Click ⏮ (First) to rewind the model to the beginning of the update cycle.

4. Click ▶| (Next) to display the first feature in the update cycle. The first feature in the specification tree is highlighted.

5. Click ▶| (Next) to display the next feature in the update cycle. The second feature in the specification tree is highlighted.

6. Continue to click ▶| (Next) to step through all of the features in the model.

Note that the update cycle is very different than the order in which features are listed in the specification tree. This can be the result of elements being created, deleted, changed, and reorganized.

7. Close the Scan dialog box.

## Task 5 - Use AutoSort to organize the elements of a model.

1. In the specification tree, right-click on **Geometrical Set.1** and select **Geometrical Set.1 object>AutoSort**, as shown in Figure 5–41.

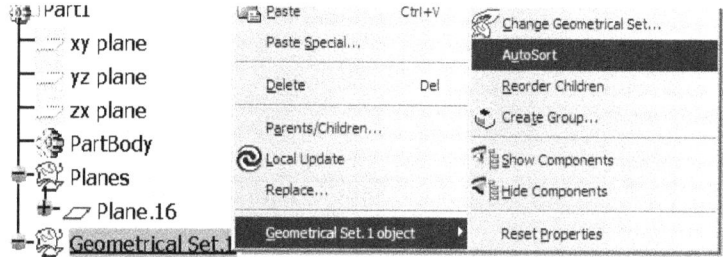

**Figure 5–41**

2. Run a **Scan or Define in Work Object** again and note how the specification tree order reflects the update cycle.

## Task 6 - Check the parents and children of features.

1. Two isolated Z-axes are not used in the model and **Geometrical Set.2** does not contain any elements. Verify that each of the three elements does not have any children, as shown in Figure 5–42.

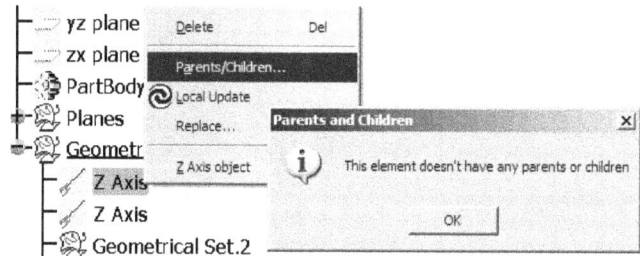

**Figure 5–42**

2. Delete the two Z-axes and the geometrical set, as shown in Figure 5–43.

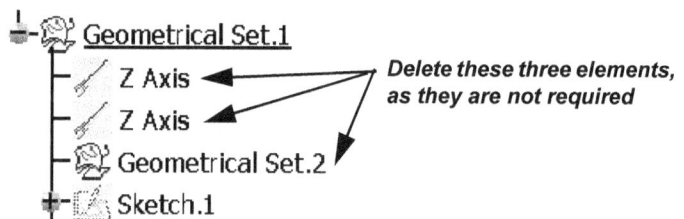

**Figure 5–43**

## Task 7 - Rename features.

**Design Considerations**

Renaming critical design elements is considered good practice. A model that contains named features helps keep the model organized and communicate design intent.

1.  Rename the following two features as shown in Figure 5–44:

    *   Rename *Sketch.1* as **Base Surface profile**.
    *   Rename *Revolute.1* as **Base Surface**.

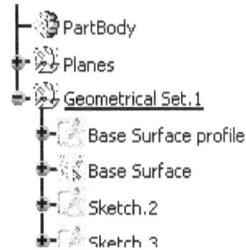

**Figure 5–44**

2.  Save the model and close the file.

## Task 8 - Open a part.

In this task, you will open a model in which many features have already been renamed to save time.

1.  Open **FeatureManagement_Renamed.CATPart**.

2.  In the specification tree, note that nine elements (sketches, surfaces, and fillets) have been renamed.

3.  Rename *Geometrical Set.1* as **Base Surface**, as shown in Figure 5–45.

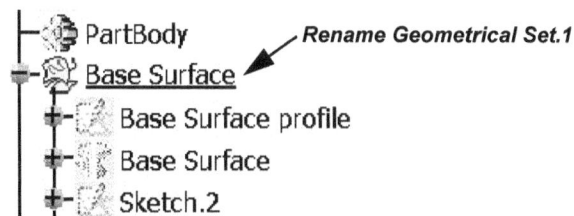

**Figure 5–45**

## Task 9 - Insert a geometrical set.

In this task, you will continue to organize the model by inserting a geometrical set and then moving features into it.

1.  Select **Insert>Geometrical Set**.

2.  Define the geometrical set as shown in Figure 5–46:

    *   *Name:* **Belt Relief**
    *   *Father:* **TrimPanel**

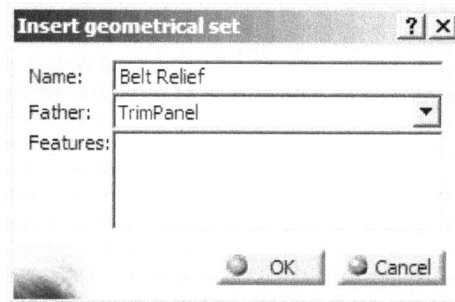

**Figure 5–46**

3.  Click **OK**.

## Task 10 - Move a feature into a geometrical set.

1.  Right-click on the Belt Relief Surface and select **Belt Relief Surface object>Change Geometrical Set**, as shown in Figure 5–47.

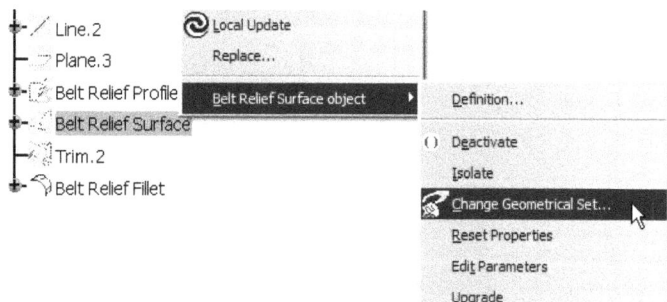

**Figure 5–47**

2.  Define the change as follows:

    *   *Destination:* **Belt Relief**
    *   Select **Move all parents**.

The dialog box and model update as shown in Figure 5–48.

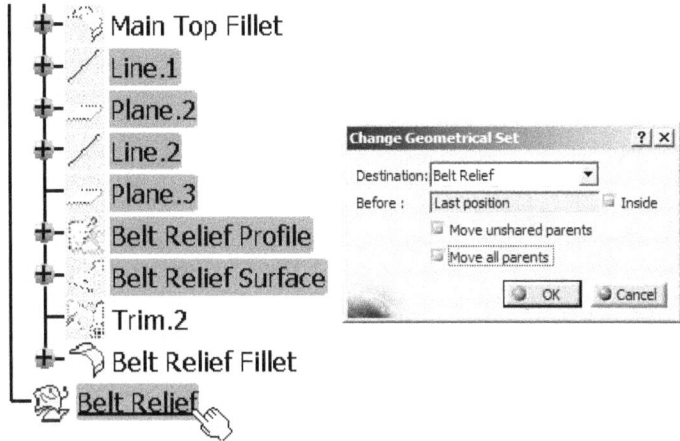

Figure 5–48

The new geometrical set and features display as shown in Figure 5–49.

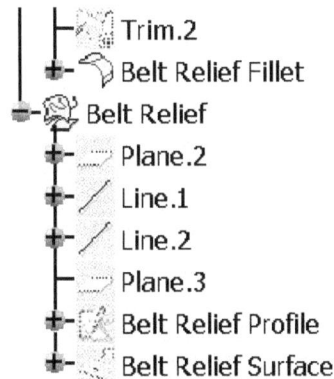

Figure 5–49

## Task 11 - Use Quick Select to find the correct feature.

**Design Considerations**

Suppose you want to modify the radius of the Main Top Fillet in the model. If you double-click directly on the geometry of the part that you think is the Main Top Fillet geometry, you might be selecting geometry that you do not want to select. Using Quick Select, you can explicitly select the intended feature.

1. Double-click on the fillet geometry as shown in Figure 5–50.

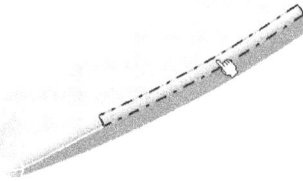

**Figure 5–50**

The Edge Fillet Definition dialog box opens and the geometry is highlighted in the display, as shown in Figure 5–51. This is not the feature that you want to select.

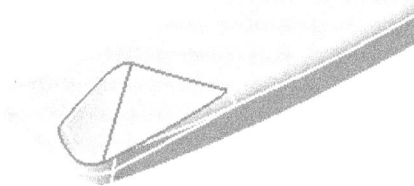

**Figure 5–51**

2. Click **Cancel**.

3. Click 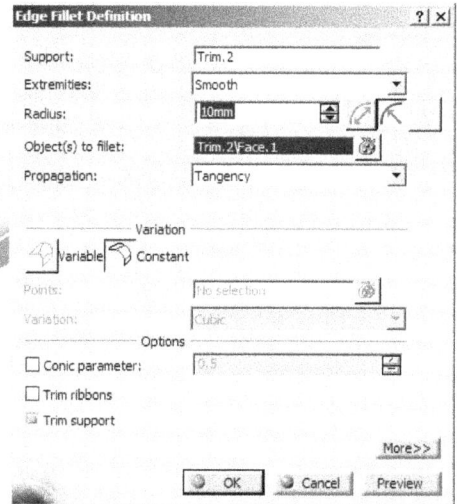 (Quick Select) and select the same fillet geometry as before, as shown in Figure 5–52.

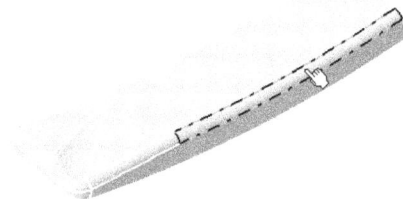

**Figure 5–52**

The Quick Select dialog box opens as shown in Figure 5–53.

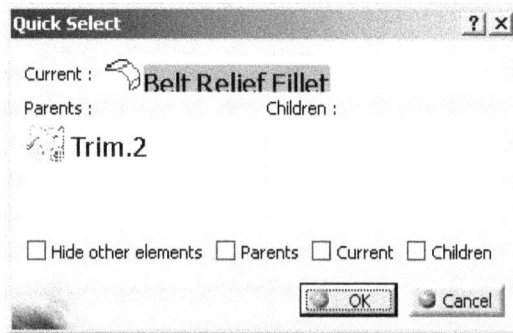

**Figure 5–53**

4. The names of the parents and children in the selected geometry are displayed. Locate the Main Top Fillet text, as shown in Figure 5–54.

*Locate the Main Top Fillet text*

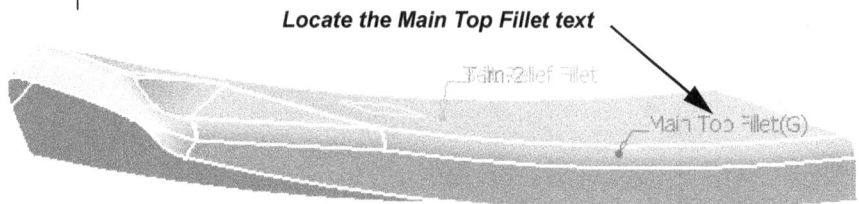

**Figure 5–54**

5. Right-click on the filleted surface area (not over the text) and select **Main Top Fillet object>Definition**, as shown in Figure 5–55.

**Figure 5–55**

6. Make the following changes to the fillet, as shown in Figure 5–56:

   • *Radius:* **15mm**

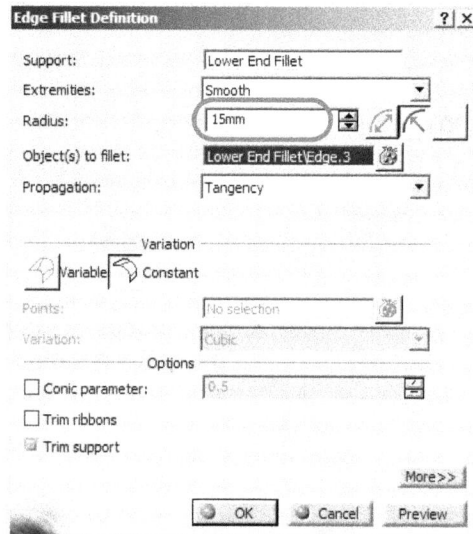

**Figure 5–56**

7. Click **OK**. The model updates, as shown in Figure 5–57.

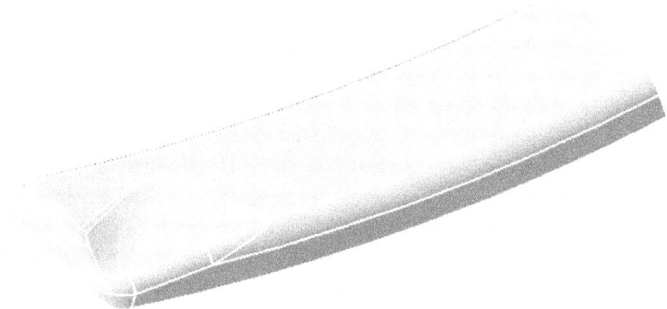

**Figure 5–57**

8. Save the model and close the window.

# Practice 5b

# Element Replacement I

## Practice Objectives

- Replace an element.
- Modify an Inverse feature.

In this practice, you will replace a curve element and observe the effects of changing the curve's orientation.

## Task 1 - Open a part.

1. Open **Replace.CATPart**. The model displays as shown in Figure 5–58. The model consists of two original curves and a hidden replacement curve.

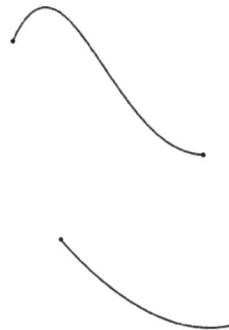

**Figure 5–58**

## Task 2 - Create a connect curve.

1. To define the Working geometrical set to be the work object, right-click on Working and select **Define In Work Object**, as shown in Figure 5–59.

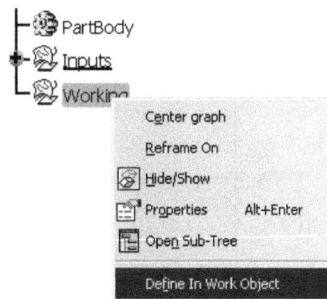

**Figure 5–59**

2. Click  (Connect Curve).

3. In the *First Curve* area, right-click in the *Point* field and select **Create Endpoint**, as shown in Figure 5–60.

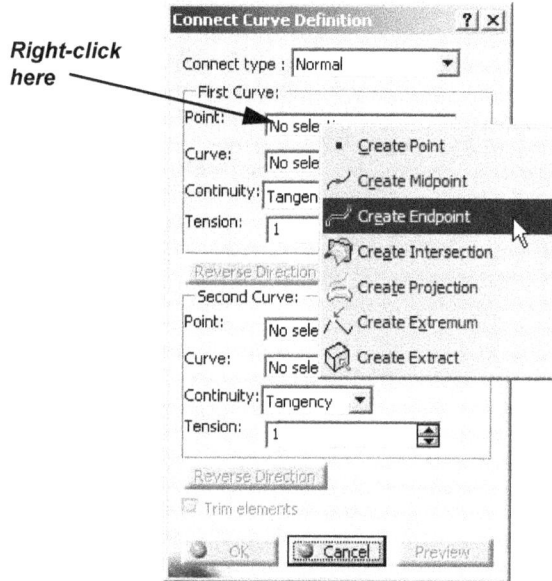

**Figure 5–60**

4. Select the end point on **Original Curve.1** as shown in Figure 5–61. Once the point has been selected, CATIA automatically recognizes the curve to which it belongs. It uses **Original_Curve.1** as the curve reference.

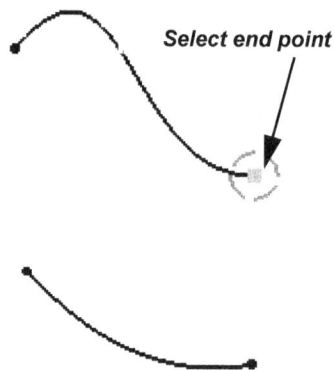

**Figure 5–61**

5. Verify that the arrow displays as shown in Figure 5–62.

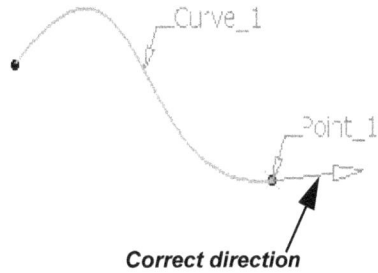

Figure 5–62

6. In the *Second Curve* area, right-click in the *Point* field and select **Create Endpoint**, as shown in Figure 5–63.

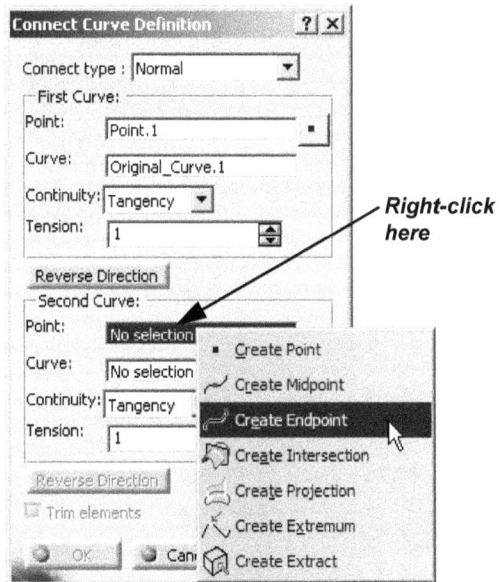

Figure 5–63

7. Select the end point on **Original_Curve.2**, as shown in Figure 5–64.

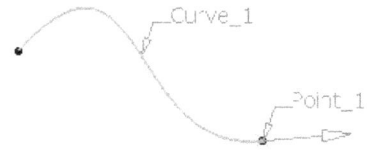

**Figure 5–64**

8. Verify that the second curve direction reference displays in the orientation shown in Figure 5–65, and select **Trim elements**.

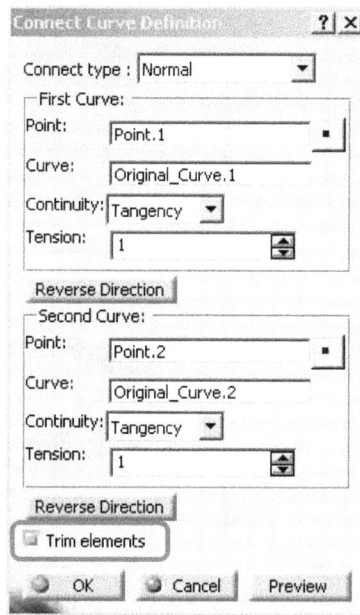

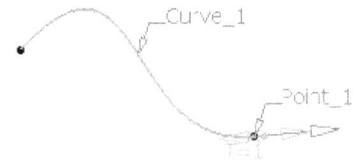

**Figure 5–65**

9. Complete the Connect Curve. The model displays as shown in Figure 5–66.

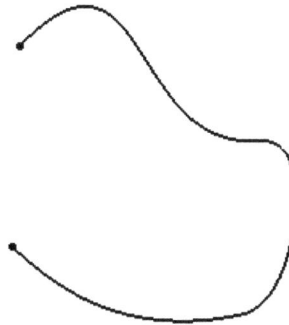

Figure 5–66

## Task 3 - Replace the original curve.

1. Show **Replacement_Curve.1**.

2. In the specification tree, right-click on **Original_Curve.1** and select **Replace**. The Replace dialog box opens as shown in Figure 5–67.

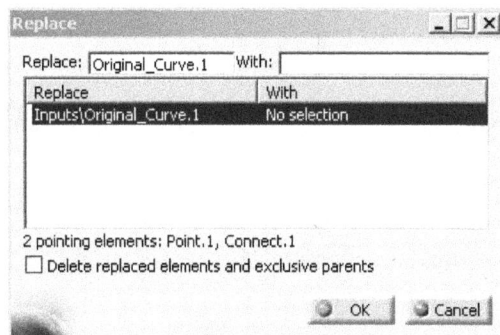

Figure 5–67

3. In the specification tree, select **Replacement_Curve.1**. The dialog box and curves update, as shown in Figure 5–68.

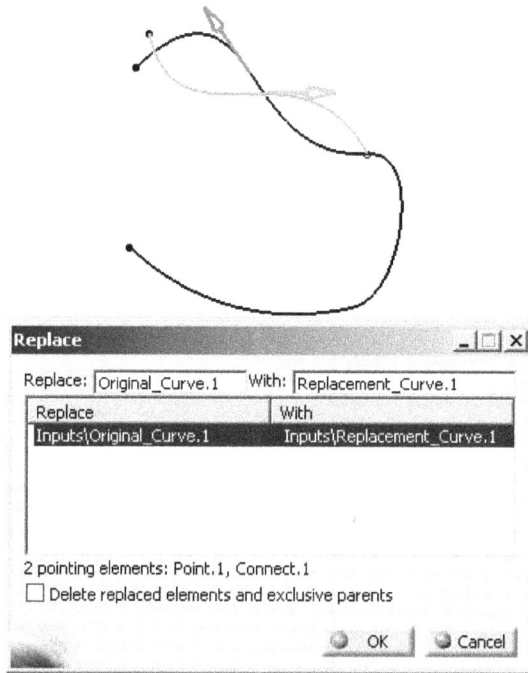

**Figure 5–68**

4. Click **OK** to complete the **Replace** operation. The result displays as shown in Figure 5–69.

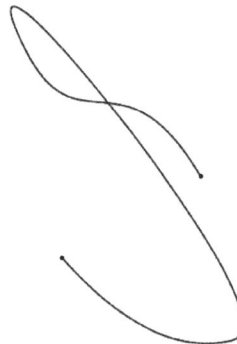

**Figure 5–69**

**Design Considerations**

The connect curve is flipped to the opposite end of the first curve. This occurs because the orientation of **Original_Curve.1** and **Replacement_Curve.1** are opposite to each another.

5. Click ![undo icon] to undo the **Replace** operation. The model returns to its original state.

## Task 4 - Replace the original curve matching the curve orientation.

1. Perform the following replace:

   • Replace *Original_Curve.1* with **Replacement_Curve.1**

   The dialog box and curves update as shown in Figure 5–70.

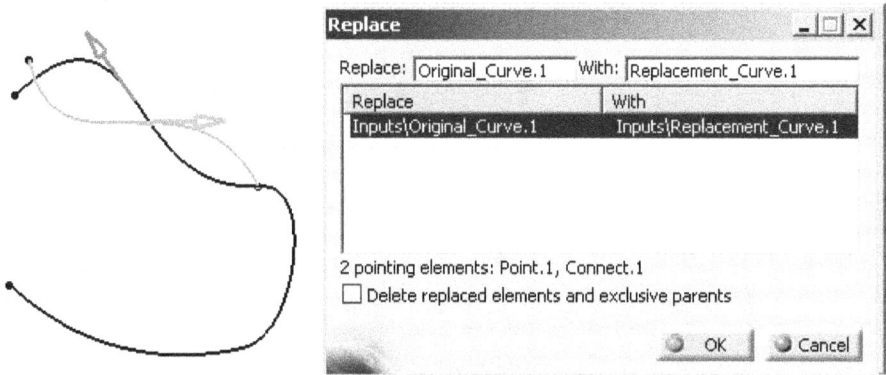

**Figure 5–70**

2. On the screen, select the green arrow on Replacement_Curve.1 to change the curve's orientation to match the original curve. The correct arrow orientation displays as shown in Figure 5–71.

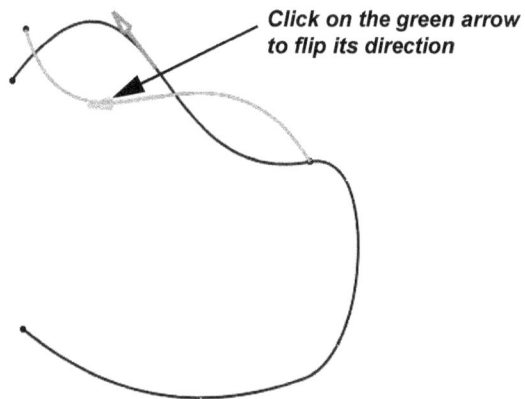

*Click on the green arrow to flip its direction*

**Figure 5–71**

3. Click **OK** to complete the **Replace** operation. The updated connect curve displays as shown in Figure 5–72.

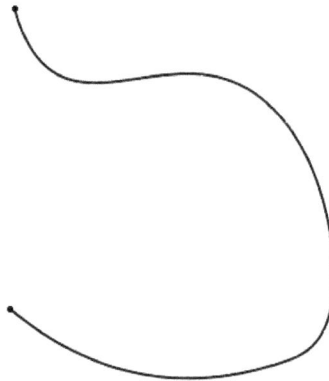

**Figure 5–72**

4. Hide **Replacement_Curve.1**.

5. Save and close the file.

# Chapter Review Questions

1. Unlike features in a solid part body, features in a geometrical set can be edited to reference features created later in the specification tree.

   a. True

   b. False

2. An example of a consumed feature is:

   a. Trim

   b. Split

   c. Join

   d. All of the above.

3. There can only be one geometrical set in a model.

   a. True

   b. False

4. A common best practice is to rename features based on their intended use.

   a. True

   b. False

5. If you change the graphical properties of a geometrical set, you can change those of the underlying features at the same time.

   a. True

   b. False

6. To hide the individual features in a geometrical set, you have to select them and hide them individually.

   a. True

   b. False

7. To search for all draft features in the model, use **Edit> Search** and enter _____ in the Input field.

   a. n:draft!

   b. n:draft*

   c. n:draft?

   d. None of the above.

8. Quick Select enables you to quickly access sub-elements in the model without having to scroll through the specification tree.

   a. True

   b. False

9. When using **Paste Special**, what does the **As Result** option do?

   a. Pastes an entity and makes it non-associative to the original.

   a. Pastes an entity and maintains the associativity between the original and the copy.

   b. Pastes an entity, maintains the associativity between the original and the copy, but makes it uneditable.

   c. None of the above.

10. When more than one possible solution exists, which option from the Multi-Result Management dialog box would you use to select the element furthest from the reference?

    a. Keep only one sub-element using a Near/Far.

    a. Keep only one sub-element using an Extract.

    b. Keep all the sub-elements.

    c. None of the above.

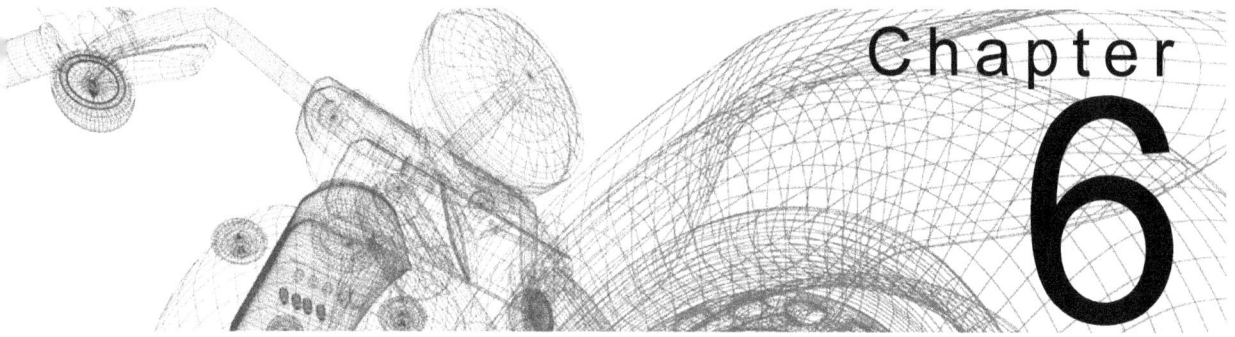

# Wireframe II

Wireframe features can form the foundation for future surface elements. The wireframe geometry can then be used to create surface features. In this chapter you learn about advanced wireframe geometry.

## Learning Objectives in this Chapter

- Create Projection, Intersection, Parallel, and Rolling Offset curves.
- Create Helix, Spiral and Contour curves.
- Create Boundary and Extract curves.
- Create Split and Trim curves.
- Create Joined curves.
- Understand Sketcher Output features.

# 6.1 Projection Curve

The Projection feature enables you to project 3D geometry onto a non-planar support. A sketch cannot be created on the non-planar surface shown in Figure 6–1, but a sketch can be projected onto it. The curve can be projected at points normal to the surface or along a direction defined by a surface plane or line.

*The direction of the projection is perpendicular to the selected Direction plane.*

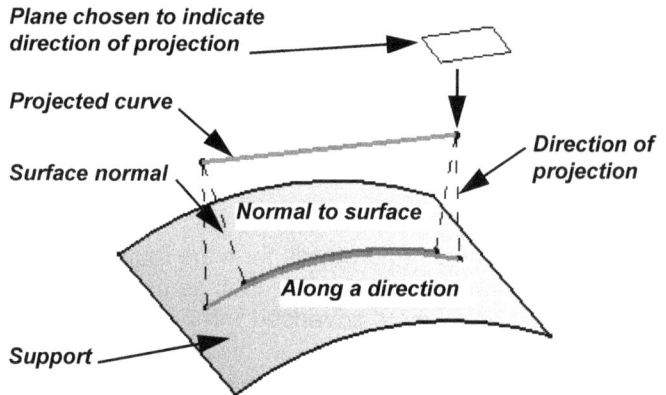

Figure 6–1

To create a projection, click  (Projection) from the Project-Combine fly-out in the Wireframe toolbar. The Projection Definition dialog box opens. You must specify a curve to be projected and a support on which to project the curve, as shown in Figure 6–2.

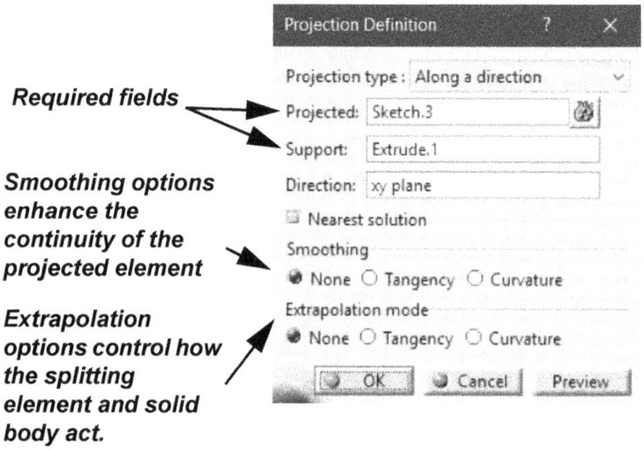

Figure 6–2

Depending on the orientation of the selected curve and support, the resulting feature could be a curve or a point.

The *Extrapolation Type* options are described as follows:

- **None**: Splits a solid when a splitting element intersects all edges of a solid body. This is the default option.

- **Tangent**: Extrapolates the splitting element tangentially and splits a solid body. You can use this option when the splitting element is too short to intersect any of the faces of the solid body.

- **Curvature**: Extrapolates the splitting element in a curvature and splits a solid body. You can use this option when the splitting element intersects at least one of the face of the solid body to split.

# 6.2 Intersection Curve

The Intersection feature enables you to create geometry at the intersection of two elements. Using this feature, a curve can be created at the intersection of two surface features, as shown in How To:Figure 6–3.

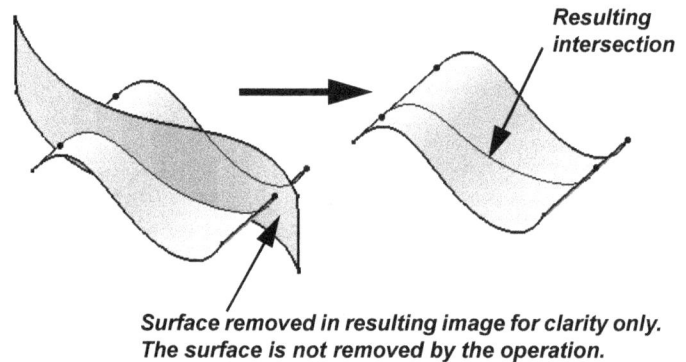

*Resulting intersection*

***Surface removed in resulting image for clarity only. The surface is not removed by the operation.***

**Figure 6–3**

## How To: Create an Intersection

1. Click (Intersection) from the Wireframe toolbar. The Intersection Definition dialog box opens as shown in Figure 6–4.

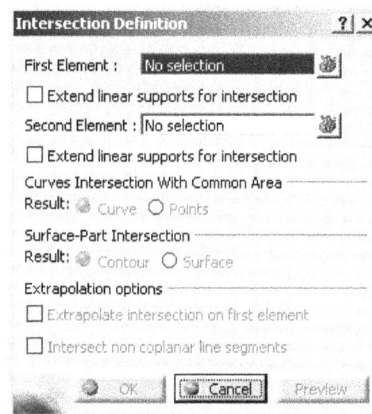

**Figure 6–4**

2. Select the two elements to intersect. Curves, surfaces, and planes are acceptable elements.
3. Click **OK** to complete the Intersect Definition. The resulting geometry can be curves, points, or a surface area, depending on the options used and the selected geometry.

# 6.3 Parallel Curve

A Parallel Curve feature enables you to create a curve that is parallel to a reference curve on a selected support plane or surface. This feature is similar to an Offset in the Sketcher workbench.

## How To: Create a Parallel Curve

1. Click ✎ (Parallel Curve) from the Curve Offsets flyout in the Wireframe toolbar. The Parallel Curve Definition dialog box opens, as shown in Figure 6–5.

**Figure 6–5**

2. Select the reference curve and the support plane or surface on which the reference curve lies, as shown in Figure 6–6.

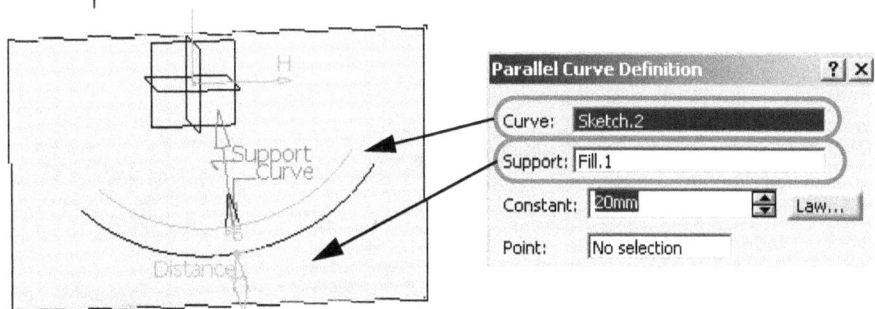

**Figure 6–6**

3. Define the parallel curve location by entering a constant offset value, or by selecting a point through which the parallel curve must pass.

4. Specify parameters for the parallel curve as shown in Figure 6–7.

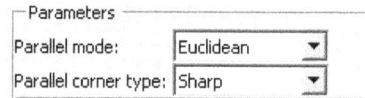

**Figure 6–7**

- **Euclidean mode:** The absolute distance between two curves is the shortest regardless of the support. In this mode, the **Sharp** or **Round** Parallel corner type must be specified.

- **Geodesic mode:** This mode takes into account the curvature of the support. Since the offset value between two curves is constant at every point, you do not need to specify the corner type.

5. Specify the **Smoothing** option as shown in Figure 6–8.

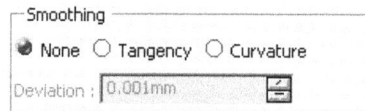

**Figure 6–8**

- **Tangency:** The continuity of the Parallel Curve improves to tangent continuity.

- **Curvature:** The continuity of the Parallel Curve improves to curvature continuity.

6. To place a Parallel Curve on the other side of the reference curve, select **Reverse Direction**. When the **Both Directions** option is selected during the creation of a parallel curve, the second parallel curve is added as a sub-element to the original parallel curve, as shown in Figure 6–9.

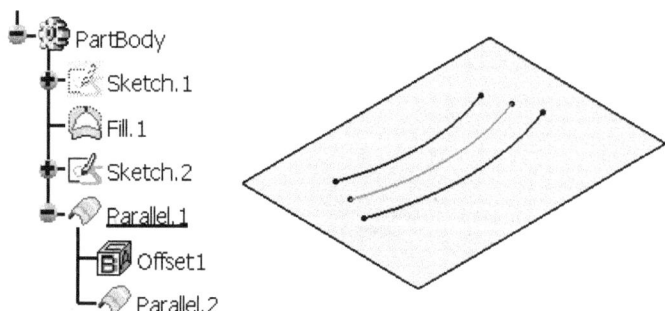

**Figure 6–9**

7. Click **OK** to complete the Parallel Curve feature.

# 6.4 Rolling Offset

A Rolling Offset curve creates a closed loop curve that is offset on both sides of a selected curve or chain of curves.

## How To: Create a Rolling Offset Curve

1. Click ⊘ (Rolling Offset) from the Curve Offsets flyout in the Wireframe toolbar. The Rolling Offset Definition dialog box opens, as shown in Figure 6–10.

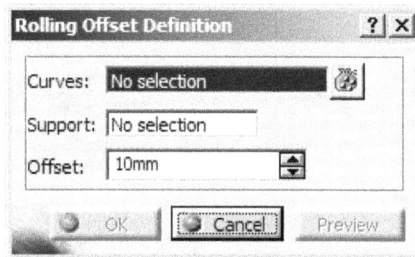

**Figure 6–10**

2. Select the reference curve, as shown in Figure 6–11.

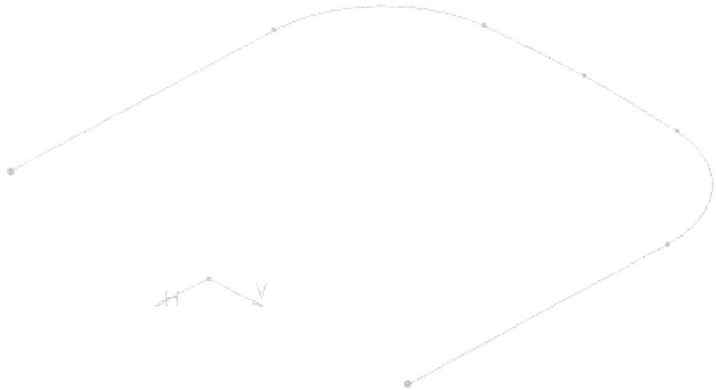

**Figure 6–11**

3. If the selected curves lie on a plane, the support is automatically selected. Otherwise, select the support.

4. Enter the *Offset* value and complete the feature. The result is shown in Figure 6–12.

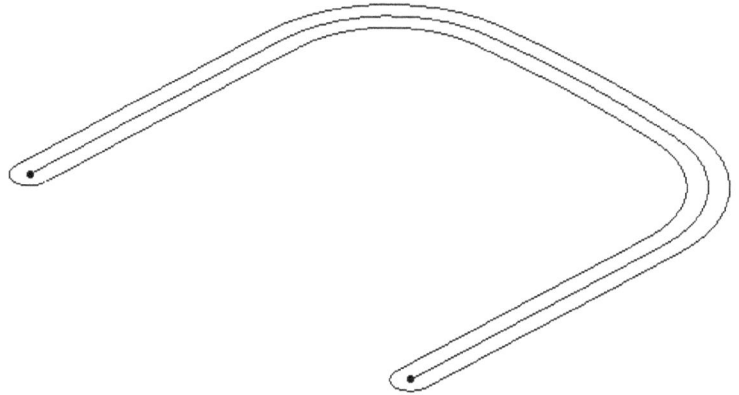

**Figure 6–12**

# 6.5 Helix Curve

To create a helix curve, click  (Helix) from the Curves flyout in the Wireframe toolbar. The Helix Curve Definition dialog box opens as shown in Figure 6–13.

**Figure 6–13**

A helix is defined by three parameters: **Pitch**, **Revolution** and **Height**. You can create a helix by any two parameters. In the Helix Type drop-down list, select one of the following helix creation methods:

- Pitch and Revolution

- Height and Pitch

- Height and Revolution

Additionally, you must select either **Constant Pitch** or **Variable Pitch**. The **Variable Pitch** option is only available for the Pitch and Revolution type of helix. When this option is selected, you can define the start pitch value and the end pitch value,

A helix can be defined by selecting a starting point and an axis. The starting point defines the radius of the helix and the axis defines the center of the helix, as shown in Figure 6–14. Once specified, you can adjust the remaining parameters to achieve the required results.

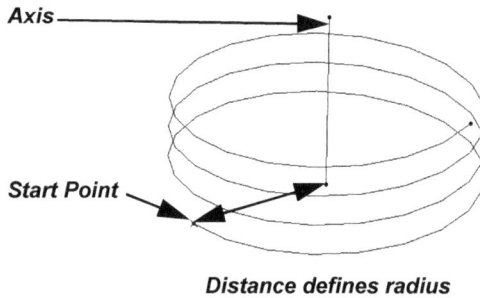

*Axis*

*Start Point*

*Distance defines radius*

**Figure 6–14**

**Pitch** defines the distance between the helix revolutions. In Figure 6–15, the helix on the left is created with a pitch smaller than the one on the right.

*You can define the pitch using a graph by clicking* **Law....**

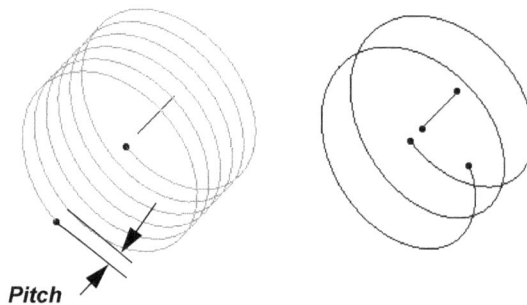

*Pitch*

**Figure 6–15**

**Height** defines the length of the axis from the start point of the helix. In the helix shown on the right in Figure 6–16, a smaller height has been defined.

*Height is not controlled by the selected axis.*

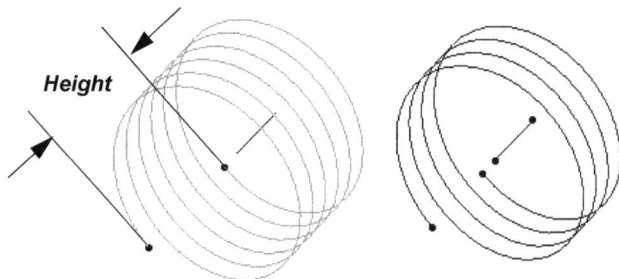

*Height*

**Figure 6–16**

**Taper** defines whether the helix has a linearly increasing or decreasing diameter. The taper can be defined **Inward** or **Outward** at a specified angle. In Figure 6–17, the helix on the right tapers inward by 15°.

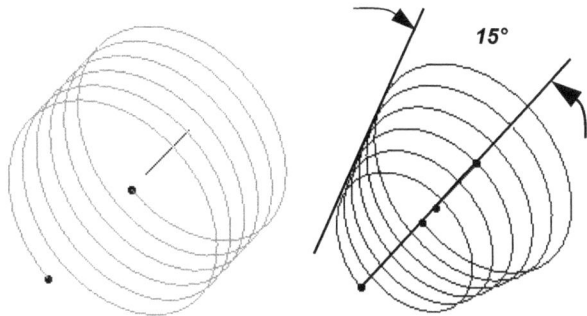

Figure 6–17

**Starting Angle** starts the helix offset from the start point, as shown in Figure 6–18.

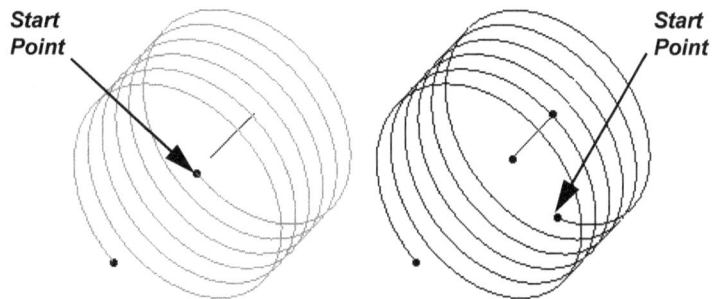

Figure 6–18

Use the options in the *Radius variation* area to further define the helix curve. The **Profile** option enables you to define a profile curve for the helix to follow. An example is shown in Figure 6–19.

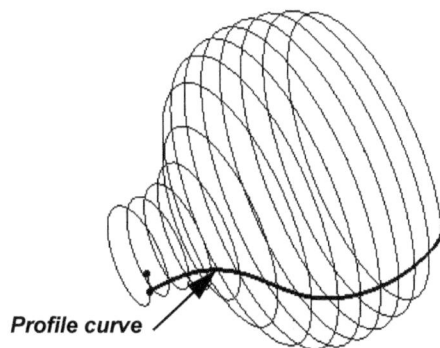

Figure 6–19

# 6.6 Spiral

A Spiral element creates a spiral curve in a plane. It is typically used as a center curve for a sweep or a profile for an extruded surface feature. An example of a Spiral element is shown in Figure 6–20.

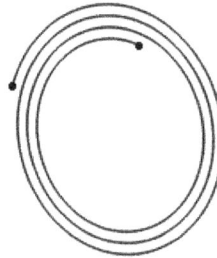

**Figure 6–20**

## How To: Create a Spiral Element

1. Click ![icon] (Spiral) from the Curves flyout in the Wireframe toolbar. The Spiral Curve Definition dialog box opens as shown in Figure 6–21.

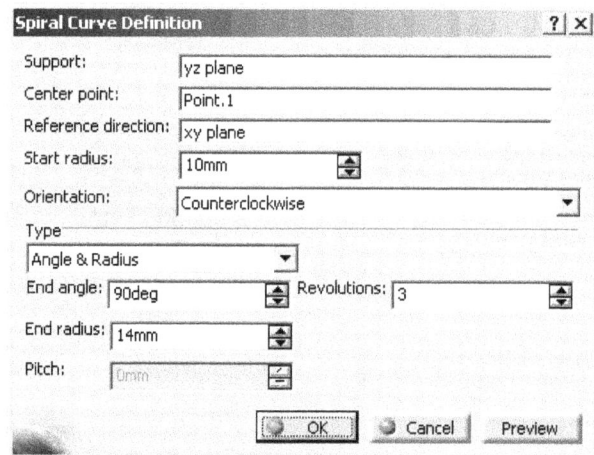

**Figure 6–21**

2. Select the following references:
   - Point to define the center of the spiral
   - Support for the spiral
   - Direction for the spiral (the directional reference is normal to the spiral)
   - Start radius
   - Orientation
3. Define the type of spiral by specifying the following parameters:
   - End angle or Pitch
   - End Radius
   - Revolutions

   An example is shown in Figure 6–22.

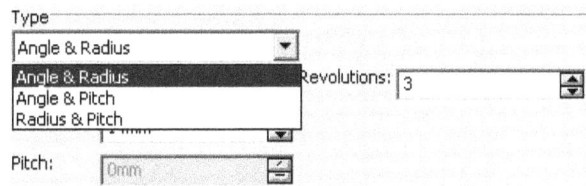

Type
Angle & Radius

Angle & Radius
Angle & Pitch
Radius & Pitch

Revolutions: 3

Pitch: 0mm

**Figure 6–22**

4. Click **OK** to complete the feature. Figure 6–23 shows a completed spiral wireframe feature.

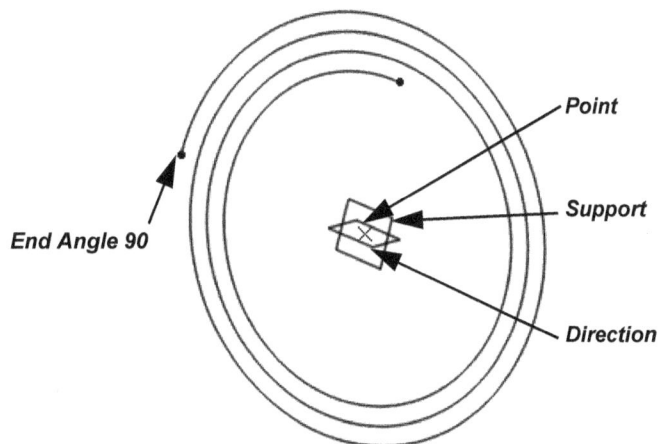

Point

Support

Direction

End Angle 90

**Figure 6–23**

# 6.7 Contour Curves

Contour curves can be created by selecting existing entities which are copied into the contour feature.

## How To: Create a Contour Curve

1. Click [Contour icon] (Contour) from the Curves flyout in the Wireframe toolbar. The Contour Definition dialog box opens, as shown in Figure 6–24.

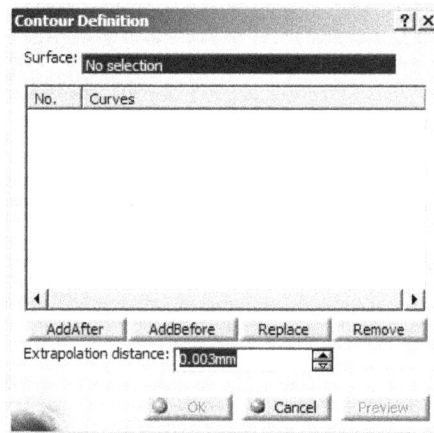

**Figure 6–24**

2. Select the support Surface, then select the curve or curves to comprise the contour, as shown in Figure 6–25.

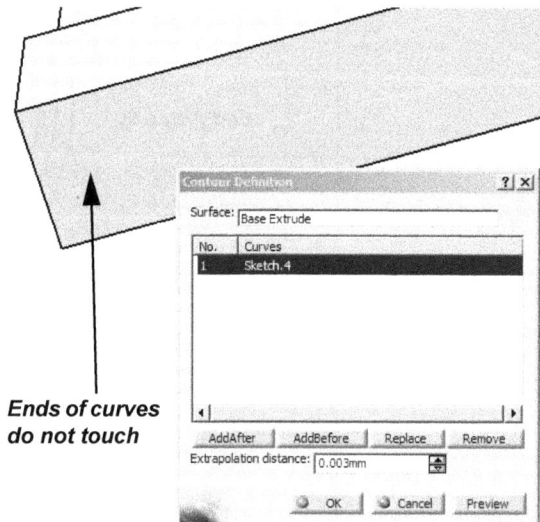

*Ends of curves do not touch*

**Figure 6–25**

3. The selected curves should form a closed loop. If you have an open loop, or if the curves cross, you can adjust the Extrapolation distance to automatically trim the resulting curves to form the closed loop, as shown in Figure 6–26.

**Extrapolated curves**

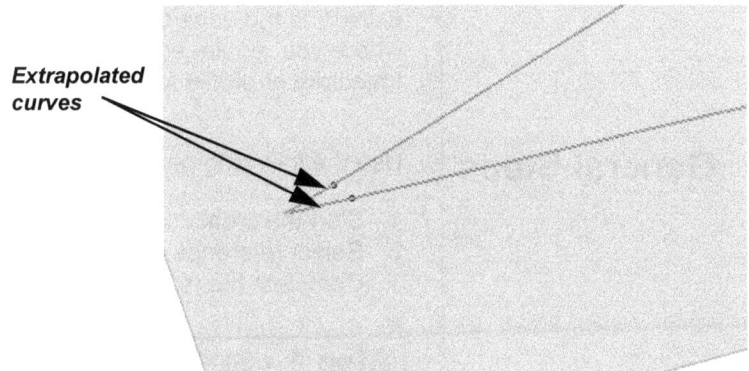

**Figure 6–26**

4. Click **OK** to complete the contour curve.

# 6.8 Boundary Curves

Boundary curves are created on the extremities of surface features. A boundary curve is a curve feature created by extracting the edge of a surface. This tool is helpful in situations where you require edges from several surfaces to use as a trajectory or profile for another feature.

**General Steps**

Use the following general steps to extract boundary curves:

1. Start the creation of a boundary curve.
2. Select reference geometry.
3. Complete the feature.

## Step 1 - Start the creation of a boundary curve.

Click ⌐ (Boundary) from the Extracts flyout in the Operations toolbar to start the creation of a boundary curve. The Boundary Definition dialog box opens, as shown in Figure 6–27.

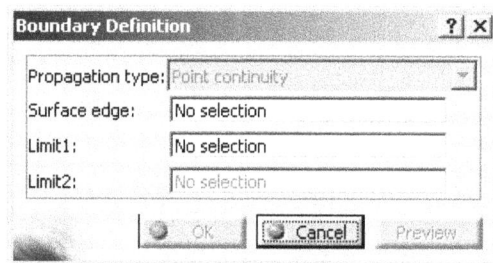

**Figure 6–27**

## Step 2 - Select reference geometry.

Select an edge belonging to a surface and specify a Propagation type. The Propagation type determines the boundaries of the selected surface that are used to generate curves.

The propagation types are described as follows:

| Propagation Type | Description |
|---|---|
| Complete Boundary | Uses the entire surface boundary. |
| Point Continuity | Uses the surface boundary starting from the selected edge until it encounters a point discontinuity. |
| Tangent Continuity | Uses the surface boundary starting from the selected edge until it encounters a tangency discontinuity. |
| No Propagation | Uses only the selected edge. |

## Step 3 - Complete the feature.

To complete the feature, click **OK**. The Propagation types you can create are shown in Figure 6–28.

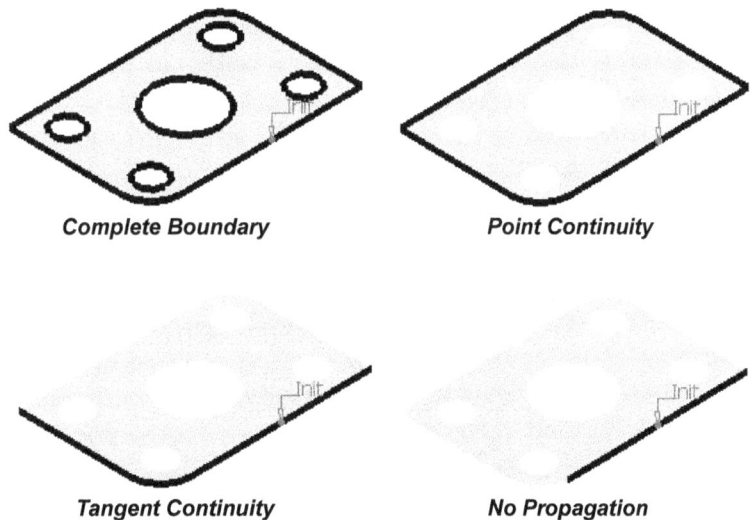

*Complete Boundary*                    *Point Continuity*

*Tangent Continuity*                    *No Propagation*

**Figure 6–28**

Limits can be defined to terminate the propagation of the boundary curve at selected points or vertices.

# 6.9 Extract Curves

The **Extract** operation creates new curve elements by copying edges or curves. Each curve selected creates a separate extract feature in the specification tree. The process of extracting edges or curves follows that of extracting surfaces. An example of an extracted curve is shown in Figure 6–29.

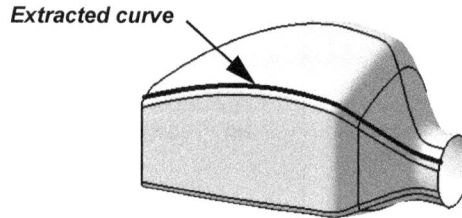

*Extracted curve*

Figure 6–29

**General Steps**

Use the following steps to perform an extract operation:

1. Start the **Extract** operation.
2. Select the entities to extract.
3. Specify the propagation type.
4. (Optional) Define the additional settings.
5. Complete the feature.

## Step 1 - Start the Extract operation.

Click  (Extract) from the Extracts flyout in the Operations toolbar. The Extract definition dialog box opens, as shown in Figure 6–30.

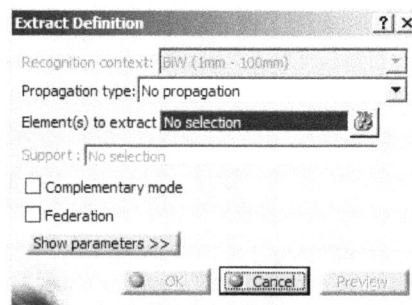

Figure 6–30

## Step 2 - Select the entities to extract.

Select an edge or curve in the model. Multiple entities can be selected using ⬚. When the Element(s) to extract dialog box opens, you can select multiple edges or curves, as shown in Figure 6–31.

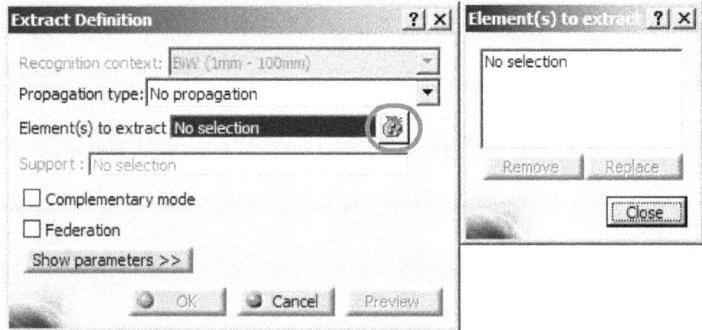

**Figure 6–31**

## Step 3 - Specify the propagation type.

In the Propagation type drop-down list, select one of the following:

- No propagation

- Point continuity

- Tangent continuity

- Curvature continuity

- Depression propagation

- Protrusion propagation

**Note:** Protrusion propagation and Depression propagation are not available for wireframe geometry (points, lines, splines or edges).

## Step 4 - (Optional) Define the additional settings.

The **Extract** tool enables you to apply optional settings, as shown in Figure 6–32.

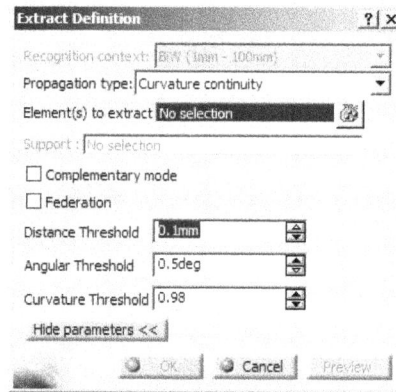

**Figure 6–32**

Select **Federation** if the resultant curve is considered to be a representation of all edges or curves added to the Extract. Clear the **Federation** option if the resultant surface is used as a collection of curves representing each curve or edge added to the Extract.

Click **Show parameters** to adjust the **Distance Threshold**, **Angular Threshold**, and **Curvature Threshold**. These options are available when extracting edges or curves, but not for surfaces.

The **Distance Threshold** is a linear value between 0.001 mm and 0.1 mm that defines the elements that are included in the Extract when point continuity is enabled.

The **Angular Threshold** is a value that defines the maximum discontinuity permitted for two tangent entities. **Angular Threshold** is available with **Tangent continuity** and **Curvature continuity** propagation.

The **Curvature Threshold** is a ratio between 0 and 1. The ratio is derived from an equation that measures the curvature vectors of two adjacent entities. The larger the curvature threshold value, the less discontinuity is permitted. This ratio is only available to adjust when **Curvature continuity** is the selected propagation type.

## Step 5 - Complete the feature.

Click **OK** to complete the feature. The number of resultant Extract features is dependent on the number of entities selected in the Element(s) to extract dialog box.

# 6.10 Split Curves

The **Split** operation divides a curve at its intersection with another curve element. An example is shown in Figure 6–33. Curve 1 is cut by Curve 2. Curve 2 is unaffected by the **Split** operation.

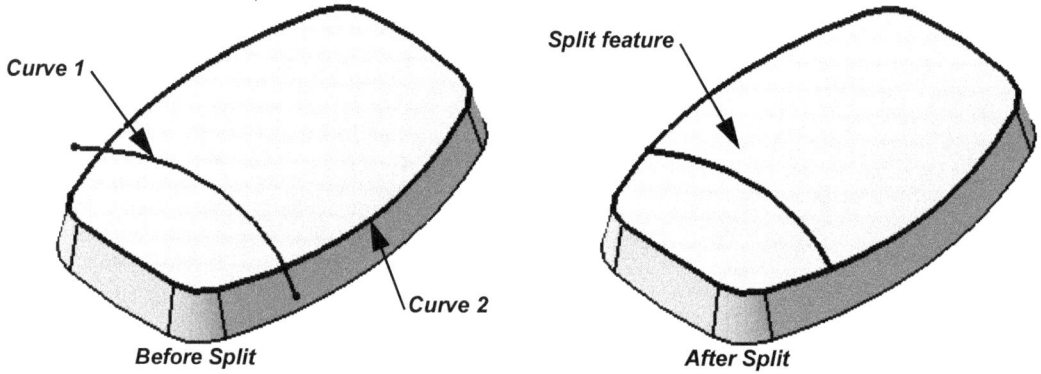

Figure 6–33

## How To: Perform a Split Operation

1. Click [Split icon] (Split) from the Trim-Split flyout in the Operations toolbar. The Split Definition dialog box opens as shown in Figure 6–34.

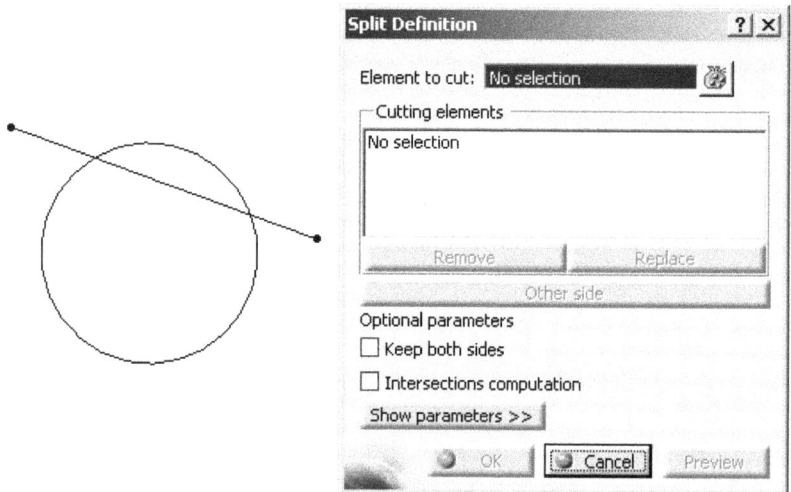

Figure 6–34

2. Select the curve or edge to be cut in the **Split** operation, as shown in Figure 6–35.
3. Select the cutting elements to intersect the curve. The curves or edges selected are affected by the **Split** operation. The cutting element and element to cut are shown in Figure 6–35.

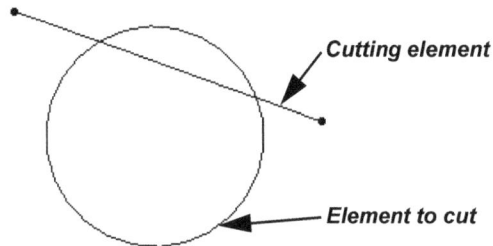

*Cutting element*

*Element to cut*

Figure 6–35

4. Click **Other side** to toggle the side to remove or select **Keep both sides** to keep both sides. **Remove** and **Replace** can be used to edit the elements added to the *Cutting elements* field. The results of toggling **Other side** are shown in Figure 6–36.

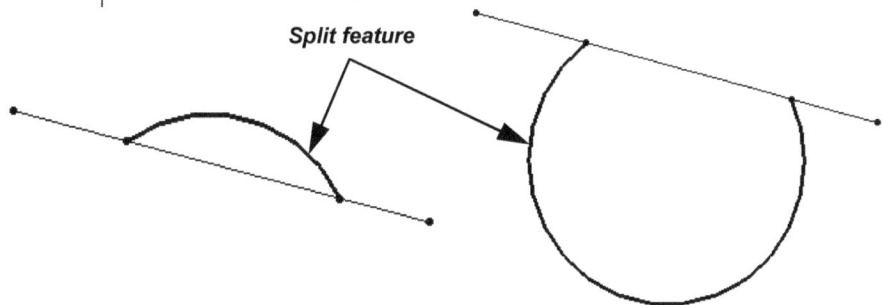

*Split feature*

Figure 6–36

5. If the **Intersections computation** option is selected, you can add an intersection curve to the feature, as shown in Figure 6–37.

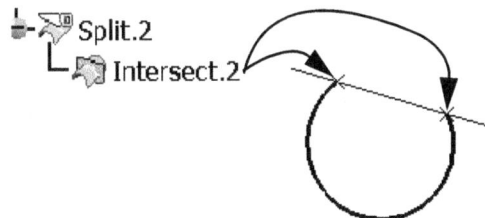

Split.2
Intersect.2

Figure 6–37

6. Click **OK** to complete the Split feature.

## Notes on Split Curves

- A curve or edge can be split by more than one cutting element, as shown in Figure 6–38.

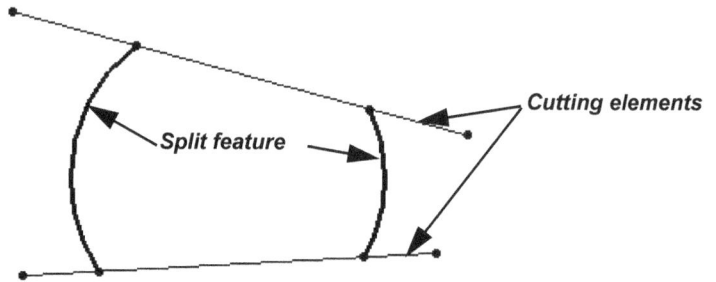

**Cutting elements**

*Split feature*

**Figure 6–38**

- Surfaces can be split by curves as shown in Figure 6–39.

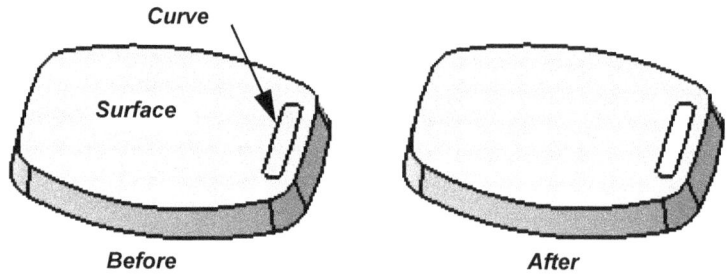

**Curve**

*Surface*

*Before*                    *After*

**Figure 6–39**

# 6.11 Trim Curves

The **Trim** operation enables you to select two (or more) curves and combine them into one curve. The input curves are cut back at their intersection. The resulting feature is one curve joining together the input elements.

## Trim (Standard)

The **Trim** operation with the Standard mode trims overlapping curves between intersecting curves.

### How To: Perform a Trim Operation

1. Click  (Trim) from the Trim-Split flyout in the Operations toolbar.
2. In the Trim Definition dialog box, expand the Mode drop-down list, and select **Standard** as shown in Figure 6–40.

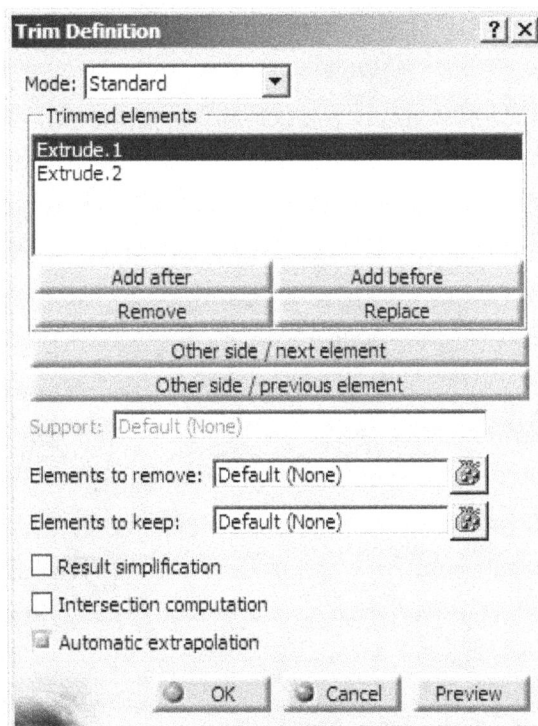

Figure 6–40

3. Select the two features with overlapping geometry for the *Element.1* and *Element.2* fields. Four different results can be achieved by clicking **Other side / next element** and/or **Other side / previous element**.

Examples of overlapping geometry are shown in Figure 6–41.

*With the **Split** operation, the cutting element stays whole. With the **Trim** operation, both elements are affected.*

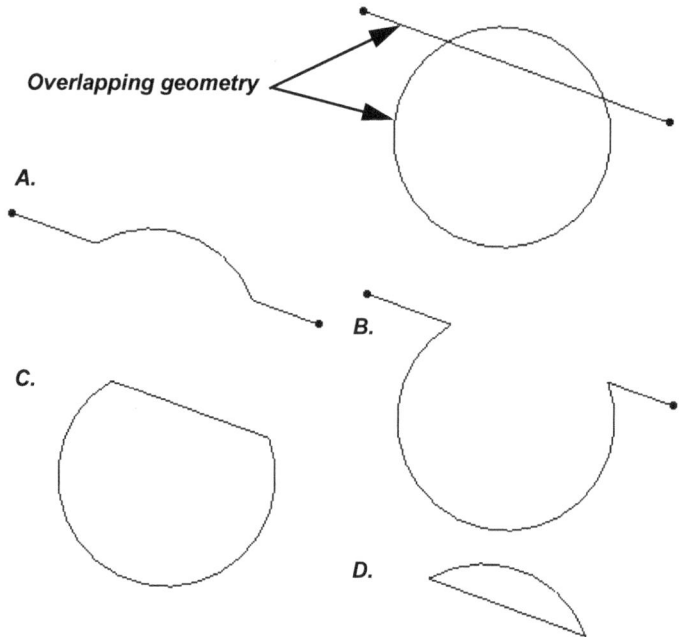

**Overlapping geometry**

A.

B.

C.

D.

**Figure 6–41**

4. Use the **Add After**, **Add Before**, **Remove**, and **Replace** buttons to modify the elements included in the **Trim** operation.
5. You can select **Intersection computation** to create wireframe geometry at the intersection of the trim elements, as shown in Figure 6–42.

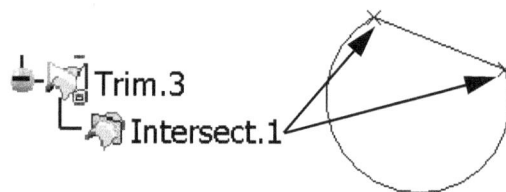

**Figure 6–42**

# 6.12 Joined Curves

Joined curves enable you to group a collection of curves into a single feature. This is useful when the profile, guide, or spine for a surface or solid feature consists of several curve features. Joining these curves enables you to select several features for a single operation.

To create a joined curve, click  (Join) in the Operations toolbar. The Join Definition dialog box opens, as shown in Figure 6–43.

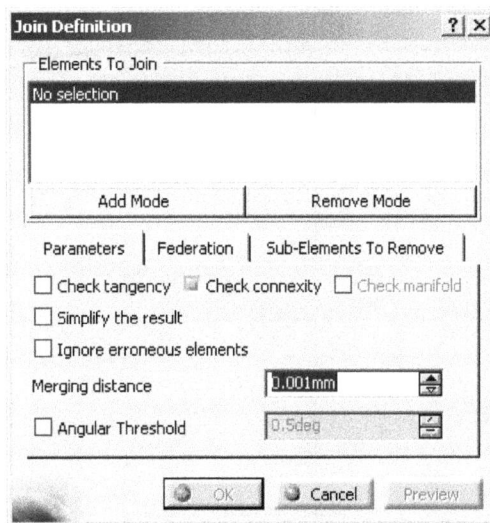

**Figure 6–43**

The curves selected for the Join must be connected at their end points to form a continuous curve. They can be G0, G1, or G2 continuous. Once the Join has been created, the selected curves are automatically hidden.

The top graphic in Figure 6–44 shows a guide consisting of two arcs and two lines. These four curves are joined to create the single guide, as shown at the bottom of Figure 6–44.

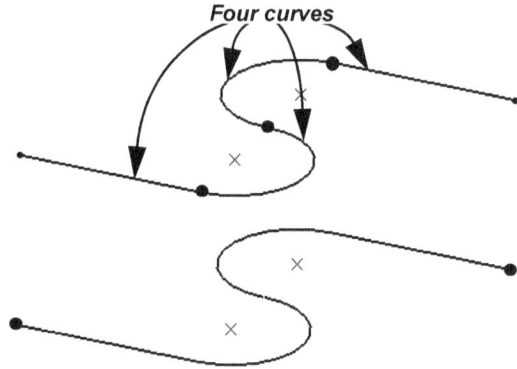

**Figure 6–44**

# 6.13 Sketcher Outputs

**Output Features**

Output features can be created in Sketcher and then used to create surfaces. They also enable you to use a portion of the sketch for your surface. In solids, multiple profile sketches can be created and then used with sketch sub-elements to use a portion of the profile. In the Generative Shape Design workbench, a single curve or profile cannot be extruded into a surface. The entire sketch is used.

The **Output feature** icon is located in the Tools toolbar in the Sketcher workbench, as shown in Figure 6–45.

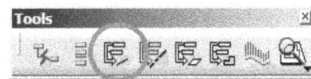

**Figure 6–45**

## How To: Create an Output Feature

1. Select the lines in Sketcher from which you want to create outputs.

2. Click  (Output Feature). The outputs are then added to the specification tree, as shown in Figure 6–46.

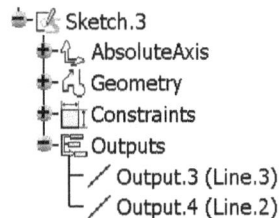

- Sketch.3
  - AbsoluteAxis
  - Geometry
  - Constraints
  - Outputs
    - Output.3 (Line.3)
    - Output.4 (Line.2)

**Figure 6–46**

The output geometry has a larger line thickness than the rest of the entities in the sketch. The geometry used to create the output is hidden after output creation, as shown in Figure 6–47.

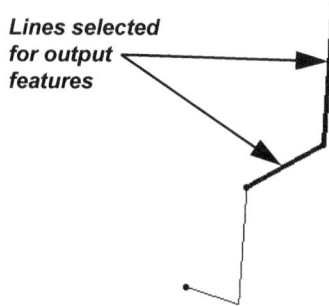

*Lines selected for output features*

**Figure 6–47**

Each output feature is regarded as an entity. For example, an output feature is used to create the surface as shown in Figure 6–48.

**Figure 6–48**

If you want to use two output features together in a **Surface** operation, you need to join them, as shown in Figure 6–49.

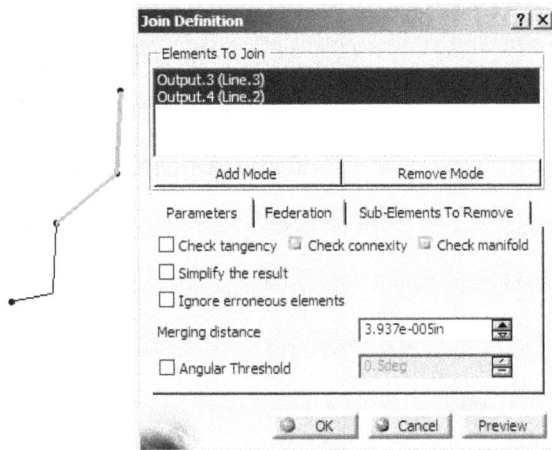

**Figure 6–49**

When the two outputs are joined and extruded they display as shown in Figure 6–50.

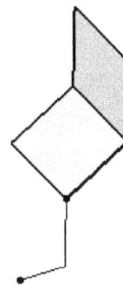

**Figure 6–50**

## 3D Axis

You can use sketch points to output 3D axes. In the Tools toolbar, click  (3D Axis) and select a point. The system generates an axis running through the point and perpendicular to the sketch support. The created output axis displays under the **Outputs** node in the specification tree, as shown in Figure 6–51.

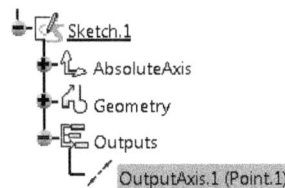

**Figure 6–51**

## 3D Plane

You can use a sketched line to output a 3D plane. In the Tools toolbar, click ⧉ (3D Plane) and select a line. The system generates a plane running through the line and perpendicular to the sketch support. The created output plane displays under the **Outputs** node in the specification tree, as shown in Figure 6–52.

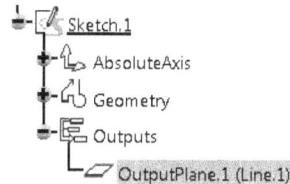

**Figure 6–52**

## Profile Features

An output Profile feature consists of a set of connected or unconnected curves that are independent of the elements from which they are created. You can create more than one Output Profile from a sketch and then use them to generate the required 3D shape.

Output Profiles can be used to create 3D features in the Part Design, Wireframe & Surface, and Generative Shape workbenches.

### How To: Use the following steps to create an Output Profile:

1. In the sketch, select the 2D elements that you want to use. In the Tools toolbar, click ⧉ (Profile Feature).
2. In the Profile definition dialog box, you can specify the following:
   - The entities for the profile.
   - A color for the profile.
   - The propagation mode.
   - Options for Tangency, Curvature, Connexity, and Manifold.

Output Profiles can only be defined from elements in the sketch. The Profile Definition dialog box and selection modes are shown in Figure 6–53. There are three ways of selecting them:

- **Point (Explicit Definition):** Adds points to the profile. Adjacent elements are not propagated with this mode.

- **Wire (Explicit Definition):** Manually select elements (such as circles, arcs, splines, lines, or ellipses) to add to the profile. Adjacent elements are not propagated with this mode.

- **Wire (Automatic Propagation):** Select an element. The connecting elements are added automatically. You can add more elements by selecting them. This is the default mode.

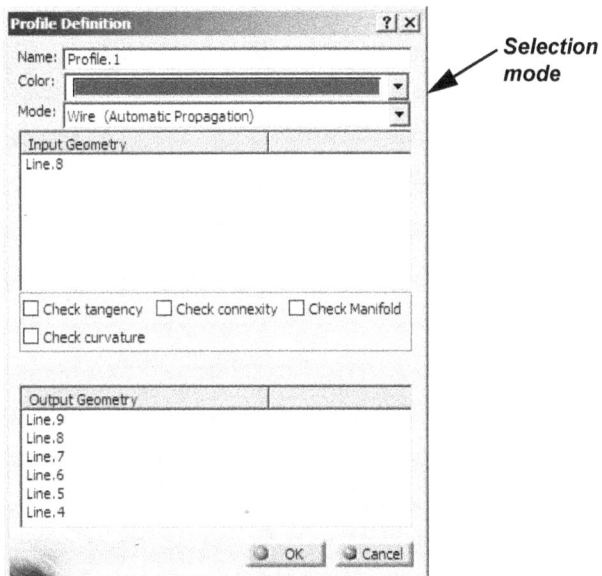

**Figure 6–53**

3. Click **OK** to complete the Output Profile. The new profile is added to the specification tree, as shown in Figure 6–54.

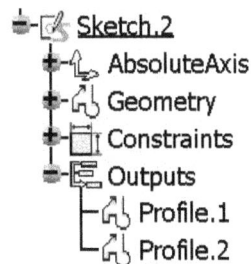

**Figure 6–54**

When you exit Sketcher the outputs can be used to create surfaces. Two Output Profiles are created from the sketch feature. Two surfaces are then created from those outputs, as shown in Figure 6–55.

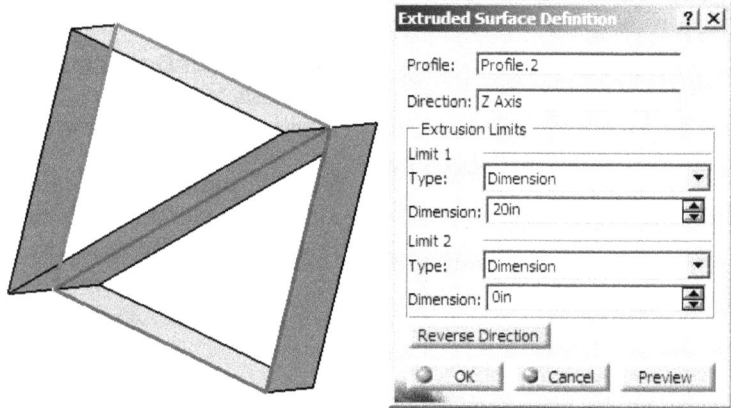

Figure 6–55

## Helpful Tips:

- In Sketcher, you cannot cut, copy, or paste Output Profiles.

- In the 3D area, you can cut or copy profiles and use them to create 3D features.

- You can only delete profiles in the Sketcher workbench. If you try to delete the profile outside the sketch, a warning message box opens as shown in Figure 6–56.

Figure 6–56

# Practice 6a | Wireframe I

## Practice Objectives

- Create a project and intersect curves.
- Create a split and trim curves.

In this practice, you will use the **Project**, **Intersect**, **Split**, and **Trim** commands to create the required wireframe geometry for an Intake House. Some solids and surfaces have already been created, which will aid in creating the geometry required for this practice. The completed model displays as shown in Figure 6–57.

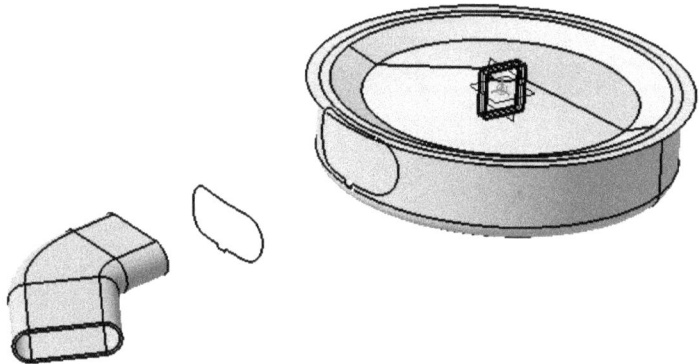

**Figure 6–57**

## Task 1 - Open a part.

1. Open **Intake_Wireframe_Start.CATPart**. The model displays as shown in Figure 6–58.

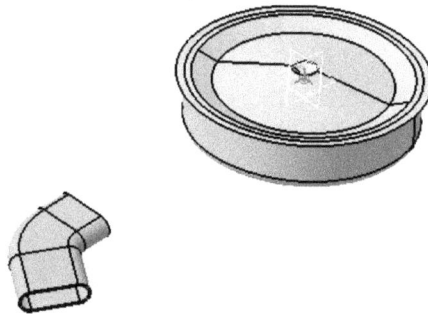

**Figure 6–58**

2. Verify that the model units are set to **mm**.

**Task 2 - Create a reference surface.**

1. Insert a geometrical set and rename it as **Intake**.

2. Define Intake as the active Work Object.

*To define the active work object, right-click on the required geometrical set and select **Define in Work Object**.*

3. Click [icon] (Extract).

4. Set the *Propagation Type* to **No Propagation**.

5. Select the surface shown in Figure 6–59.

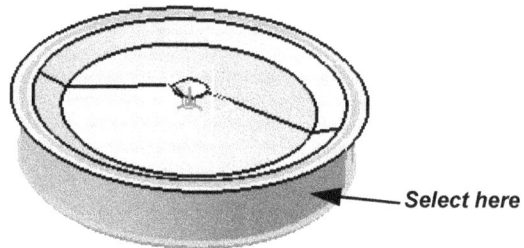

Select here

**Figure 6–59**

6. Click **OK**.

7. Click [icon] (Split).

8. Select **Extract.1** as the Element to Cut, and select the **YZ** plane as the Cutting Element.

9. Click **OK**.

10. Click [icon] (Offset).

11. Select **Split.1**.

12. Enter an *Offset* value of **100mm**.

13. Preview the result and verify that the offset direction is outward. The model displays as shown in Figure 6–60.

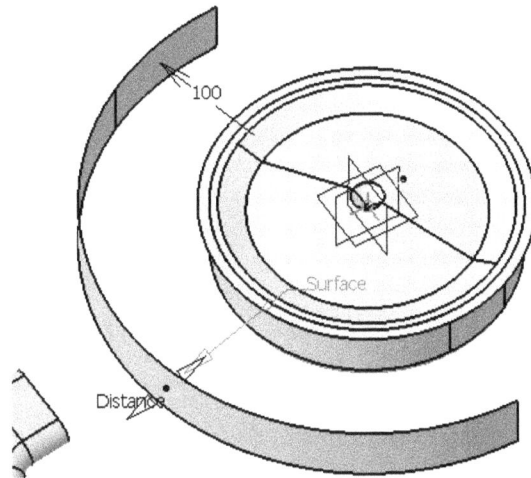

**Figure 6–60**

14. Click **OK**.

15. Hide **Split.1**.

---

**Task 3 - Extract a curve from the solid.**

---

1. In the Operations toolbar, click  (Extract).

2. In the Propagation type drop-down list, select **Tangent continuity**, as shown in Figure 6–61.

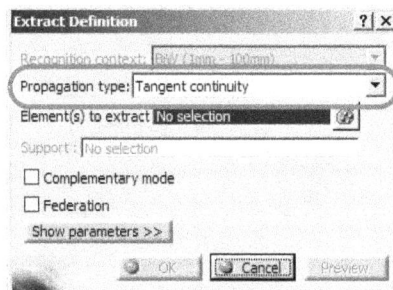

**Figure 6–61**

3. Select the edge as shown in Figure 6–62.

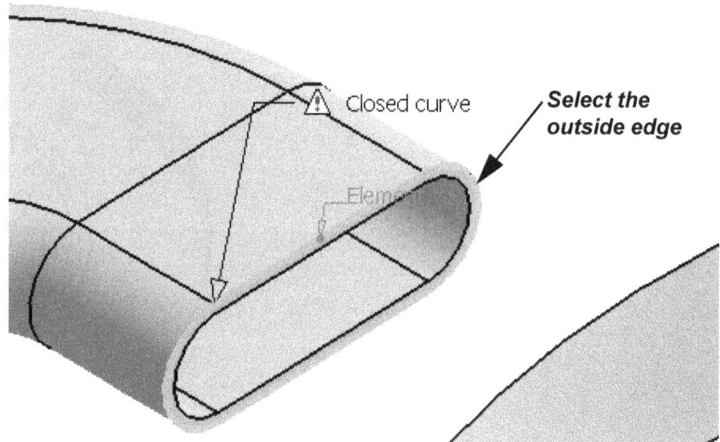

**Figure 6–62**

4. Click **OK** and rename the Extract as **Section1**.

5. Hide the **IntakeHouse** body.

## Task 4 - Project a curve.

1. Click [Extract icon] (Extract).

2. Verify that the **No propagation** type is set and select the edge shown in Figure 6–63.

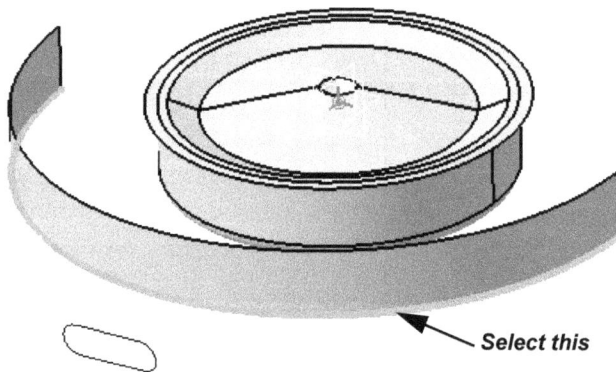

**Figure 6–63**

3. Click **OK** to complete the Extract.

4. Rename the Extract feature as **Extracted Profile**.

5. Click 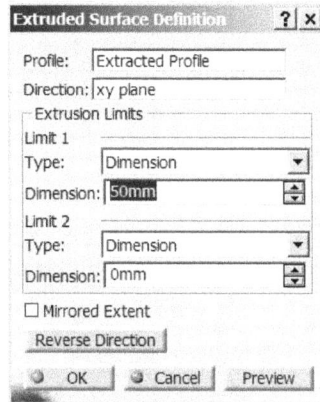 (Extrude).

6. In the *Profile* field, select **Extracted Profile**. In the *Direction* field, select **xy plane** as the reference.

7. Enter **50mm** for *Limit 1*, as shown in Figure 6–64.

**Extruded Surface Definition** ? x

Profile: Extracted Profile
Direction: xy plane

Extrusion Limits
Limit 1
Type: Dimension
Dimension: 50mm

Limit 2
Type: Dimension
Dimension: 0mm

☐ Mirrored Extent
Reverse Direction

OK    Cancel    Preview

**Figure 6–64**

8. You might need to click **Reverse Direction** so that the extruded surface displays as shown in Figure 6–65.

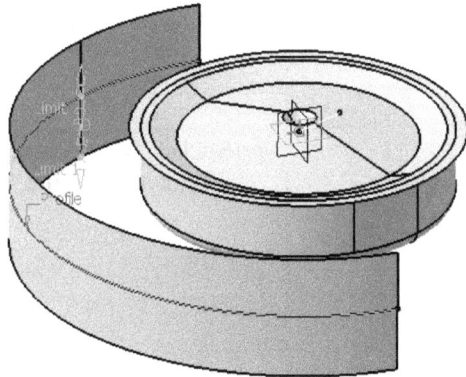

**Figure 6–65**

9. Click **OK**.

10. Join **Offset.1** and **Extrude.1**.

11. Hide **Extracted Profile**.

12. In the Wireframe toolbar, click 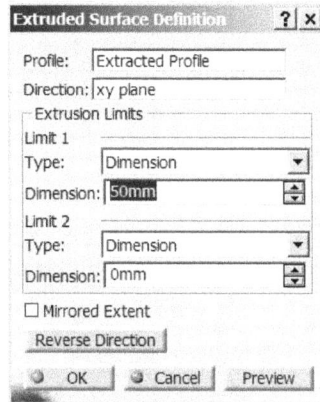 (Projection).

13. In the Projection type drop-down list, select **Along a direction** as shown in Figure 6–66.

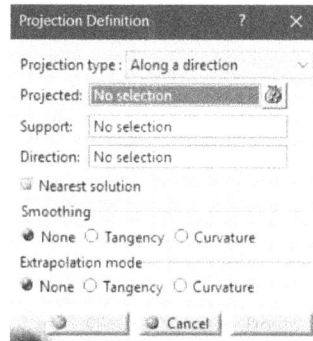

**Figure 6–66**

14. Select the references shown in Figure 6–67.

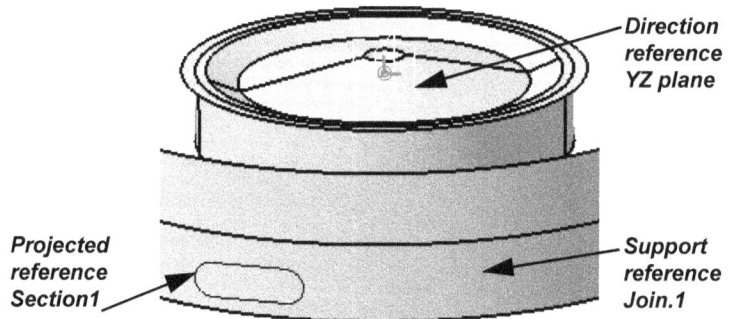

**Figure 6–67**

15. Click **OK** to complete the Projection. The model displays as shown in Figure 6–68.

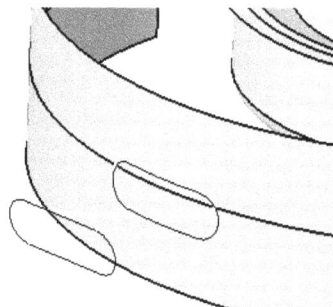

**Figure 6–68**

16. Hide **Section1**.

## Task 5 - Create parallel curves.

1. Click ![icon] (Parallel Curve). The Parallel Curve Definition dialog box opens as shown in Figure 6–69.

**Figure 6–69**

2. In the Parallel Curve Definition dialog box, enter the following references as shown in Figure 6–70:

    - *Curve reference:* **Project.1**
    - *Support reference:* **Join.1**
    - *Constant:* **4mm**
    - Select **Repeat object after OK**.

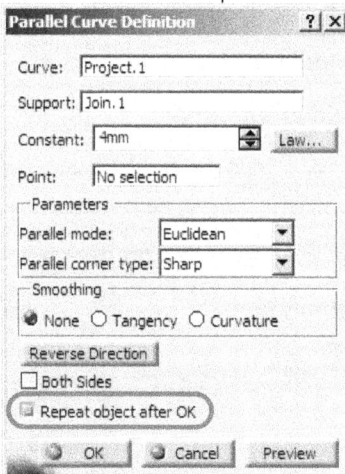

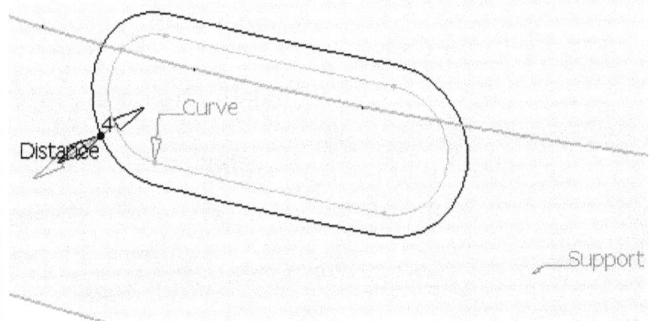

**Figure 6–70**

3. Verify that the direction is pointing outward.

4. Click **OK**.

5. In the Object Repetition dialog box, enter **1** for *Instance(s)* and clear the **Create in a new Body** option, as shown in Figure 6–71.

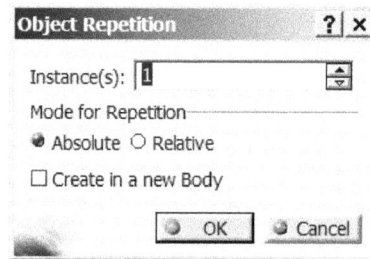

**Figure 6–71**

6. Click **OK** to complete the Parallel curve. The model displays as shown in Figure 6–72.

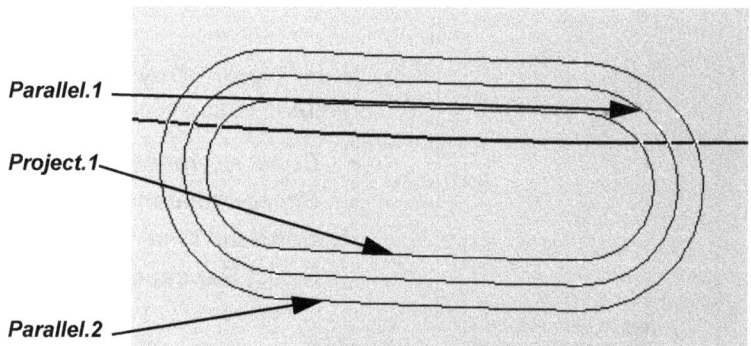

**Figure 6–72**

7. Hide **Join.1**, **Project.1**, and **Parallel.2**.

### Task 6 - Create intersection points.

1. Create a reference plane with the following parameters:

   • *Plane type:* **Offset from plane**
   • *Reference:* **ZX plane**
   • *Offset:* **4mm**

2. Create another reference plane in the opposite direction with the following parameters:

- *Plane type:* **Offset from plane**
- *Reference:* **ZX plane**
- *Offset:* **4mm**

3. Click  (Intersection).

4. Select **Plane.1** and **Parallel.1**.

5. Click **OK** to complete the Intersection.

6. Select **keep only one sub-element using an Extract**, as shown in Figure 6–73.

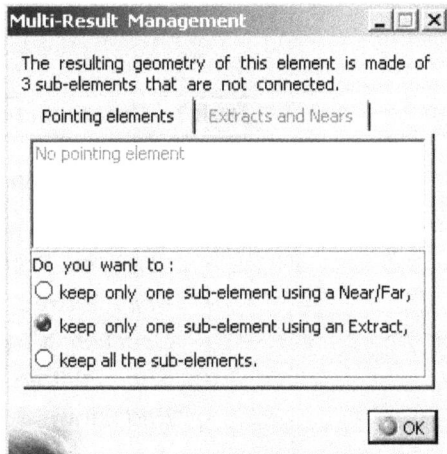

**Figure 6–73**

7. Click **OK**.

8. Select the point shown in Figure 6–74.

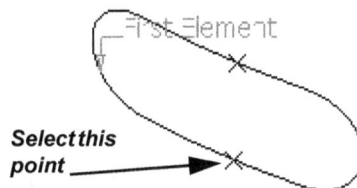

**Figure 6–74**

9. In the Extract Definition dialog box, click **OK**.

10. Rename the newly created Extract feature as **Extract Point1**.

11. Create another Intersection between **Plane.2** and **Parallel.1**. Extract the bottom point, as was done in Steps 6 to 8. Rename the Extract feature as **Extract Point2**. The model displays as shown in Figure 6–75.

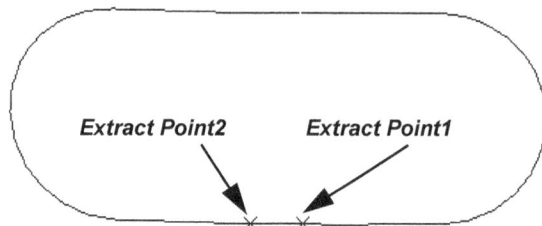

*Extract Point2*      *Extract Point1*

**Figure 6–75**

## Task 7 - Create lines.

1. Create a line with the following parameters, as shown in Figure 6–76.

   - *Line type:* **Point-Direction**
   - *Point:* **Extract Point1**
   - *Direction:* **XY plane**
   - *Support:* **Join.1**
   - *End:* **2mm**

**Figure 6–76**

2. Create another line with the following parameters, as shown in Figure 6–77.

   - *Line type:* **Point-Direction**
   - *Point:* **Extract Point2**
   - *Direction:* **XY plane**
   - *Support:* **Join.1**
   - *End:* **2mm**

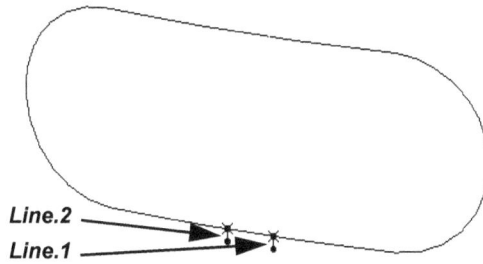

**Figure 6–77**

3. Create another line using the **Point-Point** *Line type*.

4. Right-click in the *Point 1* reference field and select **Create Endpoint**, as shown in Figure 6–78.

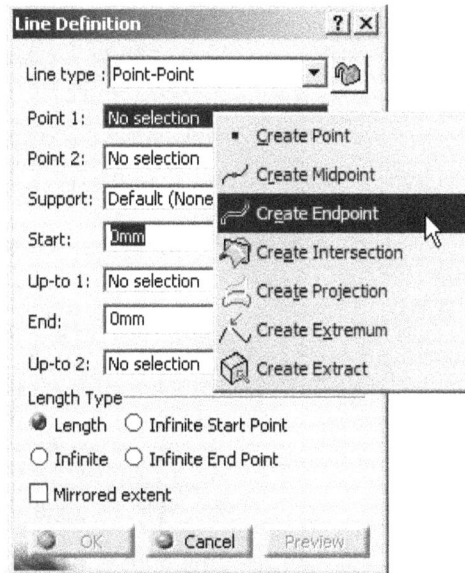

**Figure 6–78**

5. Select the end point shown in Figure 6–79.

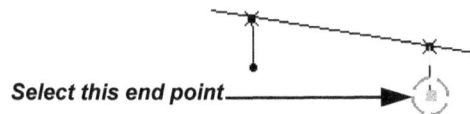

**Figure 6–79**

6. Create another end point for **Point 2**, using the end point shown in Figure 6–80.

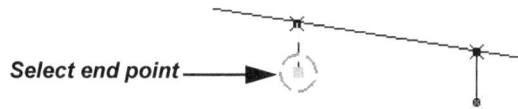

Select end point ————▶

**Figure 6–80**

7. Verify that the *Start* and *End* values are set to **0mm**.

8. Click **OK** to complete the Line feature.

9. Hide **Extract Point1** and **Extract Point2**.

---

**Task 8 - Trim curves.**

---

1. Click  (Join).

2. Select the three lines that you just created.

3. Click **OK** to complete the Join.

4. Rename the feature as **Join Curves**.

5. Click  (Trim). The Trim Definition dialog box opens.

6. Select **Parallel.1** and **Join Curves**.

7. A Warning message box opens, recommending that you use the **Elements to keep** option to obtain more stable results from future updates. Close the dialog box.

8. You might need to toggle **Other side / next element** and/or **Other side / previous element** to keep the appropriate geometry, as shown in Figure 6–81.

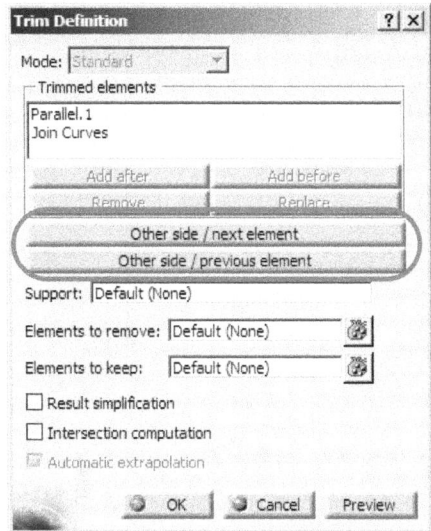

**Figure 6–81**

9. Click **OK** to complete the Trim.

10. Rename the Trim as **Section2**.

11. Hide **Section2**.

---

**Task 9 - Create the final wireframe geometry.**

---

1. Show **Parallel.2**, **Extract Point1**, and **Extract Point2**.

2. Create a line with the following parameters:

*You might need to reverse the direction to obtain the same result.*

- *Line type:* **Point-Direction**
- *Point:* **Extract Point1**
- *Direction:* **XY plane**
- *Support:* **Join.1**
- *End:* **8mm**

3. Rename the Line as **Trim Line1**.

4. Create another line with the following parameters:

*You might need to reverse the direction to obtain the same result.*

- *Line type:* **Point-Direction**
- *Point:* **Extract Point2**
- *Direction:* **XY plane**
- *Support:* **Join.1**
- *End:* **8mm**

5. Rename the Line as **Trim Line2**. **Trim Line1** and **Trim Line2** display as shown in Figure 6–82.

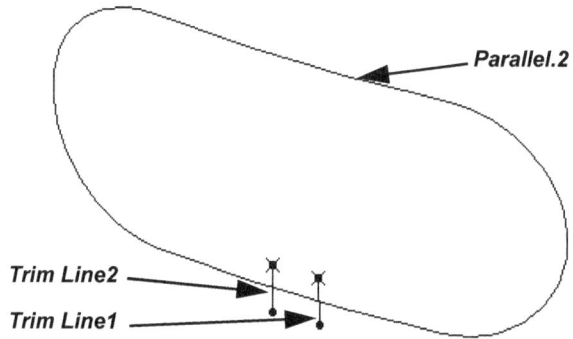

Figure 6–82

6. Create a line using the **Point-Point** *Line type*.

7. Right-click in the *Point* field and select **Create Endpoint**, as shown in Figure 6–83.

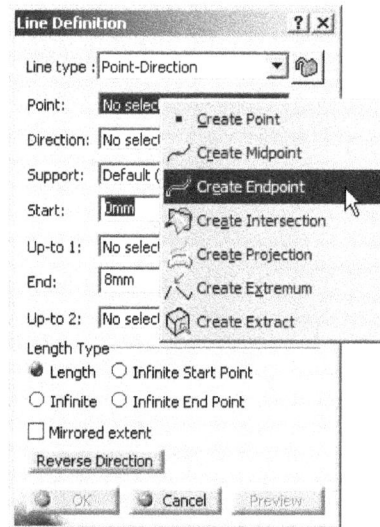

Figure 6–83

8. Select the end point shown in Figure 6–84.

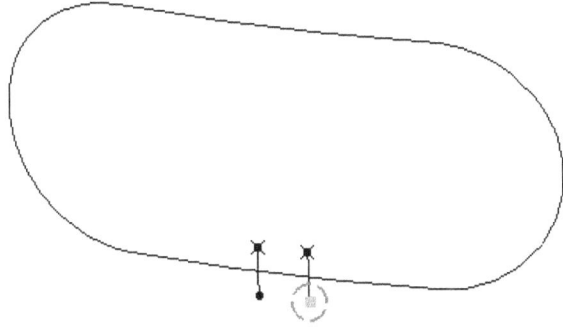

**Figure 6–84**

9. Create another end point for Point 2 as shown in Figure 6–85.

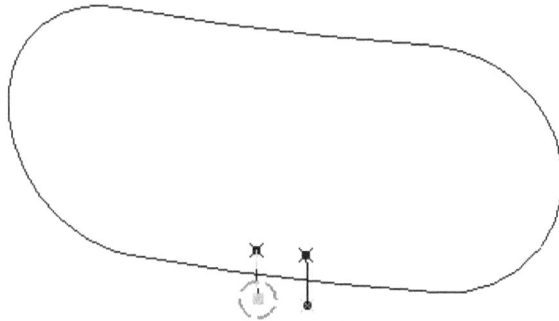

**Figure 6–85**

10. Verify that the *Start* and *End* values are set to **0mm**.

11. Join the three lines that you just created.

12. Hide **Extract Point1** and **Extract Point2**.

13. Click  (Trim).

14. Select the **Join feature** created in Step 11 and select **Parallel.2**. Toggle **Other side / next element** and/or **Other side / previous element**. to keep the appropriate geometry.

15. If a warning message box opens, close it. This message is not important.

16. Click **OK** to complete the Trim. The completed Trim displays as shown in Figure 6–86.

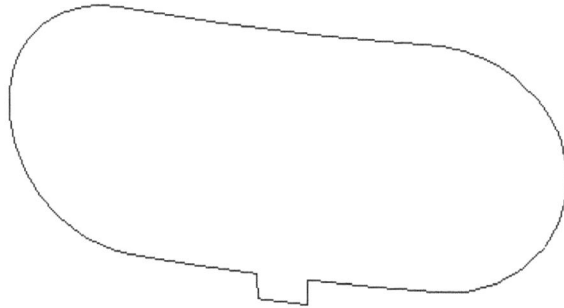

**Figure 6–86**

17. Rename the Trim curve as **ProjectCurve**.

18. Click  (Projection).

19. In the drop-down list, select **Along a direction**.

20. Select **ProjectCurve** as the Projected reference.

21. Select **Side** in the **AirFilterHousing** geometrical set for the support surface.

22. Select **Ref Direction** in the **AirFillterHousing** geometrical set as the *Direction* reference.

23. Clear the **Nearest solution** option.

24. Click **OK**. The Multi-Result Management dialog box opens.

25. Select **keep only one sub-element using an extract** and click **OK**.

26. In the Propagation type drop-down list, select **Point continuity**.

27. Select the curve as shown in Figure 6–87.

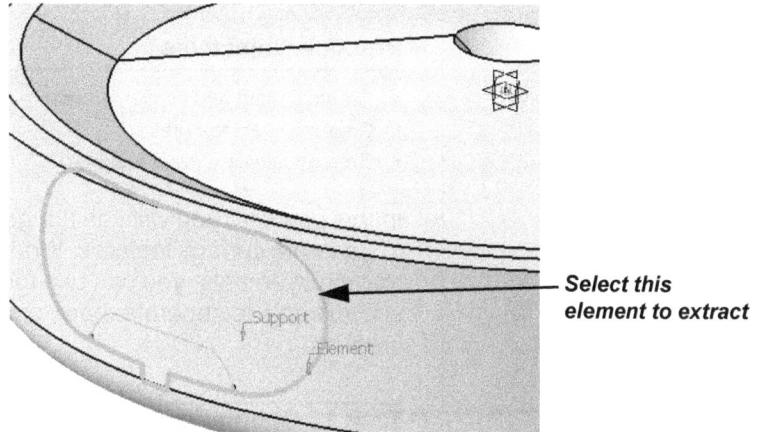

Select this
element to extract

**Figure 6–87**

28. Click **OK**.

29. Rename the Project curve as **Section3**.

30. Show the **IntakeHose** body. The completed model displays as shown in Figure 6–88.

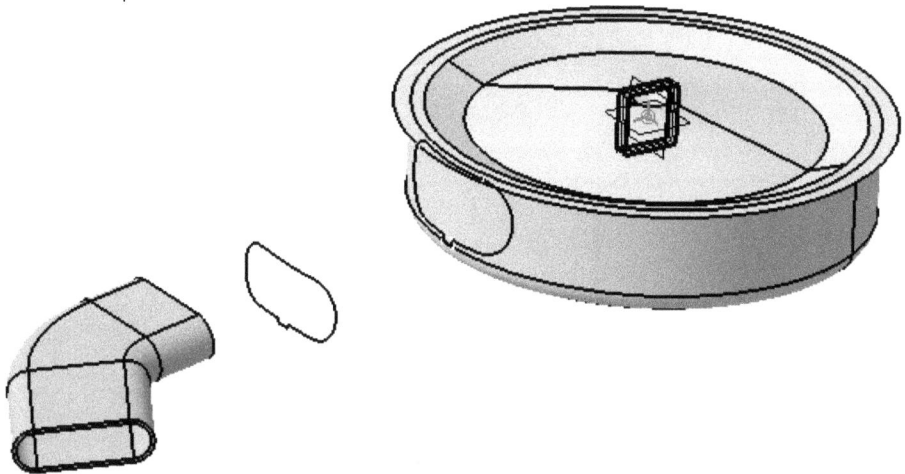

**Figure 6–88**

31. Save the model and close the file.

# Practice 6b

# Outputs and Profiles

### Practice Objectives

- Create Output and Profile features.
- Create Extract features.
- Create multiple Extract features.

In this practice, you will use the geometry of an imported sketch to generate surface features. When a sketch contains profiles for multiple elements, you can use tools (such as outputs), profiles, and extracts to separate these profiles for use in 3D geometry creation.

### Task 1 - Open a part.

1. Open **Bolt.CATPart**. The model displays as shown in Figure 6–89.

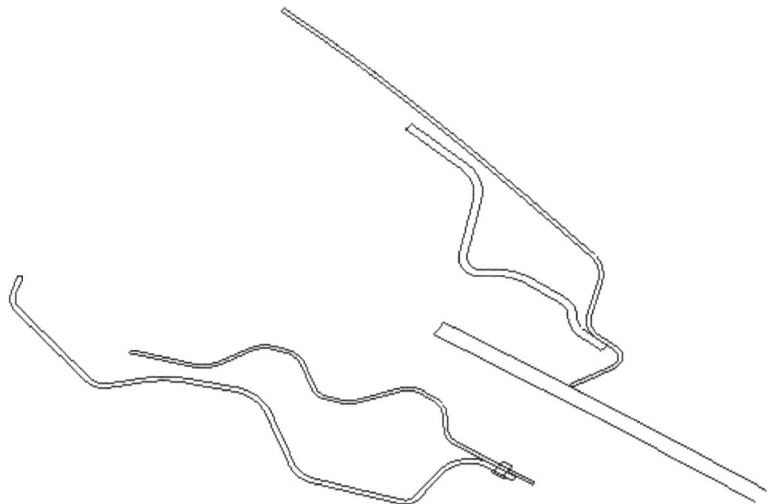

**Figure 6–89**

### Design Considerations

The model contains a single sketch that has been imported from another model. The elements contained in this sketch were created using a 2D sectioning technique. Each set of curves represent the section of a solid part. The technique brings all curves together to perform distance and clearance analysis.

Now that the sections have been approved, you will create surface and solid geometry from this data.

2. Click  (Revolve).

3. To define the profile for the revolved surface, attempt to select one of the edges belonging to the bolt section, as shown in Figure 6–90.

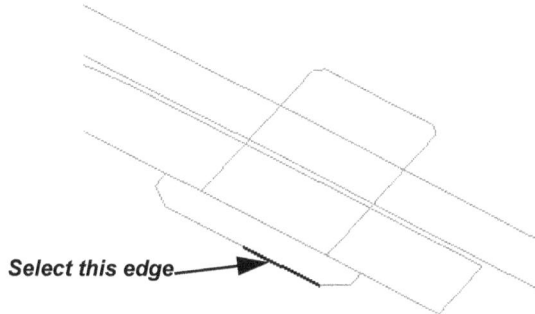

Select this edge

**Figure 6–90**

A sub-element of a sketch cannot be selected directly, so the system tries to revolve the entire sketch. Therefore, the error message shown in Figure 6–91 displays. Click **OK** to close the Update Error dialog box.

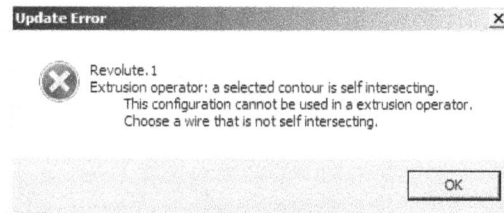

Update Error

Revolute.1
Extrusion operator: a selected contour is self intersecting.
This configuration cannot be used in a extrusion operator.
Choose a wire that is not self intersecting.

OK

**Figure 6–91**

4. Cancel the creation of the revolved surface.

**Design Considerations**

Two methods can be used to separate the sketched entities so that specific profiles can be selected to create 3D geometry.

The first method uses the **Extract** or **Multiple Extract** tool to create an associative copy of specific elements in the sketch. The result is a new feature in the specification tree. The **Extract** tool adds a unique feature for each selection, and the **Multiple Extract** tool groups all of the selections into a single feature.

The second method is to edit the sketch and use the profile and output features. This method places the resulting features beneath the sketch in the specification tree, and permits the selection of construction geometry. This method is used to develop the curves for the revolved bolt surface.

## Task 2 - Create profiles and outputs.

1. Edit the SectionProfile sketch.

2. Zoom in on the bolt geometry as shown in Figure 6–92. Note that an axis has been added to the profile. You will output the axis for use in creating the revolved surface.

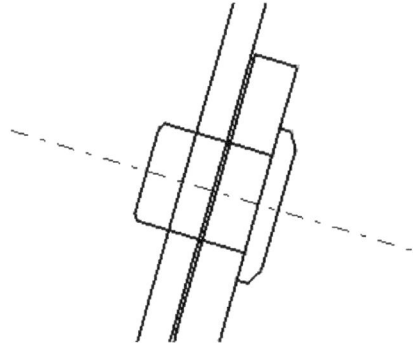

*The display of constraints and dimensions has been disabled in the Visualization toolbar to simplify the display of the section.*

**Figure 6–92**

3. In the Tools toolbar, click  (Output feature).

4. Select the axis. The system adds the profile to the **Outputs.1** branch beneath the sketch in the specification tree.

5. Rename the output as **Rotational Axis**. The specification tree displays as shown in Figure 6–93.

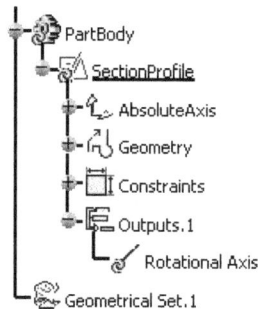

**Figure 6–93**

6. In the Tools toolbar, click  (Profile feature).

7. Select an edge in the bolt profile. The Profile Definition dialog box opens as shown in Figure 6–94.

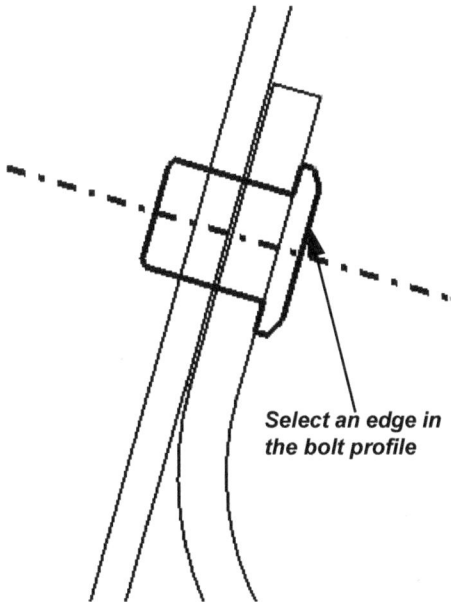

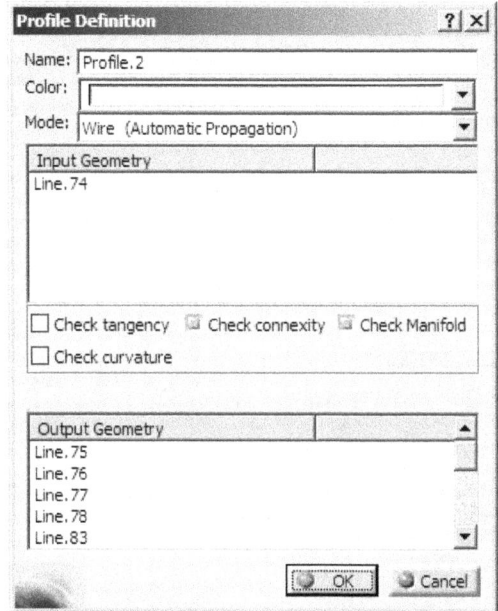

**Select an edge in the bolt profile**

**Figure 6–94**

**Design Considerations**

By default, the mode is set to **Wire (Automatic Propagation)**. Because of this, the entire bolt profile is selected. To create a revolved surface, all geometry must be to one side of the rotational axis. Therefore, you must explicitly define the elements for the profile.

8. In the Mode drop-down list, select **Wire (Explicit Definition)**. In the *Output Geometry* field, the system now only displays the selected line.

9. Select the six additional edges highlighted in Figure 6–95.

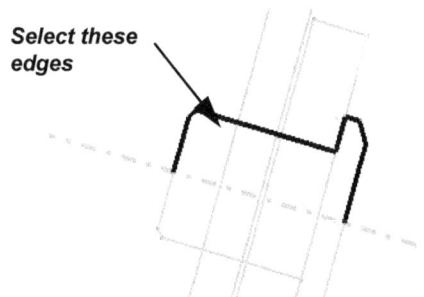

**Select these edges**

**Figure 6–95**

10. In the Color drop-down list, select the orange swatch.

11. In the *Name* field, enter **BoltProfile**. The Profile Definition dialog box updates as shown in Figure 6–96.

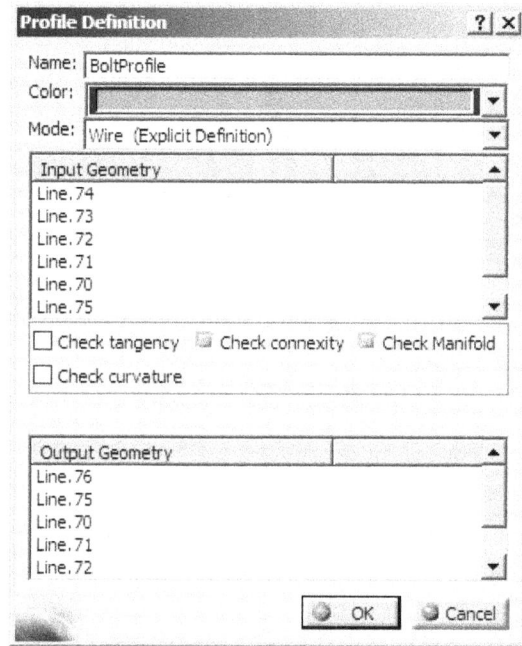

**Figure 6–96**

12. Click **OK** to complete the operation.

13. Exit Sketcher. The model displays as shown in Figure 6–97.

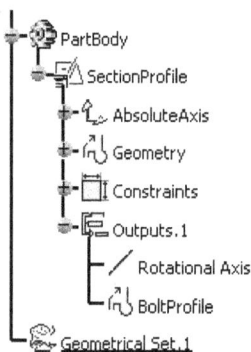

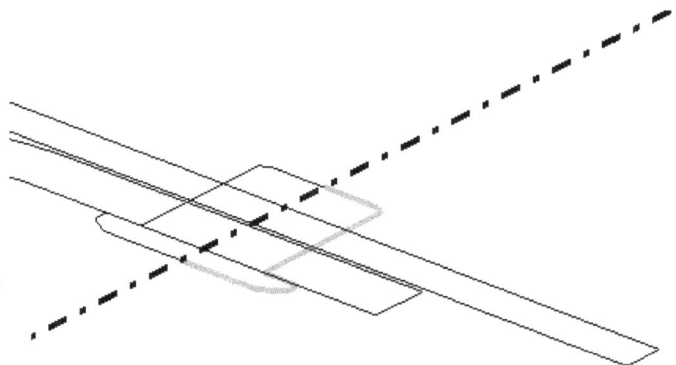

**Figure 6–97**

## Task 3 - Create a revolved surface.

1. Click  (Revolve) and specify the following parameters:

   - *Profile:* **BoltProfile**
   - *Revolution axis:* **Rotational Axis**
   - *Angle 1:* **360deg**

   The completed feature displays as shown in Figure 6–98.

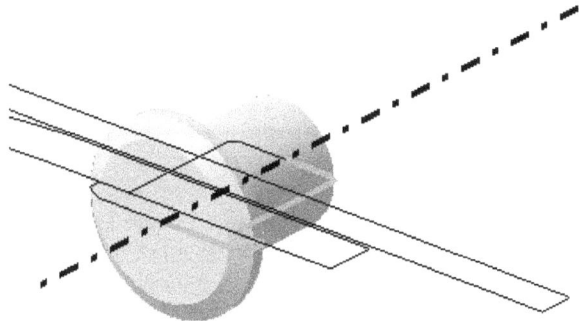

**Figure 6–98**

## Task 4 - Extract the remaining curves.

In this task, you will create a series of extract features. One extract is generated for each closed chain of curves in the sketch. This enables the extract elements to be used to develop 3D geometry for each panel in the section.

1. Click  (Extract). The Extract Definition dialog box opens, as shown in Figure 6–99.

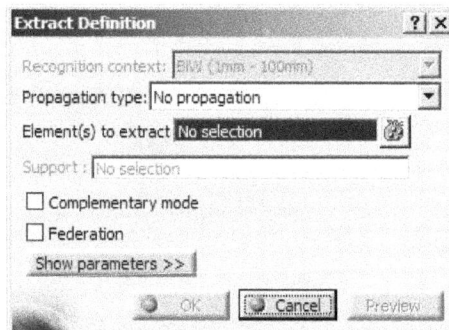

**Figure 6–99**

2. In the Propagation type drop-down list, select **Point continuity**.

3. Select the sketched edge shown in Figure 6–100. The specific edge is not relevant, but you need to verify that a vertex is not selected.

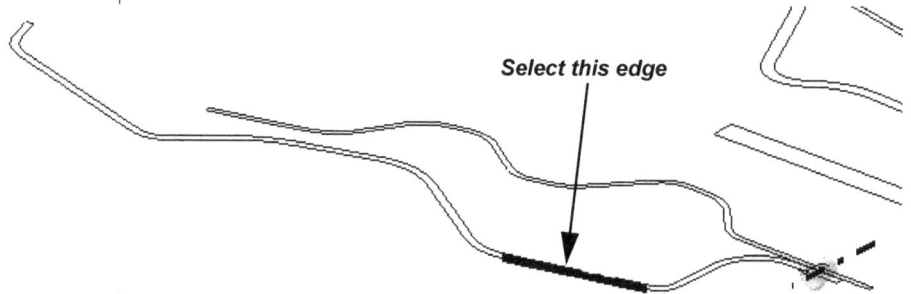

*Select this edge*

**Figure 6–100**

Based on the Point continuity propagation, the system selects all of the edges in the closed profile. Do not close the Extract Definition dialog box.

4. In the Extract dialog box, click (Choose). The Element(s) to extract dialog box opens enabling you to select multiple elements.

5. Select edges on the three other profiles shown in Figure 6–101. Based on the point continuity, the system selects the edges highlighted in Figure 6–101.

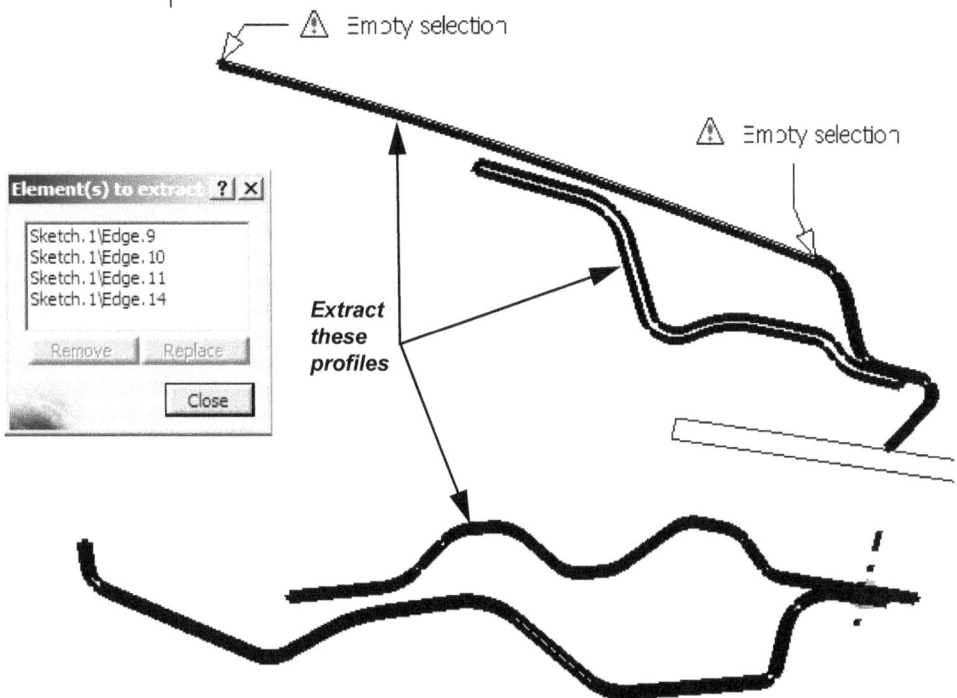

⚠ Empty selection

⚠ Empty selection

**Element(s) to extract** ? X

Sketch.1\Edge.9
Sketch.1\Edge.10
Sketch.1\Edge.11
Sketch.1\Edge.14

Remove | Replace

Close

*Extract these profiles*

**Figure 6–101**

6. Select the final edge shown in Figure 6–102.

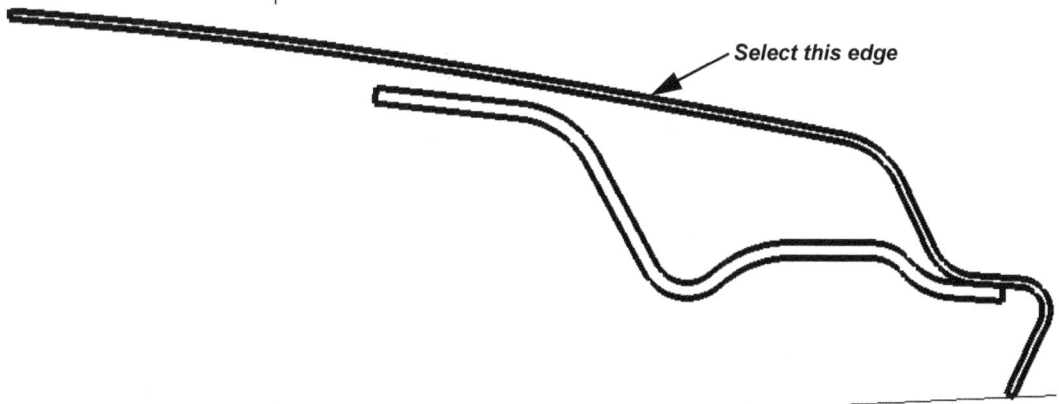

*Select this edge*

**Figure 6–102**

7. Close the Element(s) to extract dialog box and complete the Extract feature. The specification tree displays as shown in Figure 6–103. When multiple elements are extracted using the **Extract** tool, a separate feature is developed for each element.

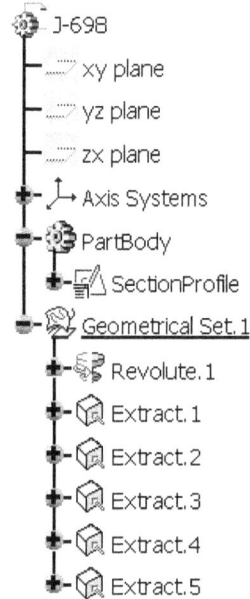

**Figure 6–103**

## Task 5 - Join curves to form the final profile.

In this task, you will join two of the extract curves to form the last profile. This profile is different than the others as the entire profile cannot be extracted together in one selection. The way the elements were created stops the profile from being selected as a continuous closed chain of edges. To resolve this, you will join two of the extract curves.

1. Click  (Join). The Join Definition dialog box opens as shown in Figure 6–104.

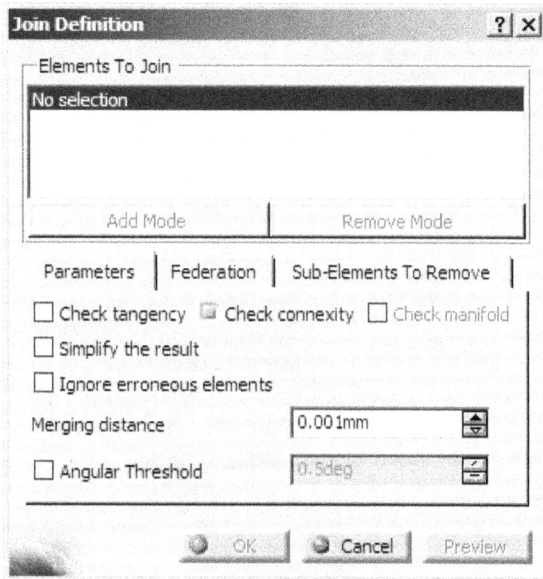

**Figure 6–104**

2. Select the appropriate extract features to create the profile shown in Figure 6–105.

3. Complete the feature.

4. Hide **PartBody**. The model displays as shown in Figure 6–105.

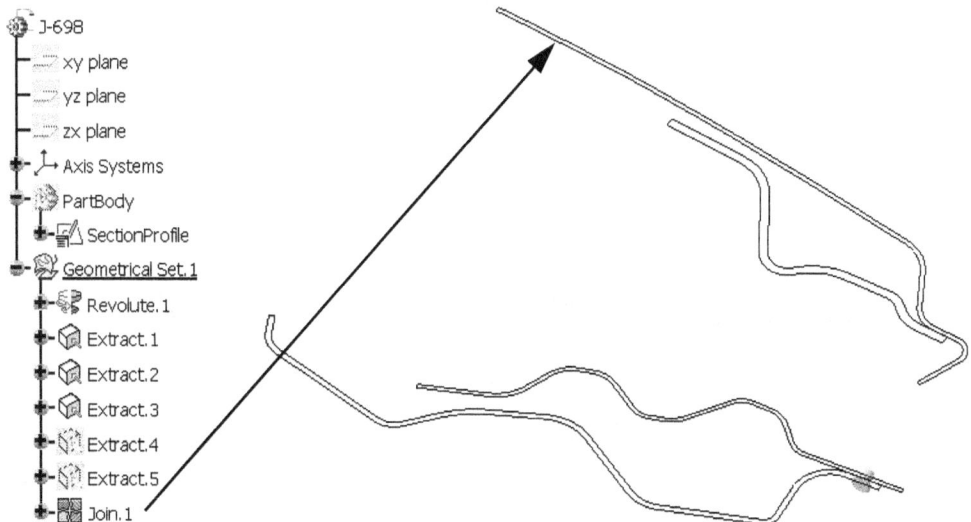

**Figure 6–105**

5. Save the model and close the window.

# Practice 6c

# Wireframe II

### Practice Objectives

- Create Output and Profile features.
- Create a helix.
- Replace wireframe elements.

In this practice, you will create a solid model of a spring. The shape of the spring is defined using a helix element that is driven by a profile to control its diameter. The helix will become the center curve for a Rib feature. Additionally, you will use Profile and Output features from the Sketcher workbench to separate elements from a *master sketch* for use in separate operations. Finally, a design change to the spring requires you to replace the profile driving the diameter of the helix with a new curve. The completed model displays as shown in Figure 6–106.

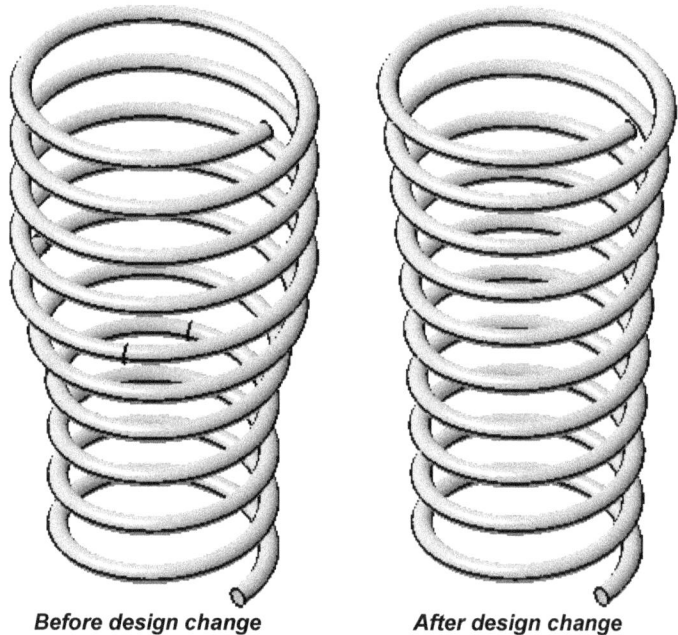

*Before design change*          *After design change*

**Figure 6–106**

### Task 1 - Create a new part.

1. Create a new part named **Spring**.

2. Insert a new geometrical set named **Construction**.

## Task 2 - Create supporting geometry for a helix.

In this task, you will define the supporting geometry required to build a helix. As a minimum, a helix requires a start point and a rotational axis.

1. Create a Coordinates point at **0, 55, 0** from the origin. Rename the point as **StartPoint**.

2. Create a line using the **Point-Direction** type. Make the following selections:

   *Create a contextual point by right-clicking in the Point 1 field and selecting **Create Point**.*

   - *Point:* **Create a contextual point at the origin**
   - *Direction:* **XY plane**
   - *Start:* **0mm**
   - *End:* **300mm**

3. Rename the line as **Rotational Axis**. The model displays as shown in Figure 6–107.

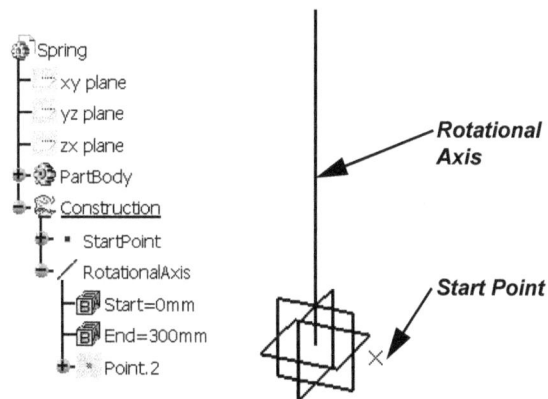

**Figure 6–107**

**Design Considerations**

The spring being created varies in diameter based on a sketched profile. The next steps generate a second point that controls the diameter at the top of the spring. A sketch is then generated that contains the profiles for the Rib feature and the helix element.

4. Create a point using the **Coordinates** option.

5. Right-click in the *Reference Point* field and select **Create Endpoint**.

6. Select the end point of the Rotational Axis line as shown in Figure 6–108.

**Figure 6–108**

7. Create the Coordinates point offset **75mm** in the Y-direction from this end point.

8. Rename the point as **EndRadius**. The model displays as shown in Figure 6–109.

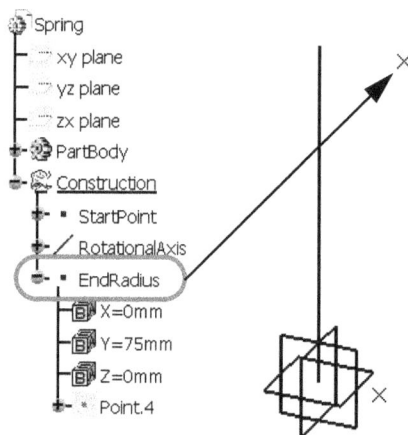

**Figure 6–109**

## Task 3 - Create a sketch containing two profiles.

In this task, you will build a sketch that contains two profiles. The first profile is used to control the shape of the helix, while the other one is used as the profile for a future Rib feature. For simplicity, these profiles are placed in the same sketch and then separated using the **Profile** and **Output** tools.

1. Create a positioned sketch on the YZ plane. Place the sketch origin on StartPoint.

2. Sketch the profile shown in Figure 6–110. Make the top of the profile coincident with EndRadius.

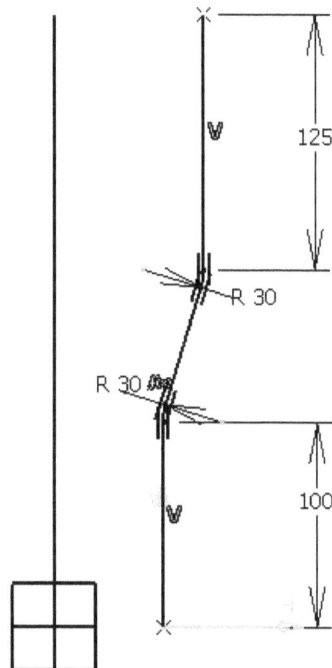

**Figure 6–110**

3. In the Tools toolbar, click  (Profile).

4. Verify that the Wire (Automatic Propagation) mode type is selected.

5. Select one of the sketched elements. The Profile Definition dialog box opens as shown in Figure 6–111. According to the current propagation mode, the system has added all of the sketched geometry to the *Output Geometry* field.

*Note that the order in which the elements display may vary depending on how you sketched the geometry.*

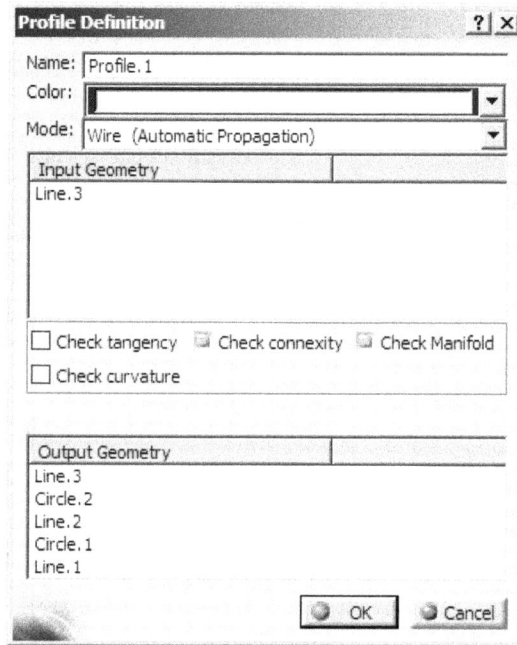

**Figure 6–111**

6. Make the following selections:

   • *Name:* **Helix Radius Profile**
   • *Color:* Select the yellow color in the drop-down list

7. Click **OK**. The new profile is added to the specification tree as shown in Figure 6–112. Do not exit Sketcher.

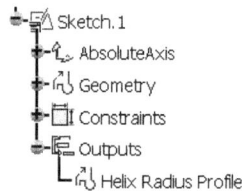

**Figure 6–112**

Note that the color change applied to the profile does not take effect until you have exited the Sketcher workbench. This is because the green color of the fully constrained profile overrides this color change in the Sketcher workbench. If you want to display the applied color, disable ⬛ (Diagnostics) in the Visualization toolbar.

8. Sketch a **10mm** diameter circle that is centered on **StartPoint**. This is the profile of the Rib feature used to create the solid spring.

9. In the Tools toolbar, click 🗎 (Output) and select the circle that you just sketched. The system adds the output to the Outputs branch in the specification tree, as shown in Figure 6–113.

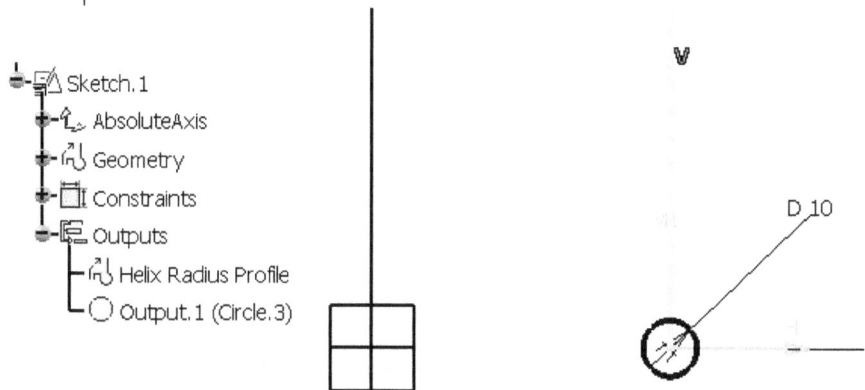

**Figure 6–113**

10. Exit from Sketcher.

11. Rename *Sketch.1* as **Profiles**.

It is important to note that the Profiles sketch might not be used to generate a feature. The Output and Profile elements are contained by this sketch and can only be modified by modifying the sketch. However, no geometry is in the actual sketch. This is because the Output elements are removed from the sketch and become unique wireframe elements.

**Task 4 - Create a helix.**

1. Click ⬚ (Helix). The Helix Curve Definition dialog box opens as shown in Figure 6–114.

**Figure 6–114**

2. Make the following selections:

   • *Helix Type:* **Height and Pitch**
   • *Pitch:* **30mm**
   • *Starting Point:* **StartPoint**
   • *Axis:* **Rotational Axis**

3. To define the height of the helix, right-click in the *Height* field and select **Edit formula**, as shown in Figure 6–115.

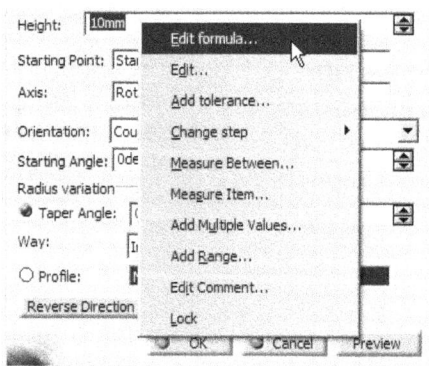

**Figure 6–115**

4.  Define a formula for the height so that it is equal to the length of the Rotational Axis by selecting the endpoint of the RotationAxis curve. The Formula Editor dialog box opens as shown in Figure 6–116.

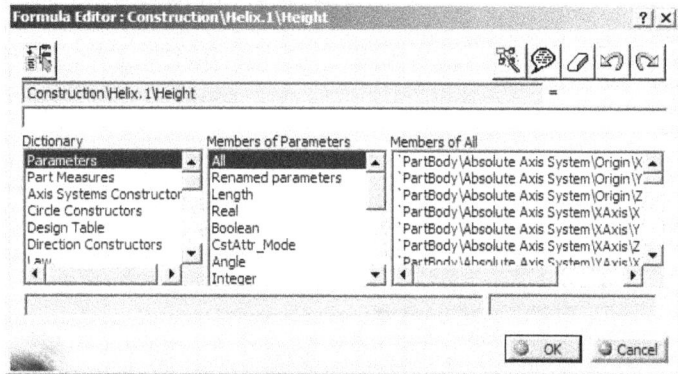

**Figure 6–116**

5.  Click **OK** in the Formula Editor.

6.  In the Helix Curve Definition dialog box, select **Profile** and select **Helix Radius Profile** in the Outputs branch in the Profiles sketch.

7.  Click **OK** and the model displays as shown in Figure 6–117.

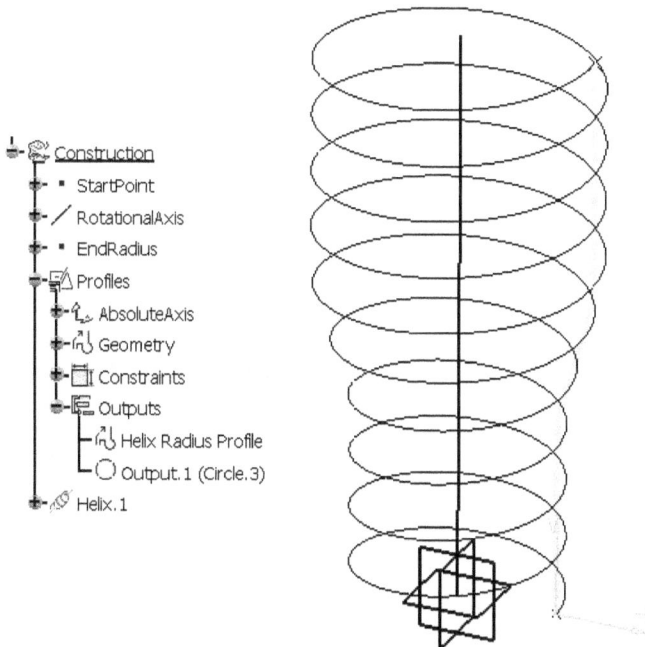

**Figure 6–117**

## Task 5 - Create a Rib feature.

In this task, you will create a solid Rib feature. The profile for the Rib uses the circle output while the center curve uses the helix.

1. Define **PartBody** as the work object.

2. Activate the Part Design workbench.

3. Create a Rib feature using the following parameters:

    • *Profile:* **Output.1**
    • *Center curve:* **Helix.1**

4. Click **OK** to complete the feature. The model displays as shown in Figure 6–118.

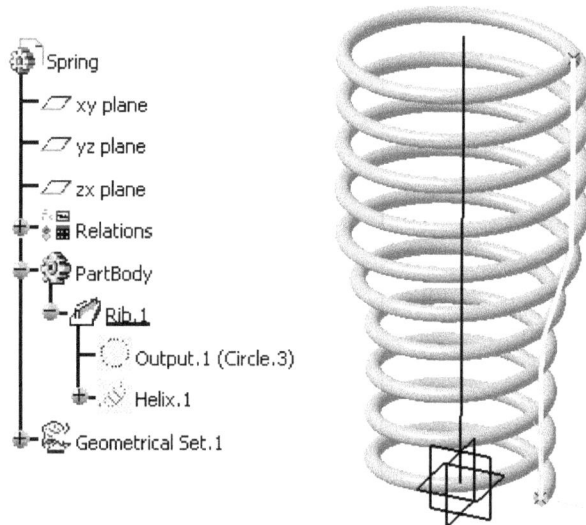

**Figure 6–118**

## Task 6 - Perform a design change.

In this task, you will create a new profile to control the radius of the helix. This curve replaces the Helix Radius Profile from the Profiles sketch.

1. Activate the Generative Shape Design workbench.

2. Create a spline using the following parameters:

    • *Point 1:* **StartPoint**
    • *Tangency reference:* **XY plan**e
    • *Point 2:* **EndRadius**

The model displays as shown in Figure 6–119.

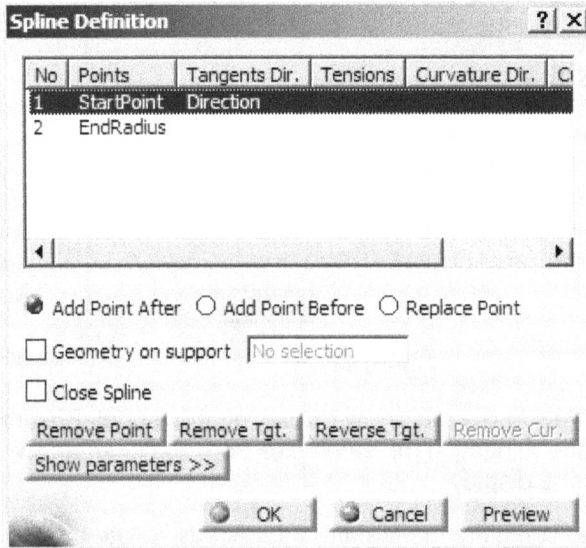

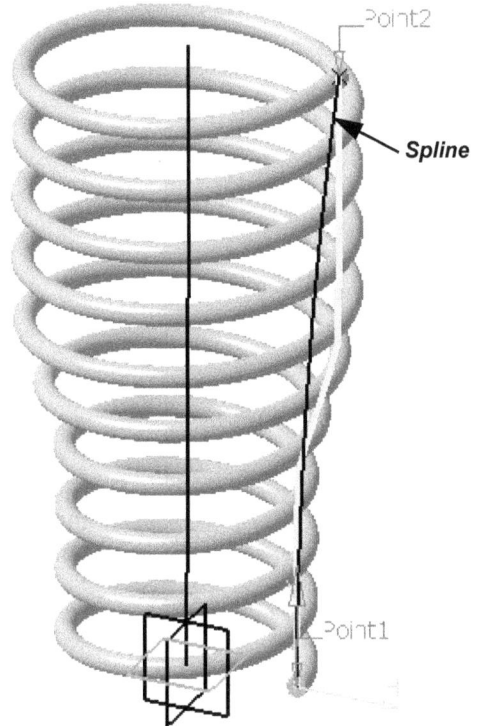

**Spline Definition**

| No | Points | Tangents Dir. | Tensions | Curvature Dir. | Cu |
|----|--------|---------------|----------|----------------|----|
| 1 | StartPoint | Direction | | | |
| 2 | EndRadius | | | | |

● Add Point After  ○ Add Point Before  ○ Replace Point

☐ Geometry on support  No selection

☐ Close Spline

Remove Point   Remove Tgt.   Reverse Tgt.   Remove Cur.

Show parameters >>

OK    Cancel    Preview

**Figure 6–119**

3. Rename the spline as **Helix Radius Profile 02**.

4. Right-click on Helix Radius Profile and select **Replace**, as shown in Figure 6–120.

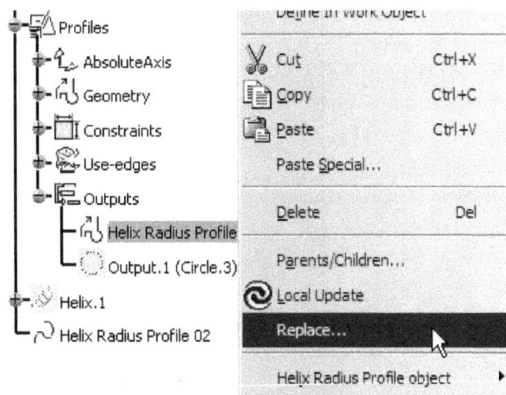

**Figure 6–120**

5. Select **Helix Radius Profile 02**. The Replace dialog box opens as shown in Figure 6–121.

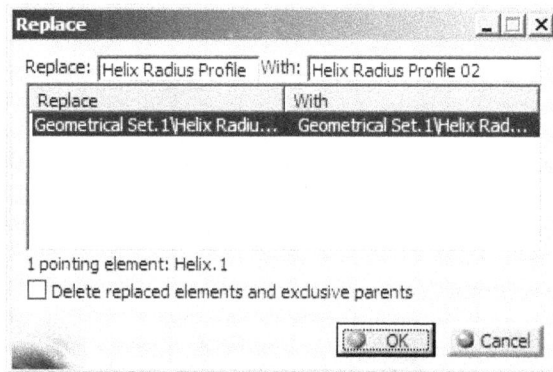

**Figure 6–121**

6. A green arrow and a red arrow display on the model. Ensure that they are pointing in the same direction. To flip an arrow, select it in the display.

7. Click **OK** to complete the feature. If required, update the model.

8. Hide all of the wireframe elements. The model displays as shown in Figure 6–122.

**Figure 6–122**

9. Save the model and close the window.

# Practice 6d

# Wireframe III

## Practice Objectives

- Intersect surfaces to develop curves.
- Project wireframe onto a surface.
- Create parallel curves.
- Trim curves using the Pieces method.
- Join curves and surfaces.

In this practice, you will create the phone cover shown in Figure 6–123.

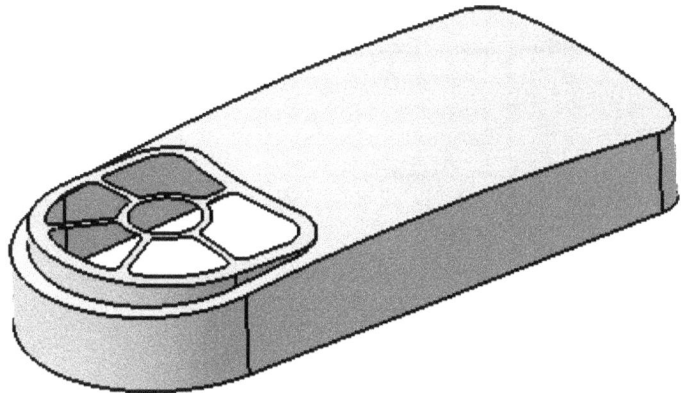

**Figure 6–123**

The cover consists of four surfaces that are trimmed and joined together. The first two surfaces, TopSurf and SideSurf, are provided with the start model for the practice. Your task is to construct the keypad surfaces using a variety of wireframe elements and operations.

## Task 1 - Open a part.

1. Open **PhoneMaster.CATPart**. The model displays as shown in Figure 6–124.

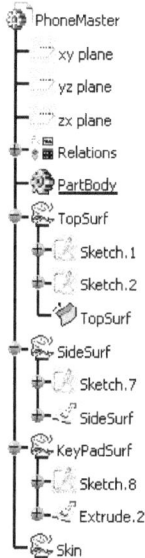

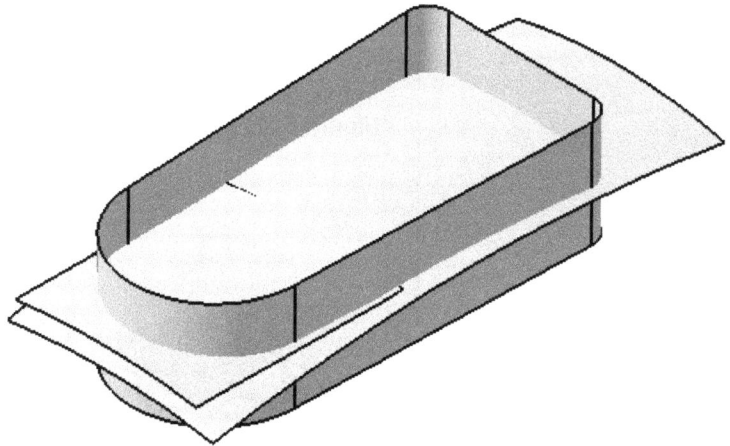

Figure 6–124

2. Investigate the model by expanding the various geometrical sets. The model consists of three surfaces that are used to create **TopSurf**, **SideSurf**, and **Extrude.2** (which will be used to create the keypad surfaces), as shown in Figure 6–125. An empty geometrical set named **Skin** will be used to contain the finished cover surface.

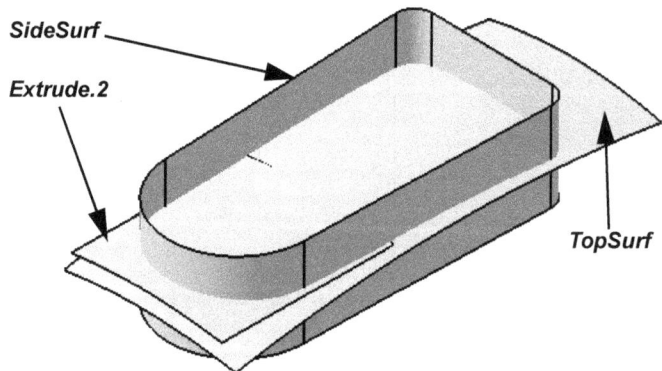

Figure 6–125

3. Activate the **KeyPadSurf** geometrical set.

## Task 2 - Define the profile for the keypad surface.

In this task, you will use a variety of wireframe and operation tools to create the shape of the keypad surface. The completed curve displays as shown in Figure 6–126.

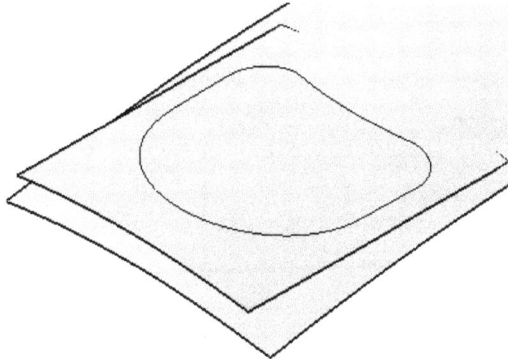

**Figure 6–126**

1. Hide **Extrude.2**.

2. Click [icon] (Intersection) and specify the following parameters:

   • *First Element:* **TopSurf**
   • *Second Element:* **SideSurf**

   The model displays as shown in Figure 6–127.

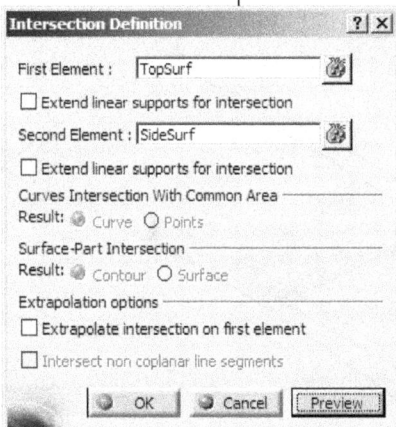

**Intersection Definition**

First Element : TopSurf
☐ Extend linear supports for intersection
Second Element : SideSurf
☐ Extend linear supports for intersection
Curves Intersection With Common Area
Result: ⦿ Curve ○ Points
Surface-Part Intersection
Result: ⦿ Contour ○ Surface
Extrapolation options
☐ Extrapolate intersection on first element
☐ Intersect non coplanar line segments

OK     Cancel     Preview

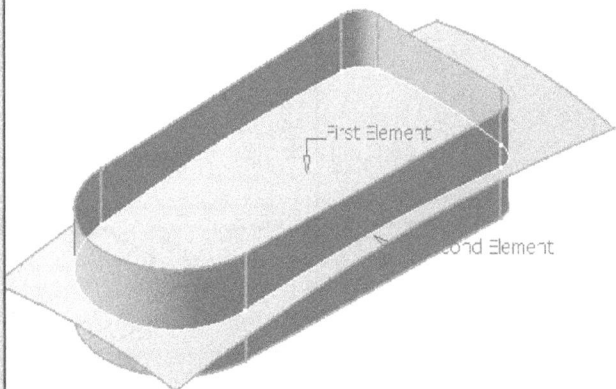

**Figure 6–127**

3. Hide the **SideSurf** geometrical set.

4. Click  (Parallel Curve) and specify the following parameters:

- *Curve:* **Intersect.1**
- *Support:* **TopSurf**
- *Constant:* **2mm**

Verify that the direction arrow is pointing to the inside of the profile, as shown in Figure 6–128.

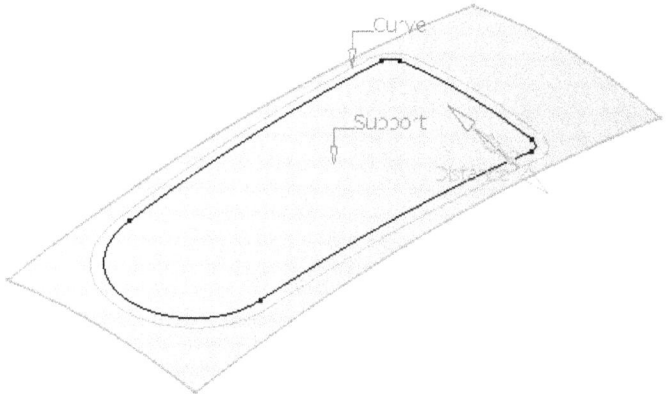

**Figure 6–128**

5. Hide **Intersect.1**.

6. Show **Extrude.2** in the **KeyPadSurf** geometrical set.

7. Create an intersection between **Extrude.2** and TopSurf. The model displays as shown in Figure 6–129.

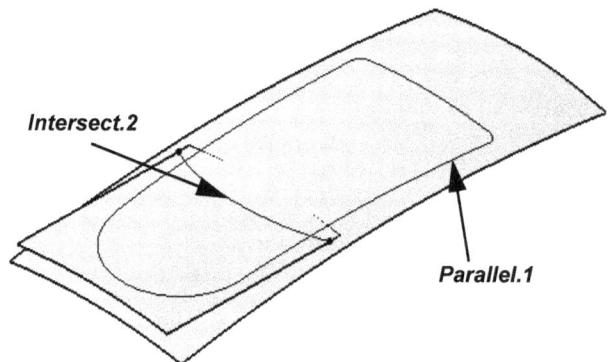

**Figure 6–129**

8. Click [icon] (Corner) and specify the following parameters as shown in Figure 6–130:

- *Corner Type:* **Corner On Support**
- *Element 1:* **Parallel.1**
- Clear the **Trim element 1** option.
- *Element 2:* **Intersect.2**
- Clear the **Trim element 2** option.
- *Support:* **TopSurf**
- *Radius:* **5mm**

The model displays as shown in Figure 6–130.

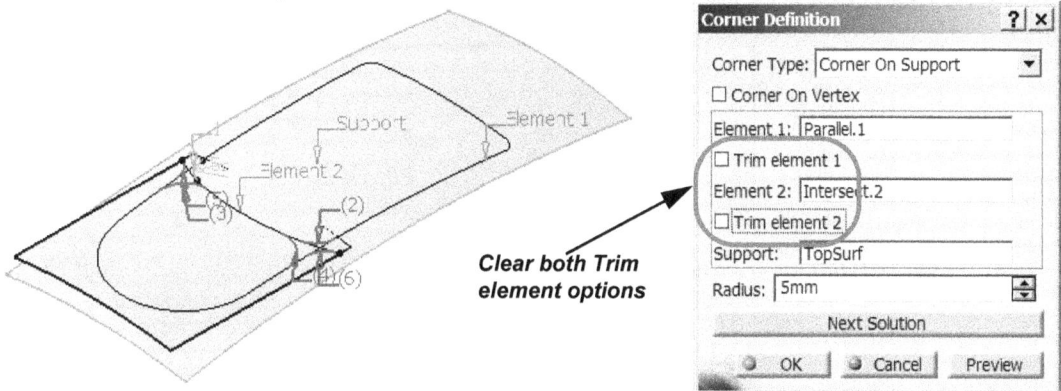

**Figure 6–130**

9. Click **Next Solution** to obtain the result shown in Figure 6–131.

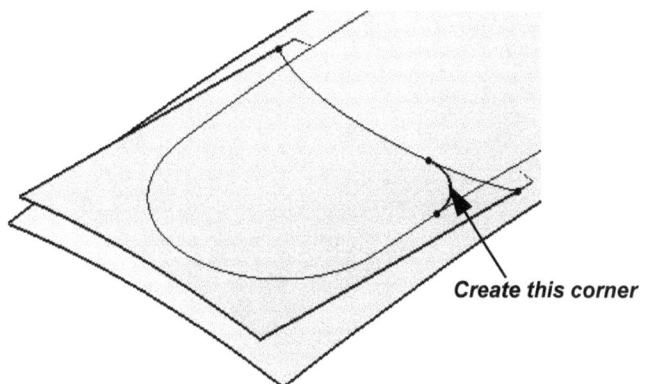

**Figure 6–131**

10. Copy the new corner feature and paste it into the model. This creates **Corner.2**.

11. Edit **Corner.2** and use **Next Solution** to create the result shown in Figure 6–132.

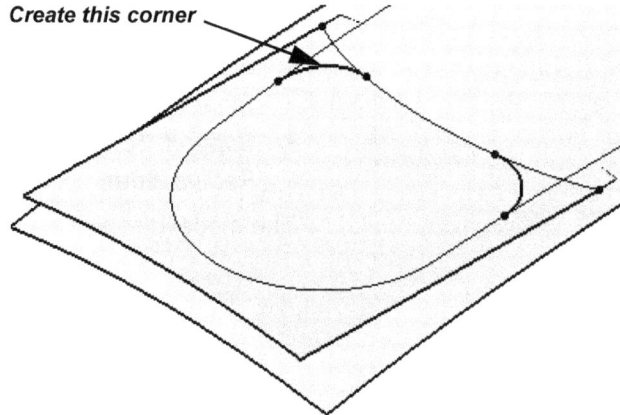

*Create this corner*

**Figure 6–132**

12. Click ⬚ (Trim). In the Mode drop-down list, select **Pieces**. The Trim Definition dialog box opens as shown in Figure 6–133.

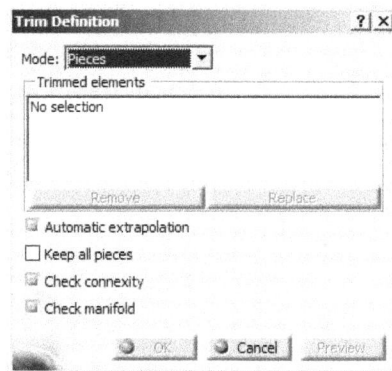

**Figure 6–133**

13. Select the elements shown in Figure 6–134. Although the order of selection is not important, verify that you have selected the indicated side of each element. The **Trim Pieces** tool keeps the side of the element that is selected.

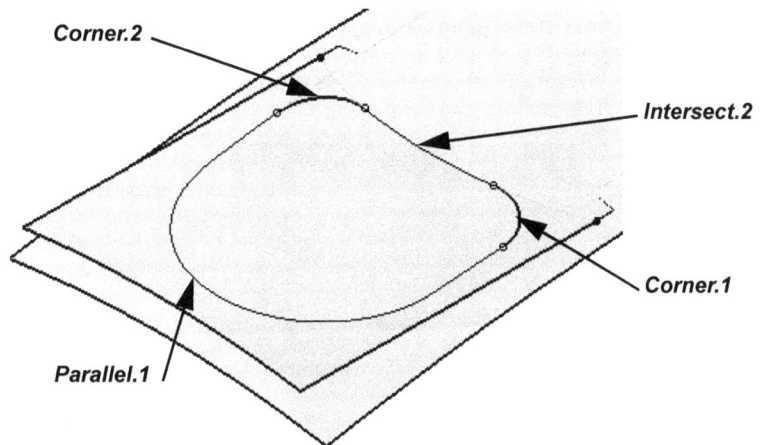

**Figure 6–134**

14. Complete the feature. The model displays as shown in Figure 6–135.

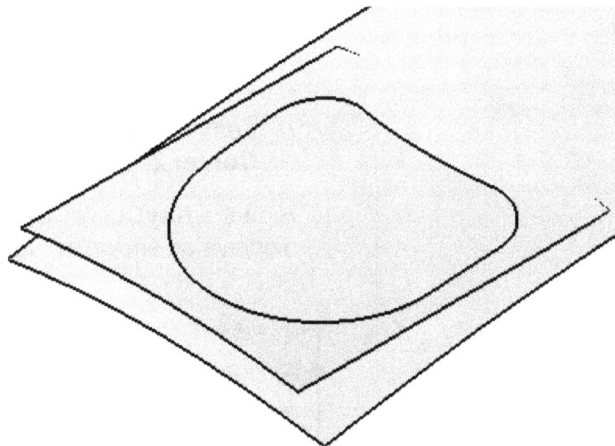

**Figure 6–135**

15. Click  (Projection) and specify the following parameters:

- *Projection type:* **Normal**
- *Projected:* **Trim.1**
- *Support:* **Extrude.2**

The model displays as shown in Figure 6–136.

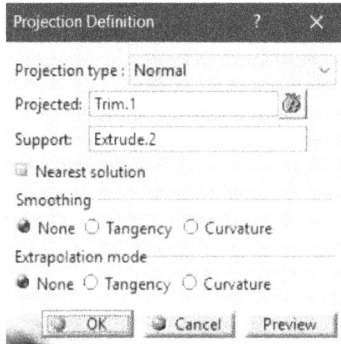

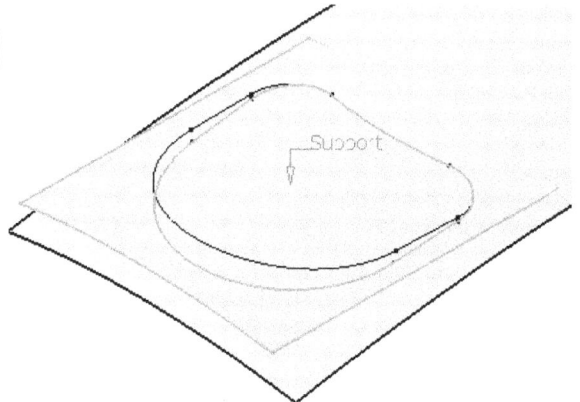

**Figure 6–136**

16. Create a new geometrical set using the following parameters:

- *Name:* **KeyCurveConstr**
- *Father:* **KeyPadSurf**
- *Features:* **Intersect.1**, **Parallel.1**, **Intersect.2**, **Corner.1**, **Corner.2**, or **Trim.1**

17. Hide the **KeyCurveConstr** geometrical set. The model displays as shown in Figure 6–137.

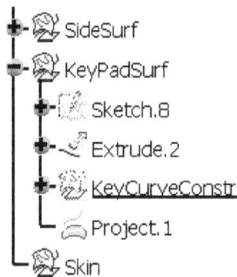

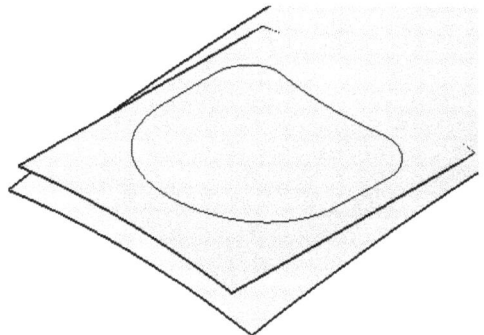

**Figure 6–137**

## Task 3 - Create the keypad geometry.

In this task, you will incorporate geometry for the keypad buttons into the keypad surface. The button geometry is imported into the model using a STEP file. The curves are then grouped using extract features and projected onto **Extrude.2**, so that they can be trimmed from the surface.

1. Open **KeyPad_Profiles.CATPart**. The model displays as shown in Figure 6–138.

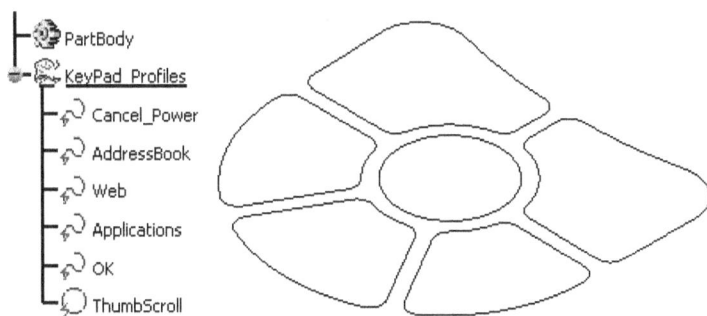

**Figure 6–138**

2. Copy the **KeyPad_Profiles** geometrical set.

3. Activate the **PhoneMaster.CATPart** window and paste the geometrical set into the **KeyPadSurf** geometrical set. The specification tree displays as shown in Figure 6–139.

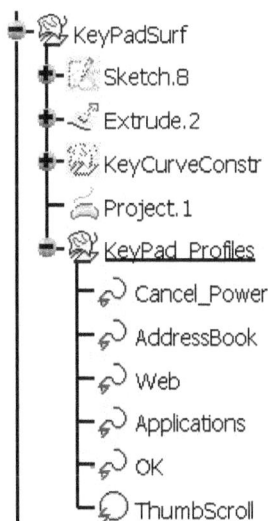

**Figure 6–139**

4. Click ⬛ (Join). The Join Definition dialog box opens, as shown in Figure 6–140.

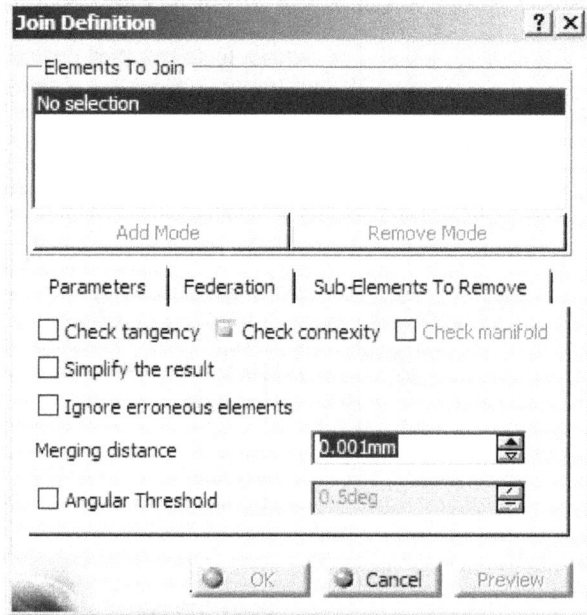

**Figure 6–140**

5. Select the six isolated curves contained in the **KeyPad_Profiles** geometrical set.

6. Click **Preview**. The error message shown in Figure 6–141 opens. By default, the **Join** tool checks that all of the selected elements are connected. Since the keypad curves are disconnected, you need to configure the tool to enable this.

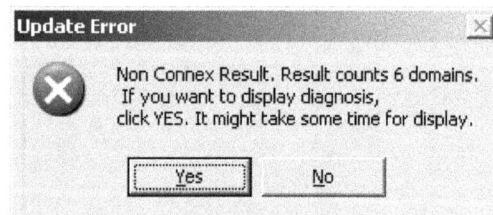

**Figure 6–141**

7. Click **No**.

8. Clear the **Check Connexity** option and complete the feature.

9. Rename the Join feature as **KeyPadProfiles**. The model displays as shown in Figure 6–142.

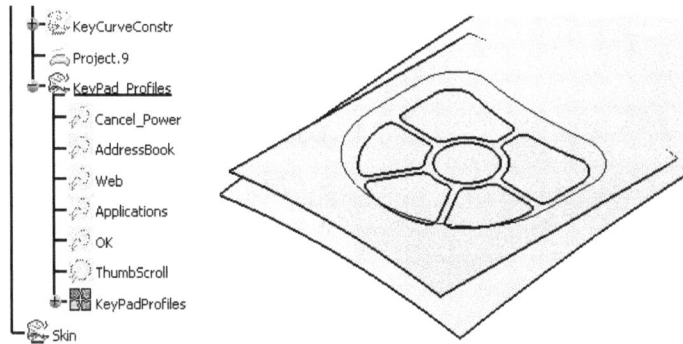

**Figure 6–142**

10. Activate the **KeyPadSurf** geometrical set.

11. Click ⬚ (Projection) and specify the following parameters:

- *Projection type:* **Normal**
- *Projected:* **KeyPadProfiles**
- *Support:* **Extrude.2**
- Verify that the **Nearest solution** option is disabled.

12. Complete the feature.

13. Select the **keep all sub-elements** option and click **OK**.

14. Hide the **KeyPad_Profiles** geometrical set. The model displays as shown in Figure 6–143.

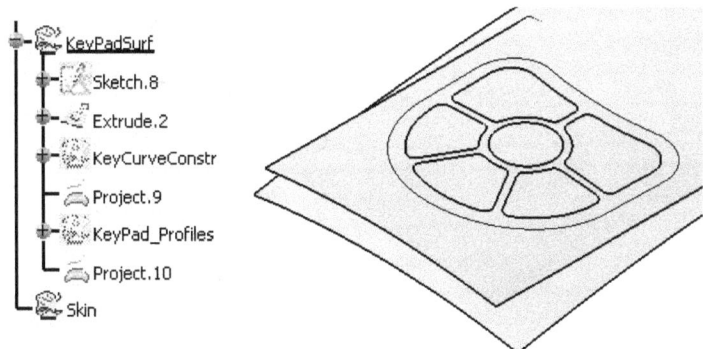

**Figure 6–143**

*For multiple closed profiles, the **Nearest Solution** option must be disabled.*

## Task 4 - Split the keypad surface.

In this task, you will use the two projected curves to split the keypad surface.

1. Click ![Split icon] (Split) and specify the following parameters:

   • *Element to cut:* **Extrude.2**
   • *Cutting elements:* **Project.1, Project.2**

   Select the correct side to obtain the result shown in Figure 6–144.

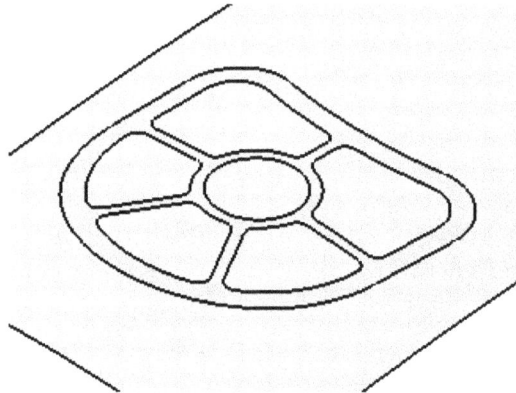

**Figure 6–144**

2. Rename the Split feature as **KeyPadSurf**.

## Task 5 - Create additional surfaces.

1. Show **Project.1**. This is the curve that defines the outside profile of the keypad surface. This profile is extruded downward to create the side surface of the keypad.

2. Create an extruded surface using the following parameters:

   • *Profile:* **Project.1**
   • *Direction:* **XY plane**
   • *Limit 1:* **10mm**

Verify that the direction arrow is pointing downward and complete the feature. The model displays as shown in Figure 6–145.

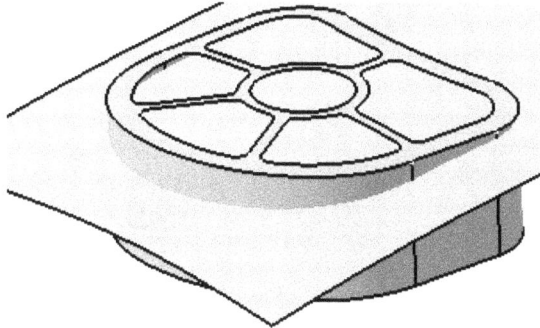

**Figure 6–145**

3. Rename the extruded surface as **KeyPadSide**.

## Task 6 - Trim the surfaces.

1. Activate the **Skin** geometrical set.

2. Click ⬚ (Trim). Verify that the mode is set to **Standard**.

3. Select **TopSurf** and **KeyPadSide**. Toggle **Other side / next element** and/or **Other side / previous element** to obtain the result shown in Figure 6–146.

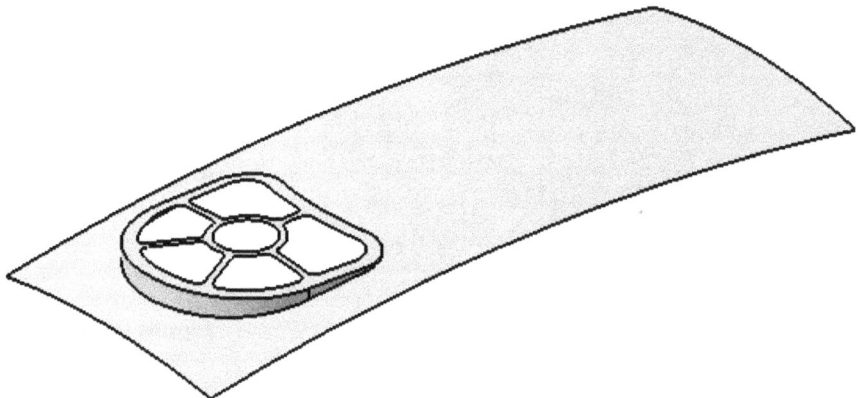

**Figure 6–146**

4. Show the **SideSurf** geometrical set.

5. Trim SideSurf to Trim.2 (just created). The model displays as shown in Figure 6–147.

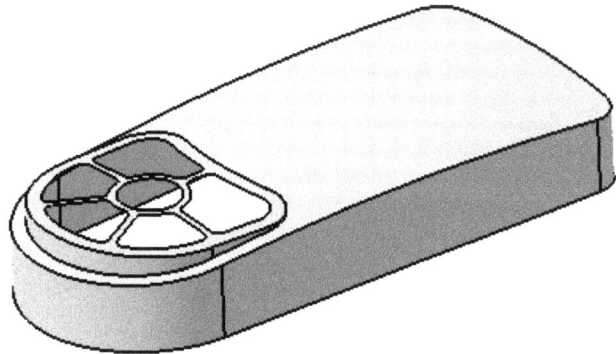

**Figure 6–147**

6. Click [icon] (Join) and join **Trim.3 to KeyPadSurf**.

7. Rename the Join feature as **PhoneMaster**. The model displays as shown in Figure 6–148.

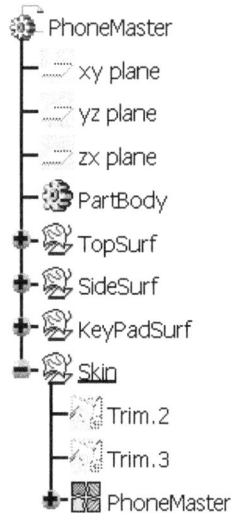

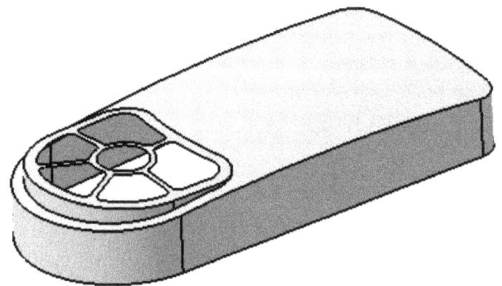

PhoneMaster
- xy plane
- yz plane
- zx plane
- PartBody
- TopSurf
- SideSurf
- KeyPadSurf
- Skin
  - Trim.2
  - Trim.3
  - PhoneMaster

**Figure 6–148**

8. Save and close the file.

# Chapter Review Questions

1. A Projection curve enables you to project a curve onto a surface, provided that surface is planar.

   a. True

   b. False

2. The following is used to create an Intersection curve:

   a.

   b.

   c.

   d. None of the above.

3. When creating a Helix, the _____ represents the distance between helix revolutions.

   a. Height

   b. Taper

   c. Pitch

   d. Profile

4. When creating a Contour curve, if the curves do not form a closed loop, you must manually create additional curves to close the loop.

   a. True

   b. False

5. When creating an Extract curve, each selected curve creates a separate extract feature in the specification tree.

   a. True

   b. False

6. With the **Split** operation, the cutting element stays whole. With the **Trim** operation, both elements are affected.

   a. True

   b. False

7. The **Join** option connects multiple curves end to end.

   a. True

   b. False

8. A sketcher Output feature lets you output selected entities from a sketch, rather than the entire sketch, for use in feature creation.

   a. True

   a. False

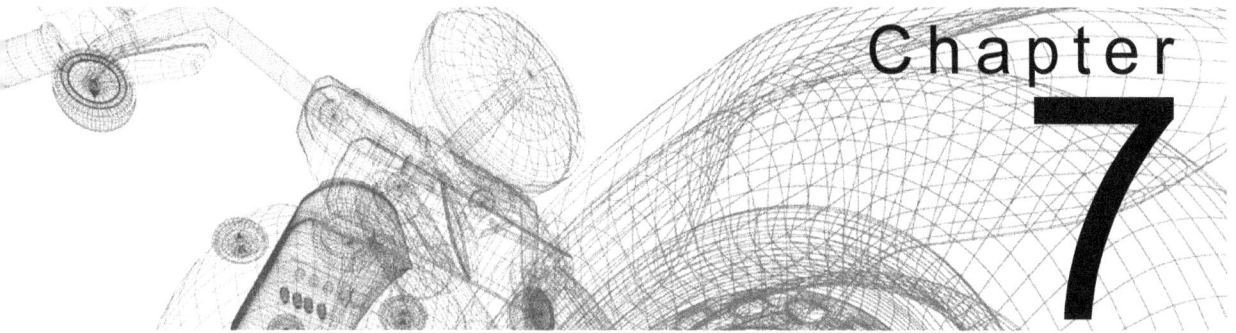

# Chapter 7

# Complex Surfaces I

Complex surfaces are created similar to simple surfaces. They enable you to add more control and definition to a part. This chapter discusses the methods used to create complex surfaces.

## Learning Objectives in this Chapter

- Create Swept surfaces.
- Create Explicit Profile surfaces.
- Use Line Profiles.
- Use Circle Profiles.

# 7.1 Swept Surfaces

The **Advanced Swept Surface** options enable you to use a variety of reference geometry to further control the swept feature.

**General Steps**

Use the following general steps to create an Advanced Swept Surface feature:

1. Start the creation of a swept surface.
2. Select curve geometry to define the sweep.
3. Specify optional elements.
4. Complete the feature.

> **Step 1 - Start the creation of a swept surface.**

To start the creation of a swept surface feature, click

 (Sweep) in the Surfaces toolbar. The Swept Definition dialog box opens as shown in Figure 7–1.

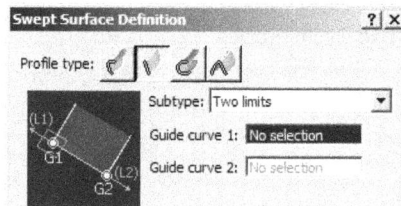

**Figure 7–1**

Select a *Profile type* at the top of the dialog box and a Subtype (if required).

The options available for a swept surface depend on the *Profile type* and *Subtype* selected. The common used options are described as follows:

| Profile type | Subtype | Subtype |
|---|---|---|
| (Explicit) | | Profile is defined by selecting curve in model. |
| | With reference surface | Surface is defined by selecting guide curve for profile. An angle with respect to a reference surface is also specified. |
| | With two guide curves | Surface is defined by two guide curves. |
| | With pulling direction | Surface is defined by guide curve and pulling direction for profile. |
| (Line) | | Profile is defined by straight line. The following subtypes determine how the line is generated. |
| | With reference surface | Line is defined by specifying length and angle with respect to reference surface. |
| (Circle) | | Profile is defined by arc or circle. The following subtypes determine how the arc or circle is generated. |
| | Center and radius | Profile is a circle. The center of the circle is defined by a guide curve and the radius is entered. |

## Step 2 - Select curve geometry to define the sweep.

Depending on the selections made in Step 1, the sweep definition might require you to select a variety of reference geometry. This geometry can include reference points, lines or planes, surfaces or faces, or other wireframe elements. For example, an Explicit profile requires the selection of a profile curve and guide curve.

## Step 3 - Specify optional elements.

Use the optional elements in the Swept Surface Definition dialog box to further define the shape of the swept surface. The optional elements available depend on the selections made in Step 1. Optional elements that are common to most types of swept surfaces are described as follows:

| Option | Description |
|---|---|
| **Spine** | Keeps the cross-section of the swept surface normal to the spine. To define a spine, select an edge, curve, or sketch. If a spine is not selected, the system automatically calculates a default spine. Usually, the first curve selected. |
| **Solution(s)** | Enables you to toggle between the available solutions (if more than one exists) to select the required swept surface. |

## Step 4 - Complete the feature.

Click **OK** to complete the feature. You can create the following types of swept surfaces:

- Explicit Profile - With Reference Surface

- Explicit Profile - With Two Guide Curves

- Explicit Profile - With Pulling Direction

- Line Profile - With Reference Surface

- Circle Profile - Center and Radius

# 7.2 Explicit Profile - With Reference Surface

A **With reference surface** explicit profile enables you to define the profile by selecting a curve in the model. With this type of Swept feature, you can add drafts by specifying a reference surface and an angle. An example of the required inputs is shown in Figure 7–2.

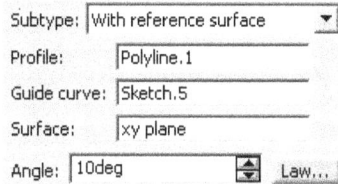

**Figure 7–2**

An explicit swept surface is shown on the left in Figure 7–3. A 10° angle is added to the surface using the top surface as a reference, as shown on the right.

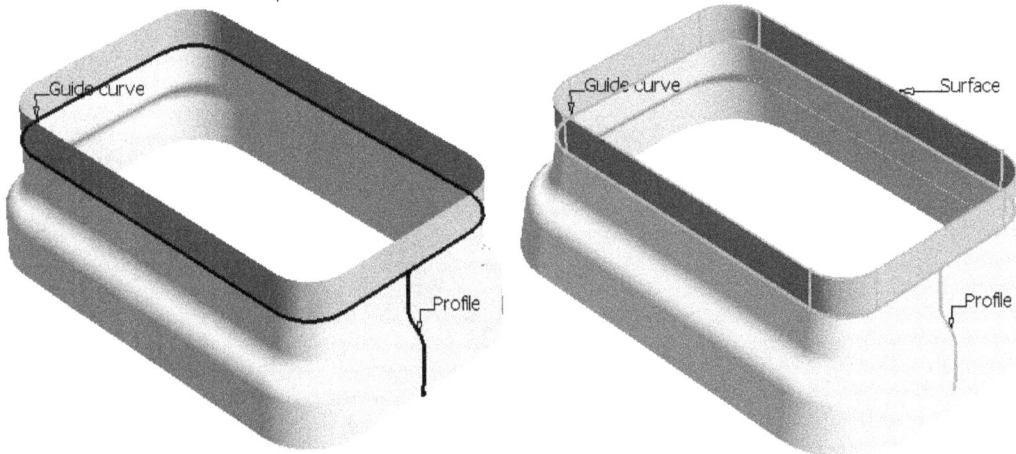

**Figure 7–3**

# 7.3 Explicit Profile - With Two Guide Curves

The **With two guide curves** explicit profile enables you to add an additional guide curve to control the shape of the swept surface at another point along the profile. An example of the required inputs is shown in Figure 7–4.

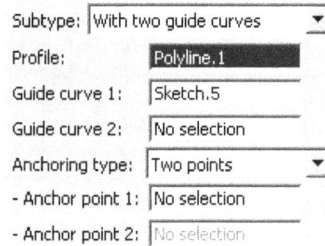

| | |
|---|---|
| Subtype: | With two guide curves ▼ |
| Profile: | Polyline.1 |
| Guide curve 1: | Sketch.5 |
| Guide curve 2: | No selection |
| Anchoring type: | Two points ▼ |
| - Anchor point 1: | No selection |
| - Anchor point 2: | No selection |

**Figure 7–4**

The selected guide curve can intersect the profile at any point. There must be an intersection between the guide curve and the profile. An example is shown in Figure 7–5.

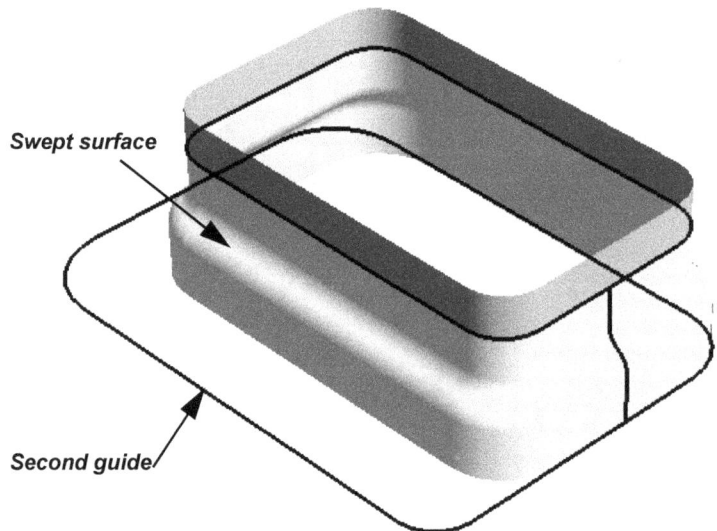

*Swept surface*

*Second guide*

**Figure 7–5**

The model updates to use the guide curve to control the shape of the resulting swept surface, as shown in Figure 7–6.

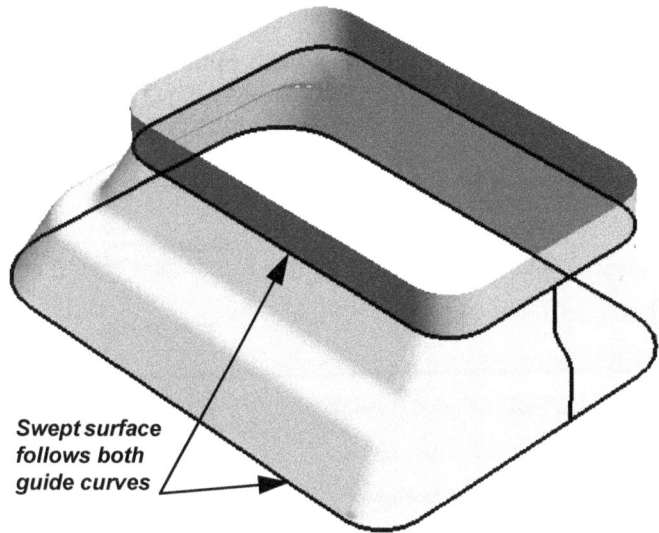

**Swept surface follows both guide curves**

**Figure 7–6**

# 7.4 Explicit Profile - With Pulling Direction

The **With pulling direction** explicit profile enables you to define the sweep using a guide curve and a direction. The profile of the swept surface is defined to follow the guide curve, at an angle to the specified direction. An example of the required inputs is shown in Figure 7–7.

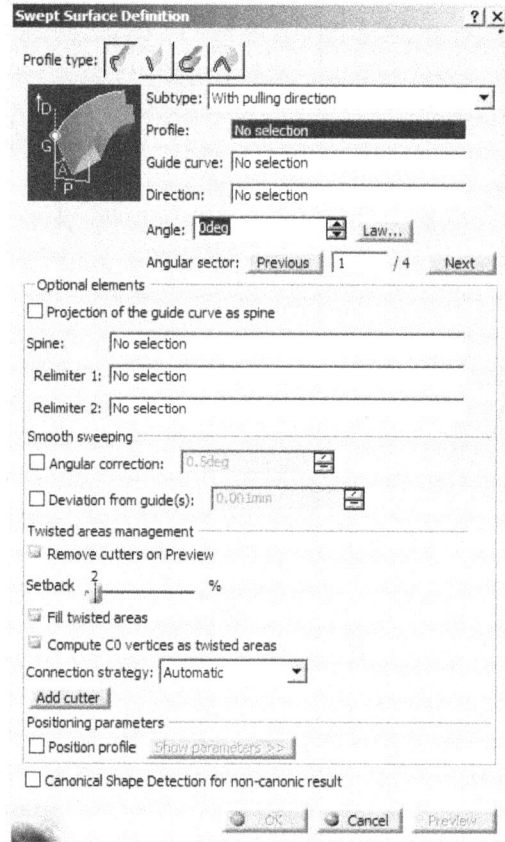

Figure 7–7

## How To: Create a With Pulling Direction Swept Surface

1. Select the Profile, Guide curve, and direction, as shown in Figure 7–8.

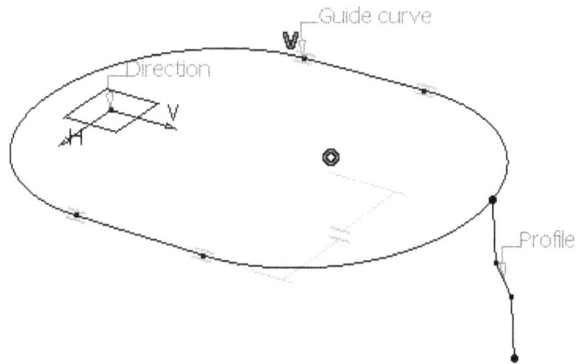

**Figure 7–8**

2. Enter the *Angle* and click **Preview** to display the surface, as shown in Figure 7–9.

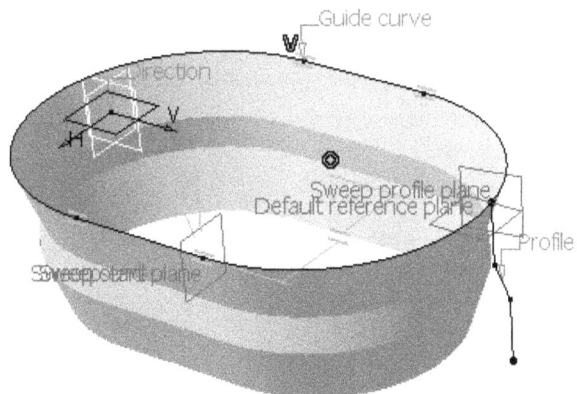

**Figure 7–9**

# 7.5 Line Profile - With Reference Surface

The **With reference surface** explicit profile creates a surface by running a line segment along one curve, while being oriented to a reference surface/plane. The required inputs for this type of sweep are a Guide curve and Reference surface, as shown in Figure 7–10.

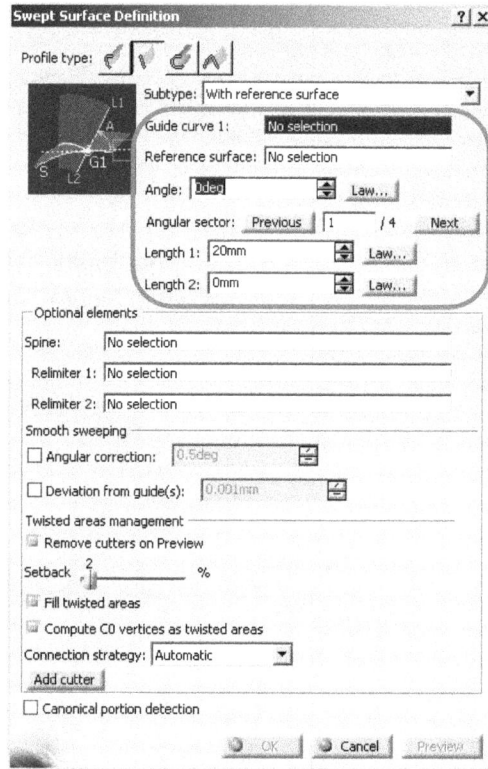

**Figure 7–10**

An example of a With reference surface swept surface is shown in Figure 7–11.

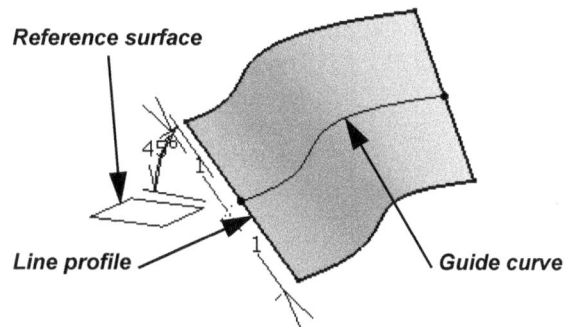

**Figure 7–11**

# 7.6 Circle Profile - Center and Radius

The **Center and radius** circle profile enables you to create a constant radius shape that is swept along a center curve. This is a simple way of creating any tubing or hoses. An example of the required inputs is shown in Figure 7–12.

**Figure 7–12**

## How To: Create a Center and Radius Swept Surface

1. Select the center curve and enter the required radius.
2. Click **Preview** to display the surface as shown in Figure 7–13.

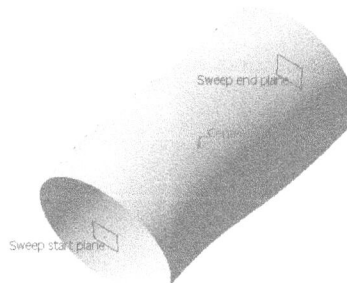

**Figure 7–13**

# Practice 7a

# Sweep Bracket

### Practice Objectives

- Create an Explicit Profile sweep.
- Create a Line Profile sweep.
- Create a Circle Profile sweep.

In this practice, you will create an irregularly shaped bracket by sweeping surfaces. You will create three types of sweeps to show their different uses in modeling. In addition, you will use surface operation tools to complete the part. The completed model displays as shown in Figure 7–14.

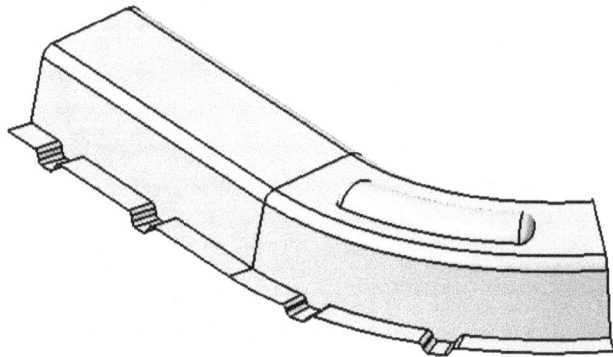

Figure 7–14

### Task 1 - Open a part.

1. Open **Sweep_Bracket_Start.CATPart**. The model displays as shown in Figure 7–15.

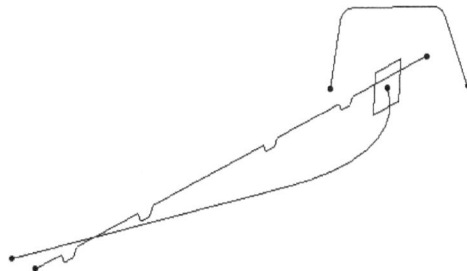

Figure 7–15

2. Ensure that the model units are set to **mm**.

3. Hide the **Sketch to Project** sketch.

## Task 2 - Create an Explicit Profile sweep.

1. Click [icon] (Sweep) in the Surfaces toolbar. The Sweep Definition dialog box opens as shown in Figure 7–16.

2. Select **Explicit** as the *Profile type* and **With reference surface** as the *Subtype*, as shown in Figure 7–16.

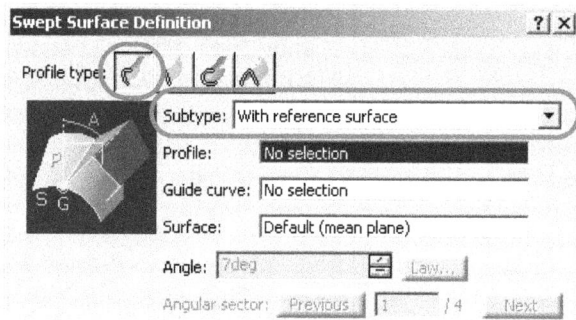

**Figure 7–16**

3. In the specification tree, select **Base Sweep Profile** as the Profile reference.

4. Select **Base Sweep Guide** as the Guide curve reference.

5. Select the **XY plane** as the Surface reference. The angle value is measured from the reference surface.

6. Ensure that **0deg** is the value for the Angle reference. If an angle is specified, the profile is rotated according to that value. The dialog box opens as shown in Figure 7–17.

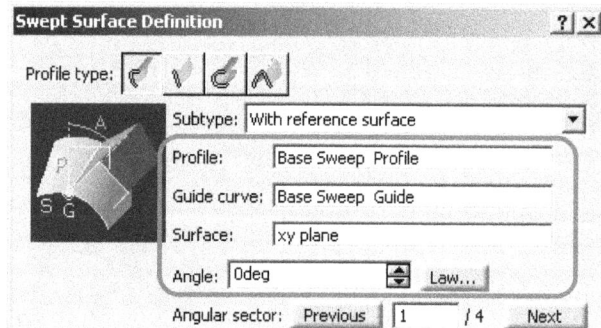

**Figure 7–17**

7. Click **OK** to complete the Sweep. The model displays as shown in Figure 7–18.

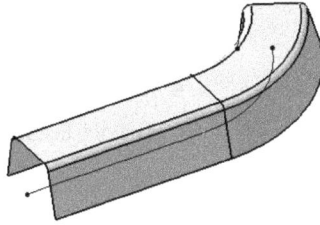

**Figure 7–18**

8. Rename *Sweep.1* as **Base Sweep**.

9. Edit **Base Sweep** by double-clicking on the feature.

10. In the Sweep Definition dialog box, change the *Angle* from *0deg* to **7deg**, as shown in Figure 7–19.

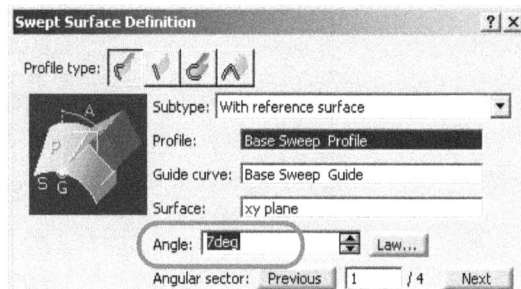

**Figure 7–19**

11. Click **OK** to accept the changes. The model displays as shown in Figure 7–20. Note the orientation of the sweep as compared to the original profile.

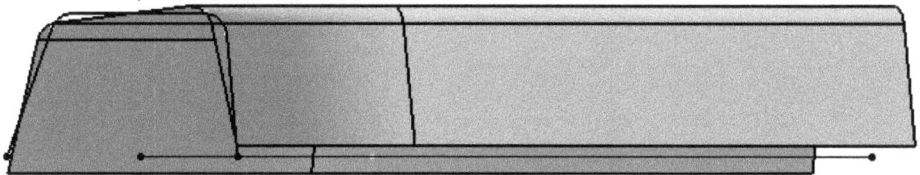

**Figure 7–20**

12. Hide **Base Sweep Guide** and **Base Sweep Profile**.

## Task 3 - Create side flange reference geometry.

1. Show **Sketch to Project**.

2. Click  (Projection).

3. Select **Along a Direction** in the Projection type drop-down list.

4. Select **Sketch to project** as the *Projected* reference.

5. Select **Base Sweep** as the *Support* reference.

6. Select **Plane.1** as the *Direction* reference.

7. Ensure that the **Nearest Solution** option is cleared. The Projection Definition dialog box opens as shown in Figure 7–21.

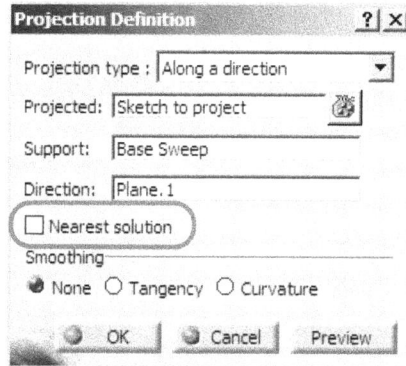

**Figure 7–21**

8. Click **OK** to completed the Projection. The Multi-Result Management dialog box opens.

9. Select **keep only one sub-element using an Extract**, as shown in Figure 7–22.

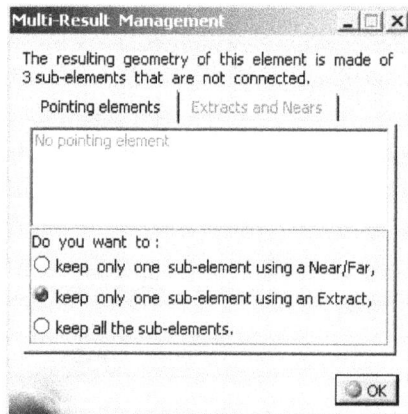

**Figure 7–22**

10. Click **OK** in the Multi-Result Management dialog box. The Extract Definition dialog box opens.

11. Select the **Tangent continuity** propagation type in the Propagation type drop-down list and select the curve shown in Figure 7–23.

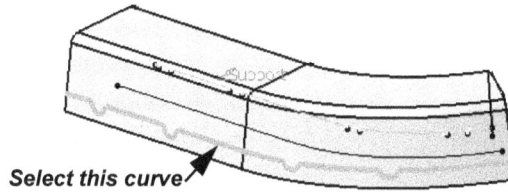

**Figure 7–23**

12. Click **OK** to complete the Extract.

13. Rename *Extract.1* as **Flange Guide**.

14. Hide **Sketch to project.**

15. Click  (Split).

16. Select **Base Sweep** as the Element to cut.

17. Select **Flange Guide** as the Cutting element.

18. Use **Other side** to ensure that the geometry displays as shown in Figure 7–24.

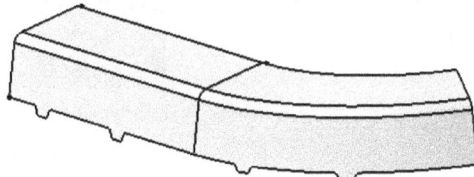

**Figure 7–24**

19. Extract the edge shown in Figure 7–25 using the **Tangent continuity** propagation type.

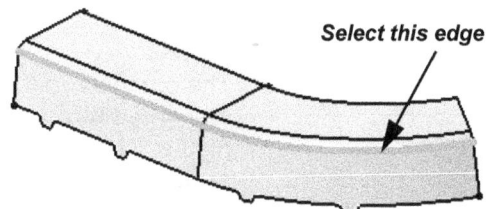

**Figure 7–25**

20. Rename *Extract.2* as **Flange Spine**.

## Task 4 - Create side flange surface geometry.

1. Click 🖉 (Sweep) and specify the following parameters:

   - *Profile type:* **Line**
   - *Subtype:* **With reference surface**
   - *Guide curve 1:* **Flange Guide**
   - *Reference surface:* **Plane.1**
   - *Angle:* **90deg**
   - *Length 1:* **10mm**
   - *Length 2:* **0mm**
   - *Spine:* **Flange Spine**

**Design Considerations**

The line profile is swept normal to Flange Spine. If you did not select a spine reference, CATIA would use a default spine. A better quality swept surface is created using this method. The Swept Surface Definition dialog box opens as shown in Figure 7–26.

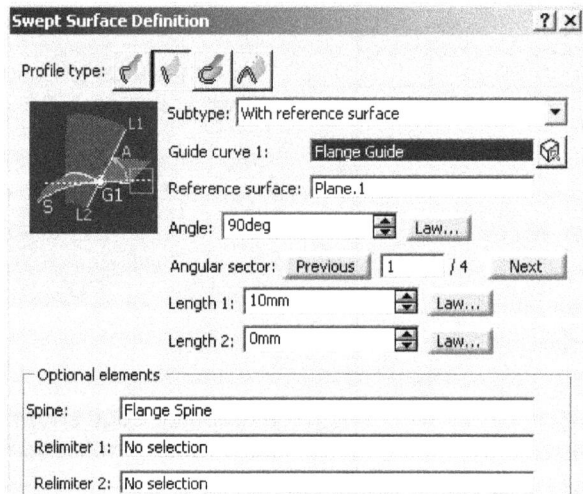

**Figure 7–26**

2. The orange arrow indicates the angle sector. Ensure that the orange arrow on your model matches the one shown in Figure 7–27. Click **Next/Previous** to change the Angular sector.

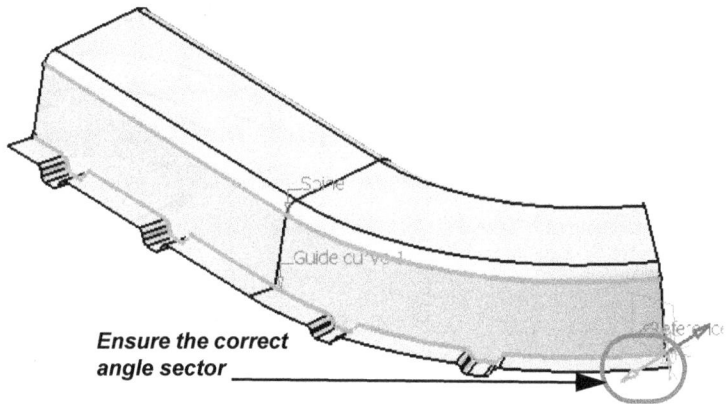

**Ensure the correct angle sector**

Figure 7–27

3. Click **OK** to complete the Sweep.

4. Rename *Sweep.2* as **Flange Sweep1**.

5. Hide **Flange Spine** and **Flange Guide**.

---

**Task 5 - Create opposite side flange reference geometry.**

1. Click 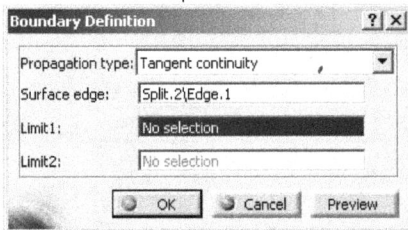 (Boundary) to create a boundary curve from the edge as shown in Figure 7–28. Use the Tangent continuity propagation type.

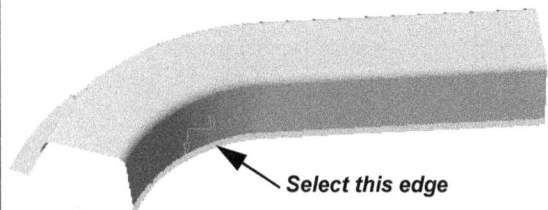

**Select this edge**

Figure 7–28

2. Rename *Boundary.1* as **Flange2 Guide**.

3. Create a point using the On Curve type and specify the following parameters:

*Select **Reverse Direction** if required.*

- *Curve:* **Flange2 Guide**
- Select **Ratio of curve length**.
- Enter a *Length* of **0**.

The model displays as shown in Figure 7–29.

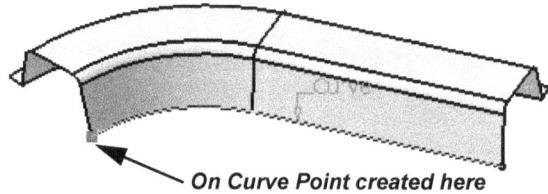

On Curve Point created here

Figure 7–29

4. Rename *Point.1* as **Flange2 Endpoint**.

5. Create a plane using the Normal to curve type and specify the following parameters:

   - *Curve:* **Flange2 Guide**
   - *Point:* **Flange2 Endpoint**

6. Rename *Plane.2* as **Flange2 Sketch Plane**.

7. Create a positioned sketch using the following parameters:

   - *Sketch Positioning Reference:* **Flange2 Sketch Plane**
   - *Origin Type:* **Projection point**
   - *Origin Reference:* **Flange2 Endpoint**

   The Sketch Positioning dialog box opens as shown in Figure 7–30.

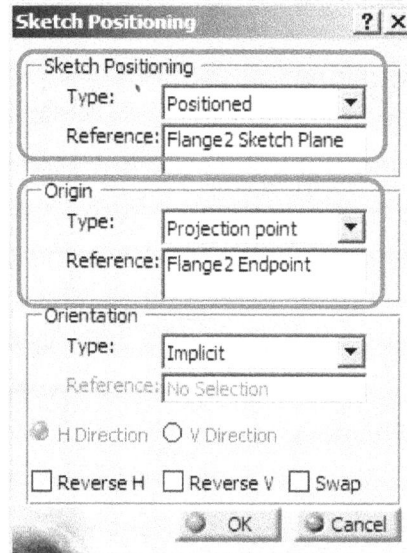

Figure 7–30

8. Click **OK** in the Sketch Positioning dialog box.

9. Create the geometry shown in Figure 7–31.

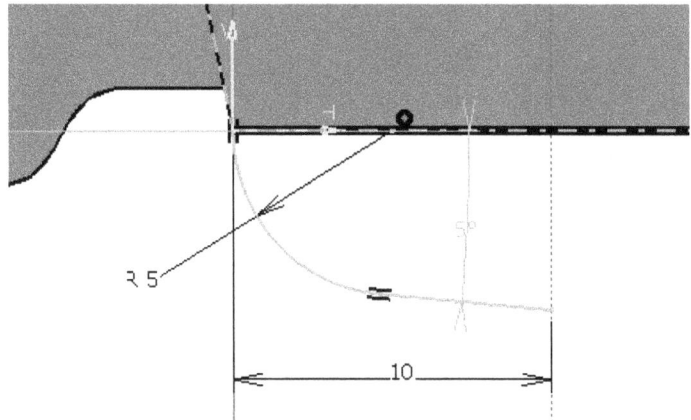

**Figure 7–31**

10. Rename the sketch as **Flange2 Profile**.

---

## Task 6 - Create the opposite side flange sweep.

---

1. Click  (Sweep) and specify the following parameters:

   - *Profile Type:* **Explicit**
   - *Subtype:* **With reference surface**
   - *Profile:* **Flange2 Profile**
   - *Guide curve:* **Flange2 Guide**

The Swept Surface Definition dialog box opens as shown in Figure 7–32.

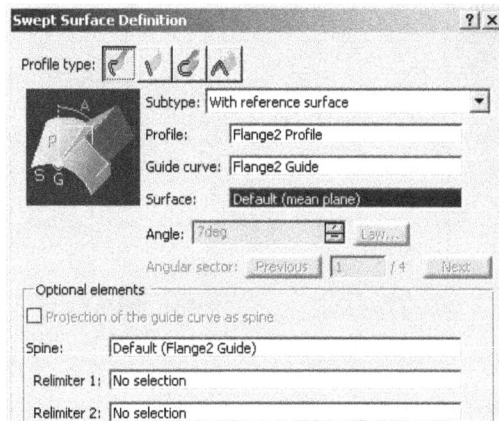

**Figure 7–32**

---

2. Click **OK** to complete the Sweep. The model displays as shown in Figure 7–33.

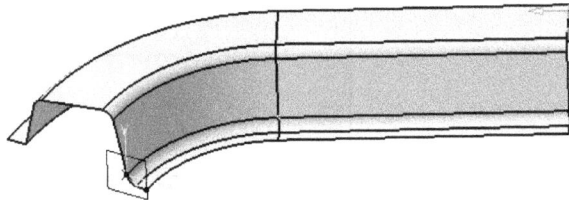

**Figure 7–33**

3. Rename the Sweep as **Flange Sweep 2**.

4. Hide **Flange2 Guide**, **Flange2 Endpoint**, **Flange2 Sketch Plane**, and **Flange2 Profile**.

5. Save the model and close the file.

# Practice 7b

# Duct & Wiring Cover

## Practice Objectives

- Create Explicit profile Sweep surfaces.
- Create Line profile Sweep surfaces.

In this practice, you will create a large diameter duct. You will also create a cover to protect the wiring running inside the duct. The protective covering consists of two flanges on each side of the cover that must have full contact with the duct's inside diameter. Because the protective covering is symmetric, you will use the copy and paste function create the surfaces more quickly. The completed model displays as shown in Figure 7–34.

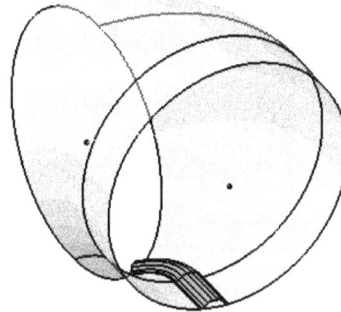

**Figure 7–34**

## Task 1 - Open a part.

1. Open **Duct-Cover-Wireframe.CATPart**. The model displays as shown in Figure 7–35.

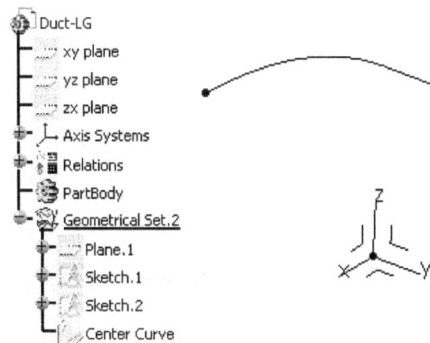

**Figure 7–35**

2. Ensure that the model units are set to **mm**.

## Task 2 - Create the duct's inside diameter.

1. Click ⬚ (Sweep) in the Surfaces toolbar and specify the following parameters:

   - *Profile type:* **Circle**
   - *Subtype:* **Center and radius**
   - *Center curve:* **Center Curve**
   - *Radius:* **2500mm**

2. Click **Preview**. The dialog box and model display as shown in Figure 7–36.

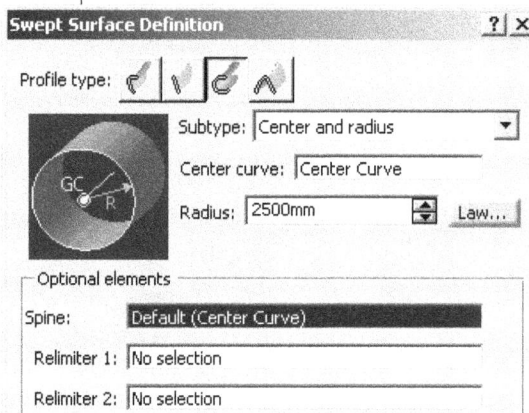

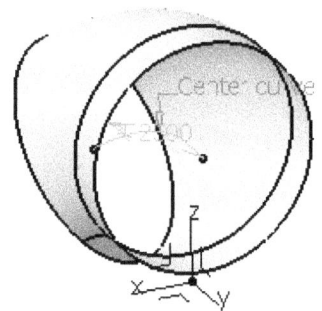

**Figure 7–36**

3. Click **OK**. Rename *Sweep.1* as **Duct**.

## Task 3 - Create the cover center curve.

1. Click ⬚ (Projection) in the Wireframe toolbar.

2. In the Projection Definition dialog box, set the *Projection type* to **Along a direction**.

3. Select **Center Curve** as the *Projected* reference.

4. Select **Duct** as the *Support* reference.

5. Right-click in the *Direction* field and select **Z Component**. The Projection Definition dialog box opens as shown in Figure 7–37.

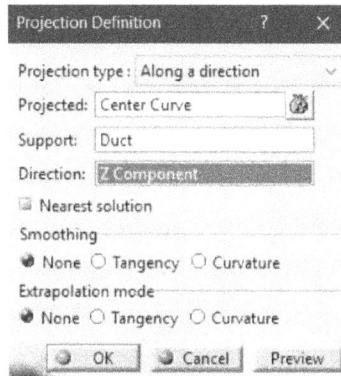
**Figure 7–37**

6.  Click **OK** to complete the Projection. The model displays as shown in Figure 7–38.

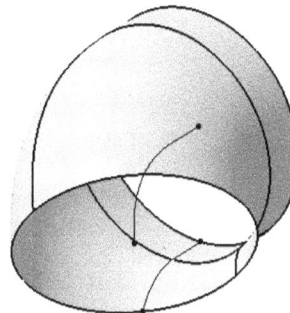
**Figure 7–38**

7.  Rename *Project.1* as **Cover Center**.

---

**Task 4 - Create the cover side curves.**

---

In this task, you will create the side curves for the cover. A swept circular surface will intersect the duct surface. The intersection of the sweep and the duct will create the required side curves.

1.  Click  (Sweep) in the Surfaces toolbar and specify the following parameters:

    *   *Profile type:* **Circle**
    *   *Subtype:* **Center and radius**
    *   *Center curve:* **Cover Center**
    *   *Radius:* **250mm**
    *   *Spine:* **Center Curve**

2. Click **OK** to complete the feature. Click **Close** in the Warnings dialog box.

**Design Considerations**

Using Center Curve as the spine ensures that the swept surface is created to the edges of the duct. An example of this is shown in Figure 7–39.

*Swept surface does not fully intersect the duct.*

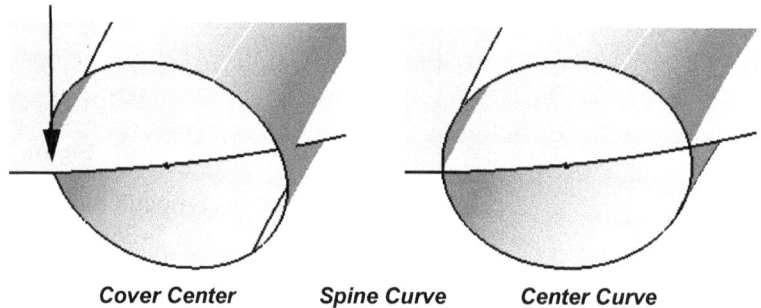

*Cover Center*          *Spine Curve*          *Center Curve*

**Figure 7–39**

3. Click  (Intersection) in the Wireframe toolbar.

4. Select **Sweep.2** and **Duct.** The intersection of the two elements creates two side curves.

5. Click **OK**. The Multi-Result Management dialog box opens as shown in Figure 7–40.

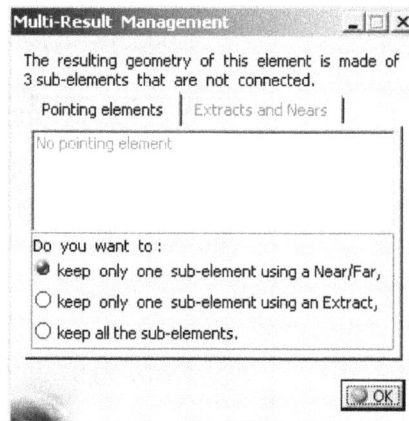

**Figure 7–40**

To create the wire housing, you will require both intersection curves. To do this, you must keep all of the sub-elements and then perform an **Extract** operation to separate the curves into two features.

6. Select **keep all the sub-elements** and click **OK**.

7. Hide **Sweep.2**.

8. Use ⬚ (Extract) in the Operations toolbar to extract the two curves (**Extract.1** and **Extract.2**, as shown in Figure 7–41) using **Tangent continuity**.

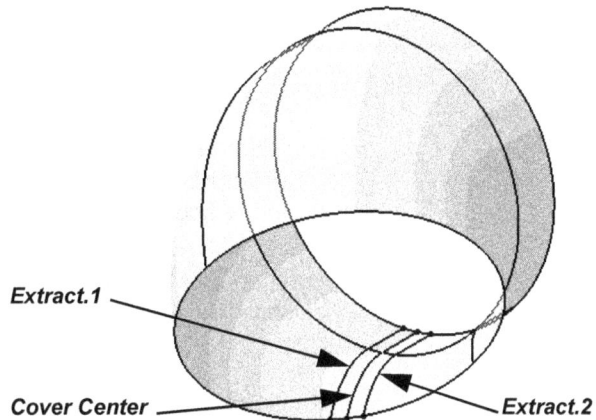

Figure 7–41

9. Hide **Intersect.1**.

---

**Task 5 - Create the cover side surfaces.**

---

1. Click ⬚ (Sweep) in the Surface toolbar and specify the following parameters:

   • *Profile type:* **Line**
   • *Subtype:* **With reference surface**
   • *Guide curve 1:* **Extract.1**
   • *Reference surface:* **Duct**
   • *Angle:* **70deg**
   • *Length 1:* **55mm**
   • *Length 2:* **0mm**
   • *Spine:* **Center Curve**

2. Set the angle sector as shown in Figure 7–42.

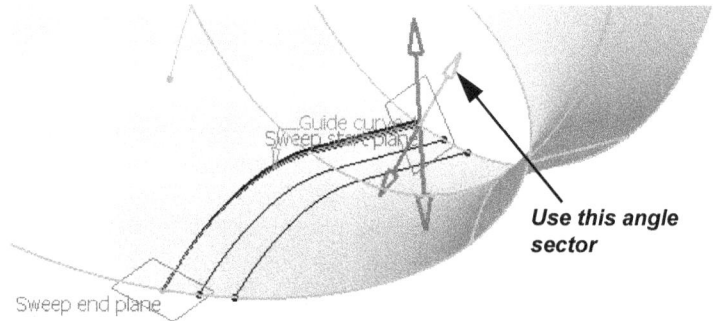

**Figure 7–42**

3. Click **OK** and click **Close** in the Warnings dialog box.

4. Copy **Sweep.3**.

5. Right-click on **Sweep.3** and select **Paste**. The copied sweep is automatically named **Sweep.4** and located below **Sweep.3** in the specification tree.

**Design Considerations**

You can create a new feature more quickly by copying an existing one that is similar and then modifying the copied feature, rather than creating it from scratch.

6. Double-click on **Sweep.4** to edit the surface.

7. Change **Guide curve 1** from *Extract.1* to **Extract.2**.

8. Change the *Angle* from *70deg* to **50deg**.

9. Ensure that the correct angle sector is set, as shown in Figure 7–43.

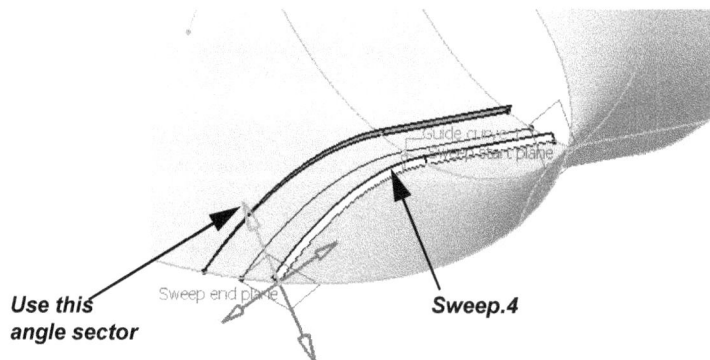

**Figure 7–43**

10. Click **OK** to complete the feature.

## Task 6 - Create the cover flange curves.

In this task, you will create another set of curves that are required for the practice. To start, you will copy and paste the existing sweep features and then edit them. You will then intersect the edited swept surfaces with the duct to form the curves.

1.  Right-click on **Sweep.2** and select **Copy**.

2.  Right-click on **Sweep.4** and select **Paste**. This pastes the sweep below **Sweep.4** in the specification tree. Note that the pasted swept surface is hidden. This is because the copied swept surface was set to hide.

3.  Double-click on **Sweep.5** to make adjustments to the feature.

4.  Change the *Radius* value to **300mm**.

5.  Click **OK** to accept the change. Click **Close** to the Warnings dialog box.

6.  Right-click on **Intersect.1** and select **Copy**.

7.  Right-click on **Sweep.5** and select **Paste**. The copied sweep is automatically named **Intersect.2** and located below **Sweep.5** in the specification tree.

8.  Show **Intersect.2**.

9.  Edit **Intersect.2** so that the feature is created between **Duct** and **Sweep.5**, as shown in Figure 7–44.

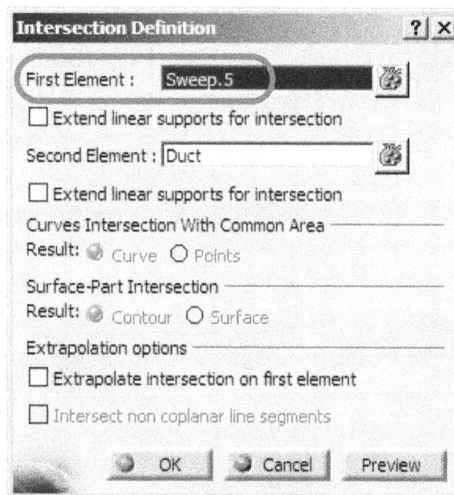

**Figure 7–44**

10. Keep all sub-elements of the intersection.

11. Create Extract features that extract the two intersection curves generated by **Intersect.2**. The model displays as shown in Figure 7–45.

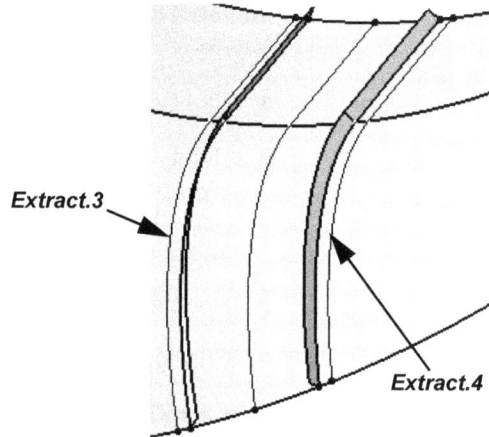

**Figure 7–45**

## Task 7 - Create the cover flange surfaces.

In this task, you will develop the flange surfaces for the wire cover. These surfaces will lie directly on top of the Duct surface. To build the flange surface, you will create a profile using the boundary of the Duct surface and sweep it along the two extract curves that were created in the Task 7.

1. Click  (Boundary). Select the boundary of the Duct surface shown in Figure 7–46.

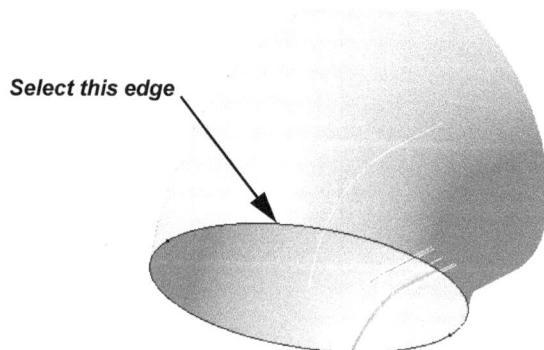

**Figure 7–46**

*You might need to flip the direction to obtain the same result.*

2. Select **Extract.1** and **Extract.3** for *Limit1* and *Limit2*. Keep the side that generates the small edge shown in Figure 7–47.

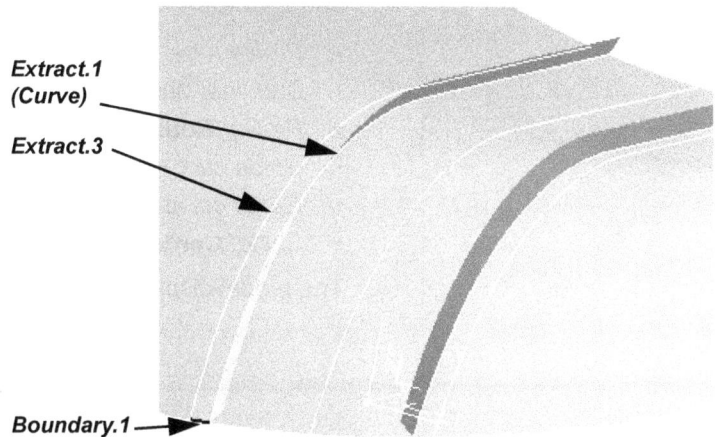

Extract.1 (Curve)

Extract.3

Boundary.1

**Figure 7–47**

3. Right-click on **Boundary.1** and select **Copy**.

4. Right-click on **Boundary.1** and select **Paste**.

5. Double-click on **Boundary.2**. Remove the limiting curves, and select **Extract.2** and **Extract.4** to obtain the result shown in Figure 7–48.

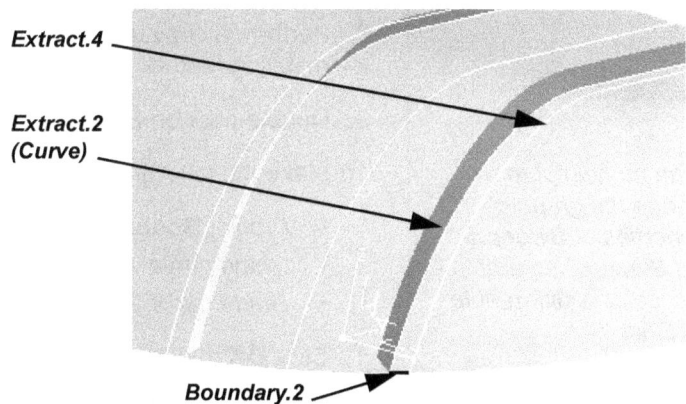

Extract.4

Extract.2 (Curve)

Boundary.2

**Figure 7–48**

6. Click **OK** to accept the change.

7. Click ![Sweep icon] (Sweep) in the Surface toolbar and specify the following parameters:

- *Profile type:* **Explicit**
- *Subtype:* **With two guide curves**
- *Profile:* **Boundary.1**
- *Guide curve 1:* **Extract.1**
- *Guide curve 2:* **Extract.3**
- *Spine:* **Center curve**

The model displays as shown in Figure 7–49.

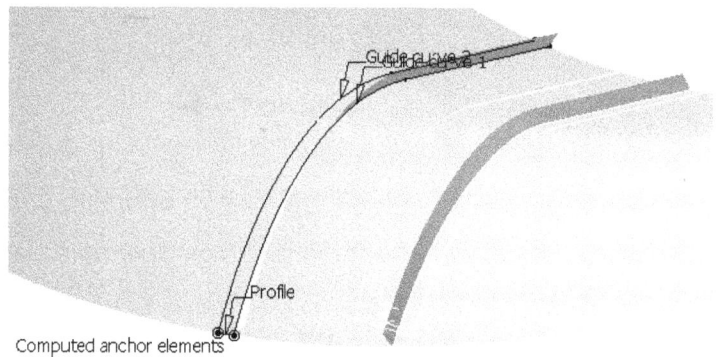

**Figure 7–49**

8. Perform a copy and paste operation on **Sweep.6**. The resulting feature will be **Sweep.7**.

9. Double-click on **Sweep.7** to edit the feature.

10. Make the following changes to **Sweep.7**:

- *Profile:* **Boundary.2**
- *Guide curve 1:* **Extract.2**
- *Guide curve 2:* **Extract.4**

11. Click **OK** to complete the Swept Surface. The model displays as shown in Figure 7–50.

*It can be helpful to change the graphic properties of Sweep.6 and Sweep.7 so that their color is different to the Duct.*

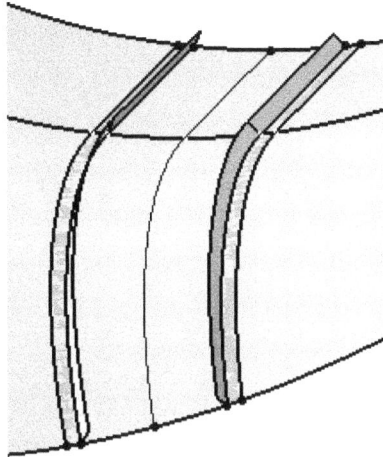

**Figure 7–50**

## Task 8 - Create the top cover surface.

In this task, you will create the top cover surface as a swept surface defined by a profile. You will need to create reference geometry before sketching the profile.

1. Hide the **Duct** surface.

2. Create a plane Normal to curve. For the Curve reference, select **Center Curve**.

3. For the Point reference, right-click in the *Point* field and select **Create Endpoint**, as shown in Figure 7–51.

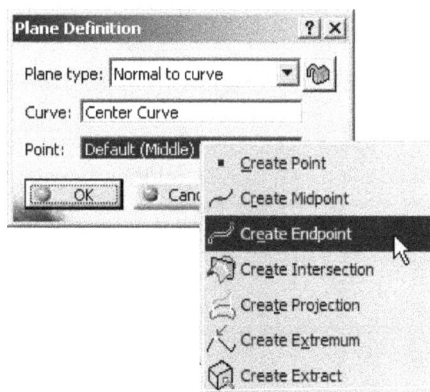

**Figure 7–51**

4. Select the point shown in Figure 7–52.

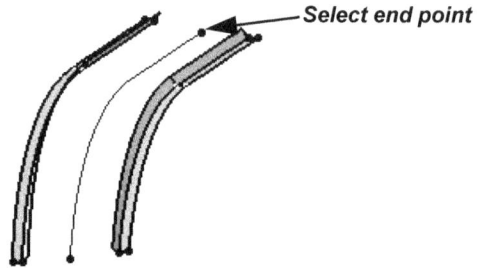

*Select end point*

**Figure 7–52**

5. Click **OK** to complete the plane. Note that the created end point is located under **Plane.2** in the specification tree.

6. Create a positioned sketch using the newly created datum plane. Use **Point.1** as the origin.

7. Begin the sketch by intersecting S**weep.3** and **Sweep.4** with the sketch plane. Ensure that you are in construction mode. Use (Intersect 3D Elements) and select the sweep features in the specification tree. The sketch displays as shown in Figure 7–53.

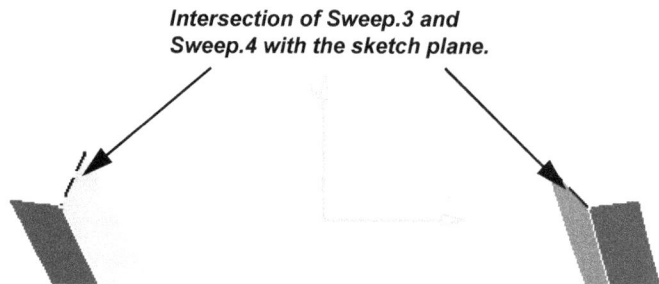

*Intersection of Sweep.3 and Sweep.4 with the sketch plane.*

**Figure 7–53**

8. Sketch the profile shown in Figure 7–54. Ensure that the sketch is fully constrained.

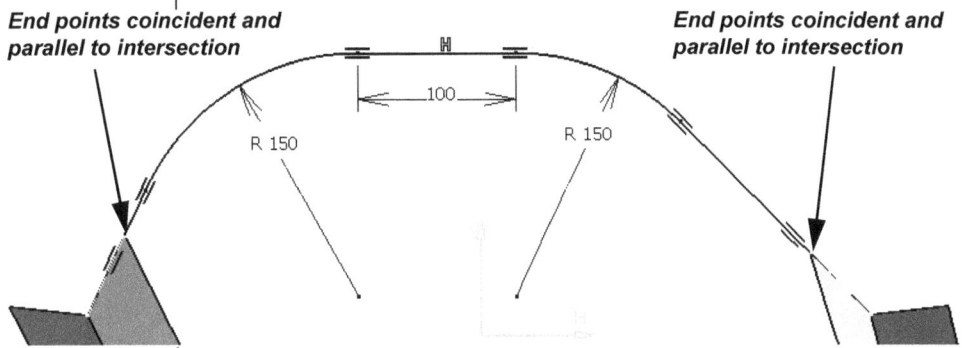

**Figure 7–54**

9. Exit Sketcher when complete.

10. Create a Sweep using the following parameters:

    - *Profile type:* **Explicit**
    - *Subtype:* **With two guide curves**
    - *Profile:* **Sketch.3**
    - *Spine:* **Center Curve**

11. Right-click in the *Guide curve 1* field and select **Create Boundary**. Set the Propagation type to **Tangent continuity**. Select the edge shown in Figure 7–55.

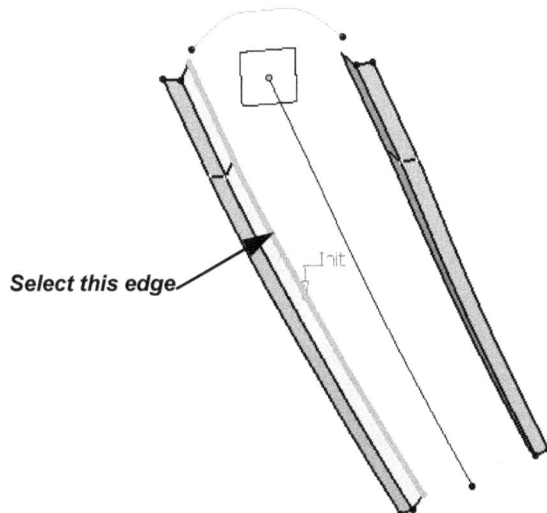

**Figure 7–55**

12. Click **OK** to complete the Boundary.

13. Follow the same procedure to create the reference for **Guide Curve 2**. Right-click in the *Guide curve 2* field and select **Create Boundary**. Ensure that the Propagation type is set to **Tangent continuity**. Select the edge shown in Figure 7–56 and click **OK** to complete the Boundary.

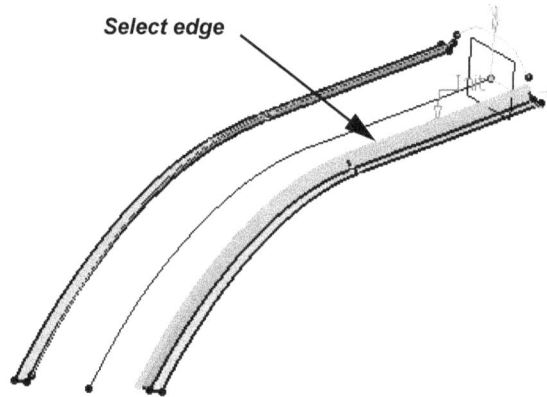

**Select edge**

Figure 7–56

14. Click **OK** to complete the Swept surface. Click **Close** in the Warnings dialog box. The model displays as shown in Figure 7–57.

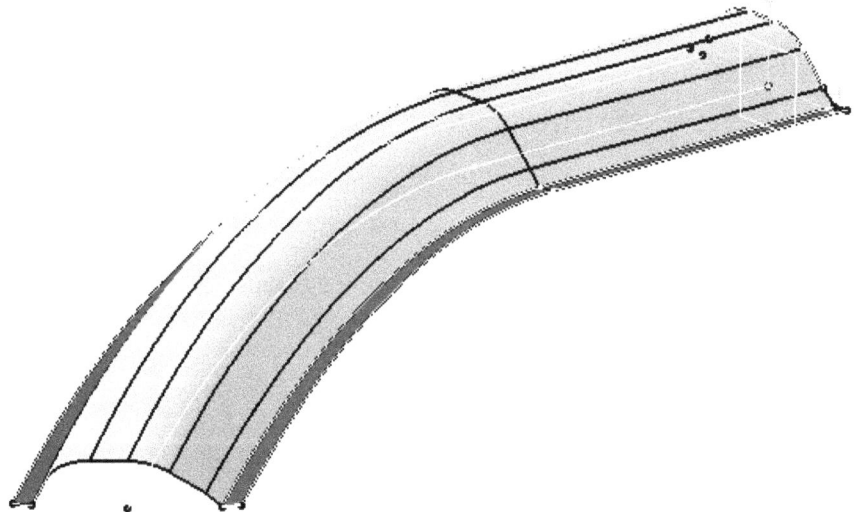

Figure 7–57

## Task 9 - Complete the model.

1. Select **Tools>Hide>All Curves**.

2. Select **Tools>Hide>All Sketches**.

3. Hide **Plane.2**.

4. Create a Join feature and select **Sweep.8** (the last surface feature created).

5. Right-click in the *Elements To Join* field and select **Distance Propagation**, as shown in Figure 7–58. This selects all of the surfaces that are point connected to Sweep.8.

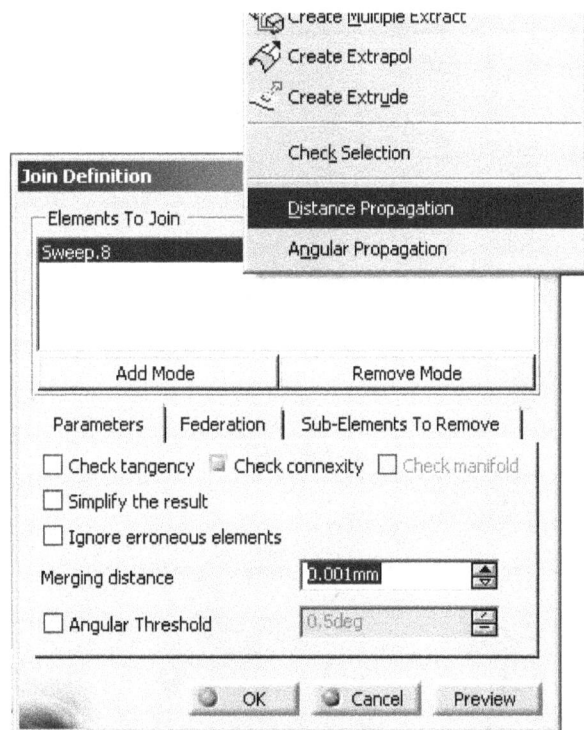

**Figure 7–58**

6. Complete the Join feature and rename it as **Wire Housing**.

7. Change the color properties of Wire Housing to blue.

8. Show the **Duct** surface.

9. Select **File>Save As**.

10. Name the file **Duct-Cover Final**. The completed model displays as shown in Figure 7–59.

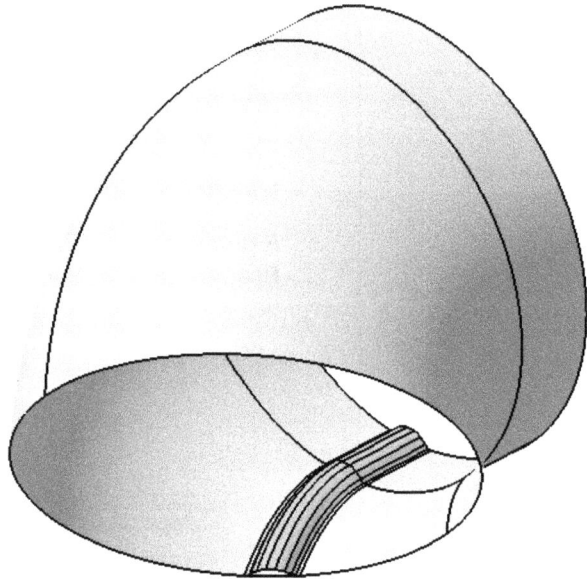

**Figure 7–59**

# Chapter Review Questions

1. When a Spine is defined for a swept surface, the cross-section of the sweep remains normal to the spine.

   a. True

   b. False

2. A **With reference surface** explicit profile sweep, you can add drafts by specifying a reference surface and an angle.

   a. True

   b. False

3. The **With two guide curves** explicit profile sweep enables you to select a curve to sweep along, and two additional curves to control the sweep shape.

   a. True

   b. False

4. With the **With pulling direction** explicit profile sweep, the profile of the swept surface is defined to follow the guide curve, at an angle to the specified direction.

   a. True

   b. False

5. Which sweep profile type would be best suited for modeling a tube or hose?

   a. Explicit

   b. Circle

   c. Line

   d. None of the above.

Chapter

# 8

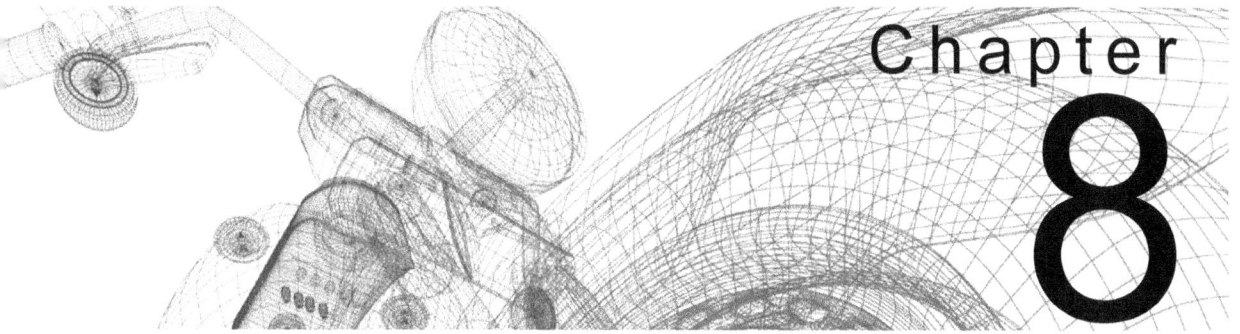

# Complex Surfaces II

This chapter discusses the methods used to create complex surfaces, such as Multi-sections surfaces and Blended surfaces. Both feature types are transitional surfaces between user-defined profiles or curves. Although similar, the Blend and Multi-sections surface features each have unique properties.

## Learning Objectives in this Chapter

- Create Multi-sections Surfaces.
- Create Blended Surfaces.

# 8.1 Multi-sections Surfaces

A Multi-sections surface consists of transitional surfaces that are created between multiple sketches, edges, or curves. Figure 8–1 shows the creation of a Multi-sections feature between two sketched sections.

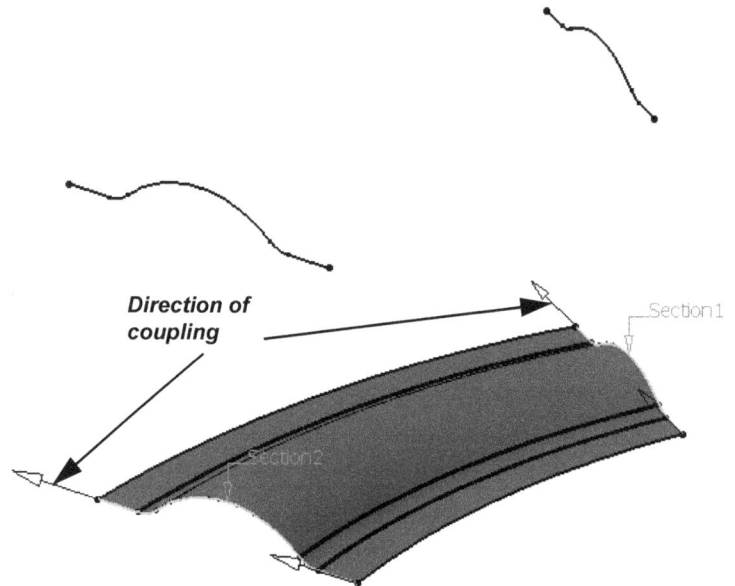

**Figure 8–1**

The transitional surfaces are created by connecting the vertices of the selected sketches with splinar surfaces. The closing points indicate the first two vertices to connect. The system couples the sections in the direction indicated by an arrow.

**General Steps**

Use the following general steps to create and control a Multi-sections feature:

1. Start the creation of the Multi-sections feature and select the sections.
2. Control the profile geometry with guides and spines, if required.
3. Set the **Coupling** and **Relimitation** options, if required.

## Step 1 - Start the creation of the Multi-sections feature and select the sections.

To begin the creation of a Multi-sections surface, click

(Multi-sections Surface) in the Surfaces toolbar. The Multi-sections Surface Definition dialog box opens as shown in Figure 8–2.

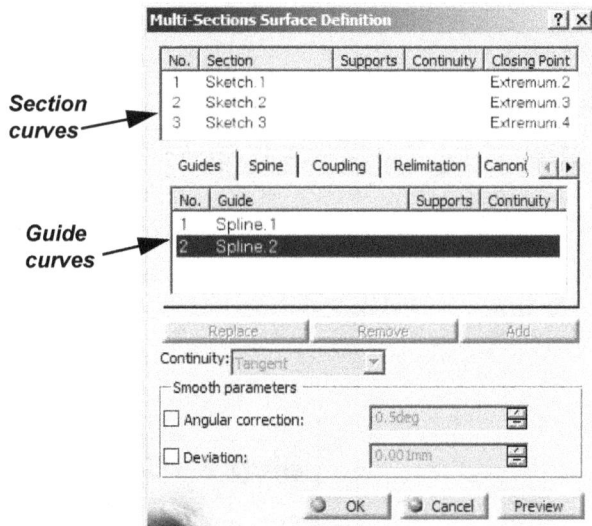

**Section curves** ⟶
**Guide curves** ⟶

**Figure 8–2**

Unlike a Multi-sections solid feature (in the Part Design workbench), the face of a solid feature (such as a pad) cannot be used as a boundary selection for a Multi-sections feature. A boundary feature must be created to generate a boundary curve for the face. This boundary feature can then be selected for the Multi-sections feature.

In the example shown in Figure 8–3, a boundary feature (**Boundary.1**) is created from the face of Pad.1 and used to create the Multi-sections feature.

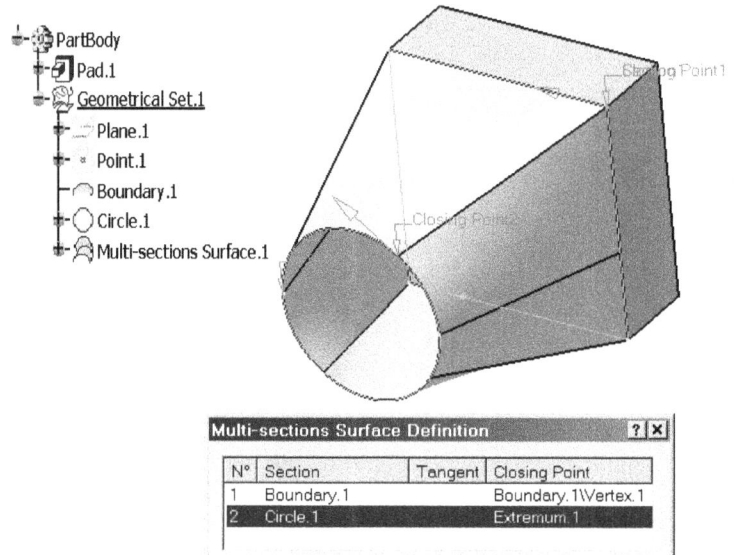

**Multi-sections Surface Definition**

| N° | Section | Tangent | Closing Point |
|---|---|---|---|
| 1 | Boundary.1 | | Boundary.1\Vertex.1 |
| 2 | Circle.1 | | Extremum.1 |

Figure 8–3

## Step 2 - Control the profile geometry with guides and spines, if required.

Once the sections have been selected, advanced options (such as guides and spines) can be added.

### Guides

A guide uses a curve or line to define an absolute path through which the Multi-sections feature travel. The wireframe geometry blends the sections of the Multi-sections surface together by connecting to each section in the Multi-sections feature. More than one guide can be used to control the feature. By default, the feature only progresses as far as the last section, regardless of the length of the guide.

In Figure 8–4, a guide curve is created that connects the two sketches and extends past the end section.

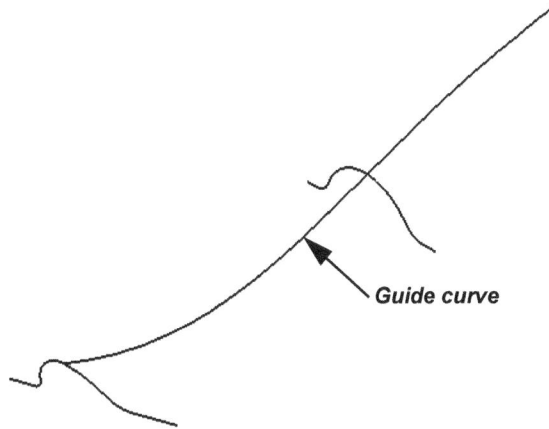

**Figure 8–4**

To use the guide in the feature, select it in the *Guides* tab in the Multi-sections Surface Definition dialog box, as shown in Figure 8–5. Then select the guide from the screen.

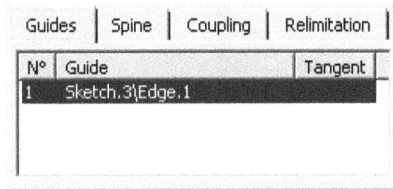

| N° | Guide | Tangent |
|----|-------|---------|
| 1 | Sketch.3\Edge.1 | |

**Figure 8–5**

The Multi-sections feature shown in Figure 8–6 is created with a guide to control the internal surface.

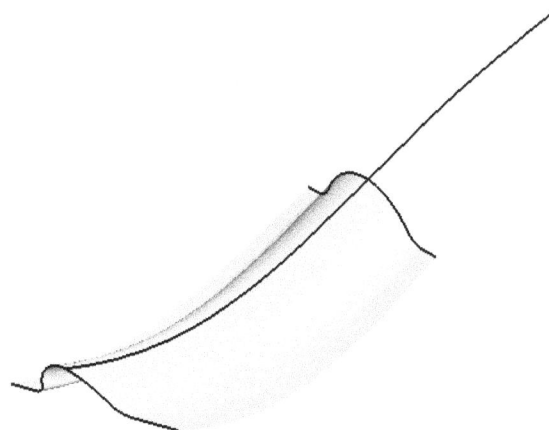

**Figure 8–6**

## Spine

A spine controls the shape of the Multi-sections feature as it progresses from one section to the next. The cross-section of the Multi-sections feature must always be perpendicular to the spine. Therefore, only one spine can be selected for a Multi-sections surface. The spine can be defined by a sketch, edge, or curve.

To specify a spine, select the *Spine* tab in the Multi-sections Surface Definition dialog box, as shown in Figure 8–7. Then select the spine geometry to be used.

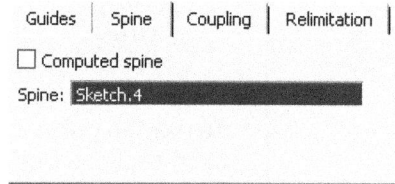

Guides | Spine | Coupling | Relimitation |

☐ Computed spine

Spine: Sketch.4

**Figure 8–7**

Figure 8–8 shows how the addition of a spine affects the shape of a Multi-sections surface. Note that the section of the Multi-sections feature is always perpendicular to the line feature used to define the spine.

*A line feature is used as a spine to control the cross-section of the Multi-sections*

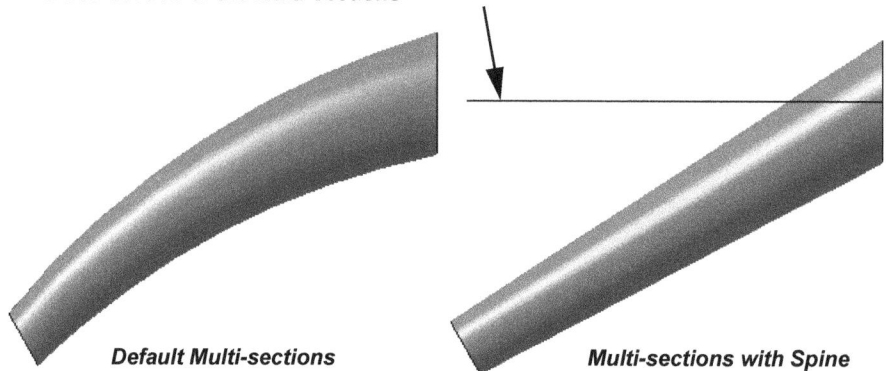

*Default Multi-sections*          *Multi-sections with Spine*

**Figure 8–8**

If a spine is not specified, CATIA computes a default spine to control the shape of the Multi-sections surface throughout its progression. To specify the system-default spine, select **Computed spine**.

# Step 3 - Set the Coupling and Relimitation options, if required.

## Coupling

You might need to change the **Coupling** option to create the Multi-sections feature. The **Coupling** option is used to define the transitions between the sections. These options are described as follows:

| Classification | Description |
| --- | --- |
| **Ratio** | If the sections are connected at positions, the ratio is computed by the percentage of the section profile. This option is recommended when non-equal numbers of vertices are present in the sketch sections. |
| **Tangency** | If the sections have the same number of tangency discontinuity points, these points are coupled together between sections. |
| **Tangency then curvature** | If the sections have the same number of tangency and curvature discontinuity points, tangency discontinuity points are coupled together between sections, and curvature discontinuity points are then coupled together between sections. |
| **Vertices** | If the sections have the same number of vertices, these points are coupled together between sections. |

If a **Coupling** option is used and the criteria described is not met, an error message box opens when attempting to generate the Multi-sections feature. For example, setting the **Coupling** option to **Vertices** results in an error message if you are attempting to create transitions between a square and a circular section. This error occurs because the circular section does not have any vertices to couple with the square section.

**Relimitation**

Relimitation controls the progression of the Multi-sections feature beyond the sections. By default, a Multi-sections surface is relimited at both the start and end sections.

By disabling Multi-sections relimitation and using a guide, the geometry can extend as far as the shortest guide. The Multi-sections shown on the right in Figure 8–9 is the same as the Multi-sections shown on the left, except that the **Relimited on end section** option is not selected.

Note how the Multi-sections extends past the last section. The shape of the Multi-sections' cross-section in this area is controlled by the last section. The trajectory of the Multi-sections is controlled by the guide.

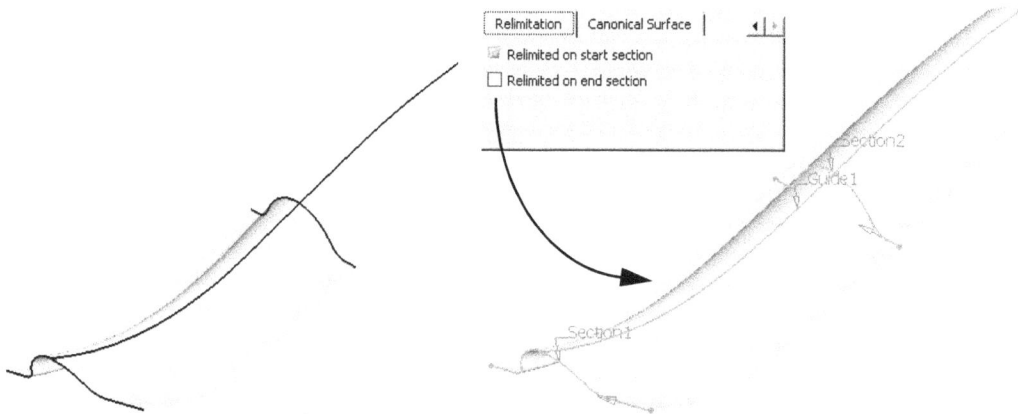

**Figure 8–9**

To specify Relimitation, select the *Relimitation* tab in the Multi-sections Definition dialog box and clear the **Relimited on end section** option.

A spine can also control the relimitation of a Multi-sections feature. Figure 8–10 shows two models created with the **Relimited on end section** option not selected. The surface shown on the left in Figure 8–10 uses the system-defined spine and a guide. Note that the cross-section at the end of the surface is parallel to the last section. The surface shown on the right in Figure 8–10 uses a selected spine. Note that the cross-section at the end is normal to the spine.

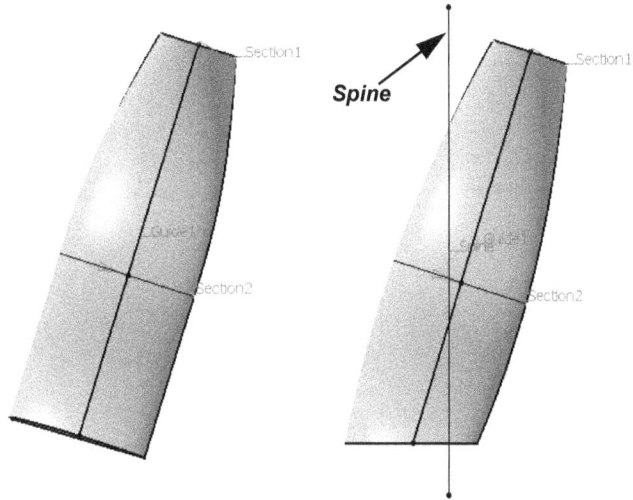

**Figure 8–10**

### Canonical Element

The *Canonical Element* tab contains the **Canonical portion detection** option, as shown in Figure 8–11.

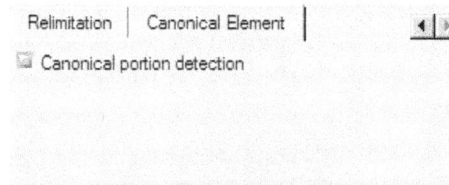

**Figure 8–11**

By default, the **Canonical portion detection** option is enabled. When this option is enabled, the system detects the planar faces of the resulting Multi-sections feature so that they can be used for downstream features. For example, the surface of the Multi-sections feature shown in Figure 8–12 can be selected as a sketch support to define the profile for another feature.

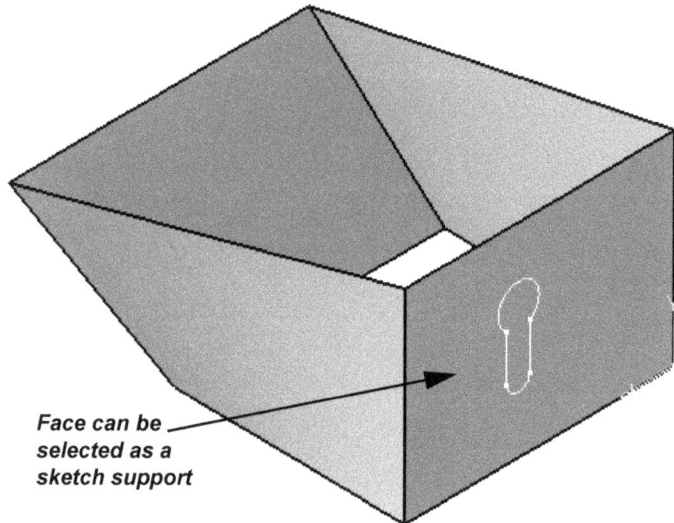

Face can be selected as a sketch support

**Figure 8–12**

If the **Canonical portion detection** option is disabled, the face cannot be selected as a planar reference, regardless of its curvature.

# 8.2 Blended Surfaces

A Blended surface connects the area between two curves or surfaces. As with the Fill surface feature, you can specify support surfaces to constrain curvature properties at the boundaries of the blended surface. Two initial surfaces are shown in Figure 8–13.

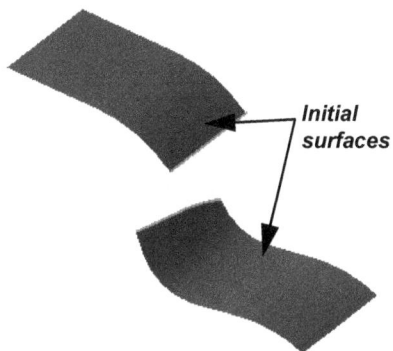

**Figure 8–13**

Two types of Blend features are shown in Figure 8–14 using the initial surfaces.

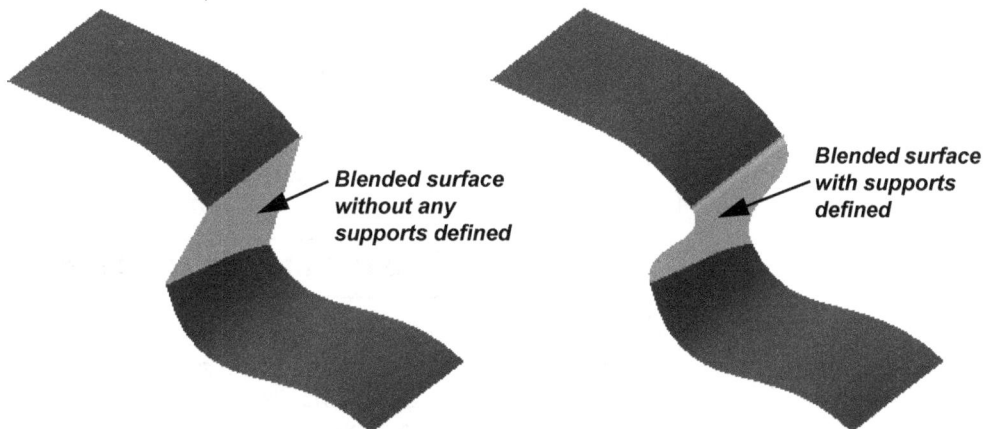

**Figure 8–14**

**General Steps**

Use the following general steps to create a blended surface:

1. Start the creation of the blended surface.
2. Define the curves to blend.
3. Specify the continuity conditions.
4. Specify the optional conditions.

## Step 1 - Start the creation of the blended surface.

To start the creation of the blended surface, click ⬙ (Blend). The Blend Definition dialog box opens as shown in Figure 8–15.

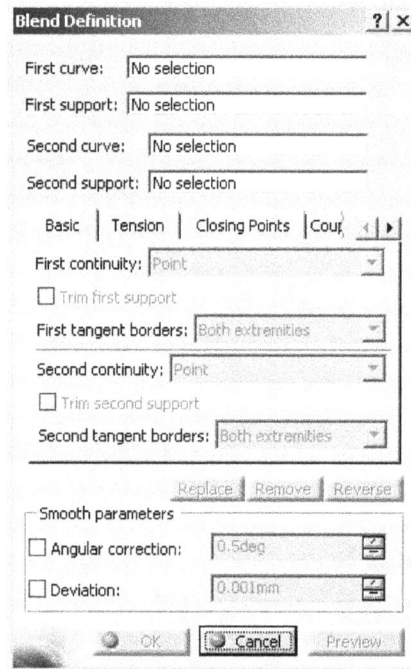

**Figure 8–15**

## Step 2 - Define the curves to blend.

Once the dialog box opens, you can define the blended surface. Select the two sections for the blend and support surfaces for each curve. These selections display in the *First curve*, *First support*, *Second curve*, and *Second support* fields.

## Step 3 - Specify the continuity conditions.

Continuity determines how the blended surface meets the support surface on either end of the feature. Continuity is controlled using the options in the *Basic* tab, as shown in Figure 8–16.

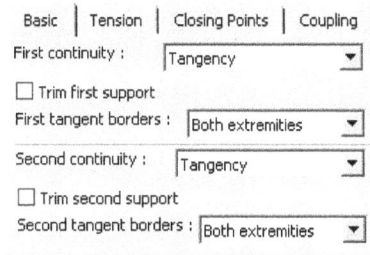

**Figure 8–16**

The options on this tab control the continuity of the first and second curves with their respective supports. The following continuity options are available:

- **Point:** Enables the blended surface and support surface to share a common boundary (also called G0 continuity).

- **Tangency:** Enables the blended surface and support surface to share a common boundary and be tangent to each other (also called G1 continuity).

- **Curvature:** Enables the blended surface and support surface to have a common curvature at their shared boundary (also called G2 continuity).

Examples of the three types of continuity are shown in Figure 8–17.

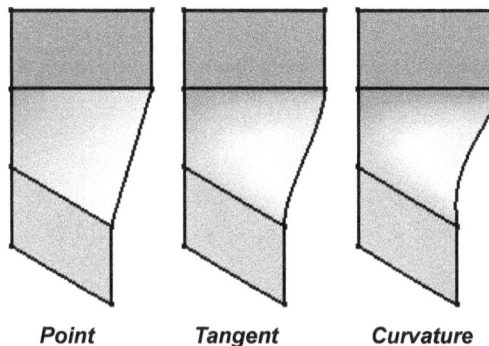

*Point*          *Tangent*          *Curvature*

**Figure 8–17**

The First and Second tangent borders drop-down lists apply the continuity setting at the start, end, both, or neither end(s) of the curve.

## Step 4 - Specify the optional conditions.

The blended surface can be further controlled using options in the following tabs: *Tension*, *Closing Points*, and *Coupling*.

**Tension**

The *Tension* tab displays as shown in Figure 8–18.

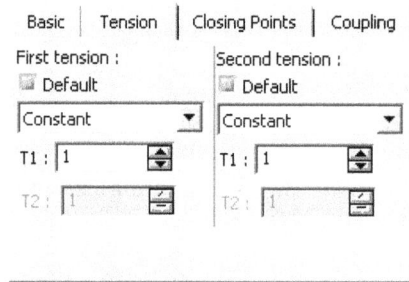

**Figure 8–18**

Tension determines how much the shape of the blended surface can change while maintaining the continuity settings defined in the *Basic* tab. The tension can be constant or vary linearly from the start to the end of the curve.

An example of how increased tension values vary is shown in Figure 8–19. The curvature continuous surface shown on the left is used to produce the surface shown on the right.

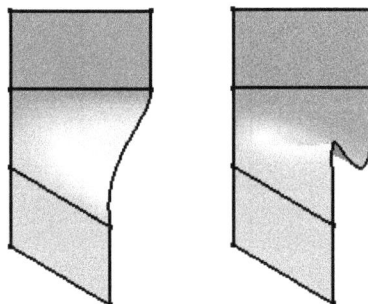

**Figure 8–19**

**Closing Points**

Use the *Closing Points* tab to determine the connection point between two closed sections. This point can be used to add a twist to a blended surface, as shown in Figure 8–20.

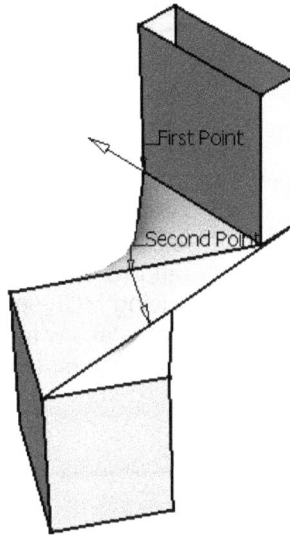

**Figure 8–20**

The closing points are automatically selected by the system. To modify the closing points, select the *First closing point* or *Second closing point* field, as shown in Figure 8–21. Then select a new vertex or reference point.

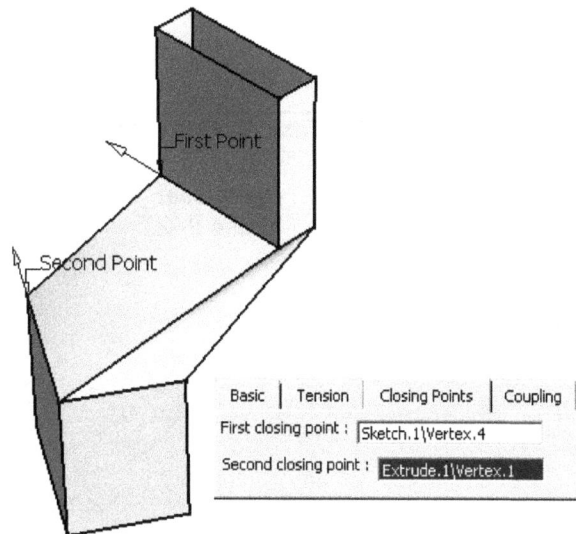

**Figure 8–21**

Click **OK** to complete the feature.

# Practice 8a | Seat Base

### Practice Objectives

- Create a Multi-sections surface.
- Create a Swept surface.
- Create a Blended surface.

In this practice, you will create the base of an automobile seat using Multi-sections and Swept surface slabs. You will then trim the slabs with a blended surface. The completed model displays as shown in Figure 8–22.

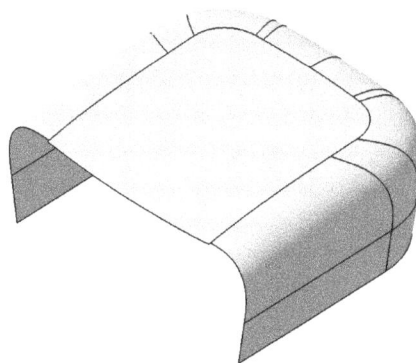

**Figure 8–22**

### Task 1 - Open a part.

1. Open **Seat_Base.CATPart**. The model displays as shown in Figure 8–23.

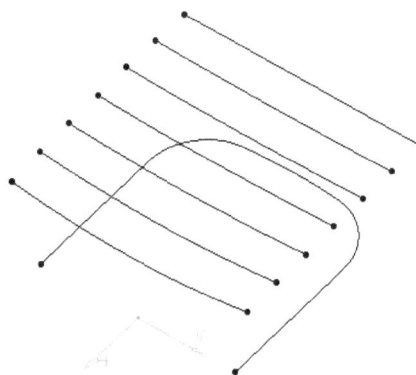

**Figure 8–23**

2. Set the units to **mm**.

**Task 2 - Create a Multi-sections surface.**

In this task, you will create a Multi-sections surface using the sections located in the **Section-Data** geometrical set.

1. Expand the **Section-Data** branch in the specification tree, as shown in Figure 8–24.

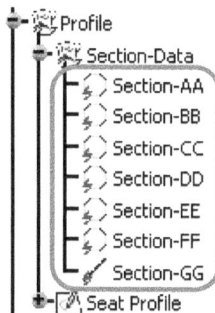

**Figure 8–24**

2. Click  (Multi-sections surface) in the Surfaces toolbar. The dialog box opens as shown in Figure 8–25.

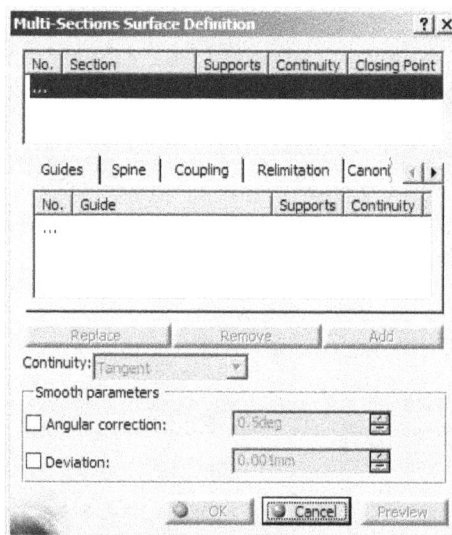

**Figure 8–25**

3. Select the sections in **Section-Data** geometrical set in alphabetical order (Section A-A to Section G-G).

4. Align the sections' coupling arrows as shown in Figure 8–26.

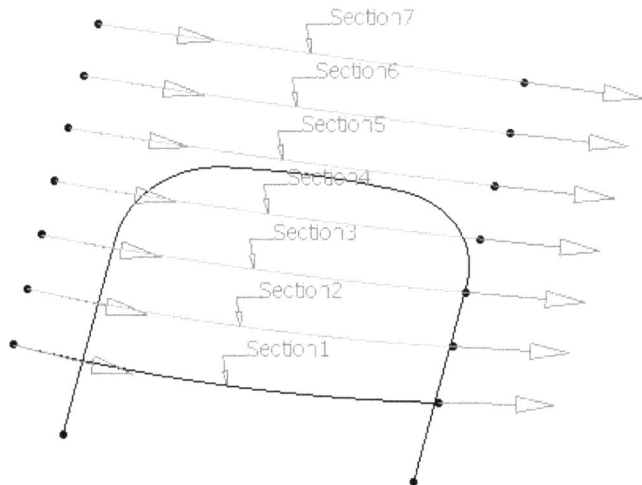

**Figure 8–26**

5. Click **OK** to complete the feature. The model displays as shown in Figure 8–27.

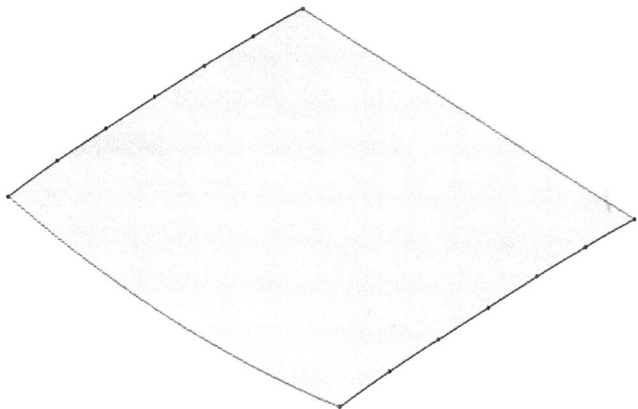

**Figure 8–27**

6. Rename the Multi-sections surface as **BottomSurf**.

7. Right-click on the **Section-Data** geometrical set and select **Section-Data object>Hide Components**.

## Task 3 - Create a Swept surface.

In this task, you will create a Line type swept surface that will form the side of the seat base. The completed Swept surface displays as shown in Figure 8–28.

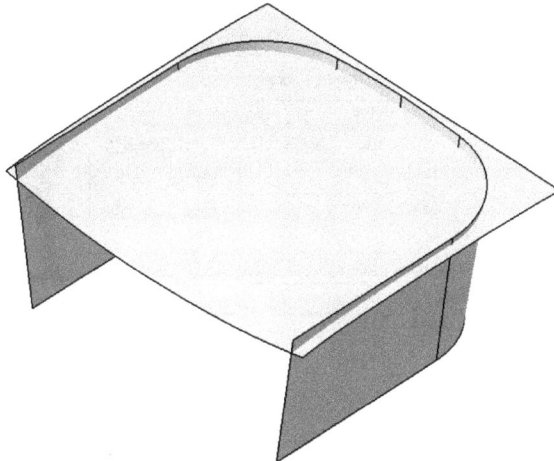

**Figure 8–28**

1. Click ⬙ (Sweep). The Sweep Surface Definition dialog box opens.

2. Click ⬙ (Line) to create a Line sweep. Select **With reference surface** as the Subtype.

3. Specify the following parameters:

   - *Guide curve 1:* **SeatProfile**
   - *Reference surface:* **XY plane**
   - *Angle:* **81deg**
   - *Length 1:* **110mm**

*The active Angular sector displays in orange.*

4. Click **Next** in the *Angular sector* area until the Swept surface feature displays as shown in Figure 8–29.

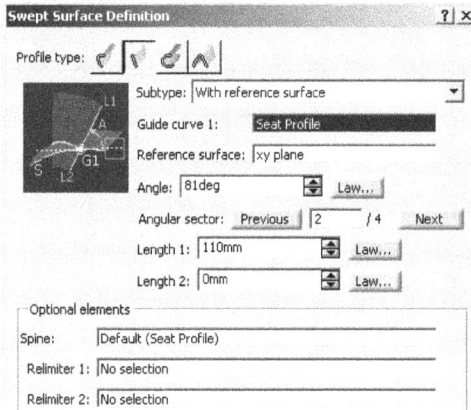

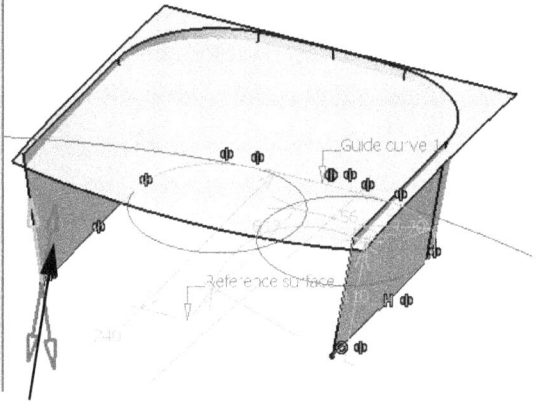

**Correct Angular sector**

**Figure 8–29**

5. Click **OK** to complete the Swept surface feature.

6. Rename the Swept surface as **SideSurf**.

---

**Task 4 - Prepare a new geometrical set.**

---

You must create reference geometry before you can construct the remaining surfaces. To maintain good modeling practice, you will create two new geometrical sets to store the reference geometry.

1. Select **Insert>Geometrical Set**.

2. Select **BottomSurf** and **SideSurf** in the specification tree.

3. Name the new set **Surface-Data** and select **Seat_Base** as the Father. The Insert Geometrical Set dialog box opens as shown in Figure 8–30.

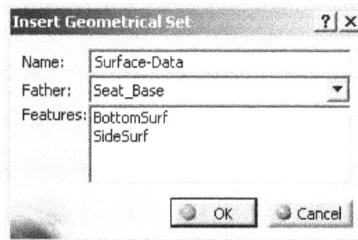

**Figure 8–30**

4. Insert a new geometrical set called **Reference-Geom** with **Seat_Base** as the *Father*. The specification tree displays as shown in Figure 8–31.

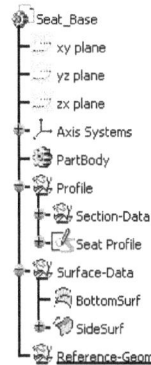

**Figure 8–31**

## Task 5 - Create an Intersection.

1. Click  (Intersection) to open the Intersection Definition dialog box.

2. Select **BottomSurf** and **SideSurf** as the *First* and *Second Elements*, as shown in Figure 8–32.

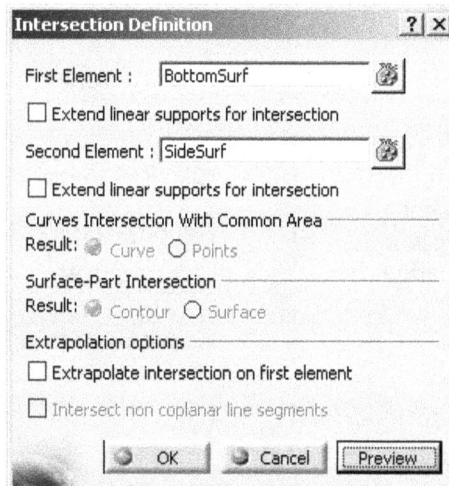

**Figure 8–32**

3. Click **OK** to complete the Intersection feature.

4. Rename the Intersection as **BottomSideIntersect**.

## Task 6 - Create two parallel curves.

In this task, you will remove the excess material from the existing surface slabs using a blended surface feature. The limits of the blended surface are defined by two Parallel Curves, which can be offset from a curve onto a support surface.

1. Click  (Parallel Curve) to open the Parallel Curve Definition dialog box.

2. Select **BottomSideIntersect** as the Curve and **BottomSurf** as the Support.

3. Enter **50mm** as the *Constant offset* value, as shown in Figure 8–33.

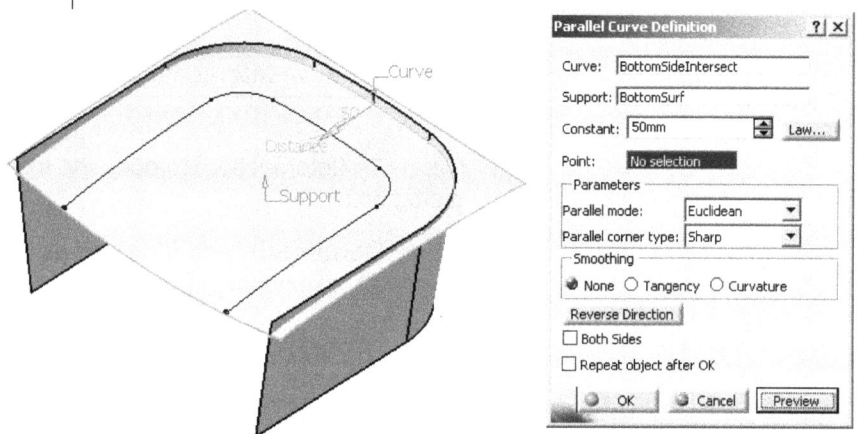

**Figure 8–33**

*If an Update Error dialog box opens, select* **Reverse Direction** *to reverse the orientation of the parallel curve.*

4. Click **OK** to complete the Parallel Curve feature.

5. Rename the Parallel Curve as **FirstCurve**.

6. Create a second Parallel Curve feature.

7. Select **BottomSideIntersect** as the Curve and **SideSurf** as the Support.

8. Enter **40mm** as the *Constant* offset value, as shown in Figure 8–34.

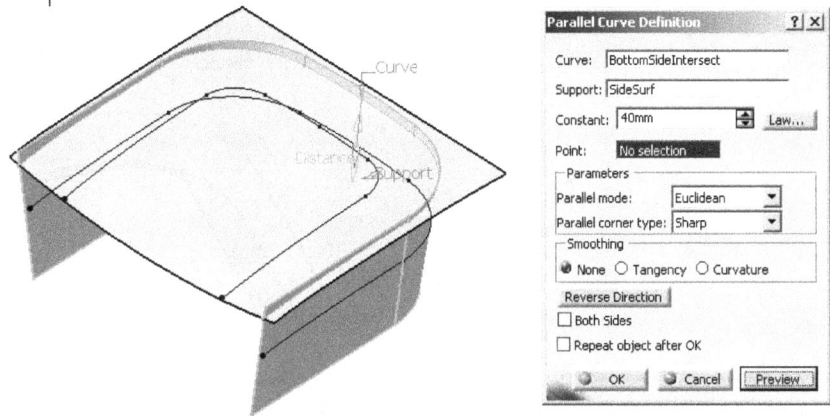

Figure 8–34

9. Rename the second Parallel Curve as **SecondCurve**.

---

**Task 7 - Split surfaces with reference curves.**

---

1. Activate the **Surface-Data** geometrical set.

2. Split **SideSurf** using **SecondCurve** as the cutting element.

3. The bottom portion of SideSurf should remain from the **Split** operation. Click **Other side** to toggle which portion of the surface to keep. The completed Split displays as shown in Figure 8–35.

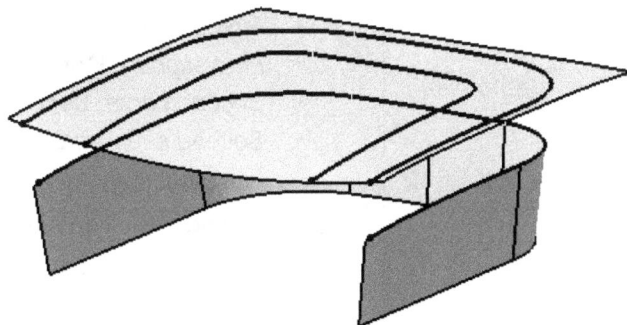

Figure 8–35

4. Rename the Split feature as **SideSplit**.

5. Split **BottomSurf** using **FirstCurve** as the cutting element.

6. If required, toggle **Other side** so that the model displays as shown in Figure 8–36.

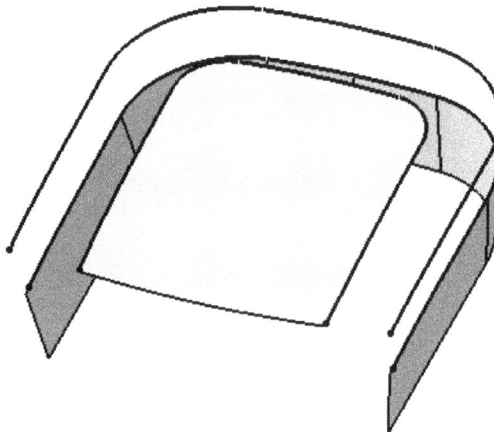

**Figure 8–36**

7. Complete the **Split** operation and rename the feature as **BottomSplit**.

## Task 8 - Create a blended surface with supports.

1. Click [icon] (Blend) to open the Blend Definition dialog box. Specify the following parameters:

- *First curve:* **FirstCurve**
- *First support:* **BottomSplit**
- *Second curve:* **SecondCurve**
- *Second support:* **SideSplit**
- *First continuity and Second continuity:* **Tangency**

The Blend Definition dialog box opens as shown in Figure 8–37.

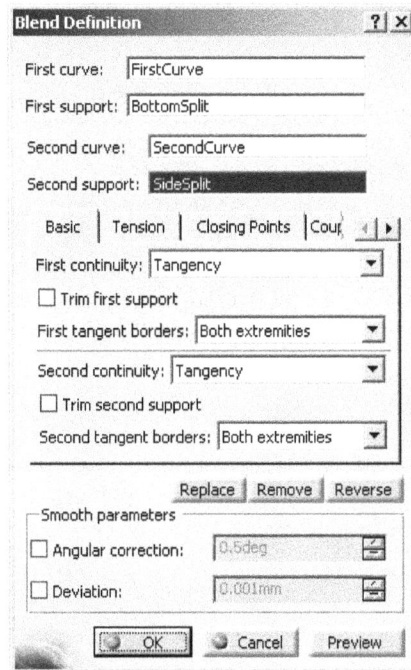

**Figure 8–37**

2. Rename the blended surface feature as **SmoothEdge**.

3. Hide **Seat Profile**, **BottomSideIntersect**, **FirstCurve**, and **SecondCurve**. The model displays as shown in Figure 8–38.

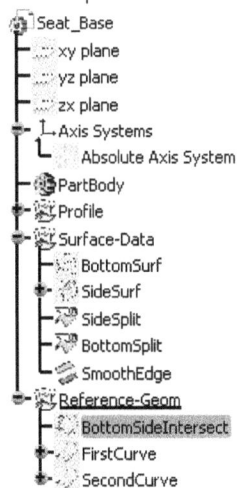

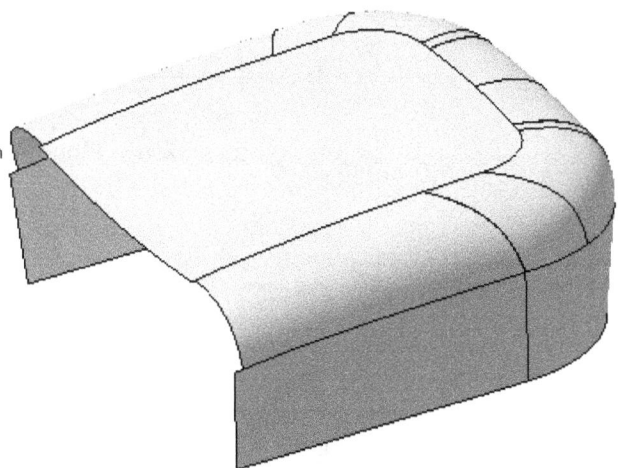

**Figure 8–38**

4. Save and close the file.

# Practice 8b

# Side Mirror

### Practice Objective

- Create a Multi-sections surface.

In this practice, you will create Multi-sections Surface and Fill features to complete the side mirror part. The Multi-sections surface consists of profiles that have already been provided. Coupling curves are established to meet the design intent of the model. The completed model displays as shown in Figure 8–39.

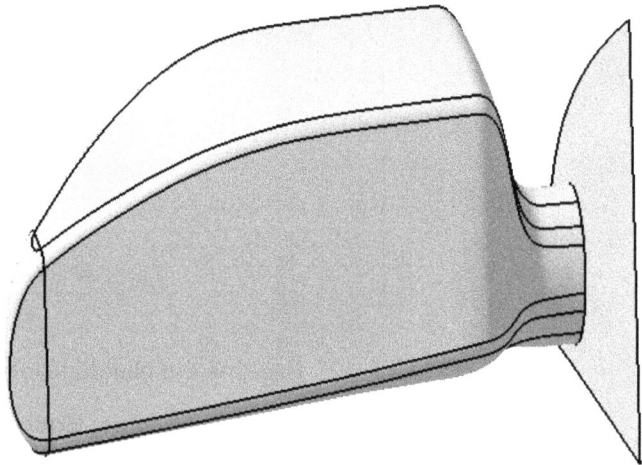

Figure 8–39

### Task 1 - Open a part.

1. Open **MSS_Side Mirror_Start.CATPart**. The model displays as shown in Figure 8–40.

Figure 8–40

Note there are two axis systems in the model. One represents the part's origin, while the other is used to create wireframe geometry and surfaces for the side mirror. All wireframe geometry and surfaces in the model are linked to the Mirror Axis system. This axis system can be moved to accommodate design changes, bringing the mirror geometry with it.

2. Hide both axis systems and **Split.1**. **Split.1** is located in the **Window Base** geometrical set.

---

**Task 2 - Investigate the model.**

---

1. Show all of the sketches belonging to the **MSS Profiles** geometrical set. The model displays as shown in Figure 8–41. The five sketches were created on planes offset from the ZX plane of the Mirror Axis system. Each sketch has six points that were created as Output features.

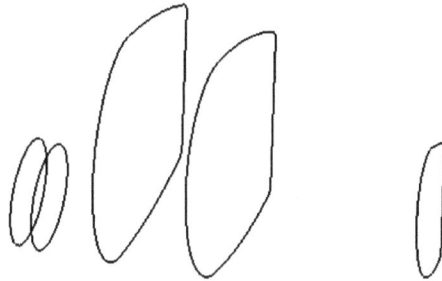

**Figure 8–41**

2. If you expand each of the sketches in the **MSS Profiles** geometrical set, the Output features are displayed as shown in Figure 8–42.

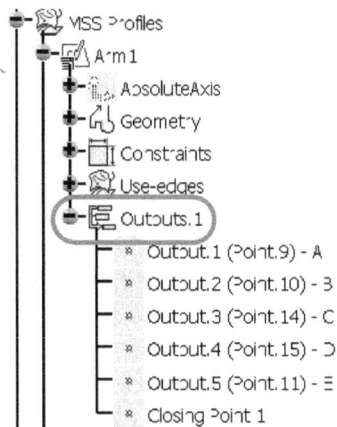

MSS Profiles
Arm1
AbsoluteAxis
Geometry
Constraints
Use-edges
Outputs.1
Output.1 (Point.9) - A
Output.2 (Point.10) - B
Output.3 (Point.14) - C
Output.4 (Point.15) - D
Output.5 (Point.11) - E
Closing Point 1

**Figure 8–42**

---

*Another method of showing every Output feature is to select* **Edit>Search***.*

3. To make all of the Output features visible quickly, enter **sketcher.output,all** in the *Power input* field. The *Power input* field is located at the bottom right corner of the CATIA window, as shown in Figure 8–43.

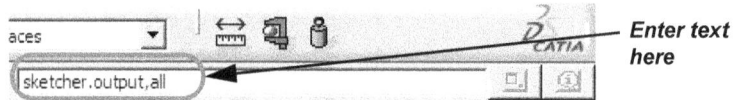

— **Enter text here**

**Figure 8–43**

After entering the text, press <Enter>. Entering a search string in the *Power input* field will run a search for the specified elements. In this case, the search will locate and highlight all of the Output features in the model.

4. Click  (Hide/Show). The Output features become visible, as shown in Figure 8–44.

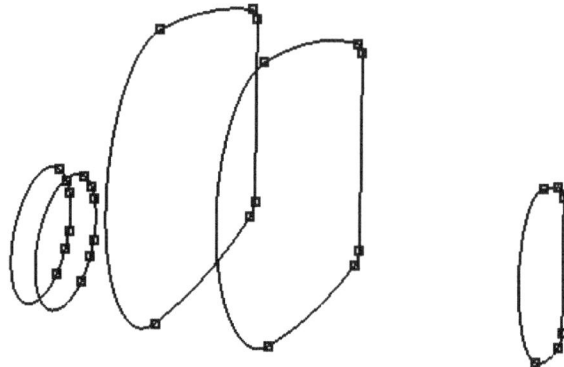

**Figure 8–44**

## Task 3 - Create a Multi-section surface.

1. Click  (Multi-section Surface) in the Surfaces toolbar. The Multi-section Surface Definition dialog box opens as shown in Figure 8–45.

**Figure 8–45**

2. Select the following profiles:

- **Arm1**
- **Arm2**
- **Body3**
- **Body4**
- **Body5**

**Design Considerations**

The closing points' position and direction match appropriately by default. Note the sub-elements (vertices) that are referenced for each closing point, as shown in Figure 8–46. To create a more stable model, you need to have the closing point for each section reference the point from the Output feature instead of a vertex.

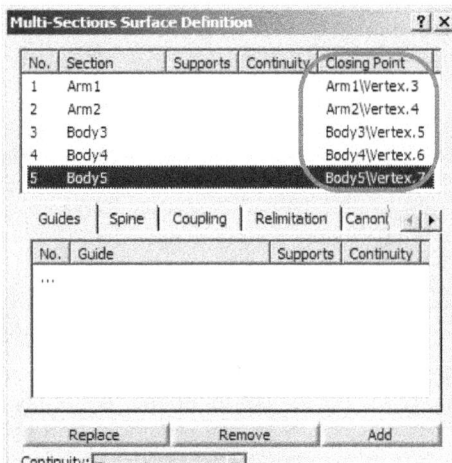

**Figure 8–46**

3. To change the closing point reference, right-click on **Arm1** in the dialog box and select **Replace Closing Point**, as shown in Figure 8–47.

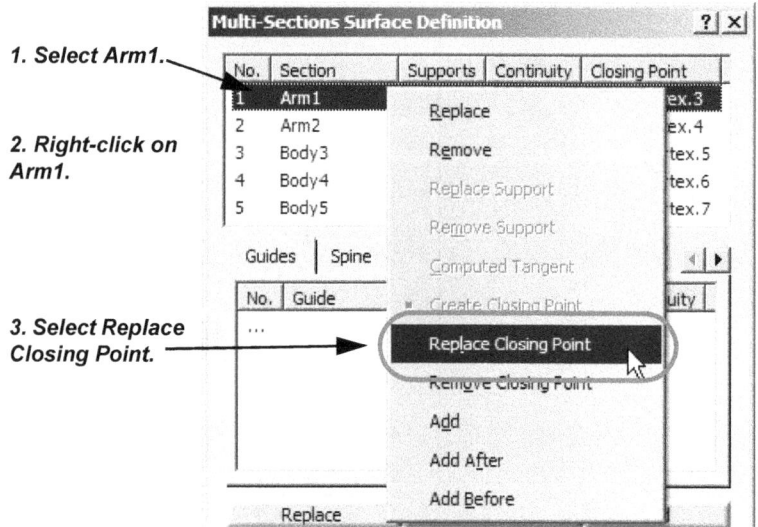

Figure 8–47

4. Expand **Arm1** in the specification tree. Expand **Outputs**.

5. Select the point named **Closing Point 1** in the specification tree, as shown in Figure 8–48.

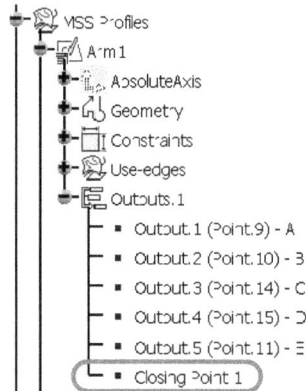

Figure 8–48

**Design Considerations**

The closing point now references the output point instead of the vertex. Because the output point is an explicitly created entity, it is listed in the specification tree and is easily modifiable, enabling a more robust and stable design. However, the vertex has not been explicitly created. If the design changes, the vertex might be altered or lost, causing the Multi-sections feature to fail.

6. Repeat Steps 3 to 5 for each of the four remaining profiles selected for the Multi-sections surface. The Multi-sections Surface Definitions dialog box opens as shown in Figure 8–49.

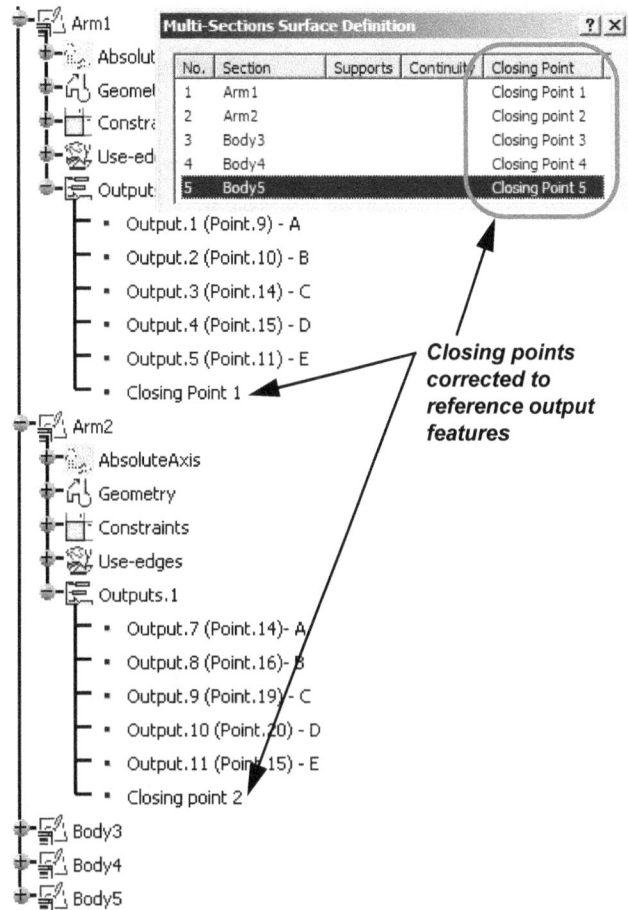

Figure 8–49

7. Select the *Coupling* tab in the dialog box.

8. Ensure that the **Sections coupling** option is set to **Tangency** as shown in Figure 8–50.

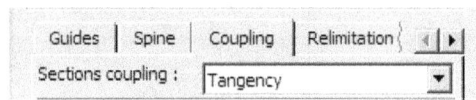

Figure 8–50

9. Click **Preview**. The model displays as shown in Figure 8–51.

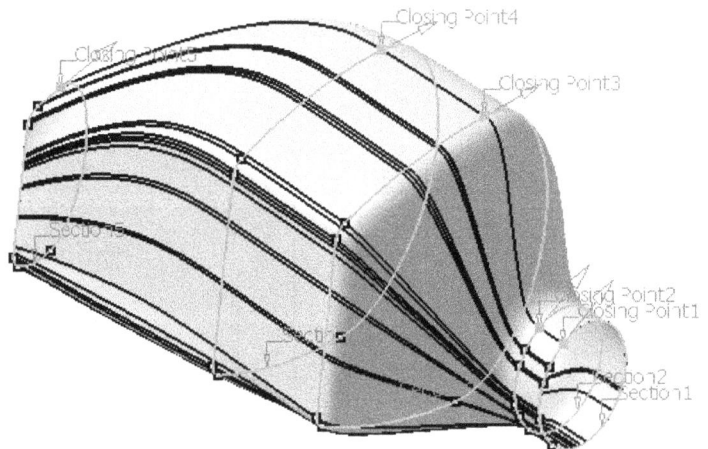

**Figure 8–51**

10. Coupling curves are required to create a better quality Multi-sections surface. Activate the *Coupling* field and click **Add**, as shown in Figure 8–52.

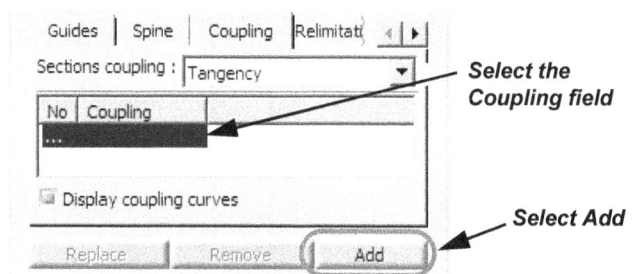

**Figure 8–52**

The Coupling dialog box opens as shown in Figure 8–53.

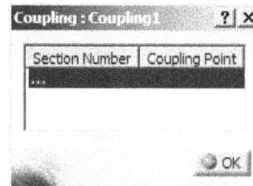

**Figure 8–53**

11. Inside each sketched section is an output point labeled **A**, as shown in Figure 8–54. You might need to expand each sketch in the specification tree to display the outputs.

12. Select each output point labeled **A** in the order shown in Figure 8–54. These output points create the first coupling curve.

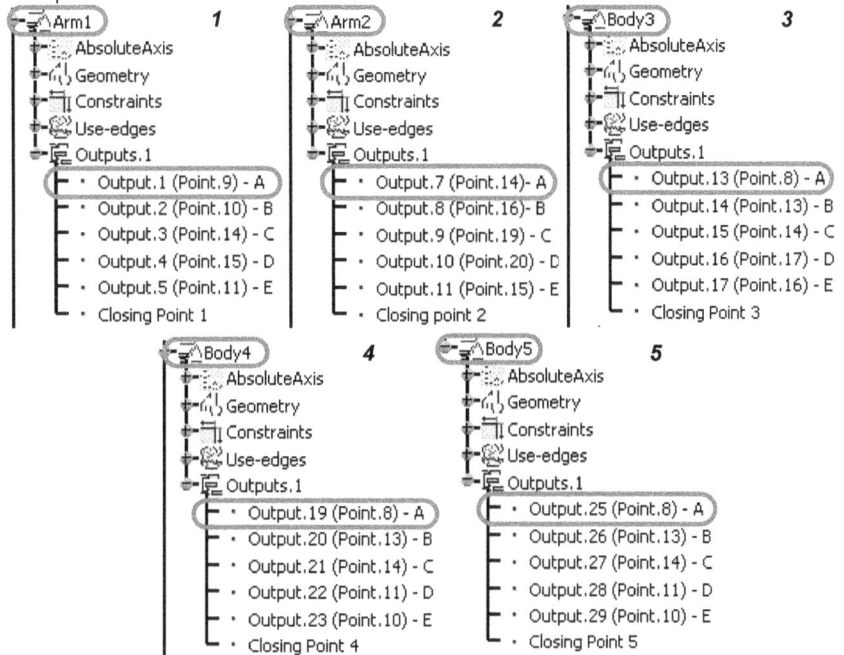

**Figure 8–54**

*Remember that the coupling points must be selected in the following order: **Arm1**, **Arm2**, **Body3**, **Body4**, and **Body5**.*

13. Repeat Steps 10 to 12 to create five more coupling curves. All of the output points labeled **B** go in one coupling curve, **C** in the next coupling curve, etc. The output points labeled *Closing Point* should also be placed in one of the five remaining coupling curves.

When the coupling curves are completed, the Multi-sections Surface Definition dialog box opens as shown Figure 8–55.

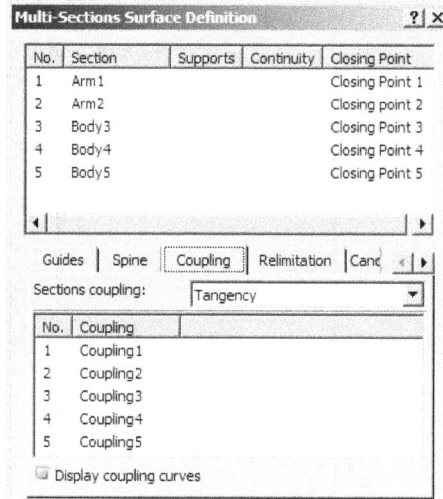

**Figure 8–55**

14. Click **Preview**. The model has changed with the coupling curves, as shown in Figure 8–56.

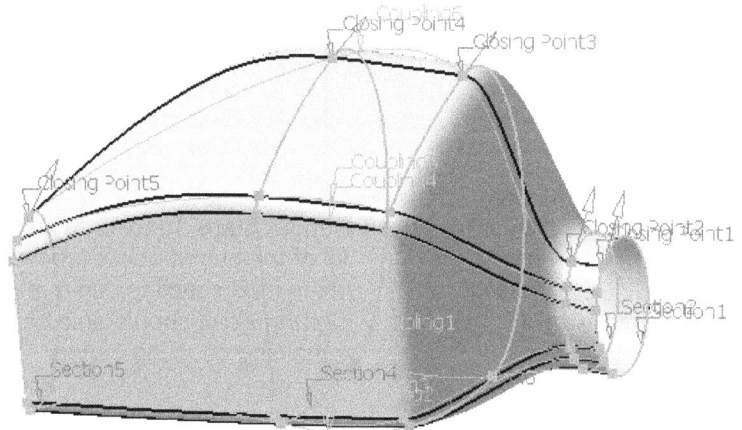

**Figure 8–56**

15. Click **OK** to complete the Multi-sections surface.

16. Using the graphic properties, make the Multi-sections Surface.1 yellow. The model displays as shown in Figure 8–57.

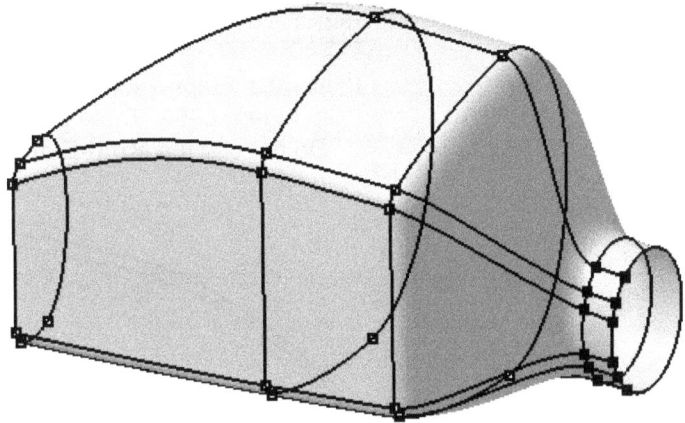

**Figure 8–57**

## Task 4 - Extract curves.

1. Hide the **MSS Profiles** geometrical set.

2. Click  (Extract).

3. Using **No Propagation**, select the edge shown in Figure 8–58.

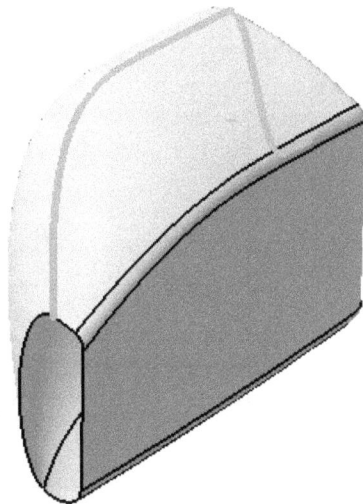

**Figure 8–58**

4. Click **OK** to complete the Extract.

## Task 5 - Create splines.

1. Repeat Steps 2 to 4 from Task 4 to create the curves shown in Figure 8–59. There should be a total of six extract curves. Do not use the **Multi-Extract** tool.

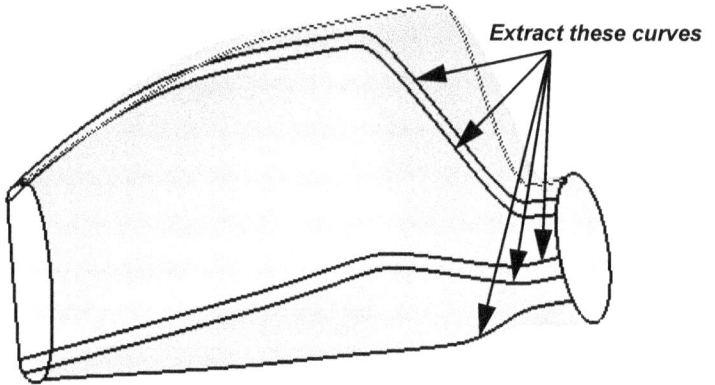

*Extract these curves*

Figure 8–59

2. Click [⌇].

3. Right-click in the Spline Definition dialog box and select **Create Endpoint**, as shown in Figure 8–60.

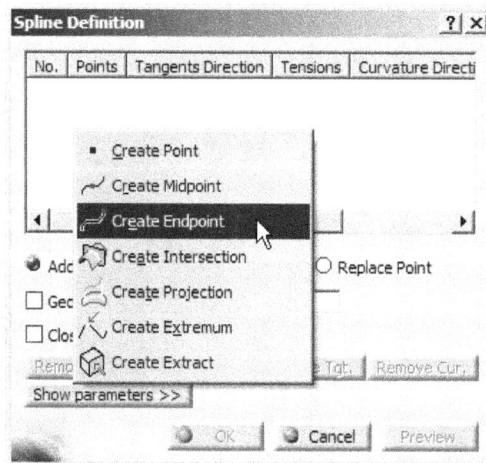

Figure 8–60

4. Select the end point shown in Figure 8–61.

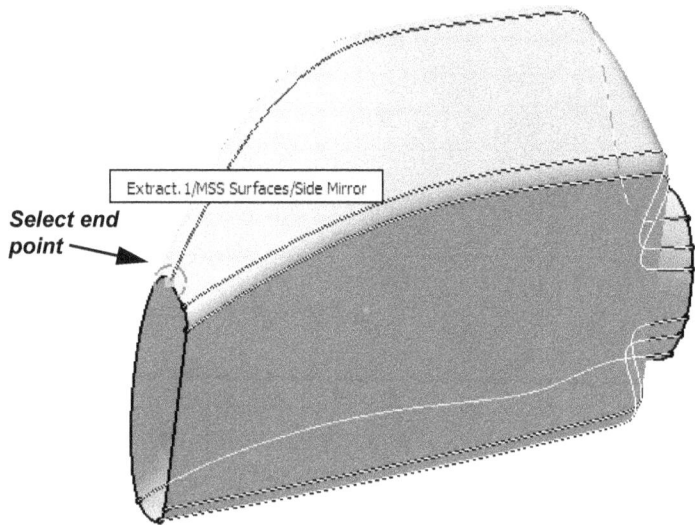

**Figure 8–61**

5. Select **Extract.1** to specify the tangency.

6. Right-click in the dialog box and select **Create Endpoint**.

7. Select the end point shown in Figure 8–62.

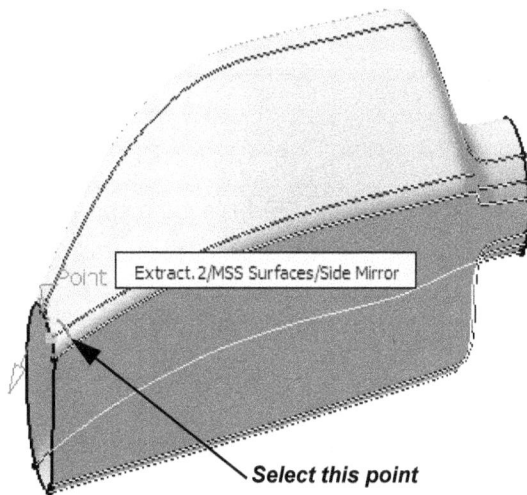

**Figure 8–62**

8. Select **Extract.2** as the tangent reference. The spline displays as shown in Figure 8–63. You might need to flip the tangency arrows. To do so, select the arrow to toggle the tangent direction.

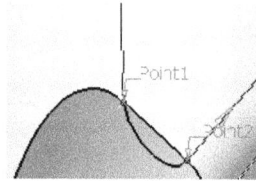

Figure 8–63

9. Click **OK** to complete the Spline.

10. Create two more splines using the same process so that the model displays as shown in Figure 8–64.

Figure 8–64

## Task 6 - Create remaining surfaces.

1. Click  (Fill).

2. Select the spline shown in Figure 8–65.

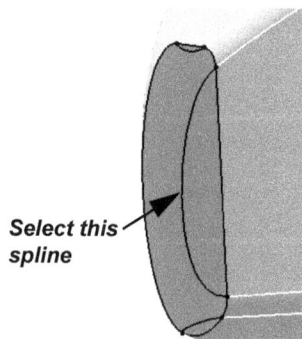

Figure 8–65

3. Right-click in the Fill Definition dialog box and select **Create Boundary**, as shown in Figure 8–66.

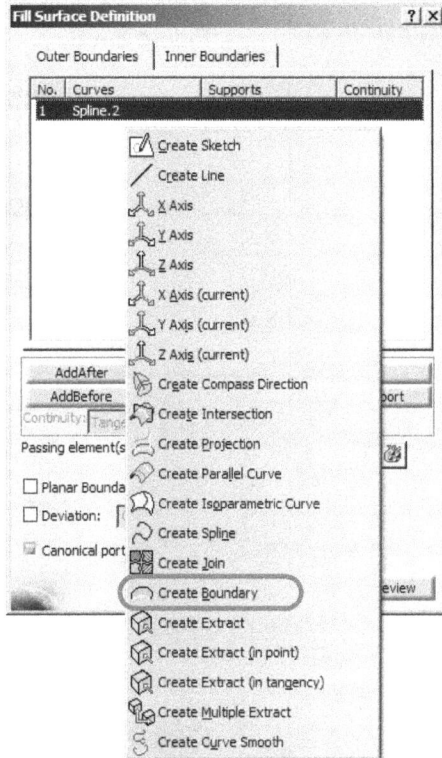

**Figure 8–66**

4. Ensure that **No Propagation** is selected in the Propagation type drop-down list. Select the edge shown in Figure 8–67.

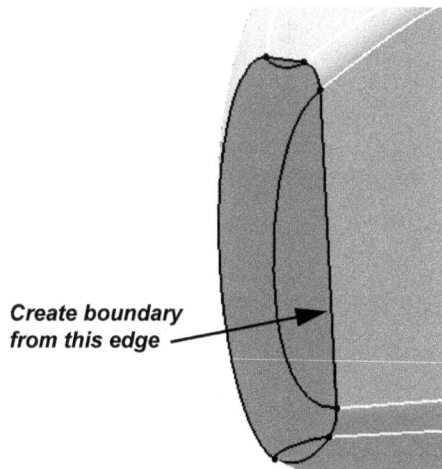

*Create boundary from this edge*

**Figure 8–67**

*Ensure that the continuity is set to **Tangent** for the Fill surfaces.*

5. Click **OK** to complete the Boundary.

6. Select the Multi-sections surface. This ensures that the Fill surface is tangent to the Multi-sections surface, as shown in Figure 8–68.

**Figure 8–68**

7. Click **OK** to complete the Fill. The model displays as shown in Figure 8–69.

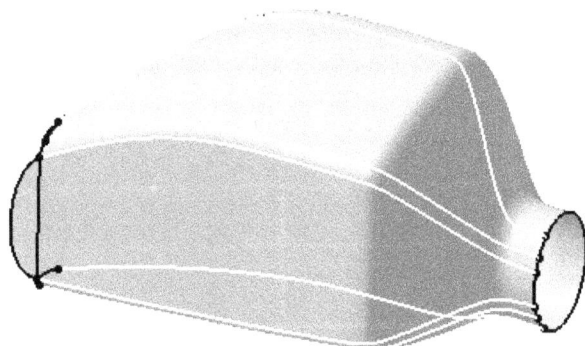

**Figure 8–69**

8. Create two more Fill surfaces using the other splines created in Task 5.

9. Rename the three fill surfaces as shown in Figure 8–70.

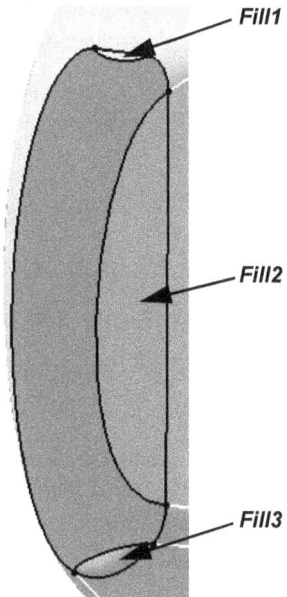

**Figure 8–70**

10. Click ⬦ (Fill).

11. Select the spline shown in Figure 8–71.

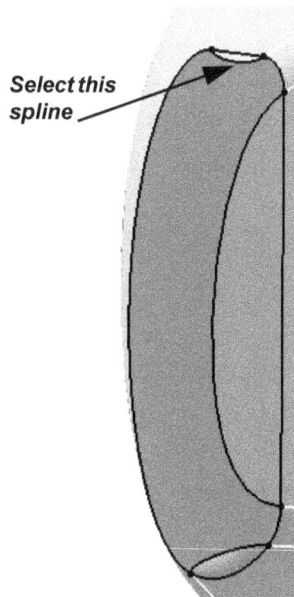

*Select this spline*

**Figure 8–71**

12. Select **Fill1**. Fill1 is the tangent reference for the previously selected spline.

13. Right-click in the Fill Definition dialog box and select **Create Boundary**.

14. With **No Propagation** selected, select the edge shown in Figure 8–72.

15. Click **OK** to complete the Boundary.

16. Select **Multi-sections Surface.1**.

17. Select the spline shown in Figure 8–72.

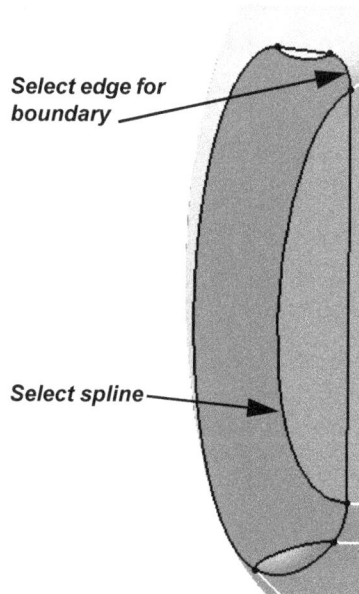

*Select edge for boundary*

*Select spline*

**Figure 8–72**

18. Select **Fill2**.

19. Create a boundary curve using the process from Steps 13 to 15 for the edge shown in Figure 8–73.

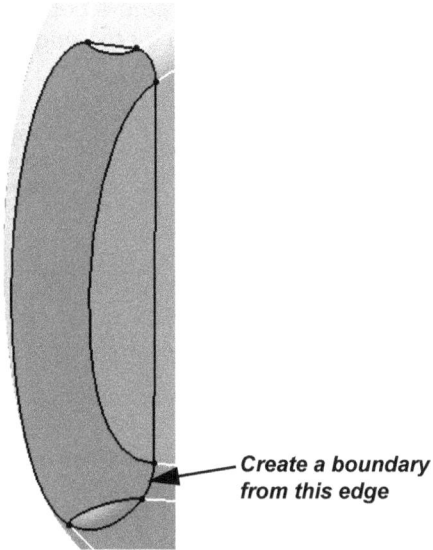

Create a boundary
from this edge

Figure 8–73

20. Select **Multi-sections Surface.1**.

21. Select the spline shown in Figure 8–74.

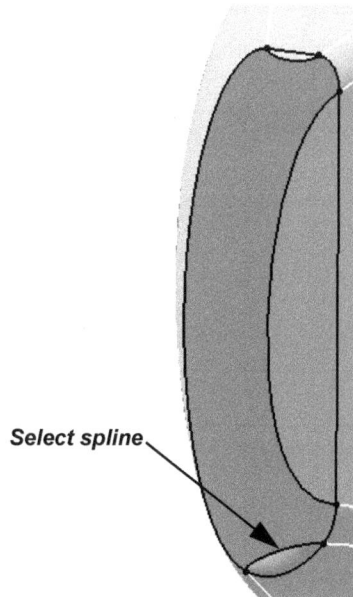

Select spline

Figure 8–74

22. Select **Fill3**.

23. Create a boundary curve using the process from Steps 13 to 15 for the edge shown in Figure 8–75.

**Create boundary curve from this edge**

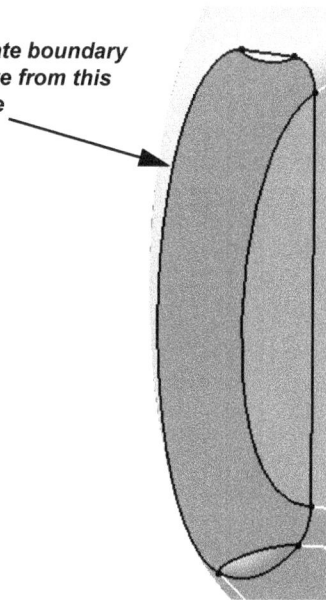

Figure 8–75

24. Select **Multi-sections Surface.1**. The Fill dialog box opens as shown in Figure 8–76.

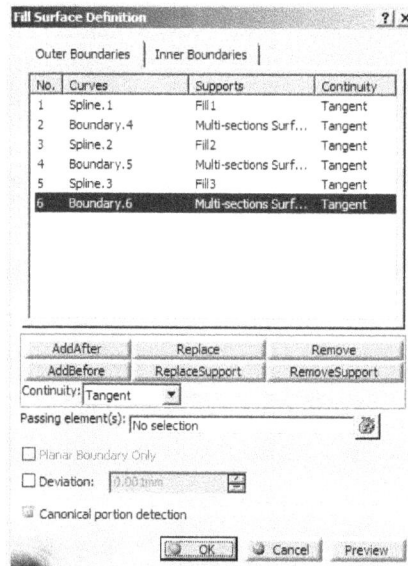

Figure 8–76

25. Click **OK** to completed the Fill.

26. Hide the extract curves and splines that you previously created. The model displays as shown in Figure 8–77.

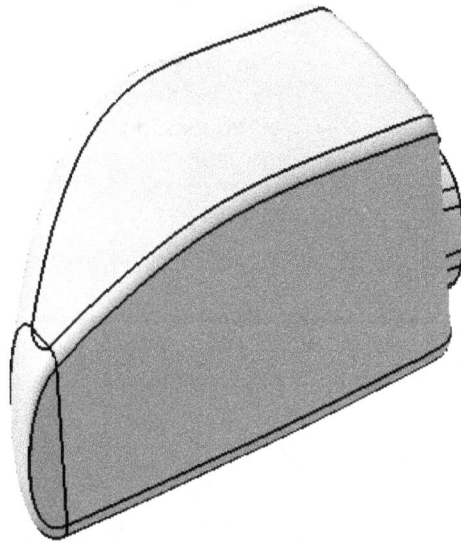

**Figure 8–77**

27. Join the four Fill surfaces and the Multi-sections Surface.

28. Show **Split.1**. The model displays as shown in Figure 8–78.

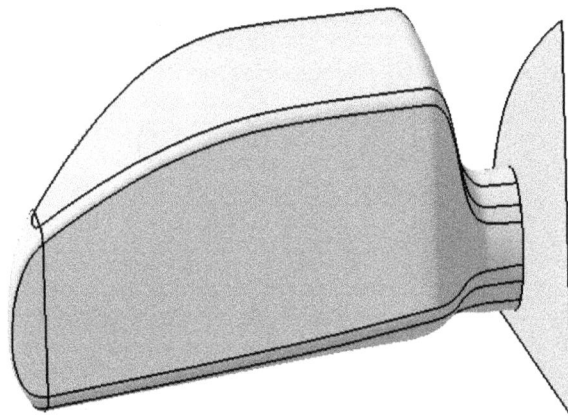

**Figure 8–78**

29. Save the model and close the window.

# Practice 8c

# Surface Design I

## Practice Objective

- Create a Multi-sections feature.

In this practice, you will work on the intake manifold. You will create the side port geometry by a Multi-sections feature with the two existing sketched profiles (shown in Figure 8–79), and ensure that the geometry is optimized for fluid flow.

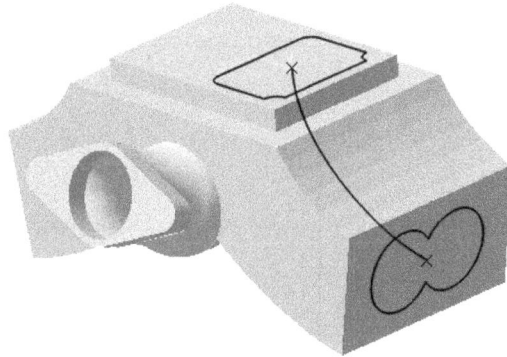

**Figure 8–79**

## Task 1 - Open a part.

1. Open **IntakeManifoldWireframe.CATPart**.

2. Set the units to **mm**.

3. Ensure that the geometry shown in Figure 8–80 is in the geometrical set.

*This geometry should be listed under Geometrical Set.1.*

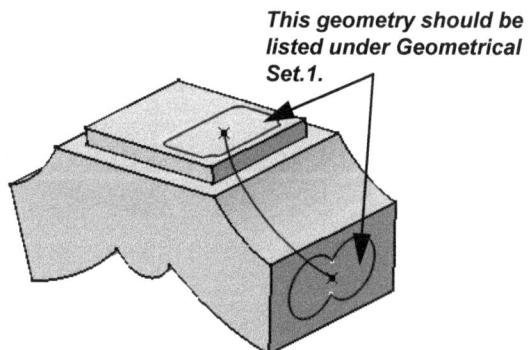

**Figure 8–80**

4. Hide the solid geometry by right-clicking on the PartBody and selecting **Hide/Show**. The wireframe elements displays as shown in Figure 8–81.

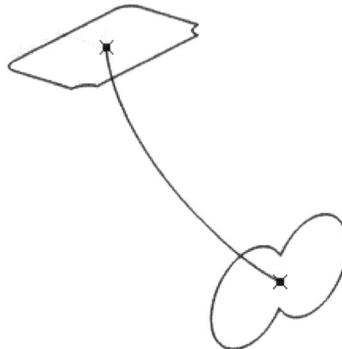

Figure 8–81

## Task 2 - Create a Multi-sections feature.

1. Click [icon] (Multi-sections Surface).

2. Select the sketch and join features for Section 1 and Section 2. Ensure that the Closing Points share the same closing points (i.e., relative vertices) and that the arrows are pointing in the same direction, as shown in Figure 8–82. If the arrows are pointing in different directions, the feature will fail.

*The **Coupling** option should be set to the default value of **Ratio**. The **Ratio** option is used to couple sections that have a different number of vertices or tangency points.*

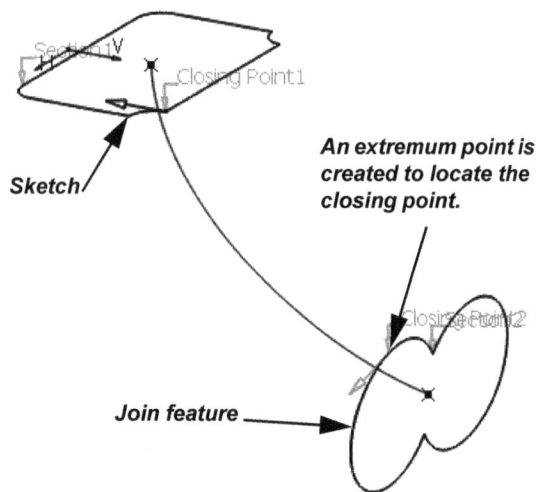

Section 1 V
Closing Point1

*An extremum point is created to locate the closing point.*

**Sketch**

Closing Point2

**Join feature**

Figure 8–82

3. Click **OK** to complete the Multi-sections feature. The model displays as shown in Figure 8–83.

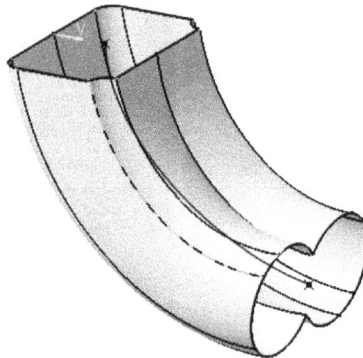

**Figure 8–83**

4. Show **PartBody**.

5. Open the Properties dialog box for the PartBody and enable transparency by dragging the handle to the right, as shown in Figure 8–84.

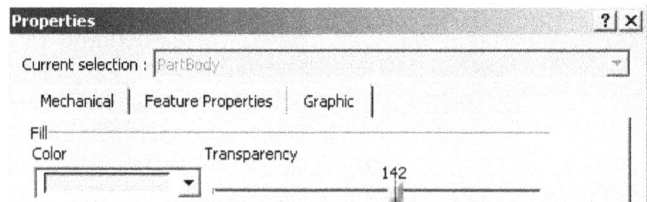

**Figure 8–84**

6. Orient the model to the Front view ( ![icon] ). The model displays as shown in Figure 8–85.

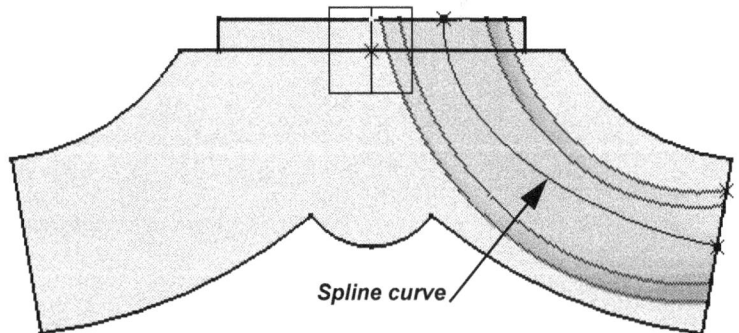

*Spline curve*

**Figure 8–85**

**Design Considerations**

The curvature of the Multi-sections feature does not match the curvature of the spline curve. When the spline was created, tangency conditions were established to make the curve normal to the solid faces at its end points. To achieve optimum flow through this port, you will add the spline curve as a spine for the Multi-sections feature. This ensures that the Multi-sections feature transitions smoothly between the two sections.

## Task 3 - Redefine the Multi-sections feature.

1. Double-click on **Multi-sections Surface.1** in the specification tree.

2. Select the *Spine* tab and select **Spline.1** as the spine for the Multi-sections feature to follow. The Multi-sections Surface Definition dialog box opens as shown in Figure 8–86.

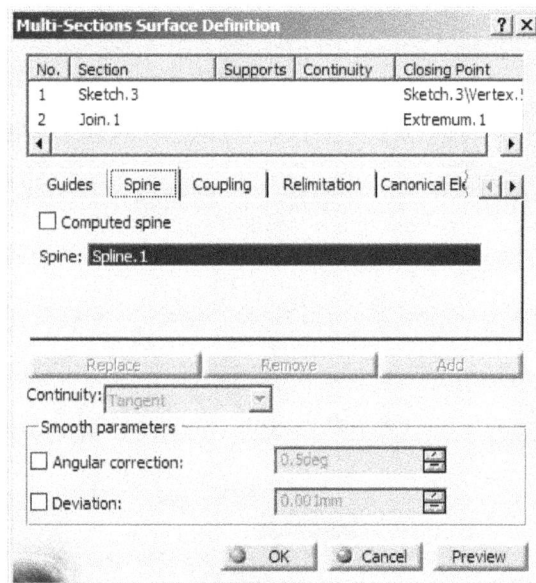

**Figure 8–86**

3. Click **OK** to complete the Multi-sections feature. The model displays as shown on the right in Figure 8–87.

*The Multi-sections surface now follows the spline curve and is centered in the part body.*

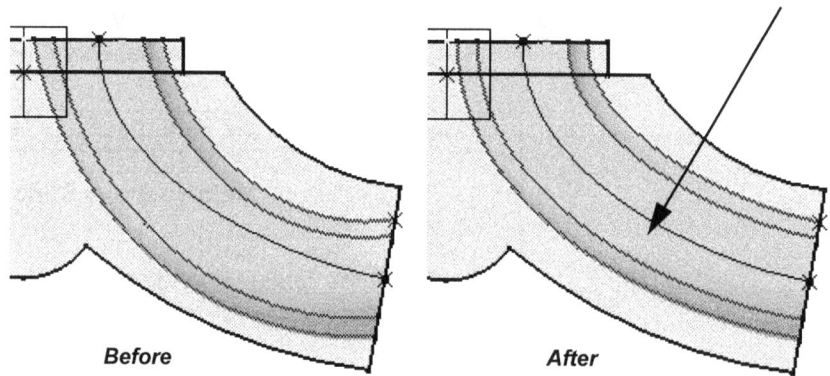

*Before*          *After*

**Figure 8–87**

4. Reset the transparency of the solid to the default value of **0**.

5. Save and close the model.

# Chapter Review Questions

1. A multi-sections surface is created by selecting a maximum of two sketches, edges or curves.

   a. True

   b. False

2. The face of a solid pad can be directly used as a boundary selection for a Multi-sections surface.

   a. True

   b. False

3. Which of the following is true regarding guides in a Multi-sections surface?

   a. Uses a curve or line to define an absolute path through which the Multi-sections feature travel.

   b. More than one guide can be used to control the feature.

   c. By default, the feature only progresses as far as the last section, regardless of the length of the guide.

   d. All of the above.

4. A spine controls the shape of the Multi-sections feature as it progresses from one section to the next.

   a. True

   b. False

5. If the **Vertices** coupling option is used to transition from a square section to a circular section _____.

   a. The system creates four vertices on the circle to transition to.

   b. The system relimits the surface to extend beyond the circle to a single point.

   c. The system displays an error message because there must be an equal number of vertices in each section.

   d. None of the above.

6. A Blended surface connects the area between two curves or surfaces.

   a. True

   b. False

7. For a Blended surface, the three continuity options are:

   a. Point, First, Second

   b. Start, End, Both

   c. Point, Tangent, Curvature

   d. None of the above.

8. To keep a Blended surface from twisting, ensure the _____ are lined up.

   a. Start Points

   b. Closing Points

   c. End Points

   d. None of the above.

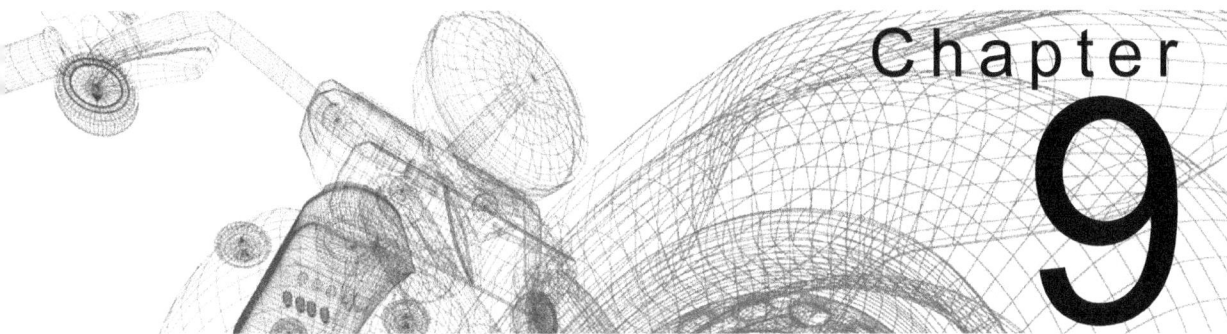

# Surface Fillets

Surface fillets work the same way as fillets in the Part Design workbench. They are used to round sharp corners on a model. This chapter introduces creating surfaces as blends. You can create several types of radius blends or fillets from surfaces.

## Learning Objectives in this Chapter

- Understand how to create surface fillets.
- Create Bi-Tangent Shape fillets.
- Create edge fillet using the Constant and Variable Radius options.
- Create Face-Face fillets.
- Review several tips and considerations.

# 9.1 Creating Surface Fillets

Surface fillets are defined by selecting the appropriate reference geometry and specifying a radius value. By default, the fillet is created tangent to the selected surfaces. An example of a Surface fillet is shown in Figure 9–1.

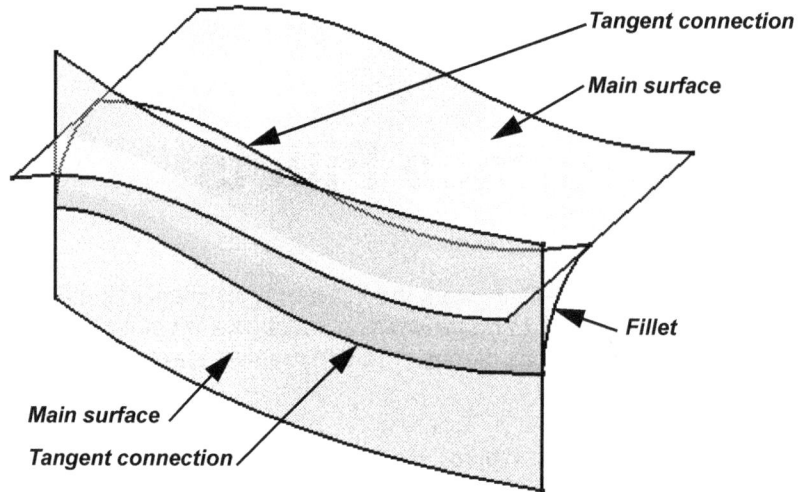

**Figure 9–1**

Fillets are created using the icons in the Operations toolbar, as shown in Figure 9–2.

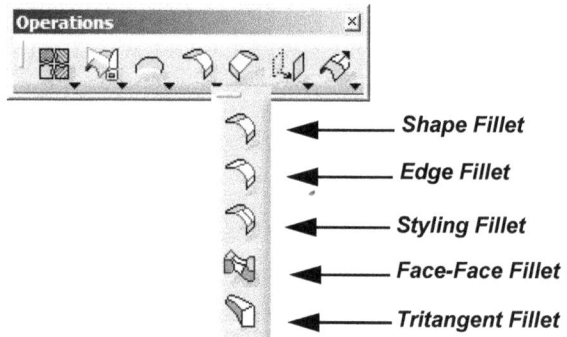

**Figure 9–2**

## General Steps

Use the following general steps to create a Surface fillet:

1. Start the creation of the feature.
2. Enter a radius value.
3. Set the extremity type.
4. Trim the support surfaces.
5. Complete the feature.

### Step 1 - Start the creation of the feature.

To start the creation of the fillet, select the appropriate icon in the Operations toolbar and select the edge or surface(s) to fillet. The feature definition dialog box opens.

The fillet types are as follows:

*Chordal and Tritangent fillets require a GSD license, which is covered in the Advanced Surface Design class. Styling fillet requires FS1 license.*

- (Shape fillet)

- (Edge fillet)

- (Styling fillet)

- (Face-Face fillet)

- (Tritangent fillet)

### Step 2 - Enter a radius value.

Enter the value for the fillet radius in the *Radius* field in the feature definition dialog box.

## Step 3 - Set the extremity type.

Set the type of extremity for the fillet using the Extremity drop-down list. By default, the fillet is created as **Smooth**. The **Smooth** option imposes a tangency constraint at the connection between the fillet surface and the support surfaces. You can also create the fillet surface without a tangency constraint by setting the extremity to **Straight**. The **Maximum** and **Minimum** options limit the surface fillet to the longest or shortest selected support edge respectively.

In Figure 9–3, the different types of extremities are applied to an edge fillet feature.

*By default, the fillet is created as **Smooth**. The **Smooth** option imposes a tangency constraint and the **Straight** option does not impose a tangency constraint. The **Maximum** and **Minimum** options limit the surface fillet to the longest or shortest selected support edge respectively.*

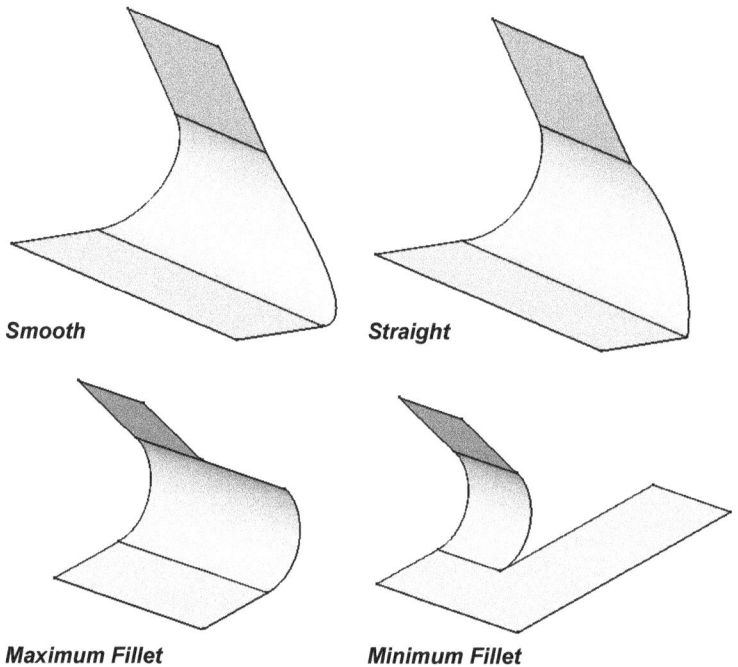

Smooth                    Straight

Maximum Fillet            Minimum Fillet

**Figure 9–3**

## Step 4 - Trim the support surfaces.

The **Trim Support** option determines the final surface composition. By default, CATIA trims the surfaces after the fillet. You can clear the **Trim Support** option for one or both surfaces so that the surface(s) are not trimmed.

In Figure 9–4, the trim options are applied to an edge fillet feature.

*By default, CATIA trims the surfaces after the fillet. You can clear the **Trim Support** option for one or both surfaces so that the surface(s) are not trimmed.*

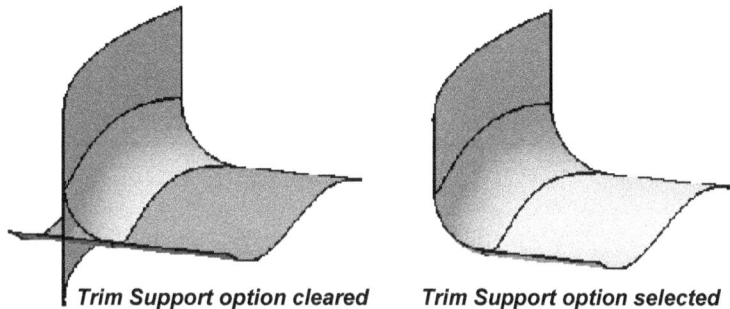

**Trim Support option cleared**          **Trim Support option selected**

**Figure 9–4**

The surfaces can be trimmed at their intersections and up to four fillet locations are possible. An arrow indicates which side of each surface is kept (while the other side is trimmed). Therefore, these arrows determine where the fillet is placed on the surface, as shown in Figure 9–5. Select the arrow to change the fillet's location.

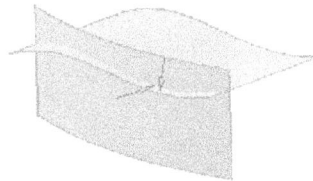

**Figure 9–5**

## Step 5 - Set the conic parameter option.

The **Conic parameter** option enables you to create conic-shaped fillets. By default, a fillet is created with a radial cross-section. To create conic-shaped fillets, the **Conic parameter** option must be activated.

The examples in Figure 9–6 show fillet geometry and their respective cross-sections to demonstrate a radial fillet versus a conic fillet.

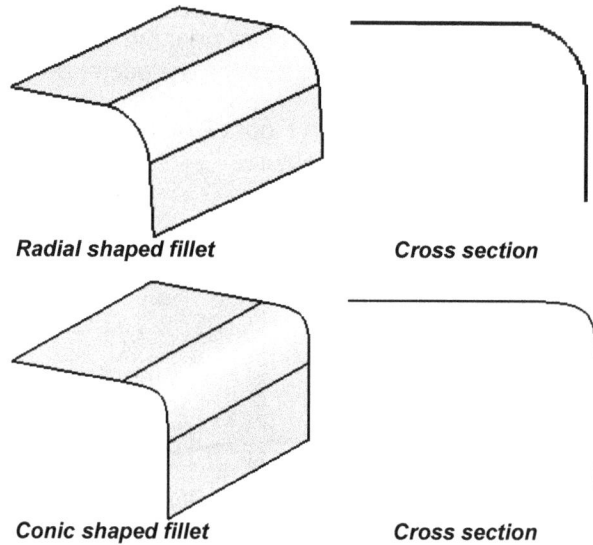

*Radial shaped fillet*                    *Cross section*

*Conic shaped fillet*                     *Cross section*

**Figure 9–6**

## Step 6 - Complete the feature.

Click **OK** in the feature definition dialog box to complete the feature.

# 9.2 Bi-Tangent Shape Fillet

A Bi-tangent shape fillet is a constant radius blend created between two surface features. An example of a Bi-tangent shape fillet is shown in Figure 9–7.

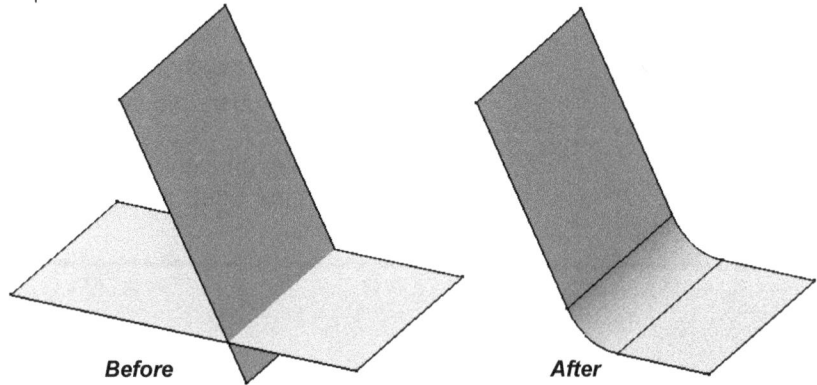

*Before*          *After*

Figure 9–7

## How To: Create a Bi-tangent Shape Fillet

1. To create a shape fillet, click  (Shape Fillet). The Fillet Definition dialog box opens as shown in Figure 9–8.

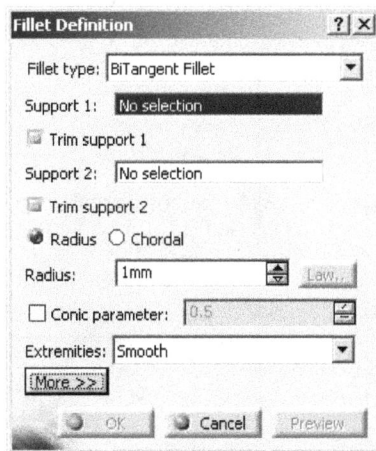

Figure 9–8

2. Select a surface for the first support element.
3. Select another surface for the second support element. The Fillet Definition dialog box updates as required.
4. Enter the value for the fillet radius in the *Radius* field.
5. Use the trim options, if required.

   • The **Trim Support** option is not available when using a GS1 license. To remove unwanted portions of the original surfaces, you must manually split or trim the surfaces using the respective tools in the Operations toolbar.

6. Set the type of extremity for the fillet using the Extremity drop-down list.
7. If required, set the conic parameter.
8. Click **OK** in the Fillet Definition dialog box to complete the feature.

# 9.3 Edge Fillet

An Edge fillet is a constant radius blend, constructed along a sharp edge on a single surface feature. Multiple edges can be selected at the same time. An example of an edge fillet is shown in Figure 9–9.

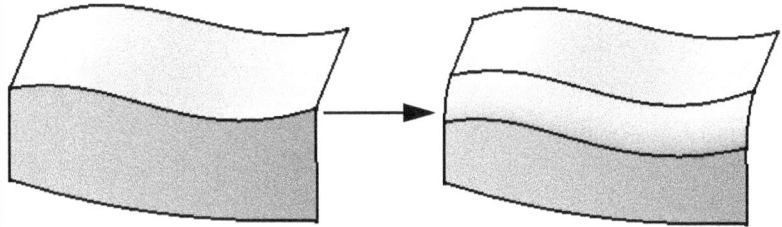

**Figure 9–9**

## How To: Create an Edge Fillet

*You can also select a surface to apply the fillet; CATIA fillets all of the sides.*

1. To create an edge fillet, click [icon] (Edge Fillet) and select an edge to apply the fillet. The Edge Fillet Definition dialog box opens as shown in Figure 9–10.

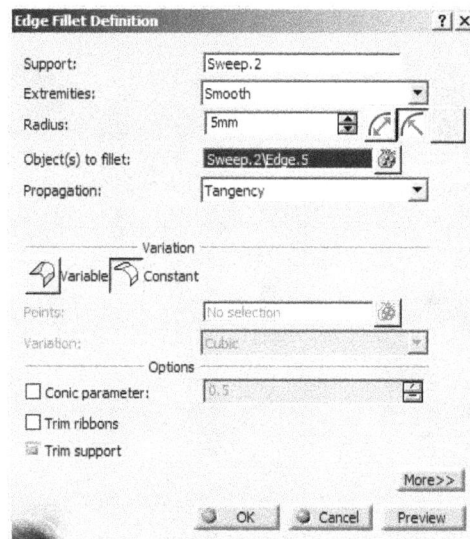

**Figure 9–10**

2. Enter the value for the fillet radius.
3. Set the type of extremity for the fillet in the Extremity drop-down list.

4. Edge fillets are created using the Selection mode drop-down list. By default, it is set to **Tangency**. This setting creates a fillet up to the first edge that is not continuous in the tangency. You can change the propagation to **Minimal**, which creates the fillet up to the first geometric limitation.

5. Use the trim options, if required.

6. If required, set the conic parameter.

7. Click **OK** in the Edge Fillet Definition dialog box to complete the feature.

# 9.4 Variable Radius Fillet

A Variable Radius fillet is a blend whose radius changes along the selected edge. This feature is created on a sharp edge of a single surface feature. An example of a Variable Radius fillet is shown in Figure 9–11.

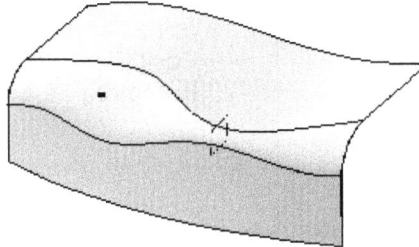

Figure 9–11

## How To: Create a Variable Radius Fillet

1. To create a Variable Radius fillet, click [image] (Edge Fillet) to open the Edge Fillet Definition dialog box, then click

   [image] (Variable), as shown in Figure 9–12.

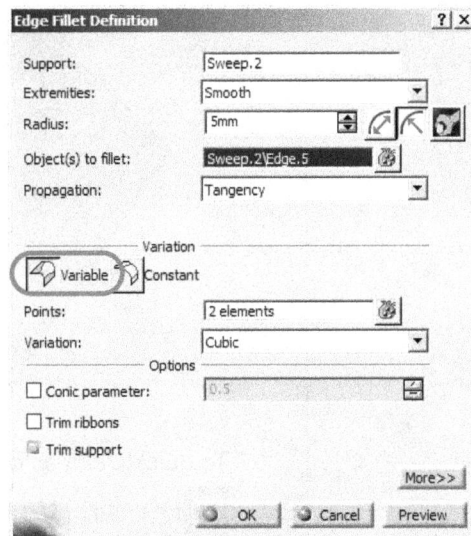

Figure 9–12

2. The system automatically defines the selected edges' end points as points to set the radius. These points can be changed by an equal value by changing the value in the *Radius* field.

To remove a point or vertex, select the point near the dimension on the model. In addition,  can be clicked in the Variable Radius Fillet Definition dialog box to display a list of points, as shown in Figure 9–13. To remove a point from the Point Elements dialog box, select the point and click **Remove**.

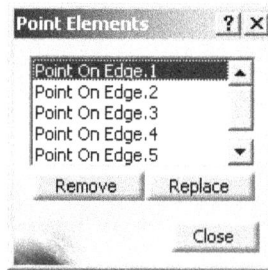

**Figure 9–13**

To vary the radius at individual points, double-click on the radius dimensions in the model and enter the radius value, as shown in Figure 9–14.

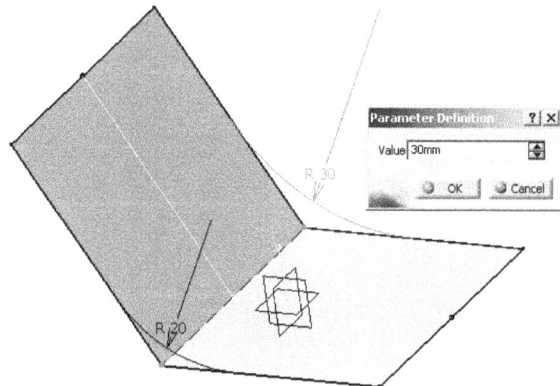

**Figure 9–14**

To quickly edit all of the variable radius values, you can click  (Edit Fillet Values) to open the Fillet Values dialog box, shown in Figure 9–15.

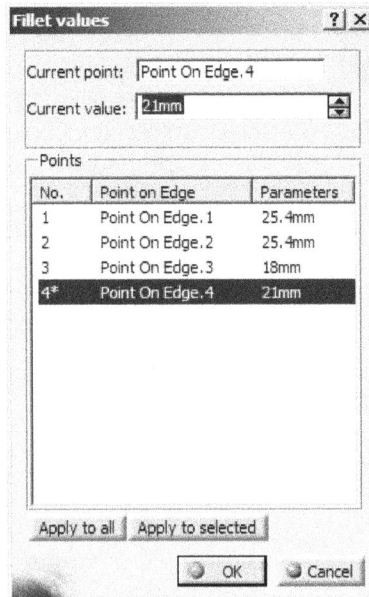

**Figure 9–15**

Here you can edit individual radius values, set all values to be the same using **Apply to all**, or select several values and set them to be the same using **Apply to selected**.

Note that you can change back to a constant radius fillet by

clicking  (Constant) in the Edge Fillet Definition dialog box. If you added any additional radius points for a variable radius round however, they will be lost.

Additional points can be added to vary the radius by selecting the *Points* field and then selecting a point on the edge. You can also select predefined points if they have been created on the edge to be filleted. Additional points added to the edge are shown in Figure 9–16.

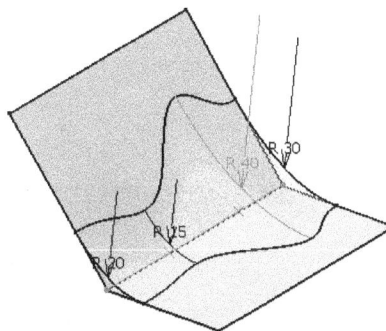

**Figure 9–16**

3. Set the type of extremity for the fillet with the Extremity drop-down list.

4. Select the Selection mode type. By default, it is set to **Tangency**. This setting creates the fillet up to the first edge that is not continuous in the tangency. You can change the propagation to **Minimal**, which creates the fillet up to the first geometric limitation.

5. If required, set the **Trim Support** and **Conic parameter** options.

6. Set the transition type. The transition between the points where the radius changes can be set to **Cubic** or **Linear**. By default, the transition from one radius to another is set to **Cubic**. The **Cubic** option creates a smoother transition between the radii, as shown in Figure 9–17.

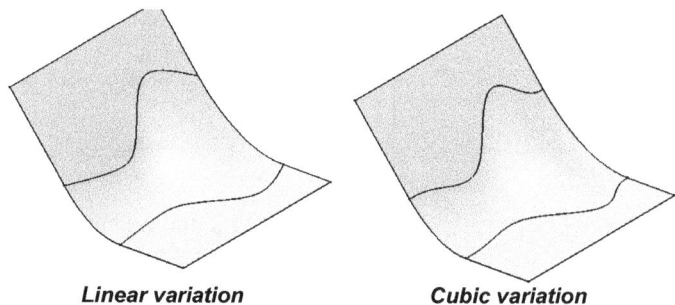

*Linear variation*          *Cubic variation*

**Figure 9–17**

7. Click **OK** in the Variable Fillet Definition dialog box to complete the feature.

# 9.5 Face-Face Fillet

A Face-Face fillet is a constant radius blend between two selected faces of a single surface feature that do not need to intersect. An example is shown in Figure 9–18.

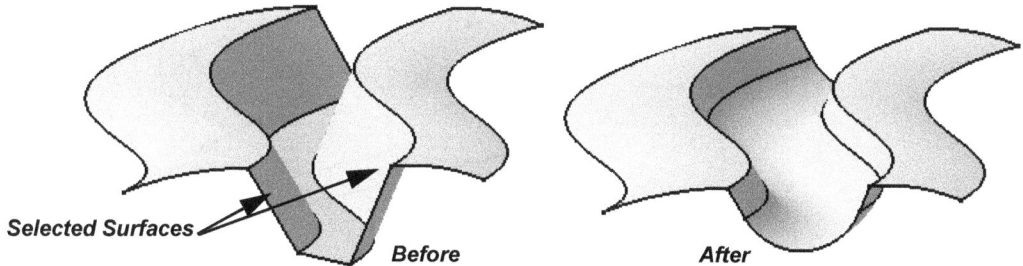

Figure 9–18

## How To: Use the following steps to create a Face-Face fillet:

1. To create a Face-Face fillet, click [icon] (Face-Face Fillet) and select the surfaces between which to apply the fillet. The Face-Face Fillet Definition dialog box opens as shown in Figure 9–19.

Figure 9–19

2. Enter the radius value and set the type of extremity for the fillet.
3. If required, set the **Trim Support** and **Conic parameter** options.
4. Click **OK** in the Face-Face Fillet Definition dialog box to complete the feature.

---

Depending on the geometry, there can be circumstances where the selection of two surfaces could result in more than one possible fillet. For example, the selection of the rounded surface and the base surface shown in Figure 9–20 could result in a fillet to one side or the other of the upper pad feature.

**Fillet could be created on either side**

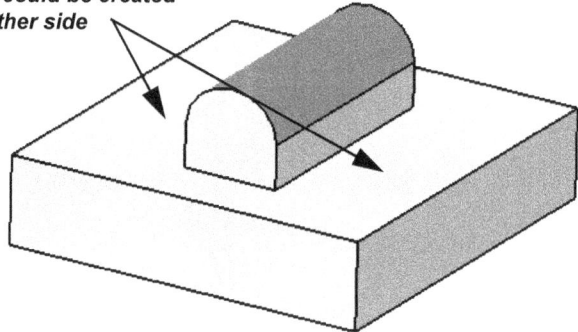

**Figure 9–20**

You can use the **Near Point** option in the Face-Face Fillet Definition dialog box to select a point which is nearest the side on which you want the round created, as shown in Figure 9–21.

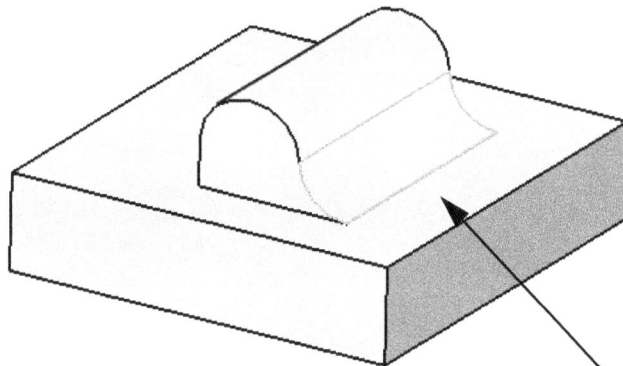

**Selected point defines fillet location**

**Figure 9–21**

# 9.6 Tips and Considerations

Fillets are typically created late in the design process. Consider the following guidelines:

- Create fillets in a dedicated geometrical set. This enables easy deactivation of the fillets if the model is used for FEA analysis or for generating NC toolpaths.

- Variable Radius fillets are difficult to manufacture. Evaluate the necessity of this feature as you are creating your model.

- Always consider the order in which features are going to be modeled. The order of fillet creation can affect the resulting geometry and is typically added from the largest radius first to the smallest radius last.

- Avoid using fillets as references for other elements in the model. A fillet might change later in the design or be completely removed. If this happens, any elements that were dependent on the fillet for placement lose their reference and fail.

# Practice 9a

# Shape Fillets - Car Hood

## Practice Objective

- Add shape fillets to surface geometry.

In this practice, you will create shape fillet features by adding fillets to existing surface geometry. The front grill of a car hood was created using an extruded surface and the top of the hood was developed using several swept surfaces that are connected by a transition surface. The geometry displays as shown in Figure 9–22.

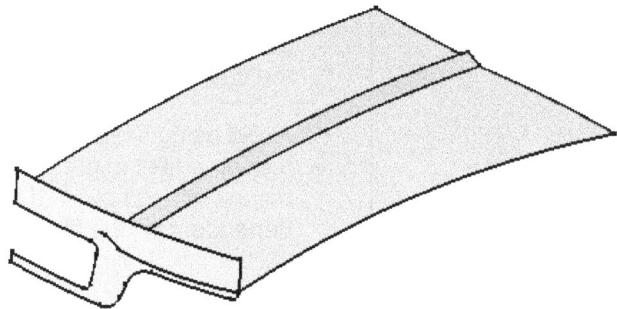

**Figure 9–22**

The edges between the transition surface and the rest of the hood, and between the hood top and the front grill, are sharp and must be rounded with shape fillets. Also, the surfaces are not trimmed and extend past their final lengths. This is a design method for the creation of surfaces, in which the surfaces are created larger than required and trimmed later when all other geometry is complete. This trimming can be accomplished after the shape fillets have been added. In the final step, you must mirror the final surfaces to model the entire hood. The completed model displays as shown in Figure 9–23.

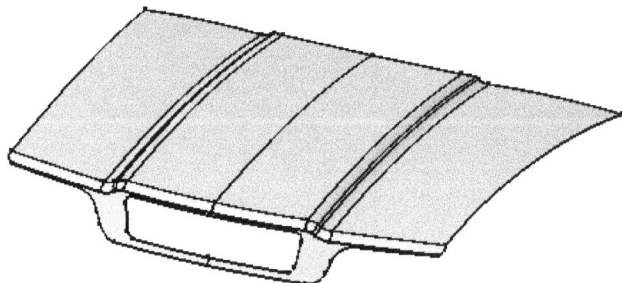

**Figure 9–23**

## Task 1 - Open a part.

1. Open **Hood.CATPart**. The model displays as shown in Figure 9–24.

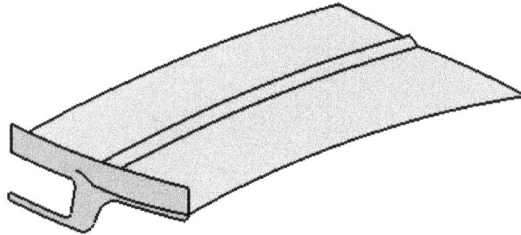

**Figure 9–24**

2. Investigate the four surfaces in the **Surfaces** geometrical set. These features represent the base surface geometry of the hood that will be filleted.

## Task 2 - Add a fillet between the hood side and transition surface.

*Fillet icons can be found in the Operations toolbar.*

1. Click ![icon] (Shape Fillet).

2. Select **Transition** as *Support 1*.

3. Select **Hood Side** as *Support 2*. The arrows indicate the location of the edge fillet. Their direction can be changed by selecting them. Ensure that the arrows point up as shown in Figure 9–25.

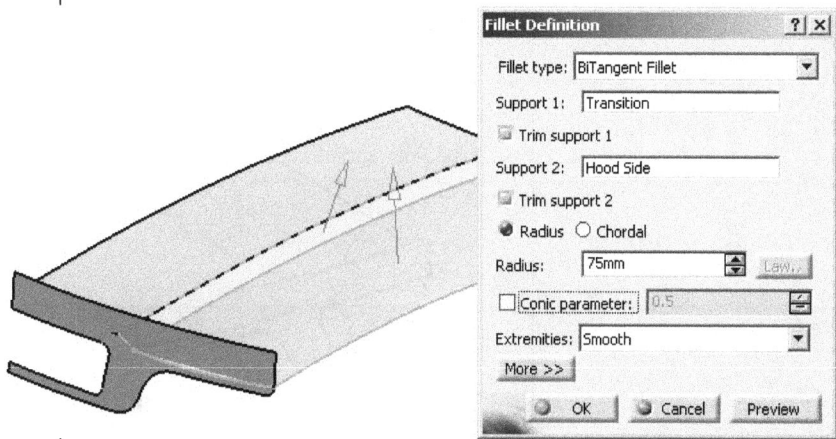

**Figure 9–25**

4. Enter **75mm** for the *Radius*.

5. Click **OK**. The model displays as shown in Figure 9–26.

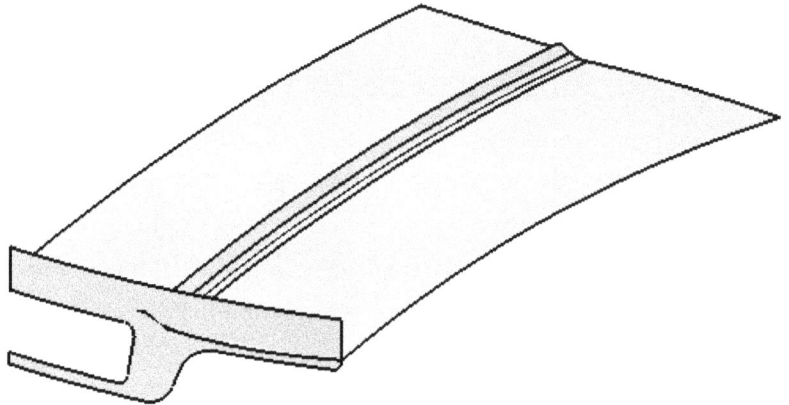

**Figure 9–26**

---

**Task 3 - Add a fillet between the hood side and the rest of the hood.**

---

1. Click  (Shape Fillet).

2. Select **Hood Top** as *Support 1*.

3. Select **Fillet.1** as *Support 2*. Ensure that the arrows point down.

4. Enter **75** for the *Radius*.

5. Click **OK**. Fillet.2 feature now represents the entire top of the hood. The model displays as shown in Figure 9–27.

**Figure 9–27**

**Task 4 - Add a fillet between the hood top and front grill.**

1. Click ⬙ (Shape Fillet).

2. Select **Fillet.2** as *Support 1*.

3. Select **Front Grill** as the *Support 2*.

4. The front grill must be trimmed by removing the section of the grill surface that is above the hood. To do this, ensure that the arrow above the hood top points down as shown in Figure 9–28.

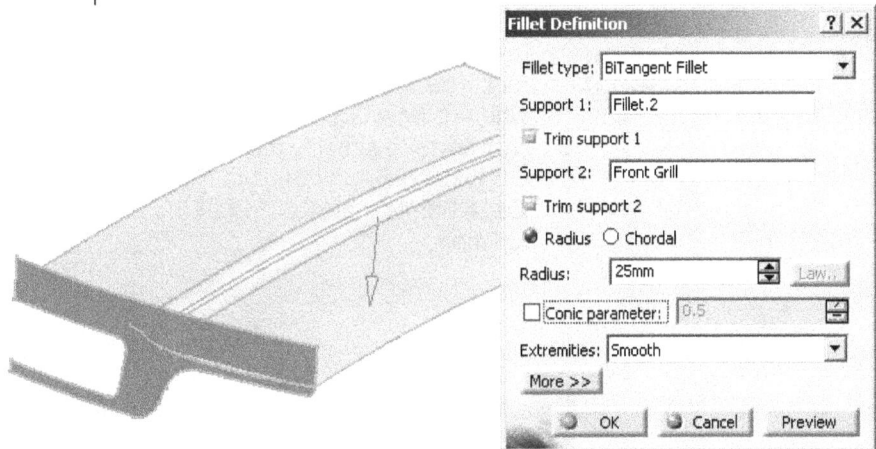

**Figure 9–28**

5. Enter **25** for *Radius*.

6. Click **OK**. The Fillet.3 feature now represents the entire hood.

**Task 5 - Mirror the surface geometry to create the entire hood.**

1. Click ⬙ (Symmetry).

2. Select **Fillet.3** as the Element.

3. Select **zx plane** in the specification tree as the Reference.

4. Click **OK**. The model displays as shown in Figure 9–29.

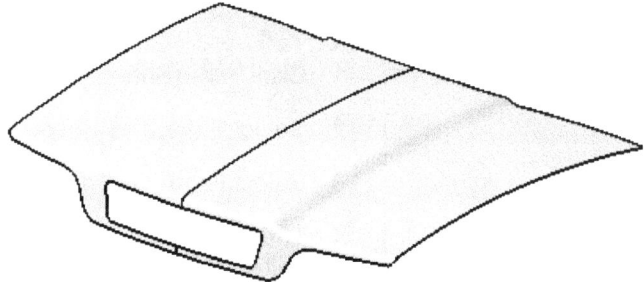

**Figure 9–29**

5. Save the model and close the file.

**Design Considerations**

In this practice, Trim supports were used with the **Shape Fillet** tool. The **Trim Supports** option is not available in Shape Fillets when using a GS1 license. The practice was created to use **Trim Supports** to simplify the filleting process. If your company has a GS1 license, and needs to fillet, it is suggested that you use **Edge Fillets** instead. **Edge Fillets** provide the **Trim Support** function.

# Practice 9b

## Shape Fillets- Bracket

### Practice Objective

- Add a variety of fillet features to a model.

In this practice, you will apply fillet features to the model shown in Figure 9–30.

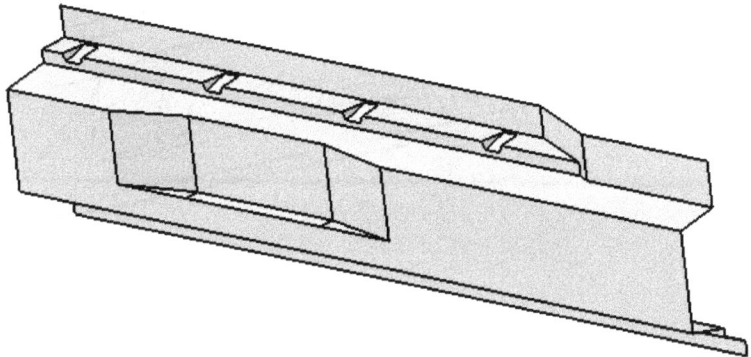

**Figure 9–30**

This practice stresses the types of decisions that need to be made when filleting a model.

For example:

- What type of fillet best captures the design intent?

- In what order should the fillets be created?

- Which references should be selected?

The completed model displays as shown in Figure 9–31.

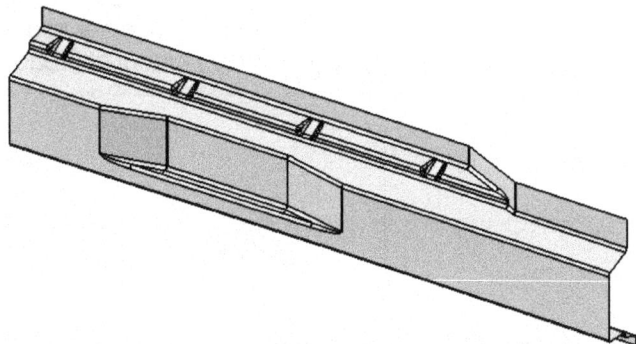

**Figure 9–31**

**Task 1 - Open a part.**

1. Open **Brace.CATPart**. The model displays as shown in Figure 9–32.

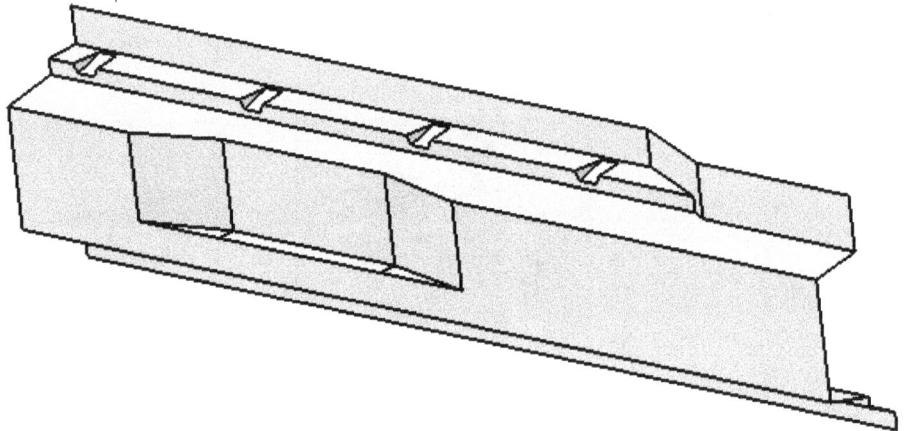

**Figure 9–32**

2. Investigate the **SharpSkin** surface in the **FilletSurf** geometrical set. This trim feature represents the base surface geometry of the brace that will be filleted.

**Design Considerations**

Before you begin to add fillets to a model, you should always review the geometry to determine the types and order of features to be added. For example, the part consists of a single surface and therefore shape fillets cannot be used. The fillet creation order also impacts the final result.

Additionally, some areas of the geometry are challenging to fillet correctly. For example, the area highlighted in Figure 9–33 shows three edges that converge on a point. As the surface is filleted, you must watch these areas to ensure that the fillet features blend together correctly to provide an aesthetically pleasing and manufactureable result.

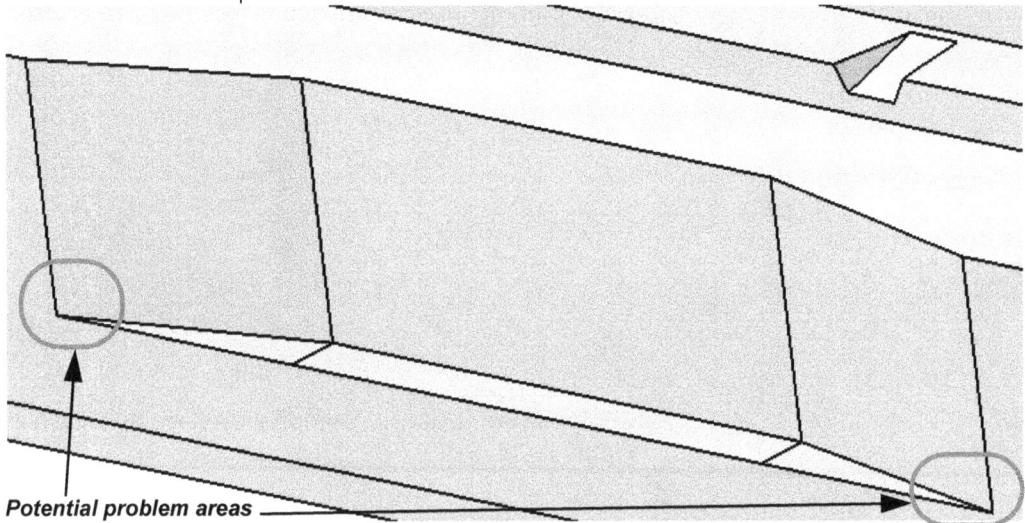

**Potential problem areas**

**Figure 9–33**

## Task 2 - Add an Edge fillet to the model.

In this task, you will begin the creation of fillets by adding an edge fillet to model that will reference a variety of edges.

1.  Click  (Edge Fillet) in the flyout in the Operations toolbar. The Edge Fillet Definition dialog box opens as shown in Figure 9–34.

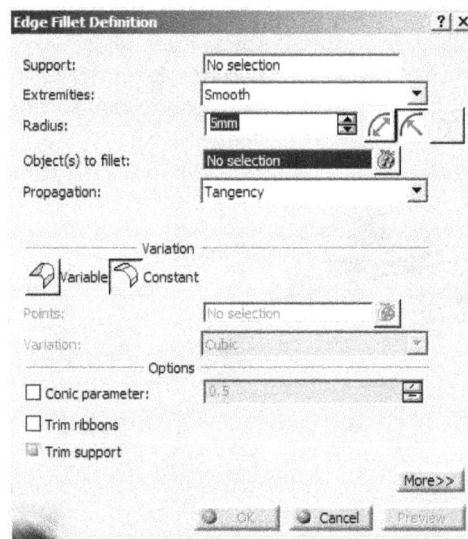

**Figure 9–34**

2. Enter **5mm** for the *Radius* and select the three edges highlighted in Figure 9–35.

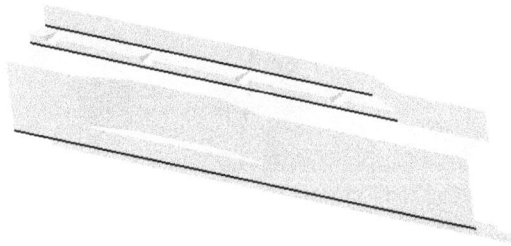

**Figure 9–35**

3. Complete the feature. The model displays as shown in Figure 9–36.

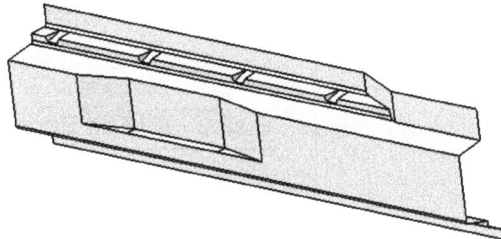

**Figure 9–36**

## Task 3 - Add a Face-Face fillet.

In this task, you will fillet the edges shown in Figure 9–37. Since this edge has been broken by the four cutouts, you will apply a Face-Face fillet. This enables you to create the fillet by selecting two non-boundary representation references. Therefore, changes to the number of cutouts will not cause a failure in the fillet.

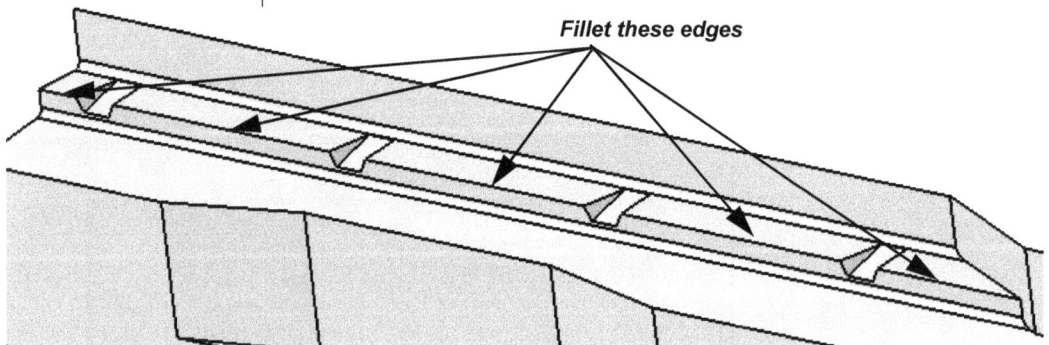

*Fillet these edges*

**Figure 9–37**

1. Click ⬚ (Face-Face Fillet). The Face-Face Fillet Definition dialog box opens as shown in Figure 9–38.

**Face-Face Fillet Definition**

| | |
|---|---|
| Support: | No selection |
| Extremities: | Smooth |
| Radius: | 5mm |
| Faces to fillet: | No selection |

Options

☐ Conic parameter: 0.5

☑ Trim support

Near Point: No selection

More>>

OK   Cancel   Preview

**Figure 9–38**

2. Enter **5mm** for the *Radius* and select the two faces highlighted in Figure 9–39.

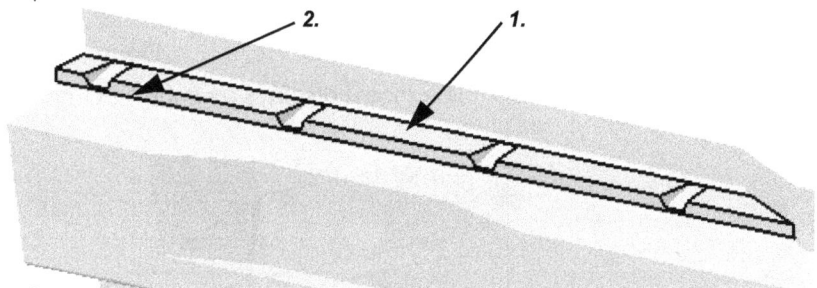

**Figure 9–39**

3. Complete the feature. The model displays as shown in Figure 9–40.

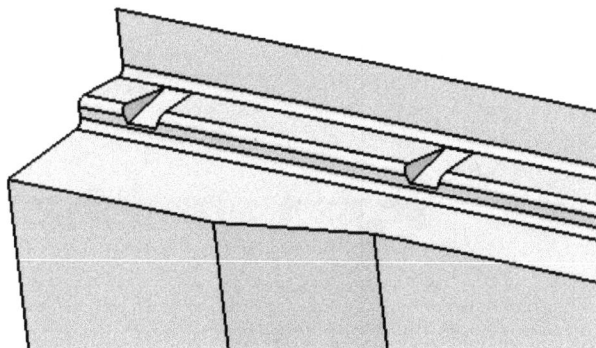

**Figure 9–40**

## Task 4 - Apply additional edge fillets.

Based on the fillet order, the tangency of edges to be filleted can be leveraged to reduce the number of selections required to create the edge fillet in this task.

1. Create a **5mm** Edge fillet using the three edges shown in Figure 9–41.

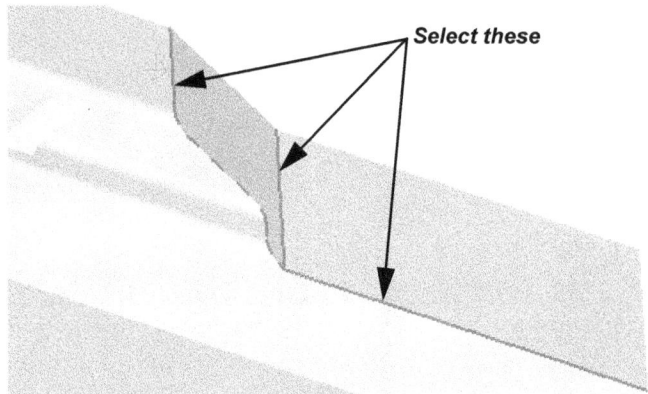

Select these

**Figure 9–41**

The model displays as shown in Figure 9–42.

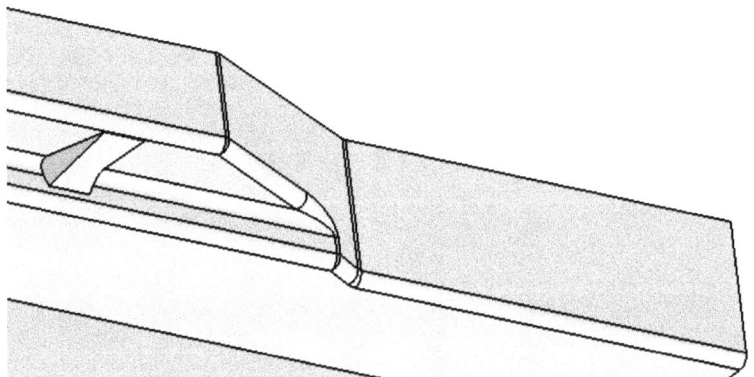

**Figure 9–42**

Note the shape of the model in the high-transition area shown in Figure 9–43. The horizontal fillet is nicely terminated by the angled edge, whose fillet flows nicely into the vertical fillet. This type of transition is preferable.

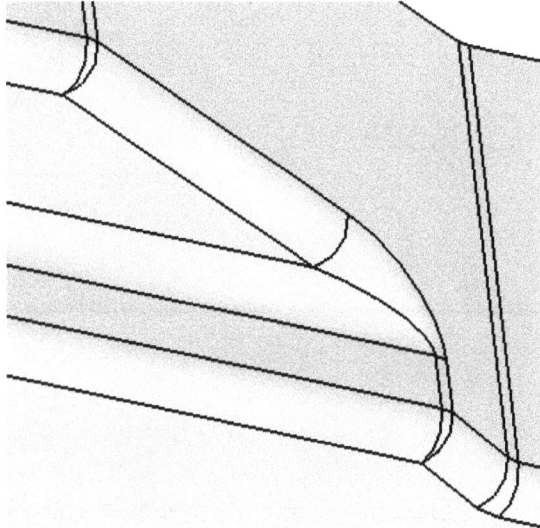

Figure 9–43

## Task 5 - Fillet the cutouts.

1. Apply a **5mm** Edge fillet to the inside edges of each cutout. You should select a total of eight edge references. The model displays as shown in Figure 9–44.

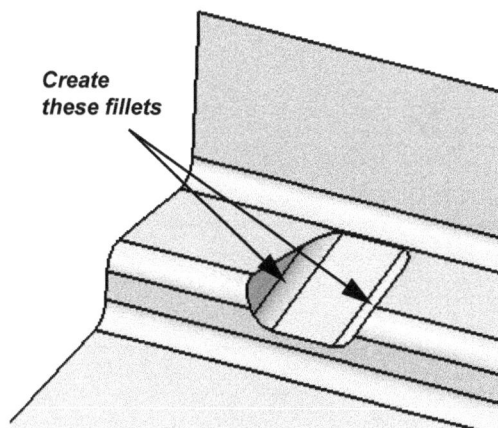

*Create these fillets*

Figure 9–44

2. Apply a second **5mm** Edge fillet to the outside edge of each cutout. You should select a total of four edge references. The model displays as shown in Figure 9–45.

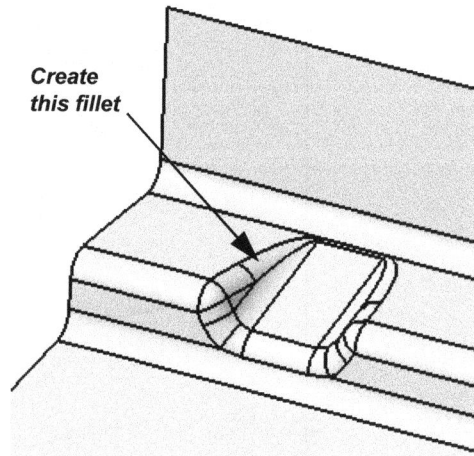

Create
this fillet

**Figure 9–45**

**Design Considerations**

For the next step, you will apply a standard 5mm fillet to the final cutout area indicated in Figure 9–46. To correctly fillet this area, the fillets must be broken across more than one feature. You can determine the order and edge references used for these features.

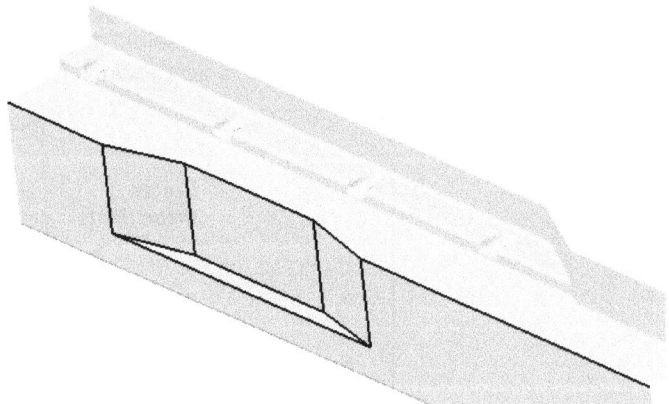

**Figure 9–46**

3. Create a **5mm** Edge fillet on the main cutout geometry. Once complete, the model displays as shown in Figure 9–47. Note the detail image on the corner. Ensure that your fillet geometry is identical to this image. If it is not, try changing the order of fillet creation or change the selected references.

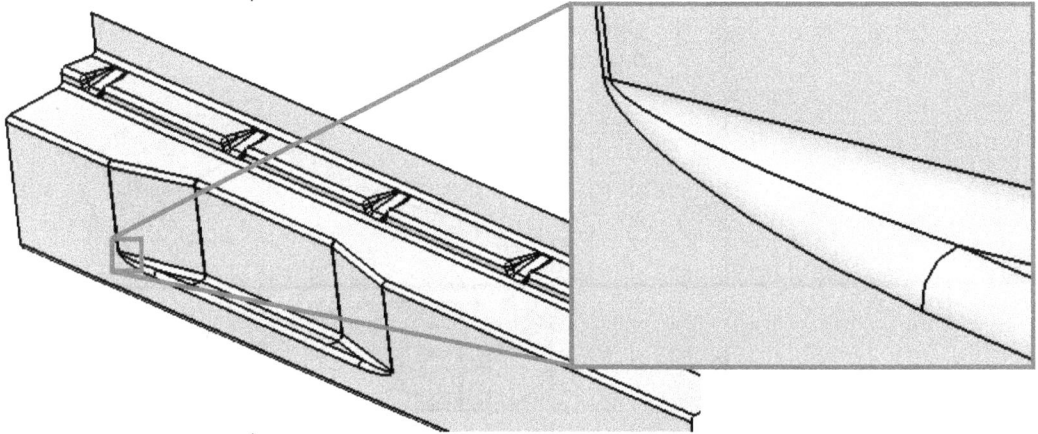

**Figure 9–47**

4. Apply **5mm** Edge fillets to any additional sharp edges in the model.

5. Save the model and close the window.

# Practice 9c | Surface Fillets - Key Fob

### Practice Objective

- Create surface fillets with no instruction.

1. Open **KeyFob_Fillet Start.CATPart**. The start model displays as shown in Figure 9–48.

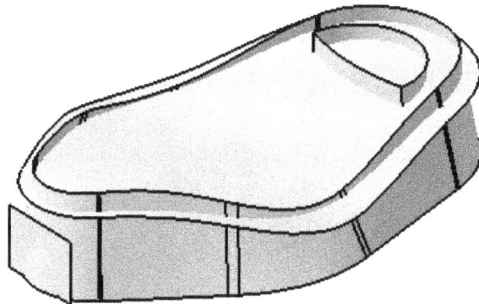

**Figure 9–48**

2. Add the appropriate fillets to the model. You might need to use Split or Trim surfaces, depending on the methods of filleting that you select.

3. Radius values for the fillets in the final model are shown in Figure 9–49.

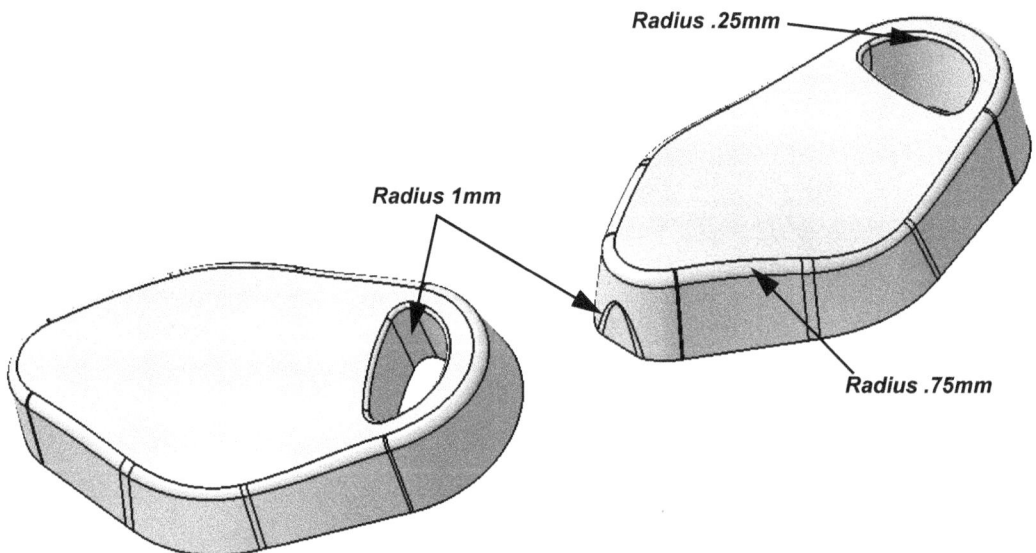

Radius .25mm

Radius 1mm

Radius .75mm

**Figure 9–49**

# Chapter Review Questions

1. By default, surface fillets are created tangent to the selected surfaces.

    a. True

    b. False

2. To create a Face-Face fillet, click:

    a.

    b.

    c.

    d.

3. To create a Bi-tangent shape fillet, you require two surfaces and a radius value.

    a. True.

    b. False

4. An edge fillet creates a constant radius along an edge formed by two separate surfaces.

    a. True

    b. False

5. What does do in the Edge Fillet Definition dialog box?

    a. Opens a dialog box enabling you to add or remove points or vertices for defining unique radii.

    b. Opens a dialog box listing the points and vertices with unique radii, enabling you to edit the values.

    c. Opens a dialog box listing the points and vertices with unique radii, but the radius values cannot be edited.

    d. None of the above.

6. When creating a Face-Face fillet, the radius value is automatically determined by the distance separating the selected surfaces.

   a. True

   a. False

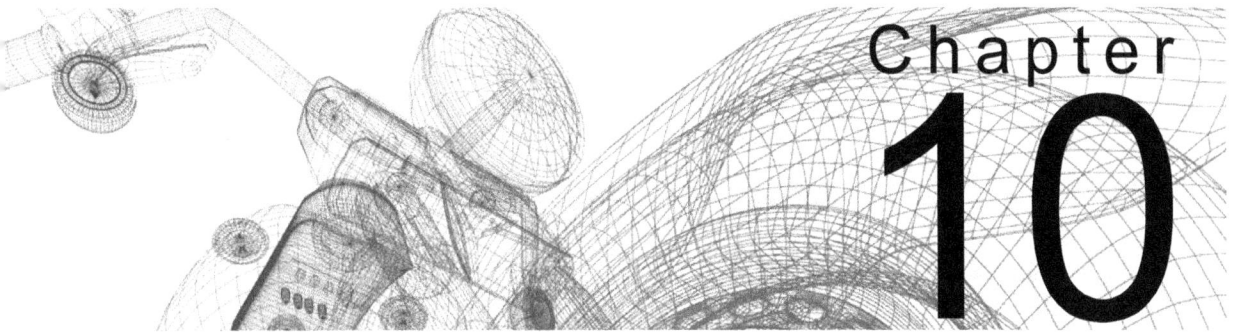

# Boundary Representations

This chapter describes the way CATIA makes references to geometry that is selected when building a feature. One reference type is called a boundary representation and involves the selection of a portion of a feature, such as the edge of a surface or a vertex on a solid. This chapter describes the advantages and disadvantages of using boundary representations and methods of avoiding this type of selection.

## Learning Objectives in this Chapter

- Use boundary representations to create surfaces.
- Understand and apply non-boundary representation modeling.

# 10.1 Boundary Representations

A boundary representation refers to the selection of any sub-element when defining references for a feature. This means a feature in the specification tree is not directly referenced. Instead, an entity belonging to a feature (such as the edge or vertex of a surface) is selected.

Whenever a boundary representation is selected, CATIA reports the reference using <feature>\<sub-element>. For example, an On Curve point is created by selecting the edge of a surface. In this case, the Point Definition dialog box opens as shown in Figure 10–1. The referenced curve is reported as *Extrude.1\ TgtEdge* indicating that a boundary representation has been used.

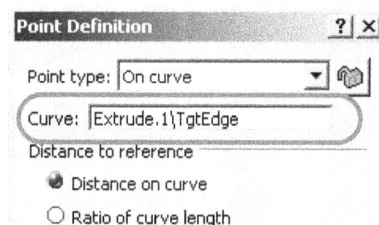

**Figure 10–1**

The methods in which a boundary representation can be created are unlimited. Various examples are as follows:

- Referencing the edge of a surface:

  - as a guide curve
  - spine
  - reference in a Fillet surface
  - fillets

- Referencing vertices:

  - creating coupling curves using the vertices of a sketch or profile
  - spline
  - line
  - polyline

The selection of a boundary representation seems typical when developing a 3D model in an associative environment. However, modeling in this way has a couple of disadvantages. The most important disadvantage is that the model is more likely to fail. The specification tree also becomes difficult to interpret.

## Feature Failure

When the referenced feature of a boundary representation is replaced or modified, the model is more likely to fail. Consider a point that is defined using the edge sub-element of an extruded surface, as shown in Figure 10–2.

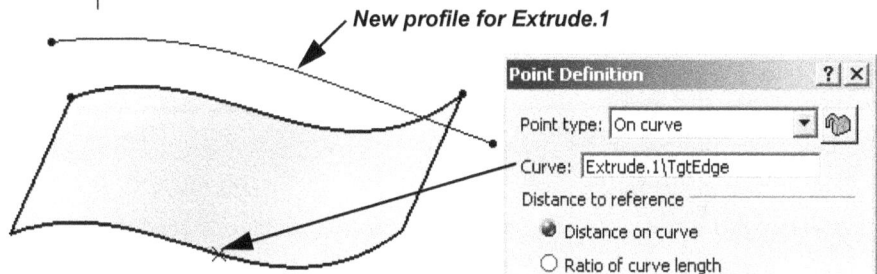

**Figure 10–2**

If the extruded surface is modified to use a different profile, the point feature fails. CATIA cannot find the edge sub-element reference on the modified surface because this edge is unique to the original extruded surface.

This failure can be confusing to some designers, because the reference that the point element requires still exists. If you were the designer who created the point, you would need to understand that the surface referenced by the point has changed and a new reference is required. If you were not the designer, the task would be more difficult.

## Model Interpretation

When a point created on the boundary representation of a surface fails, it can be difficult to determine how to resolve this failure if you did not originally create the model. The edge does not have an explicit name or ID to which the designer can refer. The designer only knows that the point was created on one of the edges belonging to **Extrude.1**.

Investigating the parents of the On curve point does not provide any additional information. Again, the only parent reported for the point feature is **Extrude.1,** as shown in Figure 10–3. This can become more confusing since the point now displays as an On Surface type instead of an On curve type.

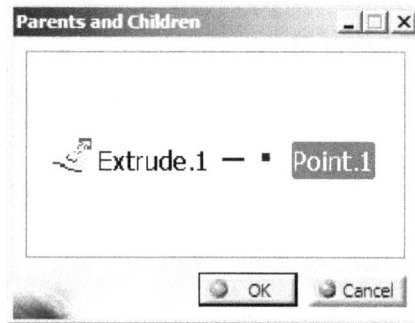

**Figure 10–3**

To resolve this failure accurately, the designer might need to undo any changes so that the point successfully updates. The point can then be modified to determine the exact edge reference that needs to be re-selected when the point fails after modifying **Extrude.1**.

Boundary representations make a model very difficult to interpret by other designers. This is an important reason for finding a more robust method of referencing sub-elements.

# 10.2 Non-Boundary Representation Modeling

The best method of creating a robust model that is easy to interpret is to not select boundary representations. Anytime a sub-element is selected, stop and think of a way the required reference can be created with a new feature. A variety of non-boundary representation modeling techniques are described as follows:

| Reference | Non-Boundary Representation Method |
|---|---|
| **Vertex** | • Intersection of two curves<br>• Extremum point<br>• On curve point |
| **Edge** | • Boundary curve<br>• Intersection of two surfaces |
| **Sketch** | • Use the output or profile tools in Sketcher to declare sub-elements. |
| **Edge Fillet** | • Always create a shape fillet instead of placing an edge fillet on a trimmed, split, or joined edge. |

It is not always possible to completely avoid creating a boundary representation. For example, if you are creating a point on the edge of a surface the edge can be obtained using a boundary curve. However, this element type requires the selection of a sub-element, as shown in Figure 10–4.

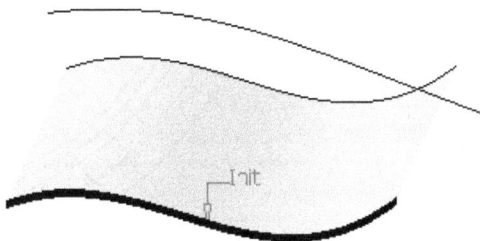

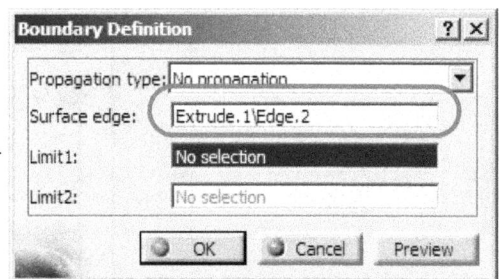

**Figure 10–4**

The method of creating a boundary element is considered better practice than creating the point directly on the edge of the surface. In this case, when a modification or replacement causes failure, the feature that fails is the actual boundary itself. This type of failure is easier for other designers to interpret and resolve than if the point failed.

There are several other possible work-arounds for this scenario. Two possibilities are as follows:

- Intersect **Extrude.1** with a new reference plane to get the edge.

- Instead of extruding one wireframe element, create the boundary of the surface with wireframe elements that defines all of the edges.

You must compare the amount of time required to create references using non-boundary representation techniques against the advantages of a more robust model. If you anticipate that a large number of changes and modifications might occur in a model, spending more time to develop robust geometry at firsts is useful when downstream modifications occur.

## Element Replacement

The **Replace** tool is another method of avoiding the errors encountered during modifications that are caused by boundary representation. This tool automatically accounts for any sub-elements that have been selected from the element being replaced.

You can access the **Replace** tool by right-clicking on the element to be replaced and selecting **Replace**.

For example, the imported surface shown in Figure 10–5 has been split by a plane. The plane was constructed using the **Normal to curve** option and a boundary representation (edge of the imported surface) was selected during creation.

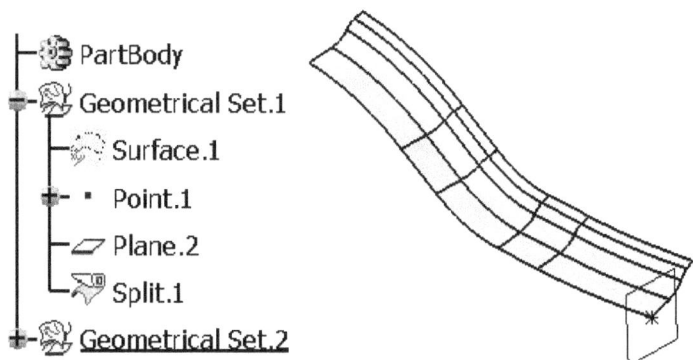

**Figure 10–5**

When this surface is replaced, the Replace dialog box prompts you to select two references: a new surface and an edge on the surface (to create the split feature). The Replace dialog box is shown in Figure 10–6.

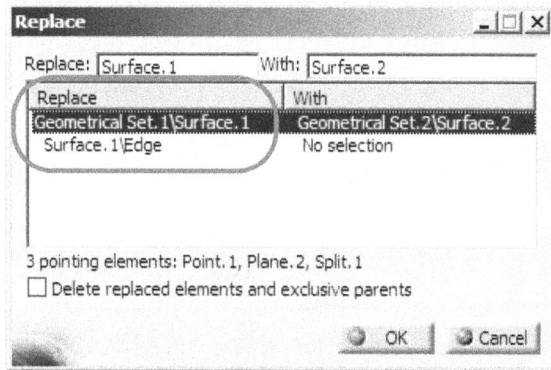

**Figure 10–6**

By forcing the designer to select all of the sub-elements that have been referenced in the replaced element, the **Replace** tool is an effective method of managing boundary representation issues.

Using non-boundary representation modeling methods creates a cleaner specification tree, which enables other designers to more easily perform predictable modifications. However, when a design has been created using boundary representations, the **Replace** tool must be used to minimize any feature failure and errors that might occur.

# Practice 10a | Boundary Representations I

## Practice Objective

• Create geometry without using boundary representations.

In this practice, you will investigate the impacts of using boundary representations on a simple model.

### Task 1 - Create a new part and add a sketch and a surface.

1. Create a new part model named **BRep Testing**.

2. Insert a geometrical set named **BASE**.

3. Create a sketch on the XY plane. Sketch the section shown in Figure 10–7.

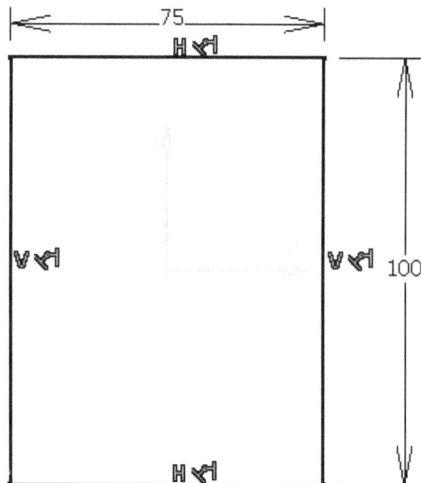

**Figure 10–7**

4. Create a fill surface using **Sketch.1** as the boundary.

5. Hide the sketch.

6. Rename the surface as **Base**. The model displays as shown in Figure 10–8.

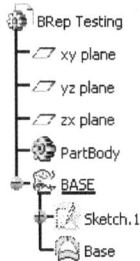

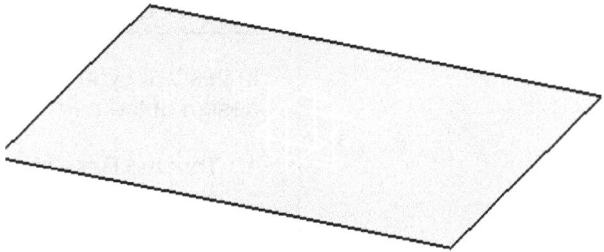

**Figure 10–8**

---

### Task 2 - Create an extruded surface from a surface edge.

In this task, you will create an extruded surface. The profile of the surface is defined by selecting an edge from the Base surface.

1. Create an extruded surface using the following parameters:

   - *Profile:* **Select the edge of Base shown in Figure 10–9**
   - *Direction:* **Z Component** (*in the shortcut menu*)
   - *Limit 1 Dimension:* **20mm**
   - Select **Mirrored Extent**.

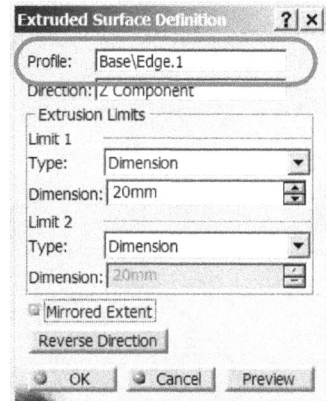

**Figure 10–9**

**Design Considerations**

Note that the system lists the profile used for the extruded surface as *Base\Edge.1*. This indicates that a boundary representation has been developed. This practice will show how this boundary representation can cause issues when modifying the part.

2. Complete the extruded surface feature and name it **Side Wall**.

---

## Task 3 - Complete the model.

In this task, you will add a Trim and Fillet feature to complete the design of the part.

1. Trim the Base and Side Wall surfaces. The model displays as shown in Figure 10–10. Note that the resulting geometry is represented by the **Trim.1** feature.

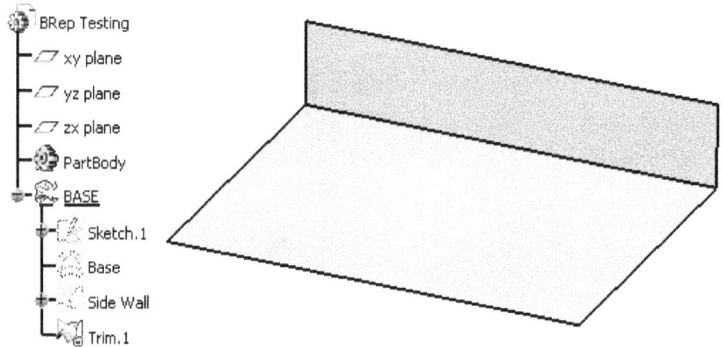

**Figure 10–10**

2. Create a **5mm** Edge fillet feature on the trimmed edge between Base and Side Wall. Note that a boundary representation is referenced to create this feature, as shown in Figure 10–11.

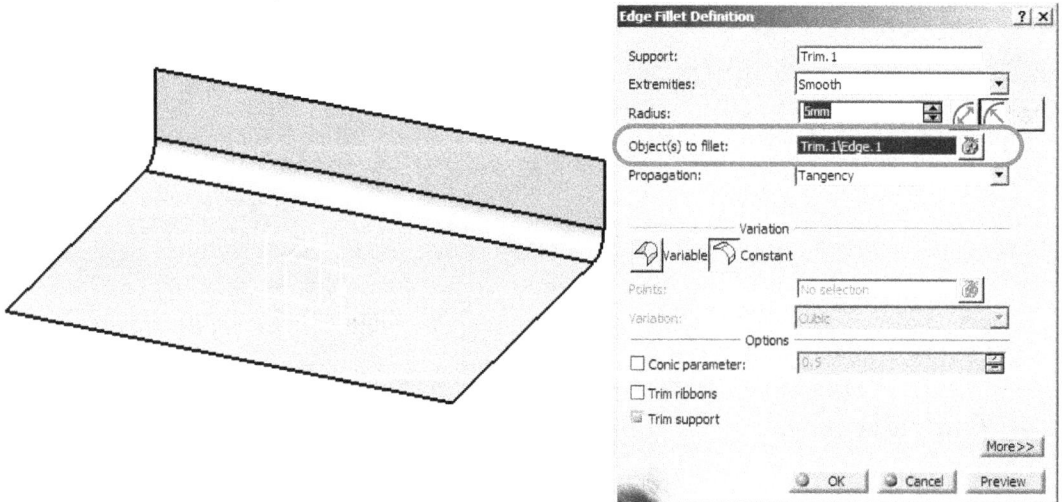

**Figure 10–11**

3. Save the model.

## Task 4 - Perform a design change by modifying the sketch.

In this task, you will simulate a design change that requires a triangular shape for the Base surface. You modify the sketch used to create the Base fill surface. This is done to observe the impact that this change will have on the Extrude, Trim, and Edge fillet features.

1. Edit **Sketch.1** and delete the rectangular profile. The entire rectangle should be deleted. If a portion of the rectangle is reused, your results will vary from those shown in this practice.

2. Sketch the triangular profile shown in Figure 10–12.

*The dimensions for this sketch are irrelevant. For the purposes of this practice, it is not important that this sketch be fully constrained.*

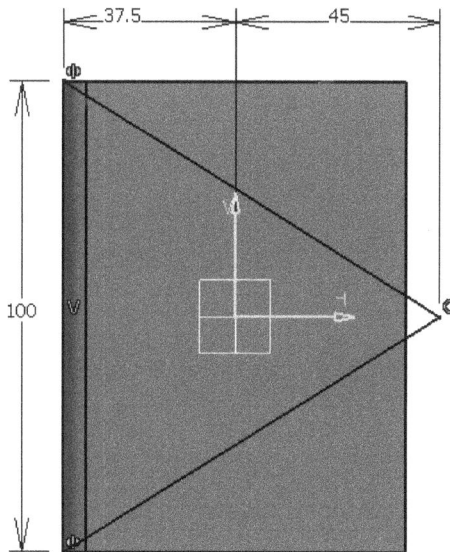

**Figure 10–12**

3. Exit Sketcher and update the model. The Side Wall feature fails.

**Design Considerations**

Why did the Side Wall extruded surface fail? The error message indicates that an edge reference no longer exists. The edge being referenced is the boundary representation *Base\Edge.1*, and is derived from the sketched edge added to **Sketch.1**. CATIA assigns a unique ID to this sketched edge. When the rectangle is deleted and the triangular profile is added to **Sketch.1**, CATIA assigns new IDs to this geometry, causing the extruded surface to fail. Note that the Base fill surface did not fail because it directly references **Sketch.1** and not a sub-element of it.

4. Close the Update Diagnosis dialog box and undo the modifications to the sketch so that it contains the rectangular section.

## Task 5 - Perform a design change by modifying the fill surface.

In this task, you will make the Base surface triangular by creating a new sketch and modifying the fill surface to use the new sketch.

1. Create a new sketch on the XY plane. Sketch the profile shown in Figure 10–13.

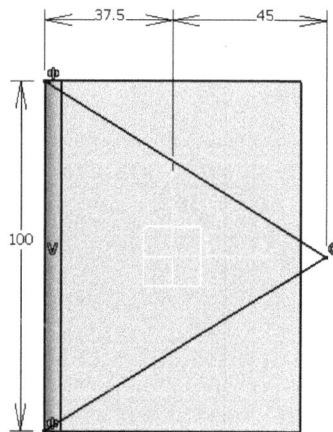

**Figure 10–13**

2. Double-click on the Base surface feature.

3. Select **Sketch.1** in the Fill Surface Definition dialog box and click **Replace**.

4. Select **Sketch.2**.

5. Complete the feature and update the model. The Side Wall extruded surface fails again due to a missing reference.

**Design Considerations**

Modifying the feature containing the element being replaced does not resolve the boundary representation issue either. This issue is best resolved by creating the geometry using as few boundary representations as possible. In the next task, you will build the geometry using a minimum number of boundary representations.

6. Close the Update Diagnosis dialog box.

7.  Undo these operations so that Base surface references **Sketch.1**. Do not undo the **Sketch.2** feature.

8.  Delete the Side Wall, Trim.1, and Edge Fillet.1 features.

9.  Hide **Sketch.2**.

---

## Task 6 - Create the model without boundary representations.

---

In this task, you will recreate the three features that you just deleted. During this modeling, you will build extra features that accurately define the required references. With these references available as separate features in the specification tree, you will reduce the chances of feature failure and greatly simplify resolving any features that do fail.

1.  Create a boundary feature using the following parameters:

    -   *Propagation type:* **No propagation**
    -   *Surface edge:* Select the edge shown in Figure 10–14

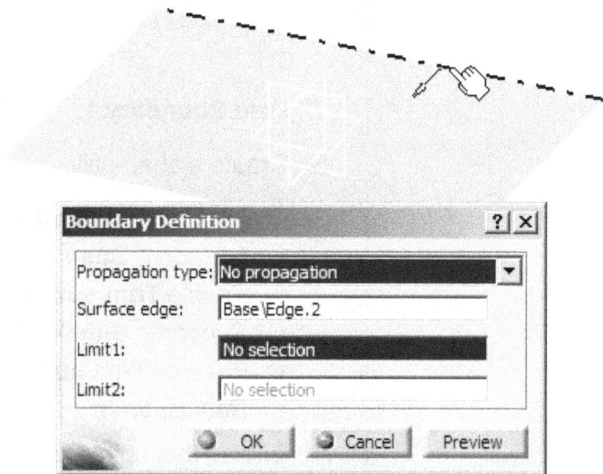

**Figure 10–14**

**Design Considerations**

Sometimes, it is not possible to avoid the creation of a boundary representation. The only way to create this boundary without selecting a sub-element would be to create the rectangular profile using a series of joined line elements. This method presents additional build time, but should be considered if model stability is critical.

In this case, the creation of the boundary feature that references a sub-element of Base will greatly simplify feature failure during the replacement of **Sketch.1**.

2.  Create an extruded surface using the following parameters:

    -   *Profile:* **Boundary.1**
    -   *Direction:* **Z Component**
    -   *Limit 1 Dimension:* **20mm**
    -   Select **Mirrored Extent**.

3.  Rename the surface as **Side Wall 2**. The model displays as shown in Figure 10–15.

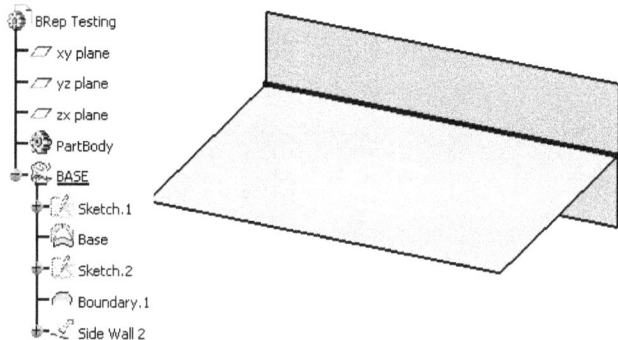

**Figure 10–15**

4.  Hide **Boundary.1**.

5.  Create a shape fillet using the following parameters:

    -   *Fillet type:* **BiTangent Fillet**
    -   *Support1:* **Base**
    -   Enable **Trim support 1**.
    -   *Support2:* **Side Wall 2**
    -   Enables **Trim support 2**.
    -   *Radius:* **5mm**

    Ensure that both arrows point in the correct direction to obtain the result shown in Figure 10–16.

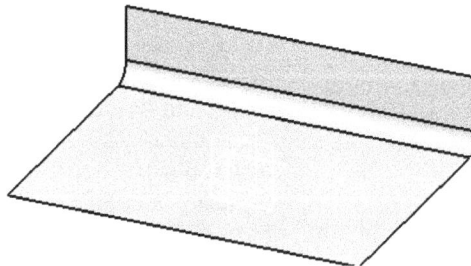

**Figure 10–16**

Previously, you trimmed the two surfaces and then created an edge fillet on their edge, creating a boundary representation. The use of shape fillets greatly reduces the creation of boundary representations, since the system calculates the edge reference based on the two surface elements selected. Therefore, the fillet will not lose its reference if either surface is replaced.

6. Save the model.

## Task 7 - Perform a design change.

1. Show the surface named **Base** and edit it.

2. Inside the Fill Definition dialog box, replace *Sketch.1* with **Sketch.2**.

3. Complete the feature and update the model. The Boundary element fails.

**Design
Considerations**

Since this boundary curve uses a boundary representation, it must be selected again after the replacement. This can be avoided by building the profile for Base using wireframe elements.

4. Edit the Boundary.1 feature and select the edge shown in Figure 10–17. Note that **Sketch.2** must be hidden, or it will be difficult to select the correct edge.

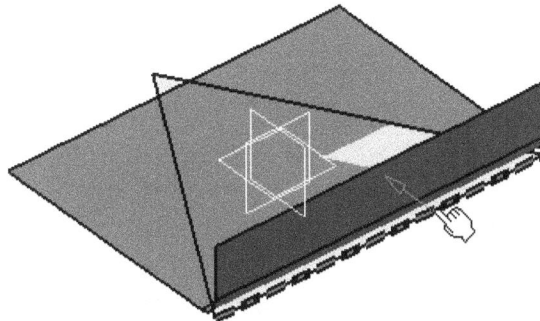

**Figure 10–17**

5. Complete the Boundary feature.

6. Hide **Base**. The model displays as shown in Figure 10–18.

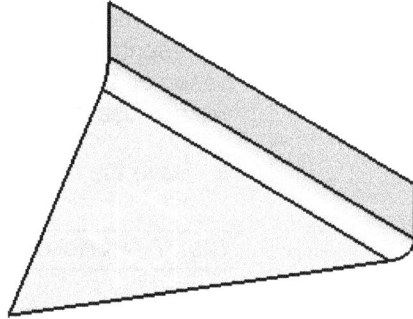

**Figure 10–18**

7. Save the model and close the window.

| Practice 10b | # Boundary Representations II |
|---|---|

## Practice Objectives

- Recognize the use of boundary element methods.
- Use the Replace tool to perform modifications.

In this practice, you will investigate the use of selecting boundary representations when building surface geometry in the surface model shown in Figure 10–19.

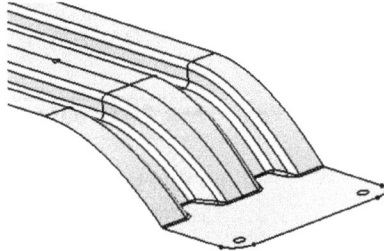

**Figure 10–19**

The model is a mounting bracket that transitions between two horizontal surfaces. First you will develop the transition and flange geometry by referencing the sub-elements (such as edges or vertices) of curves and surfaces in the model.

A design change then requires you to use a new sketch to develop the shape of the transition geometry. This replacement will cause a failure to occur as the references can no longer be updated. You will resolve this by recreating the geometry using new elements that do not require the selection of sub-elements.

## Task 1 - Open a part.

1. Open **68724Bracket.CATPart**. The model displays as shown in Figure 10–20.

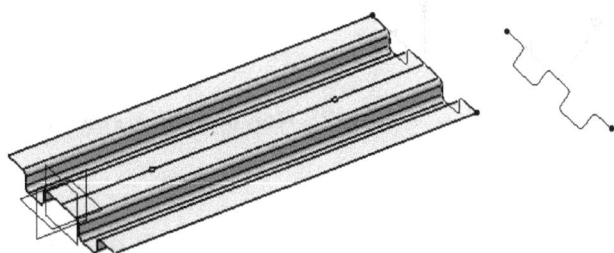

**Figure 10–20**

2. Investigate the geometrical sets and features that have been created in the model. The following data has been developed:

- **LOCATION OF BRACKET** contains a reference plane that defines the length of the base surface.
- **BODY BASE** contains the Final Base surface. This surface was created by extruding a sketch up to the ZX plane. The surface was split by two circle elements contained in the **ATTACHMENT POINTS** geometrical set.
- **TRANSITION TO FLANGE** contains a Sketch for the Multi-Sections. This sketch and the Body sketch (in BODY BASE) are used to create a multi-sections surface.

### Task 2 - Create a tangent surface.

In this task, you will create a tangent surface that is used to define tangency for a multi-sections surface.

1. Ensure that **TRANSITION TO FLANGE** is the active geometrical set.

2. Create an extruded surface using **Sketch for Multi-Section**. Extrude the surface away from Final Base to any depth. The surface displays as shown in Figure 10–21.

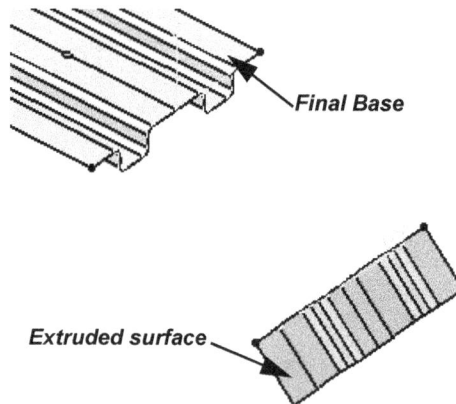

**Figure 10–21**

3. Rename the surface as **Tangency Surface**.

## Task 3 - Create a multi-sections surface.

In this task, you will create a surface that transitions between Final Base and Tangency Surface.

1. Create a multi-sections surface feature using the following parameters:

    - *Section 1:* **Body Sketch**
    - *Tangency reference 1:* **Final Base**
    - *Section 2:* **Sketch for Multi-Section**
    - *Tangency reference 2:* **Tangency Surface**
    - Sections coupling (in the *Coupling* tab): **Vertices**

2. Rename the surface as **Transition**. The resulting surface displays as shown in Figure 10–22.

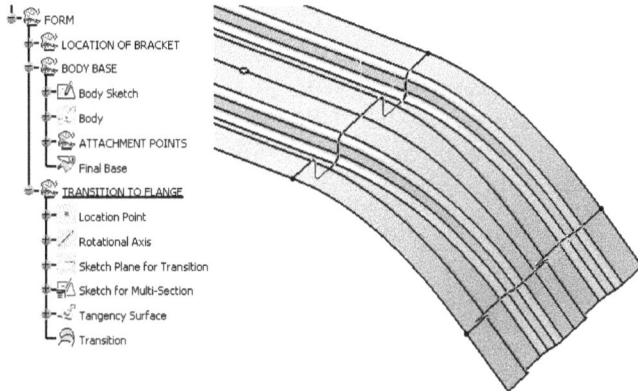

**Figure 10–22**

3. Hide the two sketches and **Tangency Surface**.

## Task 4 - Create an extruded surface.

In this task, you will create an extruded surface to define the flange geometry of the bracket. First you will define a new geometrical set and define the profile before creating the surface.

1. Create a new geometrical set beneath **FORM** named **FLANGE CONSTRUCTION**.

**Design Considerations**

The profile of the extruded surface is defined by a Point-Point line element. You will start by creating two points on the edge of the Transition surface.

2. Create a point using the **On curve** option. Place the point on the edge of Transition, **10mm** from the end point, as shown in Figure 10–23.

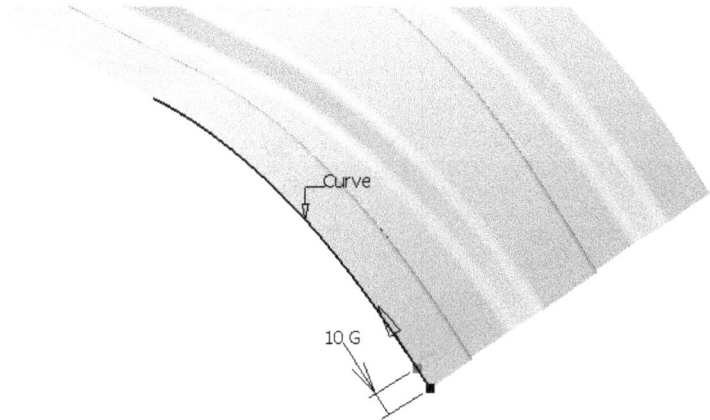

**Figure 10–23**

**Design Considerations**

When the edge of the Transition surface is selected, the system indicates that a sub-element of a surface is being used by displaying *Transition\Edge.1* in the *Curve* field in the Point Definition dialog box, as shown in Figure 10–24. When a sub-element is selected, there is a possibility that the feature might fail during a replacement or modification operation.

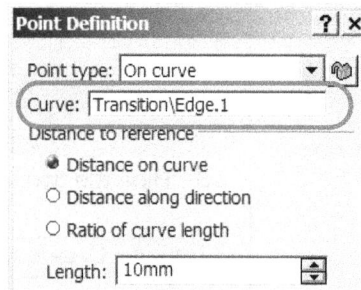

**Figure 10–24**

3. Create a second point on the opposite side of the transition surface, **10mm** from the bottom edge. Select the edge of the surface to create the point. The two points display as shown in Figure 10–25.

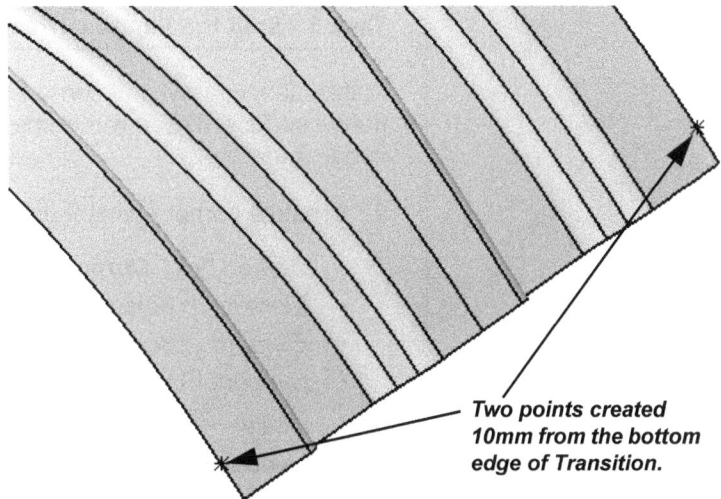

**Two points created 10mm from the bottom edge of Transition.**

**Figure 10–25**

4. Create a Point-Point line element between the two points that you just created. Rename the line as **Flange Profile**.

5. Create an extruded surface using the following parameters:

   - *Profile:* **Flange Profile**
   - *Direction:* **ZX plane**
   - *Limit 1 Dimension:* **100mm**
   - *Limit 2 Dimension:* **60mm**

   Ensure that Limit 1 points away from Final Base.

   The model displays as shown in Figure 10–26.

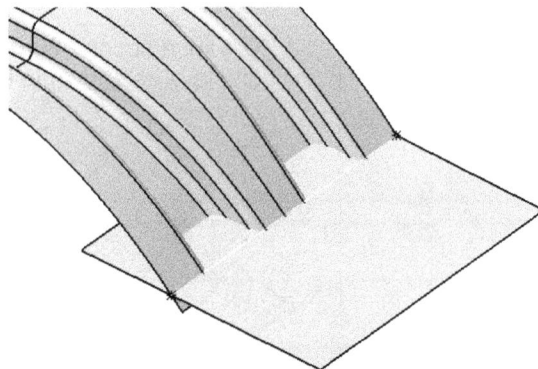

**Figure 10–26**

6. Rename the extruded surface as **Flange**.

7. Hide the two points and the line.

## Task 5 - Split the flange surface.

In this task, you will add corners and attachment holes to the flange surface. These wireframe elements are used to split the flange surface.

1. Create a corner element using the following parameters:

   - *Corner Type:* **Corner On Support**
   - *Element 1:* **Select the edge of the flange surface**
   - *Element 2:* **Select the edge of the flange surface**
   - *Support:* **Flange**
   - *Radius:* **20mm**

   The model displays as shown in Figure 10–27.

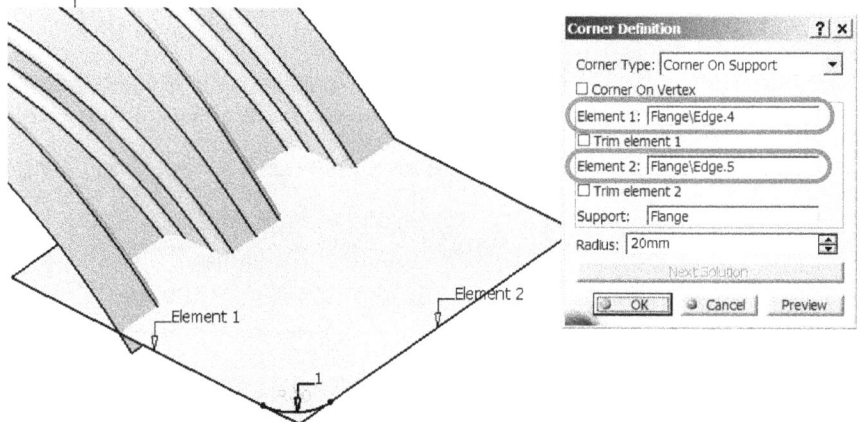

**Figure 10–27**

2. Create a second **20mm** corner element so that the model displays as shown in Figure 10–28.

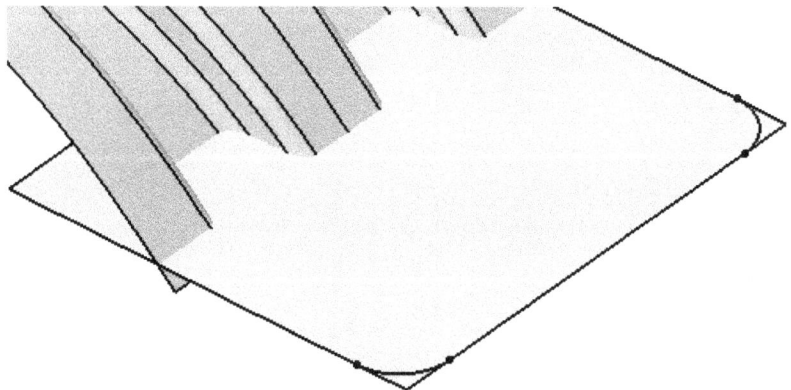

**Figure 10–28**

3. Split the flange surface using the two corners as cutting elements. The model displays as shown in Figure 10–29.

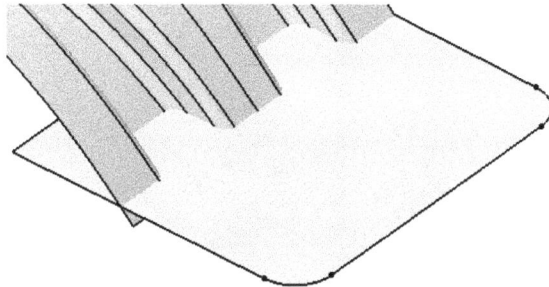

**Figure 10–29**

4. Hide the two corner features.

5. Create a sketch on the flange surface and sketch the two points shown in Figure 10–30.

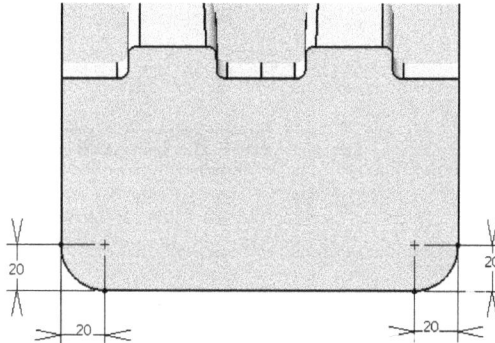

**Figure 10–30**

6. Create two circle elements using the **Center and radius** option. Center the circle on the points that you just sketched and select the flange surface (now named **Split.1**) as the support. Enter a *Radius* of **5mm**. The model displays as shown in Figure 10–31.

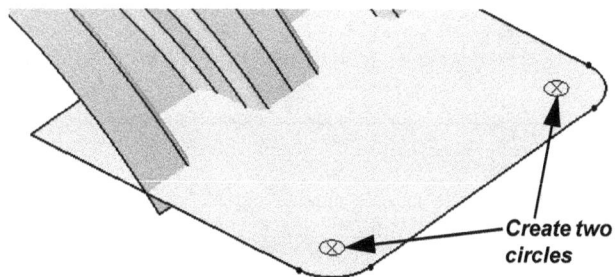

Create two circles

**Figure 10–31**

7.  Split the flange surface by the two circle elements. The model displays as shown in Figure 10–32.

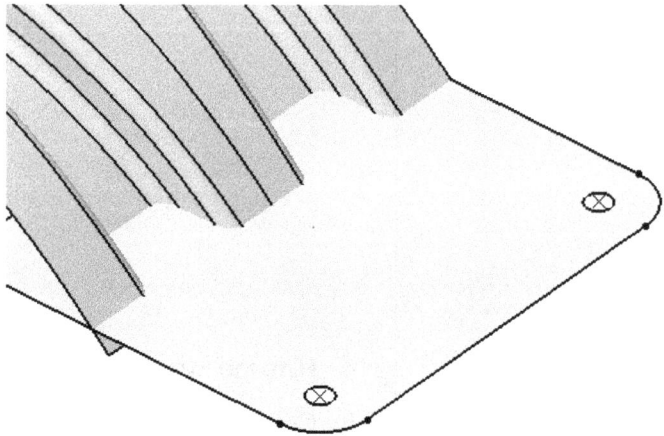

**Figure 10–32**

8.  Rename the Split feature as **Final Flange**.

9.  Hide the sketched points and circle elements.

---

**Task 6 - Complete the model.**

---

In this task, you will trim and join the surfaces to complete the model.

1.  Insert a geometrical set beneath **FORM** named **FINAL SHAPE**.

2.  Trim the Transition and Final Flange as shown in Figure 10–33.

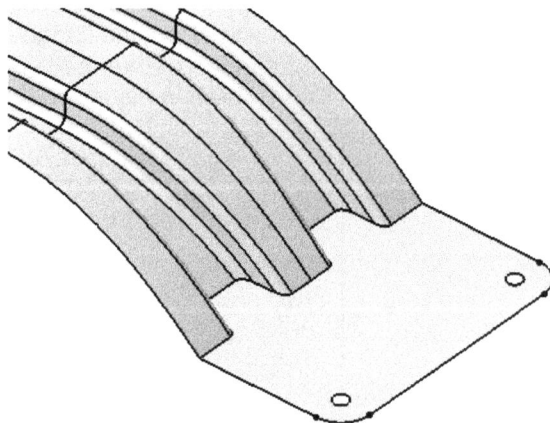

**Figure 10–33**

3. Create a **3mm** Edge fillet on the edge generated between the Transition and Final Flange trim, as shown in Figure 10–34.

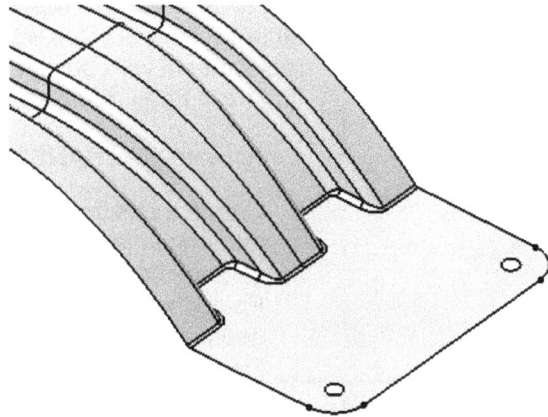

**Figure 10–34**

4. Join Final Base and EdgeFillet.1.

5. Create a symmetry element that mirrors Join.1 about the ZX plane.

6. Join Symmetry.1 and Join.1.

7. Rename the Join element as **Final Skin**. The model displays as shown in Figure 10–35.

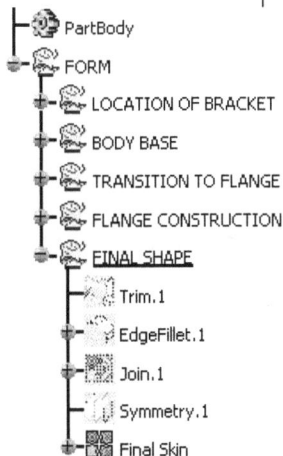

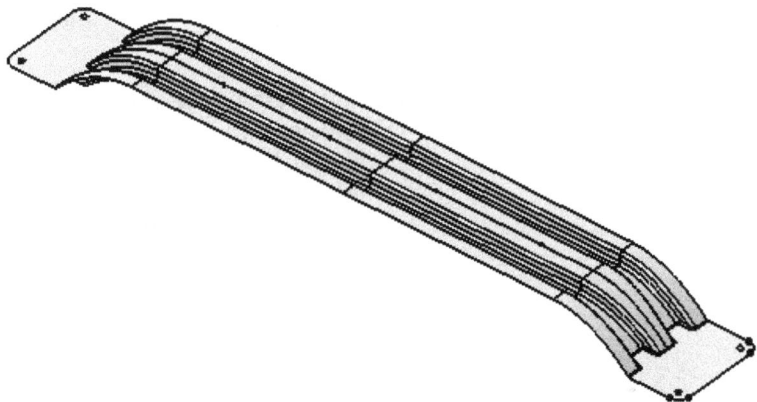

- PartBody
- FORM
  - LOCATION OF BRACKET
  - BODY BASE
  - TRANSITION TO FLANGE
  - FLANGE CONSTRUCTION
  - FINAL SHAPE
    - Trim.1
    - EdgeFillet.1
    - Join.1
    - Symmetry.1
    - Final Skin

**Figure 10–35**

8. Save the model.

## Task 7 - Perform a design change.

In this task, you will replace the sketch used to build the Multi-sections surface with a newly sketched profile. This replacement will cause feature failure due to the sub-elements that have been referenced in the model.

1. Activate the **TRANSITION TO FLANGE** geometrical set.

2. Create a positioned sketch on the Sketch Plane (the reference plane in the **LOCATION OF BRACKET** geometrical set). Locate the sketch origin on the Location Point (the reference point in the **LOCATION OF BRACKET** geometrical set.) The model displays as shown in Figure 10–36.

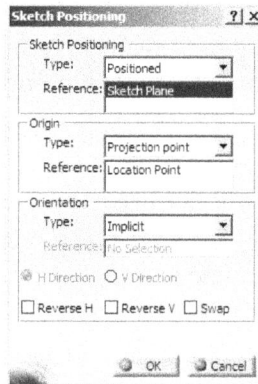

Figure 10–36

3. Sketch the profile shown in Figure 10–37. Use  (No 3D Background) in the Visualization toolbar to simplify the display. Note that all of the radii are 6mm and all of the entities are tangent to each other (the constraint symbols are hidden to simplify the display).

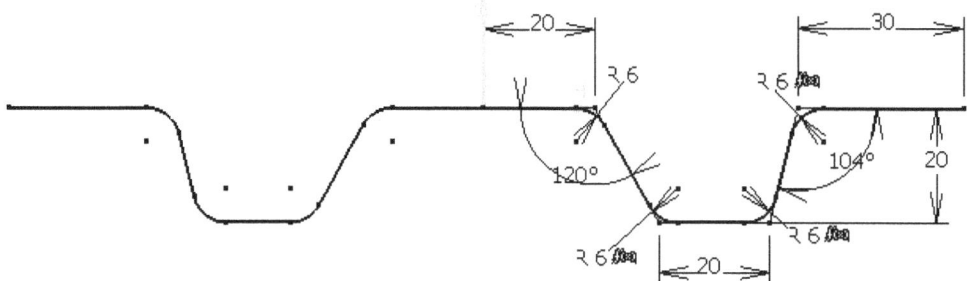

Figure 10–37

4. Rename this sketch as **Replacement Sketch**.

5. Save the model. You might need to return to this model state later in the practice.

**Design Considerations**

At this point, the part is complete. Sub-elements were selected during the creation of this model in the following instances:

- Creation of points in Task 4.

- Creation of corners in Task 5.

- Dimensions for two sketched points in Task 5.

- Creation of edge fillet in Task 6.

It is important to note when sub-elements are selected, so that you can be aware of where the model might fail when replacements and modifications are made. Although this practice forces you to reference these sub-elements, you should always make a conscious decision on whether you want to select a sub-element or create a boundary representation. In general, if a boundary representation can be created that avoids the sub-element selection, it should be created.

In the remainder of this practice, you will perform a design change using two methods: modifying the Transition surface to use a new sketch, and using the **Replace** tool to perform the modification. The **Replace** tool considers all children of the feature being replaced and prompts you to select corresponding references on the new geometry. Using the **Replace** tool enables you to resolve issues that would typically fail when a modification is performed.

### Task 8 - Modify the Transition surface.

In this task, you will modify the Transition surface to use the newly created Replacement Sketch. Before this can be done, you need to create a second tangency surface using the new sketch.

1. Create an extruded surface using Replacement Sketch. Extrude the sketch by **20mm**.

2. Rename this surface as **Replace Tangency**.

3. Modify the Transition multi-sections surface and remove the Body Sketch profile.

4. Add Replacement Sketch and make the surface tangent to Replace Tangency.

5. Ensure that the closing points and directions match. Complete the surface.

6. Update the model. The model fails on the first boundary representation created. These are the points from Task 4 that were used to build the flange.

**Design Considerations**

The use of boundary representations typically leads to model failure when changes occur. In the next task, you will perform the design change using the **Replace** tool to see how it avoids failure caused by boundary representations.

7. Close the Update Diagnosis window.

8. Undo all of the modifications. Since you can only undo up to the last save, this removes all changes including the Replace Tangency surface.

**Task 9 - Modify the part using the Replace tool.**

1. Right-click on Body Sketch and select **Replace**. The dialog box lists all of the referenced sub-elements of the Body Sketch. In this case, you must also tell the system what to use for the two vertices and edge reference.

2. Select **Replacement Sketch** as the new element to replace Sketch for Multi-Section as shown in Figure 10–38.

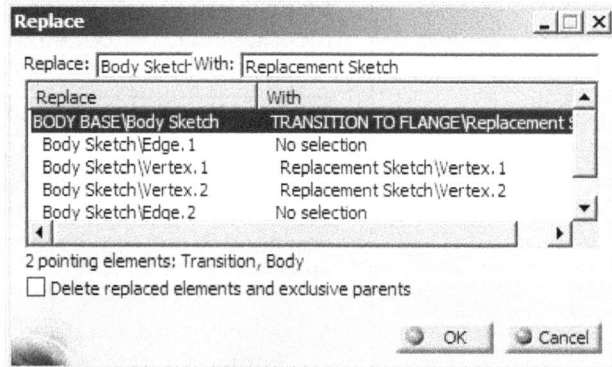

Figure 10–38

The Replace Viewer window is used in conjunction with the Replace dialog box to define the new sub-elements. The system has located replacement references for the two vertices. You must now define the replacement reference for the two edges.

3. The Replace Viewer window opens as shown in Figure 10–39. Select the edge shown on the right in the Replace Viewer window.

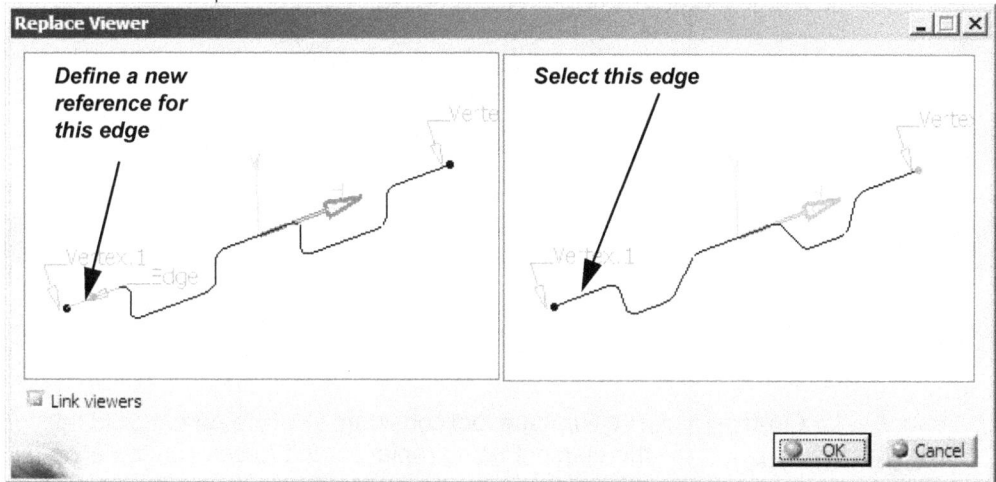

**Figure 10–39**

4. One reference edge still needs to be defined. Select the edge shown in Figure 10–40.

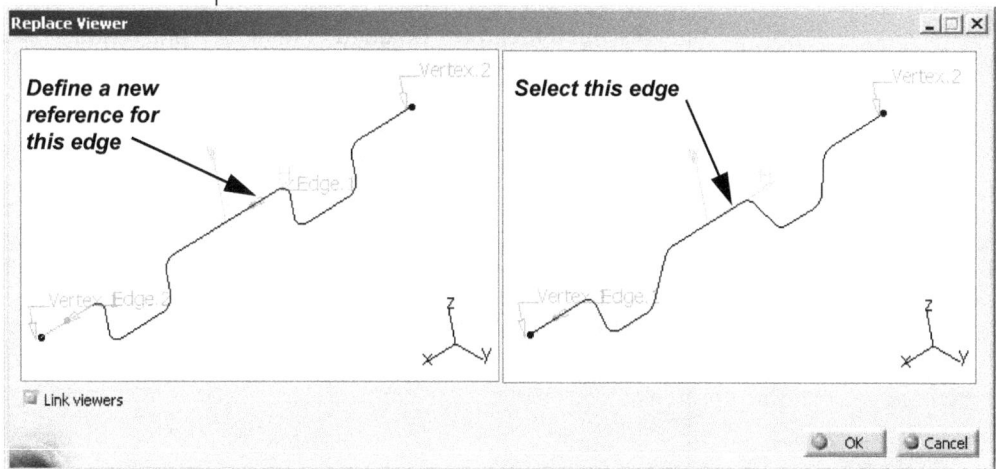

**Figure 10–40**

5. With all of the references defined, click **OK** in the Replace dialog box.

6. Update the model. It updates successfully, as shown in Figure 10–41.

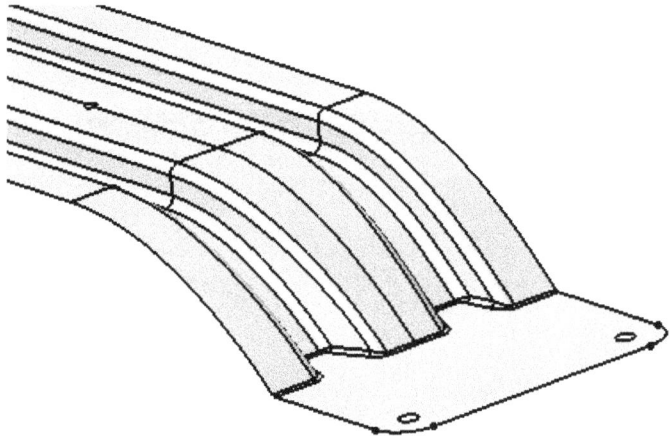

**Figure 10–41**

**Design Considerations**

The **Replace** tool considers all of the parent/child relationships of the element being replaced and forces you to define those references in the new geometry.

Using non-boundary representation modeling methods creates a cleaner specification tree, which enables other designers to perform predictable modifications more easily. However, when a design has been created using boundary representations, the **Replace** tool must be used to minimize and feature failures and errors that might occur.

7. Save the model and close the window.

# Chapter Review Questions

1. A boundary representation can be created by referencing the edge of a surface _____.

   a. As a guide curve

   b. As a Spine curve

   c. As a reference in a Fillet surface.

   d. All of the above.

2. When creating a boundary representation, an entity belonging to a feature is selected, rather than the feature itself.

   a. True

   b. False

3. As a best practice, it is important to avoid boundary representations whenever possible.

   a. True

   b. False

4. When modifying boundary references, you should use the _____ option whenever possible.

   a. **Substitute**

   b. **Swap**

   c. **Replace**

   d. **Repair**

5. When using a vertex as a reference, which is a viable Non-Boundary Representation method?

   a. Intersection of two points.

   b. Extremum point.

   c. On curve point.

   d. All of the above.

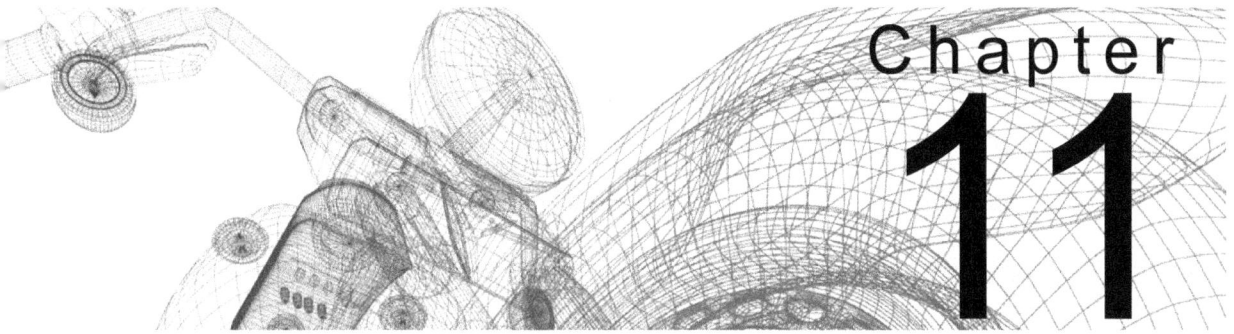

# Chapter 11

# Surface-Based Solid Features

When the surfacing operations are complete, the last step is to make the geometry solid or modify the solid model using a surface. The Part Design workbench contains various tools that make surface geometry solid and features that modify the solid model with a surface.

## Learning Objectives in this Chapter

- Understand Surface-Solid integration.
- Create Split surfaces.
- Create Thick surfaces.
- Create Close surfaces.
- Create Sew Surfaces.

# 11.1 Surface-Solid Integration

Once surfaces have been created in the GSD workbench, the resulting geometry can be used to create and manipulate solid geometry in the Part Design workbench. Using the Surface-Based Features toolbar as shown in Figure 11–1, you can use a surface to add or remove solid material from your model.

**Figure 11–1**

Since solid features are affected by operations on this toolbar, the surface-based features display in the specification tree in the *PartBody* area, as shown in Figure 11–2.

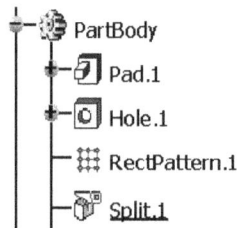

**Figure 11–2**

This section discusses the following methods that are used to create and manipulate solid geometry:

- Split

- Thick Surface

- Close Surface

- Sew Surface

# 11.2 Split

The **Split** option enables you to remove solid material based on the intersection of the solid with a surface. An arrow indicates the side of the solid that is going to be kept.

The surface shown in Figure 11–3 is used to shape the solid geometry.

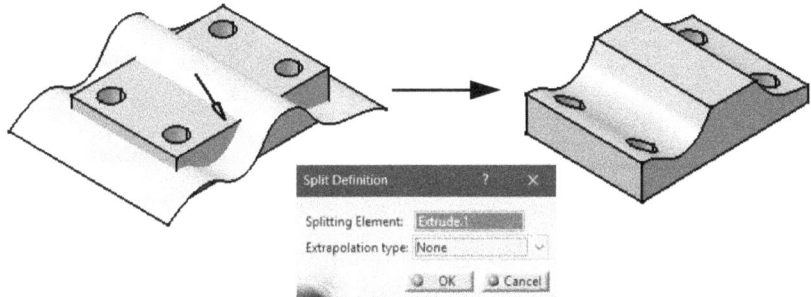

**Figure 11–3**

Although the surface does not have to intersect the solid geometry at all locations, it must cut across the entire volume. For example, the surface shown in Figure 11–4 would be an invalid split surface since it only partially defines the region to be split from the solid.

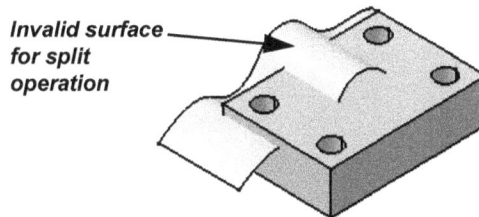

**Figure 11–4**

The *Extrapolation Types* are described as follows:

- **None**: Splits a solid when a splitting element intersects all edges of a solid body. This is the default option.

- **Tangent**: Extrapolates the splitting element tangentially and splits a solid body. You can use this option when the splitting element is too short to intersect any of the faces of the solid body.

- **Curvature**: Extrapolates the splitting element in a curvature and splits a solid body. You can use this option when the splitting element intersects at least one of the face of the solid body to split.

# 11.3 Thick Surface

The **Thick Surface** option creates a solid feature by adding thickness to a surface by a specified offset distance. All of the surface contours are offset normal to the selected surface. The result of thickening a revolved surface is shown in Figure 11–5.

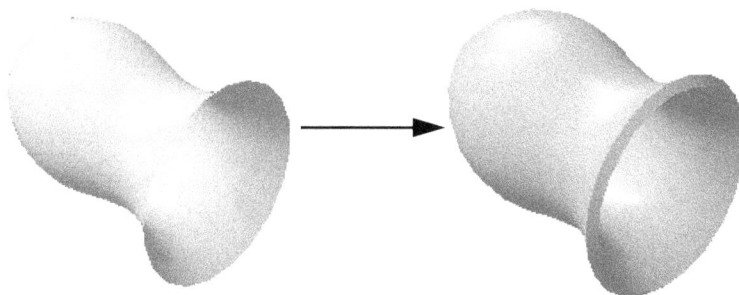

**Figure 11–5**

Overlapping geometry causes a thick surface operation to fail. Watch for small edges or small radii values that become negative or overlap when the offset occurs.

# 11.4 Close Surface

The **Close Surface** option creates solid geometry by closing a surface contour. For this feature to work, the closing areas must be planar or the surface contour must be comprised of a closed group of joined surfaces that do not have any gaps. In the revolved surface shown in Figure 11–6, the open contour lies in a plane. Therefore, the surface can be closed.

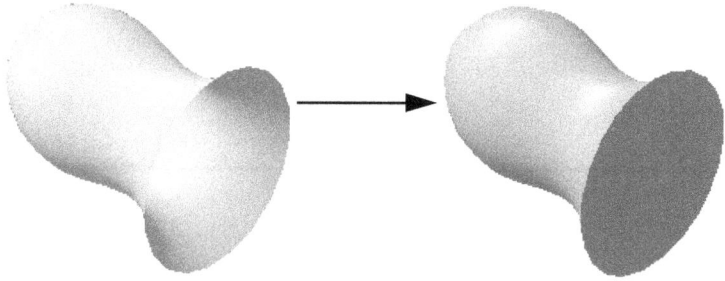

**Figure 11–6**

# 11.5 Sew Surface

The **Sew Surface** option uses a surface that has its boundaries lying on solid geometry to add and remove material. For example, the surface shown in Figure 11–7 is used to create more solid material in the model.

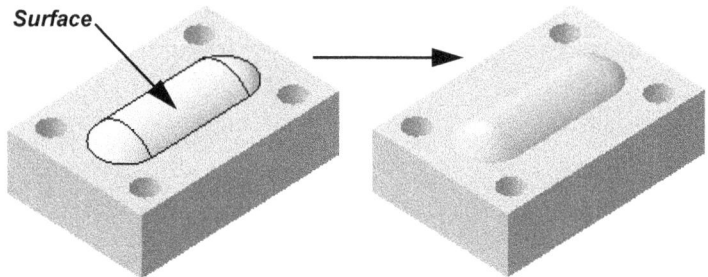

**Figure 11–7**

The surface shown in Figure 11–8 is used to remove material from the model.

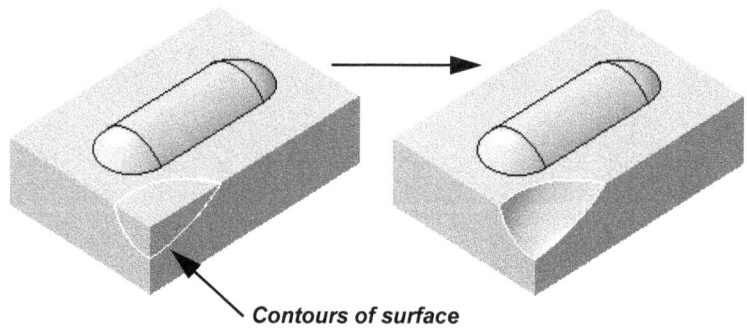

**Figure 11–8**

# Practice 11a | Aircraft Wing Spars

## Practice Objectives

- Create Thicken surfaces.
- Split solid geometry with a surface.

In this practice, you will create wireframe and surface geometry. These entities are then used to create solid geometry that represents the spars in a aircraft wing. The completed model displays as shown in Figure 11–9.

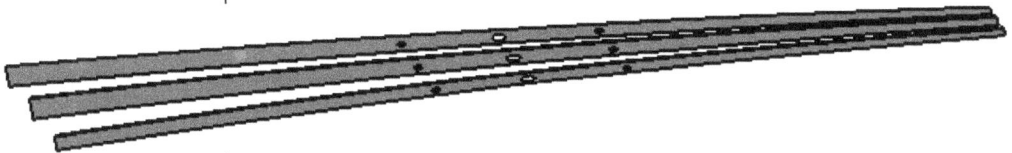

Figure 11–9

## Task 1 - Open a part.

1. Open **WingSpars_Start.CATPart**. The model displays as shown in Figure 11–10.

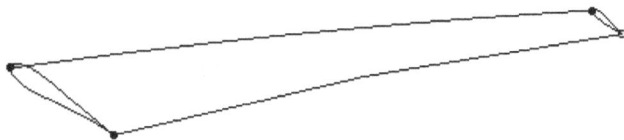

Figure 11–10

2. Geometry has already been created and organized, as shown in the specification tree in Figure 11–11. The model does not contain any solid geometry. Three working supports have been created, but none are currently active. All of the working supports are hidden.

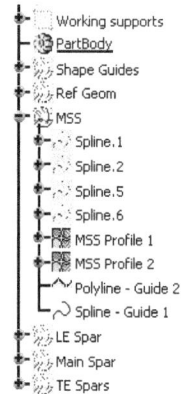

**Figure 11–11**

3. Show the following geometrical sets:

- **LE Spar**
- **Main Spar**
- **TE Spars**

4. Note the surfaces and wireframe created in each set. The model displays as shown in Figure 11–12. The wing will consist of three spars: one at the leading edge of the wing, a main spar, and a trail edge spar.

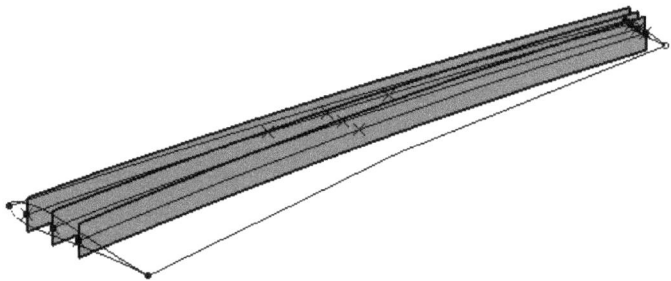

**Figure 11–12**

5. Hide the three geometrical sets from Step 3.

6. Ensure that the model units are set to **mm**.

## Task 2 - Create the remaining wing surfaces.

1.  If not already done, activate the **MSS** geometrical set.

2.  Click ▨ (Multi-sections Surface).

3.  Select **MSS Profile 1** and **MSS Profile 2** as the sections.

4.  Select **Spline - Guide 1** and **Polyline - Guide 2** as the two guide curves.

5.  Ensure that the **Sections coupling** option is set to **Tangency then Curvature**. The completed Multi-sections surface displays as shown in Figure 11–13.

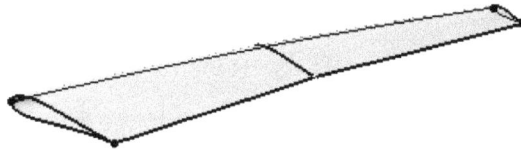

**Figure 11–13**

6.  Hide **Spline - Guide 1** and **Polyline - Guide 2**.

7.  Create two fill surfaces at each end of the wing using **MSS Profile 1** and **MSS Profile 2**. The completed fill surfaces display as shown in Figure 11–14.

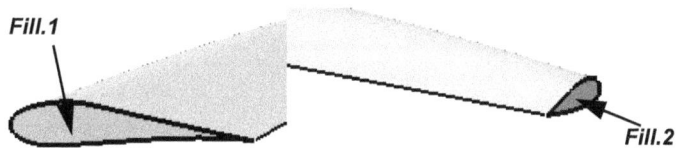

**Figure 11–14**

8.  Hide **MSS Profile 1** and **MSS Profile 2**.

9.  Join the two fill surfaces and the Multi-sections surface. Do not select the **Check Tangency** option in the Join Definition dialog box.

10. Rename the join as **Wing Skin**.

## Task 3 - Create the Lead Edge Spar.

1. Show the **LE Spar** geometrical set. The model displays as shown in Figure 11–15.

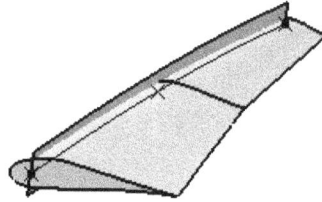

**Figure 11–15**

2. Select **Insert>Body**. The new body created is automatically made the active In work object. The Lead Edge Spar solid geometry will be placed here.

3. Rename the newly created body as **LE Spar Solid**.

4. Switch to the Part Design workbench.

*Select **Start> Mechanical Design> Part Design**.*

5. Click  (Thicken) in the Surface-Based Features toolbar. The ThickSurface Definition dialog box opens as shown in Figure 11–16.

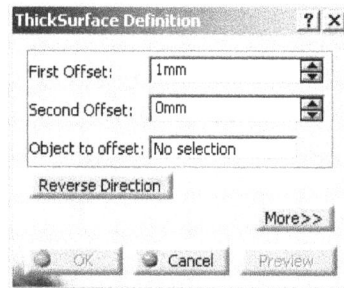

**Figure 11–16**

6. Enter the value **20mm** for the *First Offset*. Leave the *Second Offset* value as **0mm**.

7. Select **Surf - Lead Edge Spar** in the specification tree. This is a Swept surface in the **LE Spar** geometrical set.

8.  Ensure that the Thicken arrow is pointing in the direction shown in Figure 11–17. If the arrow is pointing in the wrong direction, click **Reverse Direction**.

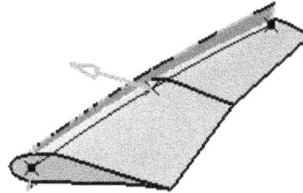

**Figure 11–17**

9.  Click **OK** to complete the thicken feature.

10. Hide the **LE Spar** geometrical set. The model displays as shown in Figure 11–18. Note that the solid geometry is indicated in gray and the surface geometry is in gold.

ThickSurface.1 ──

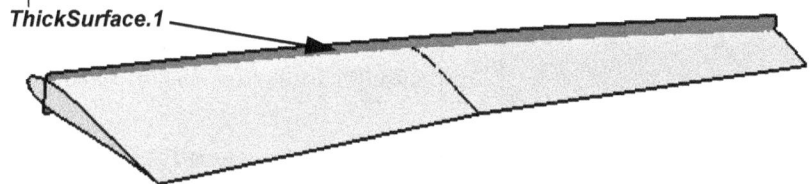

**Figure 11–18**

11. Click (Split) in the Surface-Based Features toolbar. The Split Definition dialog box opens as shown in Figure 11–19.

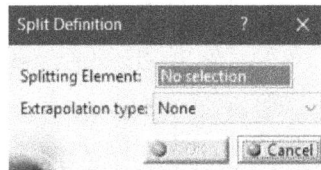

**Figure 11–19**

12. Select **Wing Skin** in the **MSS** geometrical set. The Splitting Element cuts the solid in the active body.

13. The orange arrows need to point to the inside of the Wing Skin surface. If they do not, click any of the arrows to flip the direction. The arrows' direction determines the part of the solid that is kept in the **Split** operation. The appropriate arrow direction is shown in Figure 11–20.

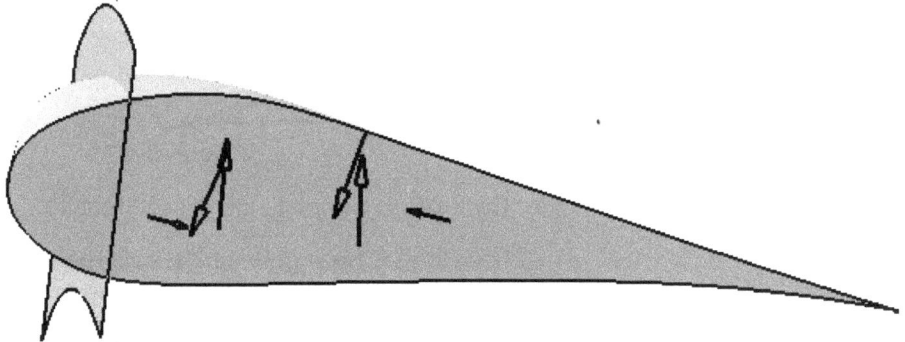

Figure 11–20

14. Hide **Wing Skin** in the **MSS** geometrical set. The resulting geometry displays as shown in Figure 11–21.

Figure 11–21

---

**Task 4 - Create the Main Spar.**

---

1. Show the **Main Spar** geometrical set.

2. Create a new body and name it **Main Spar Solid**.

3. Thicken the surface named **Surf - Main Spar** with a *First Offset* value of **20mm**. Surf - Main Spar is a Swept surface in the **Main Spar** geometrical set. Ensure that the thicken direction displays as shown in Figure 11–22.

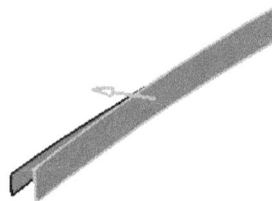

Figure 11–22

4. Hide the **Main Spar** geometrical set. The model displays as shown in Figure 11–23.

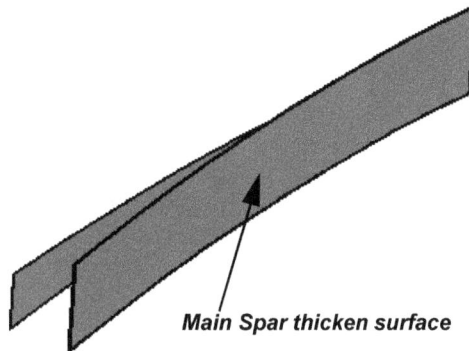

*Main Spar thicken surface*

**Figure 11–23**

5. Show **Wing Skin** in the **MSS** geometrical set.

6. Click  (Split). The Split Definition dialog box opens as shown in Figure 11–24.

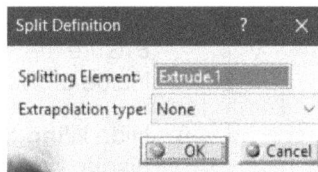

**Figure 11–24**

7. Select **Wing Skin** in the **MSS** geometrical set. The Splitting Element cuts the solid in the active body, which is **Main Spar Solid**. The orange arrows need to point to the inside of Wing Skin.

8. Click **OK** to complete the Split.

9. Hide **Wing Skin**. The model displays as shown in Figure 11–25.

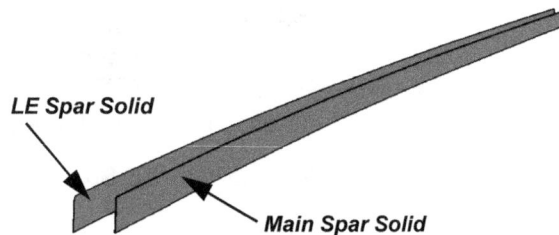

*LE Spar Solid*

*Main Spar Solid*

**Figure 11–25**

## Task 5 - Create the Trail Edge Spar.

1. Show the **TE Spars** geometrical set named.

2. Create a new body named **TE Spar Solid**.

3. Thicken **Surf - Trail Edge Spar** with a *First Offset* value of **20mm**. Surf - Trail Edge Spar is located in the **TE Spars** geometrical set. Ensure that the thicken direction displays as shown in Figure 11–26.

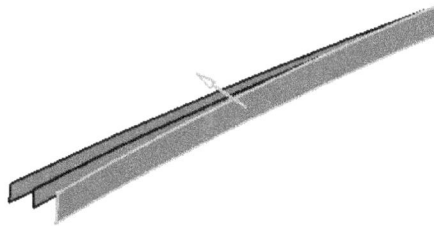

**Figure 11–26**

4. Show **Wing Skin** in the **MSS** geometrical set.

5. Split the Thick Surface created in this task with **Wing Skin**. Ensure that the arrows in the **Split** operation point toward the inside of Wing Skin.

6. Hide **Wing Skin**. The completed Thick and Split features display as shown in Figure 11–27 for the TE Spar Solid.

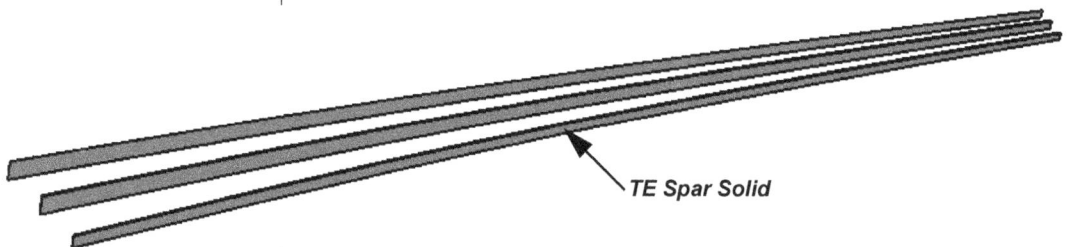

TE Spar Solid

**Figure 11–27**

## Task 6 - Create holes from wireframe and surface references.

1. Hide the bodies named **Main Spar Solid** and **TE Spar Solid**.

2. Show the **LE Spar** geometrical set.

3. Define the active work object as **LE Spar** so that any feature created will be placed here.

4. Click ⬚ (Isometric View). This is done to help you determine where the references are located in the following steps.

5. Create an **On Curve** type point using **Spline - Lead Edge Spar** as the curve reference.

6. Enter a *Ratio* of **0.4** using the point shown in Figure 11–28 as the zero reference. Based on the Isometric view, the zero reference is on the left of the curve.

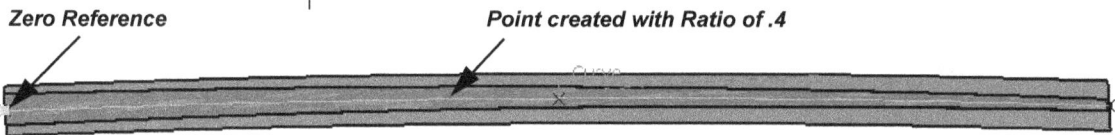

*Zero Reference*                    *Point created with Ratio of .4*

Figure 11–28

7. Create another **On Curve** type point using **Spline - Lead Edge Spar** as the curve reference.

8. Enter a *Ratio* of **0.6** using the zero reference that was used in the previous steps.

9. Rename the points as shown in Figure 11–29. The two completed points display as shown.

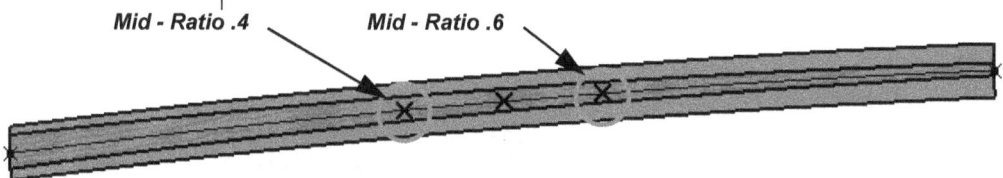

*Mid - Ratio .4*          *Mid - Ratio .6*

Figure 11–29

**Design Considerations**

The points created in this task are used to locate hole features that will be created. Using a locating point and a surface, the hole can be placed.

10. Define the active work object as **LE Spar Solid**.

11. Select the following elements:

- **Mid - Ratio .4**
- **Surf - Lead Edge Spar**

12. Click  (Hole).

13. Enter a *Diameter* of **150mm**.

*You might need to reverse the direction of the hole creation arrow.*

14. Select **Up To Last** in the drop-down list.

15. Click **OK** to complete the hole.

16. Hide **Surf - Lead Edge Spar**. The model displays as shown in Figure 11–30.

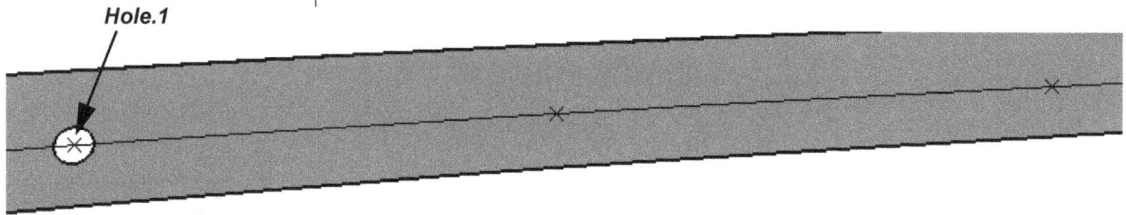

Hole.1

**Figure 11–30**

17. Create another hole, as shown in Figure 11–31. Use **Surf - Lead Edge Spar** and the point named **Mid Ratio .125** as the locating references for the hole. Enter a *Diameter* of **250mm**. Use the **Up To Last** depth option.

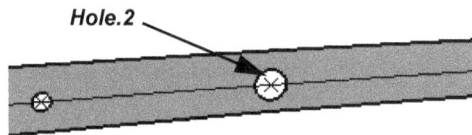

Hole.2

**Figure 11–31**

18. The last hole is created using **Surf - Lead Edge Spar** and the point named **Mid Ratio.6** as the locating references. Enter a diameter of **150mm**. Use the **Up To Last** depth option. The completed three holes display as shown in Figure 11–32.

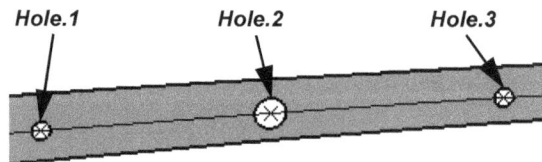

Hole.1     Hole.2     Hole.3

**Figure 11–32**

19. Save the model.

## Task 7 - (Optional) Create the remaining holes.

1. Create three holes using the steps from Task 6 for the **Main Spar** and the **TE Spar**. The completed model displays as shown in Figure 11–33.

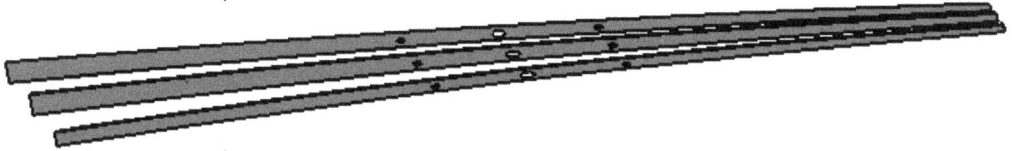

**Figure 11–33**

# Practice 11b | Side Mirror

### Practice Objectives

- Create Thicken surfaces.
- Create Close surfaces.

In this practice, you will compare two methods of solidifying surfaces. One method uses the Close feature followed by a shell, while the other method uses the Thicken feature. Although the results are similar, the difference in geometry between the two is important to note. The completed model displays as shown in Figure 11–34.

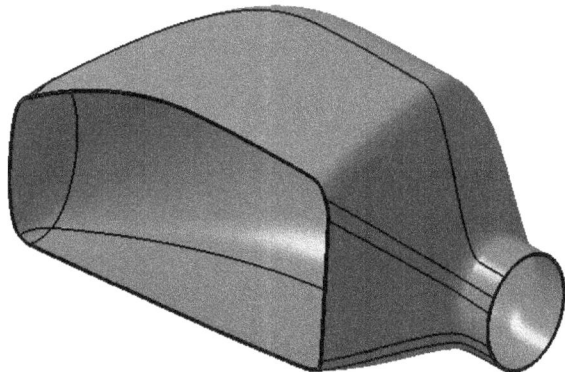

**Figure 11–34**

### Task 1 - Open a part.

1. Open **Solid_Side Mirror Start.CATPart**. The model displays as shown in Figure 11–35.

**Figure 11–35**

2. Ensure that the model units are set to **mm**.

3. Note that the **Surfaces for Solid** geometrical set is the active work object. All of the wireframes and surfaces created in this practice are placed in this set.

## Task 2 - Split the side mirror surfaces.

1. Show **Mirror Axis System** under the Axis Systems branch in the specification tree.

2. Create a positioned sketch on Mirror Axis System's ZX plane. Orient the Absolute Axis of the sketch as shown in Figure 11–36.

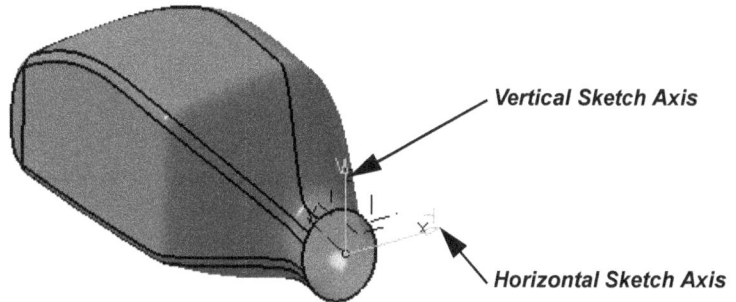

**Figure 11–36**

3. Sketch a vertical line and dimension it as shown in Figure 11–37.

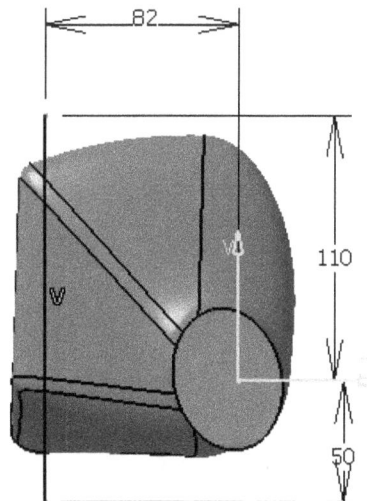

**Figure 11–37**

4. When completed, exit the sketch and rename the newly created sketch as **Split Profile**.

5. Ensure that Generative Shape Design is the current workbench.

*You might need to reverse the direction to obtain the same result.*

6. Create an Extrude using the following specifications:

   - *Profile:* **Split Profile**
   - *Direction:* **Default (Sketch normal)**
   - *Limit 1:* **250mm**

   The completed Extrude displays as shown in Figure 11–38.

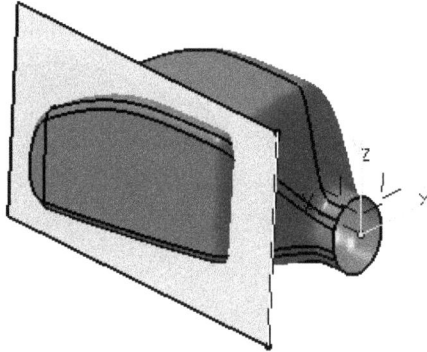

**Figure 11–38**

7. Rename the Extrude as **Split Surface**.

8. Hide **Split Profile**.

9. Create a Split using **Join.1** as the Element to cut, and **Split Surface** as the Cutting Element. The completed Split displays as shown in Figure 11–39.

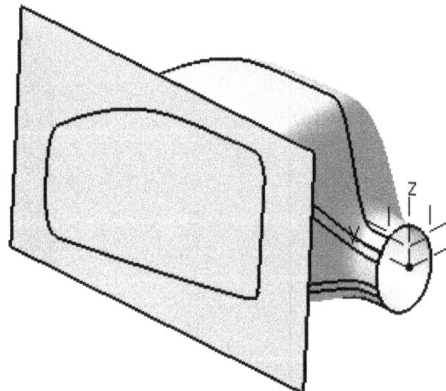

**Figure 11–39**

10. Hide **Split Surface**. The model displays as shown in Figure 11–40.

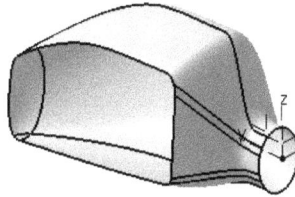

**Figure 11–40**

11. Rename the Split feature as **Split for Thicken**.

## Task 3 - Create a closed group of surfaces.

1. Hide **Split for Thicken**.

2. Show **Join.1** and **Split Surface**.

3. Create a Trim using **Join.1** and **Split Surface**, as shown in Figure 11–41.

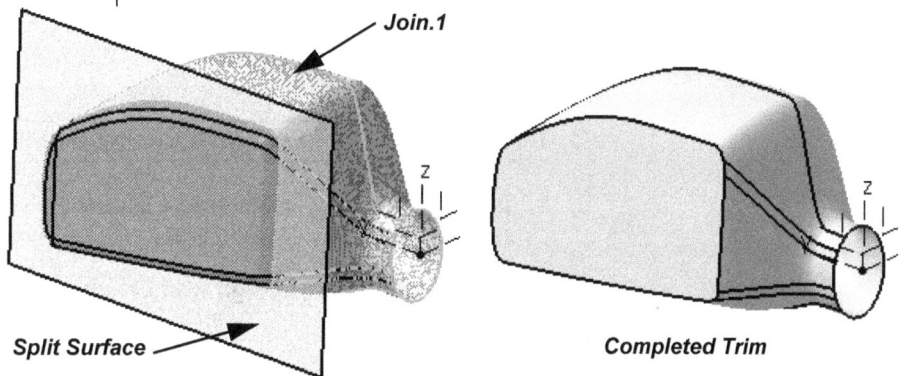

Join.1

Split Surface

Completed Trim

**Figure 11–41**

4. Using Point continuity, extract the curve shown in Figure 11–42.

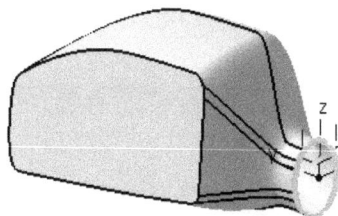

**Figure 11–42**

5. Rename the Extract feature as **Extract Curve**.

6. Create a Fill surface using **Extract Curve**. The model displays as shown in Figure 11–43.

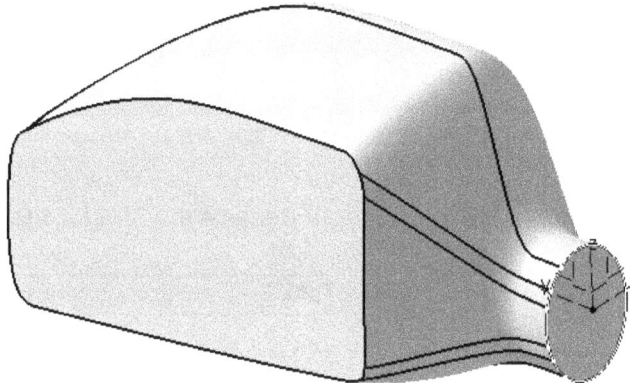

**Figure 11–43**

7. Join the newly created Trim and Fill surfaces. Do not select the **Check Tangency** option.

8. Rename the Join as **Closed Surf**.

9. Hide **Extract Curve**.

---

**Task 4 - Create solid geometry using the first method.**

---

1. Insert a new body and name it **Close**. By default, the active body is the newly created body.

2. Switch to the Part Design workbench.

3. Click  (Close) in the Surface-Based Features toolbar.

4. Select **Closed Surf**, as shown in Figure 11–44.

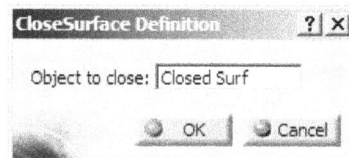

**Figure 11–44**

5. Click **OK** to complete the Close.

6. Hide **Closed Surf**. The model displays as shown in Figure 11–45.

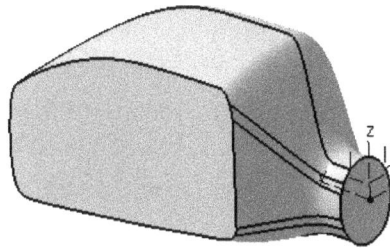

**Figure 11–45**

7. Create a shell with a **2mm** inside thickness. Leave the outside thickness at **0mm**. Remove the face shown in Figure 11–46.

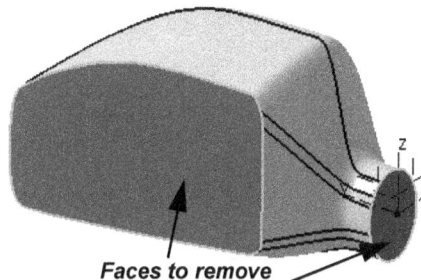

*Faces to remove*

**Figure 11–46**

---

### Task 5 - Create solid geometry using the second method.

1. Insert a new body and name it **Thicken**. By default, the active body is the newly created body.

2. Hide the body named **Close**.

3. Show the **Split for Thicken** feature. The model displays as shown in Figure 11–47.

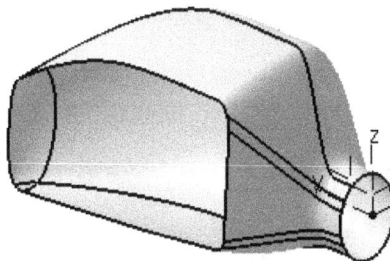

**Figure 11–47**

---

4. Create a Thick Surface from **Split for Thicken**. Enter a *First Offset* value of **2mm**.

5. Ensure that the arrows point toward the inside of the model.

6. Click **OK** to complete the Thick Surface.

7. Hide **Split for Thicken**. The model displays as shown in Figure 11–48.

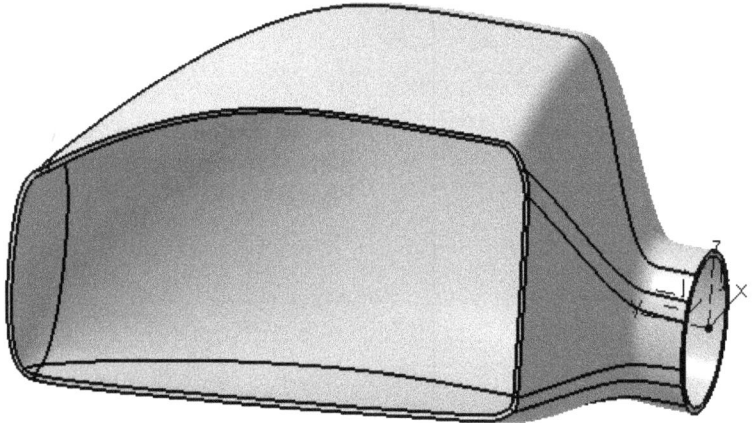

**Figure 11–48**

### Task 6 - Compare methods.

For the first method, you created solid geometry using the Close and Shell features. The second method used the Thicken feature. In this task, you will analyze the two bodies and note the differences that exist in the geometry.

1. Hide both **Close** and **Thicken** (the two bodies created in this practice).

2. Define the active work object as the **Surfaces for Solid** geometrical set.

3. Show **Plane.3**. It is located in the **MSS Planes** geometrical set.

4. Ensure that Generative Shape Design is the current workbench.

5. Create an Intersect curve using the body named **Close** and **Plane.3**.

6. Rename the Intersect curve as **X section Close**. The curve displays as shown in Figure 11–49.

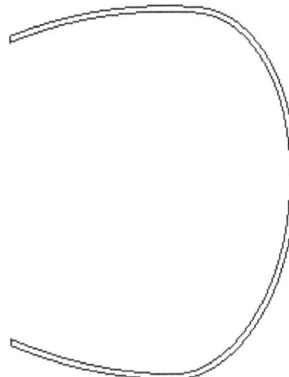

*X section Close*

**Figure 11–49**

7. Hide **X section Close**.

8. Create another Intersect curve using the body named **Thicken** and **Plane.3**.

9. Rename the *Intersect curve as X* section **Thick**. The curve displays as shown in Figure 11–50.

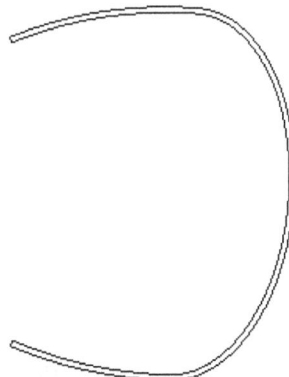

*X section Thick*

**Figure 11–50**

10. Show **X Section Close**.

11. Hide **Plane.3** and **Mirror Axis System**. They no longer need to be displayed.

12. Click ⬚ (Right View) so that the model displays as shown in Figure 11–51. Zoom in on the area shown in Figure 11–51.

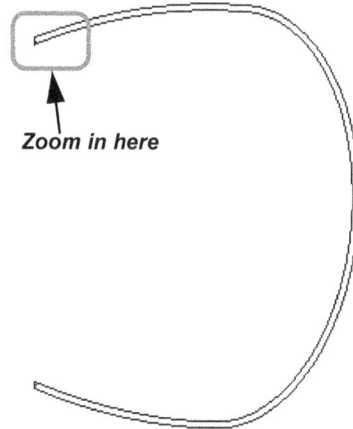

**Zoom in here**

**Figure 11–51**

Note the differences between **X section Thick** and **X section Close**, as shown in Figure 11–52.

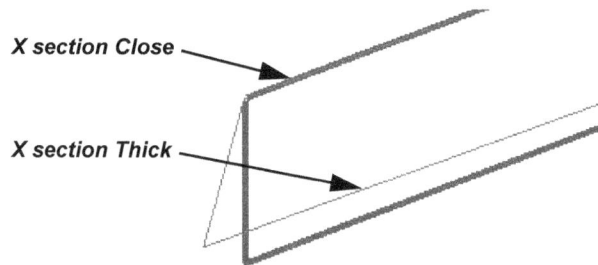

*X section Close*

*X section Thick*

**Figure 11–52**

13. Show **Close** and **Thicken**.

14. Using the graphic properties, change the color of the **Close** body to yellow, and color of the **Thicken** body to blue. The model displays as shown in Figure 11–53.

15. Zoom in on the areas shown in Figure 11–53. Note the differences between **Close** (yellow) and **Thicken** (blue) along the edges of the opening.

*Zoom in on the edges of the opening.*

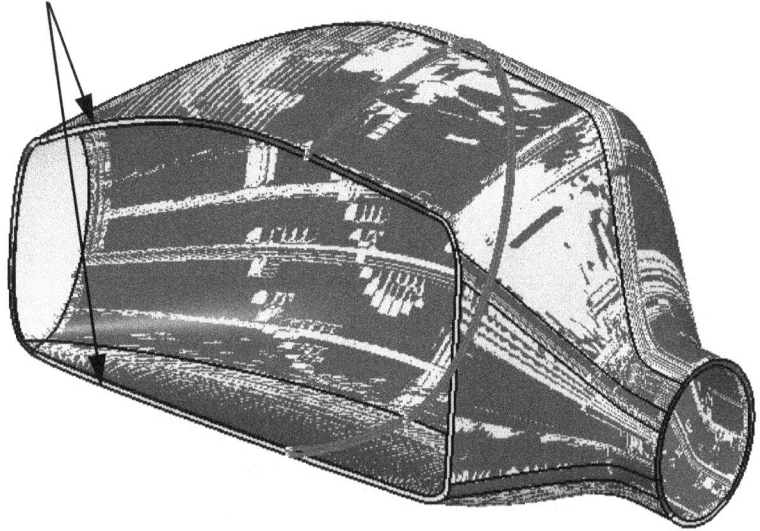

**Figure 11–53**

16. To further distinguish this difference, show **Split Surface** in the **Surfaces for Solid** geometrical set. The model displays as shown in Figure 11–54.

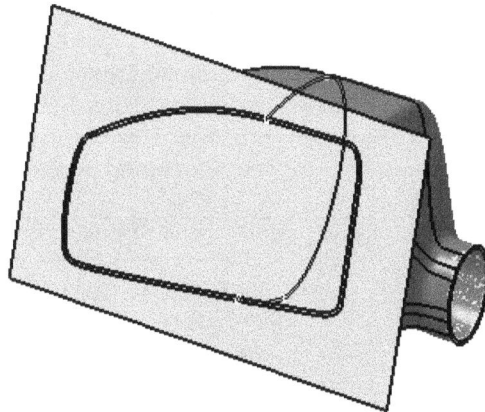

**Figure 11–54**

17. Zoom in on the area shown in Figure 11–55. The body named Close does not extend past Split Surf, but Thicken does.

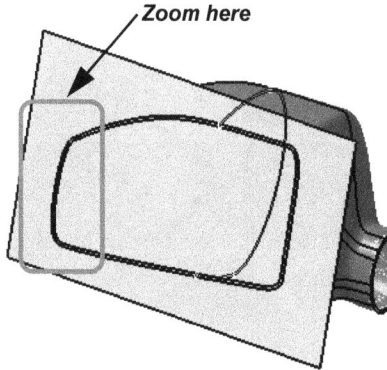

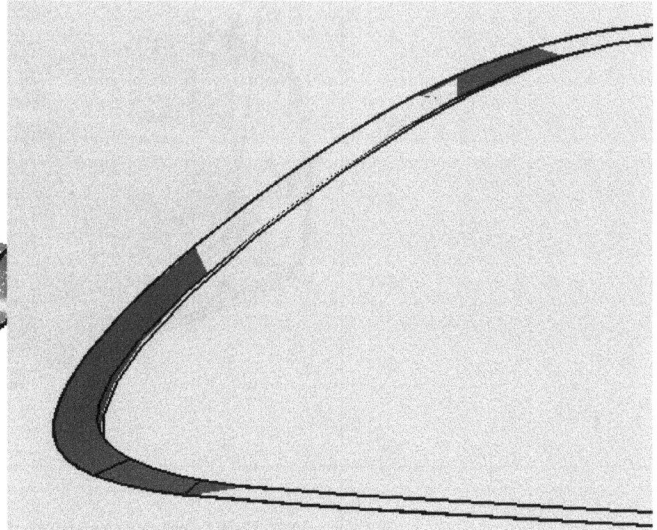

**Zoom here**

**Figure 11–55**

**Design Considerations**

By showing the intersect curves and coloring the bodies, you can see a difference at the opening of the solids.

When a surface is closed and then shelled, the resulting geometry aligns with the face(s) that were removed in the process. This result simulates a cast or injection molded manufacturing process.

The Thick Surface method of creating solid geometry does not have any references with which to align. It adds the material thickness normal to the reference surface. This can produce an uneven result that simulates a stamping manufacturing process. Use the method that is appropriate for the model that is being created.

18. Save the model and close the window.

# Chapter Review Questions

1. You can use surface geometry to create and manipulate solid geometry.

    a. True

    b. False

2. The **Split** option adds or removes material based on the intersection of the surface and the solid.

    a. True

    b. False

3. The _____ option creates a solid surface feature by adding material to a surface by a specified offset distance.

    a. **Offset Surface**

    b. **Solid Surface**

    c. **Thick Surface**

    d. **Replace Surface**

4. The **Close Surface** option creates solid geometry by closing a surface contour.

    a. True

    b. False

5. The **Sew Surface** option uses a surface to add and remove material. The surface feature boundaries need not lie on the solid surface.

    a. True

    b. False

www.ingramcontent.com/pod-product-compliance
Lightning Source LLC
Chambersburg PA
CBHW080117220326
41598CB00032B/4872